THE GAITHERS
and
SOUTHERN GOSPEL

THE GAITHERS

and

SOUTHERN GOSPEL

HOMECOMING IN THE TWENTY-FIRST CENTURY

RYAN P. HARPER

University Press of Mississippi / Jackson

www.upress.state.ms.us

The University Press of Mississippi is a member of
the Association of American University Presses.

First printing 2017

∞

Library of Congress Cataloging-in-Publication Data

Names: Harper, Ryan P.
Title: The Gaithers and southern gospel : homecoming in the twenty-first
century / Ryan P. Harper.
Description: Jackson : University Press of Mississippi, [2017] | Series:
American made music series | Includes bibliographical references and index.
Identifiers: LCCN 2016040509 (print) | LCCN 2016040698 (ebook) | ISBN
9781496810908 (hardcover : alk. paper) | ISBN 9781496810915 (epub single)
| ISBN 9781496810922 (epub institutional) | ISBN 9781496810939 (pdf
single) | ISBN 9781496810946 (pdf institutional)
Subjects: LCSH: Gospel musicians—United States—Biography. | Gaither,
Gloria. | Gaither, Bill. | Gaither Vocal Band. | Gospel music—History and
criticism.
Classification: LCC ML400 .H368 2017 (print) | LCC ML400 (ebook) | DDC
782.25/40922 [B] —dc23
LC record available at https://lccn.loc.gov/2016040509

British Library Cataloging-in-Publication Data available

"It was the excitement; all the people. And the music was—well, it was strenuous." She paused, trying to think what the music and dancing meant. "It was such an odd day," she said. "There was the outwardness, the people coming and the mass and the feasting and then the dance, and last of all the storm. Am I being silly, Joseph, or was there a meaning, right under the surface? It seemed like those pictures of simple landscapes they sell in the cities. When you look closely, you see all kinds of figures hidden in the lines. Do you know the kind of pictures I mean? A rock becomes a sleeping wolf, a little cloud is a skull, and the line of trees marching soldiers when you look closely. Did the day seem like that to you, Joseph, full of hidden meanings, not quite understandable?"

—John Steinbeck, *To a God Unknown*

CONTENTS

ACKNOWLEDGMENTS

Although the Gaithers spotlight their share of solo stars, the Homecomings are essentially ensemble affairs. The same has been true for my project. Inside the academy, this project took off at Duke Divinity School. Kate Bowler, Julie Byrne, Curtis Freeman, Mandy McMichael, Lauren Winner, and above all Grant Wacker, were my early encouragers and conversation partners. My spouse, Lynn, attended Wake Forest Divinity School at the same time, and I thank Brian Graves, Beth Honeycutt, Katharine Martin, and many other Wake Forest friends for transcending fierce ACC basketball rivalries to workshop my early ideas. Several incarnations of Princeton University's Department of Religion deeply informed and supported me. Marie Griffith brought me to Princeton and provided an important early ethnographic model. Judith Weisenfeld's tireless support and advice is becoming the stuff of legend among scholars of American religion, and I was an immediate beneficiary of her care and attention. April Armstrong, Laura Bennett, Wallace Best, Mary Kay Bodnar, Pat Bogdiewicz, Vaughn Booker, Jessica Delgado, Josh Dubler, Lorraine Fuhrmann, Eddie Glaude, Rachel Gross, Matt Hedstrom, David Jorgensen, Rachel Lindsey, Kathryn Gin Lum, Emily Mace, Caleb Maskell, Anthony Petro, Michael Robertson, Kerry Smith, Jeff Stout, and Cornel West were ever-present models, advisors, and friends. Outside of the Department of Religion, Deborah Blanks, Alison Boden, Matt Ellis, Alex Karels, Michael Lamb, Paul Raushenbush, and Hana Shepherd were trusted colleagues and companions. My dear friends at Small World Coffee deserve a special thank-you, since so many of these pages first saw the light there. I also thank a Princeton population that was largely invisible to me: the once-and-current builders and maintainers of the Delaware and Raritan Canal trail system and Princeton Community Park. The thousands of miles I logged running, hiking, and biking in these locations provided me delightful, if often strenuous, respite from writing and reading, and made my work better and more enjoyable.

Outside of Princeton, Jim Goff, Doug Harrison, and Samira Mehta devoted their thoughts, support, and infectious energy for the project. Craig Gill, David Evans, the staff, and the outside readers at the University Press of Mississippi believed in this project in its early stages, and I thank them for their advice, patience, and care. Special thanks to Debbie Upton for the fine copy-editing work as well.

The people who appear in the following pages brought a special energy to my research. I am humbled and grateful that so many fans invited me into their lives—sometimes literally into their living rooms, often sight unseen—to share their thoughts and feelings on the Homecomings. Many Homecoming musicians shared what backstage moments they had with me, and they never failed to be welcoming to a conspicuous wanderer in their world. In the Gaither offices and backstage, Teri Garner, Jeralee Mathews, Emily Sutherland, Deana Warren, and Connie Williams helped orchestrate trips to Indiana and beyond—always with a kind and prompt word. Of course, the Gaither family—especially Bill and Gloria—deserve a great deal of thanks for sharing their resources, thoughts, and time with me. This project would have been much more difficult were it not for Bill's and Gloria's willingness to talk with me, to read my work, to bring me into their work. Although as gospel music celebrities the Gaithers are used to people writing things about them that they probably would not write about themselves, as this project progressed I increasingly wondered how I would behave if I were in their shoes—with someone working on such a publication about *me*. I hope I could exhibit even a modicum of the grace and generosity they showed me.

Long before I stepped foot in the academy, this project had its origins in southeast Missouri, when as an elementary-school drummer I traveled on weekends with my family's southern gospel band, playing at church revivals and homecomings in the hinterlands of Missouri, Illinois, Kentucky, and Tennessee. Years before the first Gaither Homecomings, southern gospel was the soundtrack of my early life. Although my performing and listening tastes changed, I never forgot the genre's pull and power in particular quadrants of Christian America. I thank my parents and siblings for raising me inside this music, and I am happy to revisit the music in its—and my—later light.

The South begins and ends in the Midwest, in southeast Missouri. My family comes from the state's southernmost "Bootheel" region. My in-laws, the Casteels, come from the counties just north of the Bootheel, and always have been supportive of my study of a world that was both near to and distant from them. Lynn and I now laugh as we remember one winter afternoon, not long into our relationship, when she entered my parents' living room, where my father was watching a Gaither Homecoming video. Pointing to the screen, on which Bill Gaither was directing the ensemble, Lynn asked in her alto, middle-American accent, what she thought was a reasonable question: "Who's that?" My father grabbed the arms of his recliner and sat suddenly straight up, his eyes wide on Lynn. In his high-pitched Bootheel twang, which managed to communicate jest and sincere shock at the same time, he chirped, "You don't know who that is? *That's Bill Gaither!*" Lynn's blank face proved that his answer did not clarify matters, so she quickly found herself her future father-in-law's student in an afternoon-long crash course on gospel music.

Little did either of us know then that, one day, Lynn would be able to teach that crash course. She has been an unfailing partner in fieldwork, writing, editing, and thinking. Her willingness to be a curious, vocal, unapologetic outsider helped me—whose familiarity with gospel culture could be a blessing and a curse—to distinguish, support, and sometimes revise my hunches, intuitions, discoveries, and claims. This book is dedicated to her.

THE GAITHERS
and
SOUTHERN GOSPEL

ꙮNTRODUCTION

IN A CONVEX MIRROR

"I'm glad you were able to get down to this one. I thought you would be interested in seeing how we do one of these," Bill Gaither told me backstage. Straight out of the Gaithers' mobile makeup/hair salon, the freshly coiffed gospel music mogul talked to me as we walked through a flashing gauntlet of video equipment and be-headphoned, fast-talking stage technicians, wires flailing behind them like jellyfish tentacles. Cameras and photo-studio umbrellas diverted the seventy-one-year-old Bill—a musician-businessman already prone to the distractions of artistry and enterprise. Despite Bill's toothy smile and avuncular shoulder pats, which always helped ease my suspicions that I was a backstage nuisance, I left Bill backstage and found my seat.

The backstage buzzed with special excitement at this performance because Bill was recording it for eventual release as a DVD. We were gathered at the river: Louisville, Kentucky, that gateway city into or out of the American South, 150 miles south of the Gaithers' Indiana headquarters, somewhere between Dayton, Ohio, and Dayton, Tennessee. Two all-male quartets shared billing: Ernie Haase and Signature Sound and Bill's own Gaither Vocal Band (GVB). Bill regarded the former group as the future of southern gospel—or the most promising culmination of its past. By most metrics, the GVB sat atop the contemporary southern gospel hill. The 2,400-capacity Whitney Hall housed fewer fans than the sporting arenas and civic centers in which I had seen other Gaither concerts, but the size seemed to concentrate the ordinary enthusiasm of a Gaither concert. This parlor of the Louisville Orchestra and Ballet retained the gloss of its usual highbrow residents. An orchestra backed the quartets. The quartets would wear tuxedos for the concert's second half. This was high cotton.

With the help of an usher, I discovered that Bill had planted me in the fourth row—not far behind Gloria, his spouse and co-songwriter, who took her barely offstage front-row seat about ten minutes before show time to a small eruption of screams and applause. Knowing the camera would find Gloria numerous times during the evening, I guessed that the camera likely would find me, too, in the periphery. I was among the precious few thirty-and-unders in attendance, and I wondered if the camera might find me for that reason as well—visual proof of the Gaithers' expansive appeal. I conversed with my neighbors and learned I was seated beside one of Bill's fellow Anderson University trustees and his spouse—a pleasant, garrulous couple, not shy about their love of Anderson University, Gaither music, and the Gaithers themselves. I knew Bill was exceedingly proud of the Christian school, his alma mater. I also knew the Gaithers had helped to fund Anderson's impressive fine arts facilities. I was beginning to think that my seat location was no accident. Friendly, rural midwestern evangelical, scatter-brained artist, and shrewd industry entrepreneur, Bill Gaither blended the providential, the coincidental, the premeditated in his arrangements. It made for difficult sight-reading.

Just before the concert began, a young man stepped onto the stage and greeted the crowd through a tiny headset microphone in an animated radio deejay voice. After reminding us to turn off cell phones and to refrain from picture taking, he explained that, since the concert would become a live DVD, the crew would record some stock footage of the audience before the performance began—footage they would insert into the final edit as necessity dictated. They would make six recordings of the audience, he informed us, each approximately one-minute long. During the first three recordings, we needed to applaud at incrementally more enthusiastic levels: mild approval at first, then stronger (perhaps adding some whistles and yells), then a final crescendo to a rip-roaring standing ovation. The second three recordings would recapitulate this tripartite crescendo, only with laughter: a minute of polite giggles, then of open-mouthed chuckles, then of knee-slapping guffaws. Heavy on comedic interludes, the Gaither programs wanted laughter.

Our young emcee then led us in this bizarre audience-participation activity—bizarre not only because the secret of production was so plain, the fabrication so bare, but also because it seemed surprisingly easy for all gathered to yield to the direction of the friendly man on the gospel stage. For six minutes he harvested our pretense. A camera, perched at the end of a remote control boom arm that could stretch about thirty feet into the seats from the front of the stage, thrust and swerved across the auditorium, craning high above us to capture and create the magnitude of the venue, then sweeping just above the eyeline of the front row, left to right and back, pausing on particular sections of the crowd for a few seconds. I could not see who operated the machine. It seemed as if we were being inspected by a very expensive robotic dinosaur. Occasionally, it stopped in front of me. I returned its stare, glancing tiny, bent fragments of myself and my neighbors, in our full theater, on the surface of the glass eye, organizing everything. Imagining myself applauding at how well I applauded—how well *we* applauded—I went along with the gag, heightening my applause as the orchestra of hands and hoots built to our final scherzo. Since the absurdity of two thousand-plus people chuckling at nothing was genuinely funny to me (and got funnier and more absurd as we continued), I had no trouble producing laughter. The secret was too plain; our feigned laughter was my real object. All was totally fabricated— if pretense, blunt pretense—these our dangling modifiers, freely given, referents to be determined in the final edit.

The prospect of seeing my laughing face appear after a particularly unfunny (or dubiously tasteful) joke in the final video disconcerted me. What power the Gaithers wielded, that they would leave the concert hall that evening with armloads of images ripe for the framing, that they had been able to gain our consent so effortlessly. However, the gaze was not one-way. By granting a literal and figurative front-row seat and backstage pass to a scholar who would observe, record, and produce a text about them, the Gaithers had themselves agreed to be captured, captioned, constructed. I left with a load of artifacts for my own framing. To be sure, the Gaithers exercised a good deal of control over what I would witness, onstage and backstage; furthermore, should they not care for my eventual framings, the pair possessed sufficient resources to offer very public counterframings. But the fact that numerous concertgoers also watched the Gaithers limited the latters' ability to pose and repose for any single gaze, including mine. Being watched by and within such a mass of individuals was a blessed vast problem. From 2006 to 2012, this would be our lot, the Gaithers' and mine: this studied standoff, this infinite regression of reciprocal gazes turning and returning scrutiny, adjusting focus and posture, the Gaithers watching me watching them watching me.

*   *   *

Bill and Gloria Gaither are singer-songwriters. They have held a prominent place in the gospel music industry since the 1960s. As performers, they comprised two-thirds of the Bill Gaither Trio (Bill's brother Danny was the third member most of the time), which performed and recorded throughout the 1970s and 1980s. However, the Gaithers rose in the music industry primarily through their songwriting. Several of their approximately seven hundred songs have become canonical in Christian (especially evangelical) circles: "He Touched Me," "Let's Just Praise the Lord," The Family of God," and "Because He

Lives" are among the most popular. Before 1990, the Gaithers' songwriting and their recordings yielded them two Grammys and eighteen of the Gospel Music Association (GMA) Dove Awards—nine of the latter for being named "Gospel Songwriter of the Year."[1] In 2000, the Association of Songwriters, Composers, and Producers (ASCAP) named the pair the "Gospel Songwriters of the Century"—based on research indicating that musicians inside and outside the church performed Gaither compositions more frequently than those of any other gospel artists. In the awards ceremony, Sony-ATV CEO Donna Hilley claimed, "the Gaithers are to gospel music what the Beatles are to pop music."[2]

The Gaithers' achievements from the late 1960s to the 1980s alone would have secured their place in gospel music history. However, no single Gaither enterprise of those decades would compare in profits or in visibility to the Homecoming videos, albums, and concert series. Starting in 1991, the Gaithers regularly gathered a cadre of mostly white, middle-aged-and-older gospel musicians in their studio and on their stages to sing gospel songs. The programs were part variety show (individuals and small ensembles sang one or two songs per show), part collective sing-along. The first decade of "Homecomings" paid tribute to the landmark gospel musicians who rose to fame in the middle of the twentieth century—many of whom were present, and quite old, in the programs themselves. As the franchise entered the new millennium, the Gaithers blended "old-time" gospel music and its representatives with contemporary groups and genres.

The Homecomings succeeded. The Gaithers won four additional Grammys and dozens of additional Dove Awards for Homecoming-era videos and music albums.[3] Over fifty of the one hundred-plus Homecoming videos have reached platinum-level sales. In 2004, the Gaithers occupied the forty-seventh slot on *Rolling Stone*'s list of fifty wealthiest musicians in the world—the only gospel artists on a list that included names like Michael Jackson and Paul McCartney. The same year, the Homecoming concert tour outgrossed the "comeback" tours of Fleetwood Mac and the Eagles. On this front, "classic gospel" outdueled "classic rock."[4]

The Gaithers and the Homecomings have received little scholarly attention—a corollary to the fact that southern gospel music has drawn scholarly interest only recently. "Southern gospel" is an ill-defined subgenre of gospel music. Historically, scholars, fans, and musicians have defined southern gospel by what it is not: not black gospel, not contemporary Christian music (CCM), not high church hymnody. I will examine the varied meanings of southern gospel throughout this book, but as a starting, provisional descriptor, southern gospel is a religious form of music that arose out of shape-note singing conventions in antebellum America. It is predominantly an ensemble genre; its prototypes are the white, all-male quartets and family singing groups that flourished in the mid-twentieth-century South and Midwest. As CCM, Christian rock, and "praise-and-worship" began to make waves in post–civil-rights-era white evangelical culture, *southern gospel* came to distinguish "traditional" gospel singing from the new measures. As a cause and effect of the mid-century ensembles' usefulness as prototypes, new "traditionalists" often referred to the former as *southern gospel* musicians. In common usage, the appellation is newer than much of the music it designates.[5]

Over the past two decades, scholars have produced a number of studies on Christian rock, CCM, traditional and contemporary African American gospel, and even the Christ-inflected country genre.[6] Although southern gospel plays sometimes-significant roles in all of these traditions' histories, it receives little attention in most of these studies. However, the general interest in American Christians' music has yielded a handful of book-length treatments of southern gospel. James Goff's 2002 *Close Harmony: A History of Southern Gospel* examines the story of the music from its nineteenth-century roots through approximately the late 1980s. In 2004, Mercer University Press released *More Than "Precious Memories": The Rhetoric of Southern Gospel Music*, a collection of essays on past and contemporary manifestations of southern gospel. Doug Harrison's 2012 book, *Then Sings My Soul: The Culture of Southern Gospel Music*, opens a number of the heretofore-unexplored elements of the genre—especially the "queerness" of southern gospel music and spaces. The authors of these works are trained and teach in departments of history, rhetoric, communications, and English. Religious studies scholars have been silent on southern gospel.[7]

Each of these studies helped fill a gaping hole in scholarship on American Christians' music, but each possesses a complicated relationship to the Gaither Homecomings. Goff's history ends before the full blossoming of the Homecomings. Most of his references to the Gaithers are prospective nods. The Mercer Press collection contains two essays on the Homecomings, but they focus mostly on a handful of the early videos. *Close Harmony* and *More Than "Precious Memories"* were published the same year the Homecoming franchise exploded in notoriety and profits, so the studies could not account for the Homecomings at their most robust. Harrison devotes the fifth chapter of his book to the Homecomings; it is the best piece of scholarly writing on the Homecomings to date. But one chapter hardly can do justice to the most lucrative enterprise in gospel music history. Moreover, as Harrison seeks to call attention to the current, dynamic world of "extra-Homecoming" southern gospel, he can only pay so much attention to the Homecomings without doing a disservice to his larger aim.

One can feel the burden of the Homecomings in all three books: they each appeared at a moment when the Homecomings loomed large in American evangelical culture but when southern gospel cast a faint shadow among scholars. All of the authors were personally intimate with southern gospel (Goff and Harrison are die-hard southern gospel fans; the latter ran a major southern gospel blog during the research for his monograph). They wrote for an academic audience but also for fans who knew that the air abounded in Homecomings. The very existence of and demand for these books was due to the success of the Homecomings; Goff's book cover included an endorsement from Bill Gaither. These scholars knew that one portion of their audience needed to be told (or reminded) that southern gospel was *more* than the Homecomings, and another portion needed to recognize the significance of southern gospel— a significance proven by *but not reducible to* the Homecomings' success. The Homecoming behemoth got lost in a shuffle it created.

The scant scholarly attention paid to Bill and Gloria Gaither is more peculiar, because their impact extends beyond southern gospel. Many Gaither songs anticipated contemporary praise and worship music. Many appear in hymnals alongside the works of Charles Wesley, Fanny Crosby, and the "father of gospel music," Thomas Dorsey. The Bill Gaither Trio—not Christian rock, not hymnody, not quartet music—paved the way for "inspirational" Christian music, a subgenre that peaked in the late 1970s and 1980s, whose musicians turned the rock amplifiers down (slightly) and reorchestrated and rechanneled formal hymnody. Turn-of-the-century CCM often recapitulated inspirational music's soft grandiosity. The gospel music industry would not exist in its current form without the Gaithers' musical and even administrative contributions. Not only has Bill won numerous Dove Awards; he conceived of the Dove Awards.[8]

Still, recent studies on CCM or Christian rock barely mention the Gaithers. In their 1999 study of CCM, Jay Howard and John Streck briefly refer to Bill as a "middle of the road songwriter, a CCM forerunner who helped to bridge the gap" between traditional and contemporary forms. This reference seems dismissive, but it is telling. Indeed, the "Gaither genre" has been difficult to pin down; the Gaithers always have been transitional, synthesizing, reconciling figures—ever singing the anacrusis between past, present, and future, between Larry Norman, Charles Wesley, Andraé Crouch, George Beverly Shea, Amy Grant, Sandi Patty, and Jake Hess.

GOSPEL METHOD

This book enters this vast middle of the road. Circumscribing the time and location of my research is difficult, given the mobility and size of the

Homecoming world.[9] Stated simply, my fieldwork extended from 2006 to 2012. In 2006, during my final year at Duke Divinity School, I began watching the Homecomings. I saw rich possibilities for a large-scale project on this immensely popular franchise—a franchise that, perhaps due to its appeal to a senior demographic that American culture (academic and nonacademic) preferred not to countenance, seemed hidden in plain sight. I wrote to Bill, sharing some preliminary thoughts and my prospects for further study. His handwritten letter back to me encouraged me to proceed. A few months of correspondence with Bill led to me driving with my spouse, Lynn, to Alexandria, Indiana, to meet Bill and Gloria (it will become clear that being in a heterosexual marriage—married to a minister, no less—gave me a special kind of head start in the Gaithers' world).

After I began my doctoral studies in Princeton University's Department of Religion, I would make two more trips to Alexandria—the first a weeklong stay in 2008, the second in 2011, for Gloria's inaugural weekend-long Song-writers' Intensive workshop. My lengthiest, tape-recorded, sit-down interviews with Bill and Gloria occurred separately during the 2008 trip. Direct quotations of private conversations with the Gaithers come mostly from these recordings. A small number of quotations come from the verbatim notes I made immediately after the respective exchange.

I attended eleven Homecoming concerts over this timespan in various states: Alabama, Kentucky, Maryland, Missouri, North Carolina, Pennsylvania, and Tennessee (the last event was the annual three-day Family Fest in Gatlinburg, which was the performance equivalent of at least three concerts). I divided my time at the concerts between listening to the music, conversing backstage with performers and staff members, wandering among the merchandise tables, and talking to fans.

In addition to informal fan conversations, I conducted off-site, tape-recorded fan interviews. In the fall of 2009 and the summer of 2010, I talked to fans in Missouri, Illinois, North Carolina, Kentucky, and New Jersey—all white, approximately 60 percent women, almost entirely evangelical but spanning denominations, mostly fifty years of age and older. All of the quotations in this book from named fans come from these interviews (though I change names). Quotations from informal fan conversations come from my verbatim transcriptions.

PHRASEOLOGY: SORTS OF *HOMECOMINGS*

Long before *Homecoming* became a capitalized Gaither entity, the term *home-coming* possessed a few meanings in American evangelical culture. Even under the Gaither rubric, homecoming can signal a variety of artifacts and musical forms.

Homecomings in history: Around the time of the Great Depression, many churches in the South and Midwest began hosting annual revivalistic reunions. These gatherings typically occurred once a year, lasted from a day to a week, and revolved around preaching, praying, singing, and eating. The church invited guest preachers and some quantity of gospel singers and musical worship leaders to master the ceremonies—usually regionally renowned figures and groups (the reach of the invitations often depended on the availability of funds). The music issued from some combination of congregational singing and ensemble performances. The festivities—the *homecoming*—concluded with an often-outdoor community feast: the "dinner on the grounds."

Churches called these events *homecomings* because they sought to gather not only current but also erstwhile members of the congregation, especially those who had left the church's geographical reach but who still had familial connections to the old home place. Homecomings and rural emigration became anticipated events during the same period. Family farms faded as children moved from parents' homes and fields toward the lights in the distance—in search of employment in the industrial urban centers and on the larger proto-factory farms that increasingly dominated the rural landscape.[10] My father grew up in a southern Missouri town that had fewer than 100 citizens and that no longer exists—in a farmhouse with no electricity or indoor plumbing. After high school, he moved to and between the local "big cities" (ranging from 4,000 to 8,000 people) before becoming a manager of a grocery store in 35,000-person Cape Girardeau, Missouri. He still receives invitations to his boyhood church's annual homecoming.

This sort of homecoming is rooted in anxiety over roots. It is necessary because of dislocation, separation. People have left home and made new homes. The home to which they come for a homecoming is home no longer. On one hand, the homecoming jointly lifts up the piety and authenticity of the returned-to home. The quality and the pitch of homecoming sermons and songs testify to the vigor and durability of the old-time (religious) ways. Home is authentic *because* it is unchanged by the suffocating caprices of modern life. It is *still* home, flush with familiarity and mutual recognition. The appeal depends partly on the assumption that home is a site where dissimulation is neither possible nor desirable—a contestable assumption, given the experience of many people who lived as sexual, political, or theological exiles in their old home places, whose home survival necessitated dissimulation. But the assumption contains a kernel of truth. Effective dissimulation requires profound intimacy with the culture one is putting on. There also is a self-fulfilling edge to this assumption. If one is a candidate for a homecoming invitation, and if one accepts the invitation, one bears witness to the profound, mutual intimacy that exists between the departed characters and the old home place. It is an effective practice. Emigrants for whom return is not ideal do not return. Emigrants who hunger for former times and places were back home before they arrived.

On the other hand, the homecoming undermines the old home place because it is a *special* revival event. The "home" that the homecoming puts on is not the local church functioning in ordinary time. The invited preacher, the guest musicians, and even, paradoxically, the presence of those who have "left home," to whom the homecoming is supposed to appeal—all testify to the fabricated, extraordinary nature of this "home." The erstwhile church member, the emigrant, comes home only in the sense that a young Christian might come home to the house of her upbringing for Christmas. The glitter and tinsel do not adorn the living room most weekends. Home might include glittery, revival moments, but it includes much more, and much less. Additionally, the tightly circumscribed temporality of the homecoming indicates that it does not and cannot represent home-as-current-place-of-residence. Just as one must have left home to come home, one will depart for home once one leaves the homecoming. From the vantage point of a person who has "moved on"—for example, a person who left town and church long ago—the homecoming is an annual memorial service for a way of life that has passed away.

But the past does not pass away entirely. Memorialization is often evangelization. As revival events, homecomings seek to ignite and recharge the faiths of those gathered. While preaching and singing display homecoming evangelism most strikingly, homecomings proclaim more than belief in the unadorned, context-transcending saving gospel of Jesus Christ. Along with Jesus come the sights, sounds, tastes, and smells of the old home place. The erstwhile community member who has moved to the city or to the centralized factory farm town receives a reminder of her Christian calling couched in a set of specific (if idealized) community practices. The practice is what is preached, in the hopes that emigrants might carry some element of those nearly extinct practices to their new homes, that they might fashion their new home places in the image of the old—for their welfare, for the welfare of their new city. The past need not be dead. It need not even be past.

Homecoming in death: *Homecoming* also possesses a more otherworldly connotation. That one's true home lies in the Great Beyond, and that being at home with the Lord means being away, in some sense, from one's extant material body, are old Christian notions. New Testament passages such as the prodigal son parable and the interpretation of Abraham's journey in the eleventh chapter of Hebrews use home as a metaphor for final communion with God, the home's patriarch. The heaven-as-home motif is ubiquitous in country and gospel music, but it is not limited to them. Pop and rock songs such as Peter Schilling's "Major Tom (Coming Home)" and the Grateful Dead's "Uncle John's Band" play with the metaphor.

The home/heaven metaphor cuts two ways. Because it encourages people to extrapolate from this-worldly "homes" to the afterlife, it domesticates the eternal. Numerous popular evangelical renderings of heaven in film and literature suggest that, when evangelical Christians speculate on the furniture of heaven, it resembles the furniture of their living rooms (or that of the idealized living room of the old home place). The same people sit by the heavenly and earthly hearths. Todd Burpo's and Lynn Vincent's best-selling 2010 book *Heaven Is for Real* exemplifies how one's earthly notion of family and home can shape one's notion of heaven.[11] At the same time, the heaven/ home metaphor depends upon there being a difference between heaven and earth; the former is the real thing, the latter the shadow. A Christian resides truly in the arms of God, and in that shelter, there may be other residents—people who implicitly or explicitly are denied a place by the hearth in this world. If Christians believe they should strive to approximate the heavenly "family of God" in this world, they must assess and reassess the boundaries of their communions. Even if such assessments never occur, or even if they merely uphold old boundaries, the possibility ever exists that one's domestic arrangements will be weighed in the heavenly scales and found wanting.

Homecomings and the Gaithers: The Gaither Homecomings intentionally conjure these sorts of *homecoming*, but they also have given the term new meanings. *Homecoming* can refer to several different endeavors in the Gaither world. Most narrowly, *Homecoming* indicates the 1991 video and Gaither Vocal Band album that birthed the franchise. The Gaithers also used "Homecoming" loosely to describe the media products and the personnel on the videos that immediately followed in the 1990s and early 2000s—nearly all of which included a chorus of singers sitting in a semicircle around a piano, taking turns singing solos, and joining together to sing hymns and convention songs. These videos and albums advertised "Bill and Gloria Gaither and Their Homecoming Friends." The Homecoming concert tour began in 1995. Even after many of the performers in the first videos and concerts died or pursued other interests, and even after the Gaithers altered the design and format of the concerts and videos, "Homecoming" remained in the title or subtitle of most Gaither events and products. Gloria launched *Homecoming Magazine* in 2003. Thomas Nelson published *The Gaither Homecoming Bible* in 2012.

Eventually, Bill came to use "homecoming" to signify a particular visual and aural arrangement. The standard format for the concerts I attended from 2006 to 2011 was a split show: before intermission, individual artists and groups took turns performing two to three songs (the Gaither Vocal Band performed longer). Bill typically announced before intermission that "we would do a homecoming" when the program resumed. After intermission, all of the musicians would gather in seats onstage and perform a set of songs amenable to audience singing, trading the solo microphone.

MOTIFS AND SKETCHES

I always have liked Cleanth Brooks's idea that poetry resists paraphrase. As Brooks's New Criticism fell out of fashion in literary circles, many poets hung (and hang) on to this notion of unparaphrasability. I enjoy the certainly true, possibly factual story of the Russian ballerina Anna Pavlova, responding to a reporter who had asked her to explain the meaning of one of her performances: "if I could explain it to you, I would not have needed to dance it."[12]

Poets and dancers maintain, even accrue, authority when they give such dodgy answers concerning the propositionality—the "aboutness"—of their compositions. But one does not get away so easily with such answers when one writes a book that is supposedly *about* something. *What IS your book about? What is your argument? What can we expect? For what can we hold you responsible?* These questions burden me because I do not know who "we" are, exactly, and I probably will find out late. They burden me because they cannot be answered simply, yet they deserve a response. I believe scholarly writing on religion and art is itself an art. As such, it veers away from "aboutness" more than many in the field may care to admit. Scholars surely are charged to observe and to propose explanations about their subjects using language and categories that the subjects themselves might not possess or use. However, I believe it is only honest for scholars to produce a study whose content *and form* neighbors the often nonpropositional or trans-propositional dimensions of their subjects' worlds. It is true that scholars traffic in propositions—in self-conscious arguments that are sustained based on agreed-upon kinds of evidence. But this is what many of our religious subjects say about their endeavors, too—especially if we work on evangelical Protestants.[13] So often we listen to them politely then proceed to explain how their propositions are epiphenomenal (at best), focusing on the "significant" stuff going on behind, underneath, against, and in spite of their propositions. We should not be surprised if one day our subjects approach our "essentially propositional" scholarly self-identity with the same skepticism with which we have approached theirs.

I do not wish to rush headlong into the fallacy of imitative form. I believe responsible scholarship does not simply mirror the idiosyncrasies and aesthetic of its subjects, nor does it eschew making claims and arguments. But it should be more than this. As I searched for a voice in this project, my challenge was to write in a fashion that discharges my debt to my many different potential readers—among them, ethnographers of religion; scholars of American evangelicalism; historians of American music; theologians; ethicists; people interested in the Gaithers, Homecomings, and southern gospel; and the people about whom I write—while at the same time pushing all of these communities to wrestle with the terms of their (our) specific vocabularies and expectations. My models have been sorts of ekphrastic writers—those who write about art of all varieties, who do so in a way that melds argument with artistry, whose writing participates in, but is not confused with, the life and aesthetic of their subjects: Stanley Cavell and Jim Boon on Henry David Thoreau, Helen Vendler on Walt Whitman and John Ashbery (I might add, Ashbery himself on Parmigianino), Jeff Stout on Emerson's "Experience" (and on community organizing in the American Southwest—another kind of artistry), Amy Hungerford on Tim Lahaye's *Left Behind*, John Lardas Modern on *Moby-Dick* and "religious machines."[14] These writers transform my vision of what is operant inside and around their subjects without dictating to me an absolute argument. These are scholars who put things together and take things apart without tidying things up. These are scholars whose work leaves me admitting, it is not *merely* as they say, it is not *only* as they say, but it is *certainly* as they say.

In the spirit I find in my models, I continue to set my type against paraphrase. In the same spirit, I verge on an argument. The narratives that comprise this book typically revolve around three conflicts:

Particularity vs. universality: Most southern gospel insiders would concede that southern gospel is one form of Christian music among many. It traffics in a particular vision of a particular American "southernness." *Southern* gospel is attractive because of this particularity.

The question of southern *gospel*'s particularity is more difficult for southern gospel insiders to answer. While they would concede that there is a *demographic* particularity to the southern gospel's Christian message (obviously, not everyone in the world is a Christian), there would be more debate about its *normative* particularity. The more exclusivistic members of the southern gospel world might not concede that the "gospel" of southern gospel is one version of Christianity among many (again, except as a concession to demographics). There is only one Christian gospel; where it is absent, Christianity is also absent. There also is the question of Christianity's universal appeal. While southern gospellers might concede that there are some parochial elements of the genre that might not appeal to people outside the fold, they would maintain that the "gospel" contained in the music transcends particularity. The general message is for all, even if the particular medium is not.

The question of which aspects of *southern gospel* are universal and which are particular requires perpetual speculation from evangelicals who work to defend and disseminate their "universal" message of gospel salvation to all. Defending the gospel message means specifying a particular object for defense; such particularities always take shape in specific cultural contexts. The difference between an instrumental and a nonnegotiable particularity (substance and essence) is difficult to discern—especially in a large, nonhierarchical group of people whose religion is based largely on the Universal becoming incarnate in one transcendent-yet-historically-located man.

Preservation vs. expansion: Related to the issue of particularity and universality is preservation and expansion. The issue pertains to the musical genre. Bill Gaither's love for southern gospel means that he wants to (a) showcase it as a distinct musical form and (b) broadcast it to an audience largely ignorant of it, in the hopes of bringing more people into the fold. While Bill has confidence that the power of the music, unadulterated, will draw people to it, he is also aware that maximizing his audience requires him to push the genre's boundaries. Gaither music has always been genre-transgressive, and the Gaithers are not just able but also eager to push the boundaries; they want the southern gospel faithfuls' boundaries to be expanded as well. But how far can one push the genre's boundaries, in order to evangelize on behalf of the genre, before one has created a new genre? How far can a southern gospel soul swim away from itself and hold on to the promise of returns?

The parallels with evangelical religion are clear: when do the measures of evangelization, the will to universalize one's gospel, change the content of one's evangelizing? The theological, musical, social, and regional aspects of Homecoming production overlap as members of the Homecoming world wrestle with this inaudible question.

Authenticity vs. artifice: "I can see how you felt that way," Bill told me with a smile. I was nervous. He and Gloria had read an early draft of this book, and while they both had seemed to understand my aims in the project from the outset, part of me always wondered if they were expecting hagiography from me. This first, five-hour meeting with the pair regarding the initial draft greatly alleviated my concern. To be sure, Bill and Gloria pushed back at some of my claims—who wouldn't, in their position?—but most of their comments were matters of clarification and were immensely helpful.

Of utmost concern to Bill was my opening story about the taping in Louisville. Bill explained to me that, during that year, he had hired a production outfit he had never worked with previously. They were nice people, he said, and they worked hard for him, but he bristled at the "artificial" devices the group used to elicit appropriate responses from Gaither crowds—in other words, the preshow tactics to gather canned laughter and applause. "I tried to tell them, 'you won't need to tell our audiences when to laugh and clap,'" Bill told me with a shake of the head. "We stopped using them after that show." He pointed to my opening pages and said, "but I can see how you felt that way."

Senses of authenticity fuel the Homecomings. Being authentic—being real—is rule number one for the Gaithers and their musicians. In the Homecoming world, authenticity is a concept of multiple correspondence. The Gaithers are authentic if all of their "selves"—onstage and offstage—match with one another. The Gaithers are also authentic if their professions of Christian faith match their onstage and offstage professions and actions.

Two factors complicate Homecoming authenticity. First, when a celebrity evangelical's public face is a home(coming) face—when the public seat she occupies is a plush living-room recliner situated in the middle of a concert stage—the lines between public and private blur, and not always in the celebrity's favor. While the private-looking public stage may persuade fans that they are actually peering into the Gaithers' parlor, it also makes fans feel entitled to see the actual private spaces. Southern gospel fans—at least, many of those die-hards who publish the articles, post on the blogs, and cultivate what they feel are justifiably strong opinions about performers—tend to obsess over musicians' personal lives. The payoff for musicians can be high, but so is the price. Everything and nothing is public and private. If some prying fan or academic unearths something from the offstage private space that troubles the Homecoming décor, all is lost. It is risky business to be authentic.

The second factor relates to the preservation vs. expansion issue. In so large and protean a congregation as the Homecoming fan base, opinions abound as to what constitutes authentic Christianity. Not only do fans have differing opinions as to what constitutes right correspondence between professed Christianity and Christian behavior, they also are likely to expect all of the Gaithers' variously manifest Christianities to correspond with their own—even though theirs might not correspond to those of their fellow fans. Maintaining lines of correspondence in the Homecoming world is extremely tricky business.

This book is about how the Gaithers, Homecoming performers, and Homecoming fans work through these three nodes of tension. The first chapter focuses on the first decade of the franchise. I examine the first *Homecoming*, and the Gaithers' narrative rendering of *Homecoming*, against the backdrop of late 1980s/early 1990s American politics, economics, evangelicalism, and entertainment. Chapter 2 examines Guy Penrod—singer in the Gaither Vocal Band through the Homecomings' most successful run, the face of the franchise during its heyday. The first of three chapters that focus on a particular Homecoming figure, this chapter investigates the Homecoming "construction" of Penrod as a rugged yet sensitive family man. I bring to light the ways the Gaithers choose and contour performers to satisfy and challenge fans' expectations. Chapter 3 explores the (a)politics of the Homecomings. For several reasons, the Gaithers intend their programs to be free of politics—primarily free of the party endorsements that have saturated and often harmed the ministries of a number of their fellow public evangelicals, dating back to the Richard Nixon–Billy Graham era. While the Gaithers are relatively adept at accomplishing this sort of "apoliticism," there are other senses of "politics" resident, implicitly and explicitly, in Homecoming discourse. My analysis of the appearances and disappearances of these "politics" in the Homecoming world exposes the promises and perils that face American evangelical communities—and, more broadly, the American democratic community of which they are an important constituent.

Chapter 4 focuses on Gloria Gaither, the principal lyricist in the Gaither duo and the chief scriptwriter for most Homecoming videos and products. Gloria is a monumental yet marginal presence in the Homecoming world, as are her theological contributions. The chapter explores how Gloria simultaneously expands and fortifies the boundaries of Homecoming evangelicalism—primarily through her careful augmentations of conservative evangelical tropes. Chapter 5 picks up chronologically where chapter 1 ended: the turn of the century. In this chapter, I explore what happens to the Homecomings when the Gaithers leave the American South, when a number of the "legends" to whom the early videos pay tribute die, and when the Gaithers have a decade's worth of Homecoming social capital at their backs on which to expand. No Homecoming regular better illustrates the tension between expansion and preservation than Lynda Randle, the subject of the sixth chapter. The most pervasive African American presence in the Homecomings, Randle functions both as evidence of and catalyst to the changes the Gaithers made and make to southern gospel culture. Unlike most African American figures in the Homecomings, Randle is framed as a full member of the circle. However, even Randle's full membership is contingent upon her embodiment and narration of trace differences. The Gaithers contract Randle to enlarge the Homecoming gospel. The question of Randle's inclusion is the question that the Gaithers, the Homecoming musicians, Homecoming fans, and I, in this sort of Homecoming book, perpetually ask: in the end, which terms are binding?

1
TIME PRESENT AND TIME PAST
THE HOMECOMINGS, 1991–1999

IN THE END, THE BEGINNING

In 1990, Bill Gaither could feel an end beginning. By the end of the 1980s, Elvis Presley, Johnny Cash, and many others had recorded Bill's "He Touched Me."[1] The Gaither songs "Because He Lives," "Let's Just Praise the Lord," "There's Something about That Name," "The King Is Coming," and "The Family of God" had been recorded by countless gospel artists and anthologized in evangelical and mainline Protestant hymnals.[2] "Jesus, You're the Center of My Joy," which the Gaithers cowrote with African American gospel musician Richard Smallwood, won Gospel Song of the Year at the 1987 Stellar Awards (started in 1985, the Stellars are the premier awards program devoted to black gospel music). The song was on its way to becoming a new classic in African American churches. The Gaithers controlled the copyrights to their compositions, so Bill and Gloria, fifty-four and forty-eight years of age, respectively, would continue to collect royalties as long as their songs had public life. Things looked promising. The stylistic adaptability of many Gaither songs suggested that they could face an evangelical tomorrow in which pianos, choirs, and hymnals would give way to guitars, "praise bands," and overhead projection.

At the same time, Bill's all-male quartet, the Gaither Vocal Band (GVB), which had performed and recorded since 1981, was not performing well on the market. The GVB had been a labor of love for Bill. It provided him a way to sing in an ensemble akin to those groups he loved as a youth in the 1940s and 1950s, the heyday of what would come to be called southern gospel music. A mongrel of traditional close harmony[3] and 1980s synth-gospel, the GVB did not fit squarely in the self-consciously traditional southern gospel milieu or in the growing CCM scene. During the late 1980s, Gloria had subordinated her songwriting to her academic pursuits. The former high school French teacher taught off and on as an adjunct professor at her alma mater, Anderson University, a few miles down the road from the Gaither's Alexandria home. In 1991, Gloria earned a master's degree in English from Ball State University to go with her triple-major undergraduate degree in English, French, and sociology. By 1990, all three of the Gaithers' children had left the house (Gloria and her oldest daughter Suzanne attended graduate school together at Ball State, Suzanne earning her master's degree in English in 1990). Transitioning from hands-on parenthood to potential grandparenthood in 1990, the Gaithers were rolling back their gospel workload, seeming to prepare for a life more at ease in Alexandria—partially retired, a sort of final homecoming.

Bill thought the first "Homecoming" would be wrap-up music. He wanted to resolve the GVB melodies on an explicitly traditional note. In his 2003 book *It's More Than the Music*, Bill recalls telling Gloria in 1990, "it seems that the Gaither band is winding down, but before we quit, I'd like to record a Southern gospel classic. I've always loved that style of music, so I'd like to have all my heroes come in and sing on one song, something we all know."[4] Bill ran his idea by Darrell Harris, a respected producer at Star Song—one of the top record labels in the Christian music business, also the GVB's label. Harris liked the idea, immediately registering the similarity between Bill's proposed project and the Nitty Gritty Dirt Band's highly successful 1972 recording of A. P. Carter's "Will the Circle Be Unbroken?"—a musical encomium performed with (and for) country music legends Roy Acuff, Mother Maybelle Carter, and others.[5] With Harris's and Star Song's blessing, Gaither began making phone calls in his circle, to the "living legends" of southern gospel.

In the winter of 1991, the legends came forth—some from the evangelical-vaudeville stages of Branson, Missouri, and Gatlinburg, Tennessee, some from third-tier Nashville studios, some from the little brown churches in America's remote vales, some from near destitution resulting from mismanagement of funds or increasing musical obsolescence. Many of the artists, who once upon a time had shared stages, tour buses, and personnel, had not seen one another in years. The circle had been broken—by death, illness, professional decline, or the simple drifting apart that occurs when time and space yawn widely between the immobilized.

Through the tearful torrents of reunion, Bill ordered the proceedings. The session was designed to yield a recording of the 1940 James Coats song, "Where

Could I Go (but to the Lord)?" The song would appear on what Bill supposed would be the final GVB album, *Homecoming*. Intending to produce a music video for the song, Gaither hired a video crew to capture images of the singers "live" on the sound stage. Reminiscent of Quincy Jones's 1985 production of the collaborative "We Are the World," the studio session itself would supply most of the video footage—though the final video would contain images and archival reels of the legendary gospel quartets and singing groups performing in their mid-twentieth-century prime. A montage of decade-spanning gospel singing, the "Where Could I Go?" video would merge past and present.

By accident or design, the audio and video crews had a surplus of audio and video reels at their disposal. While the singers quickly recorded work-able tracks for the Coats song, it would take another several hours to pry the musicians, kicking and singing, from the little studio circle. No one wanted to quit. Gathered around the grand piano in the center of the studio, the assembly kept procuring and performing the gospel songs lodged in their collective memory. They shouted out "requests" to pianist Eva Mae Lefevre (of the gospel group the Lefevre Trio), who promptly plunked out an intro, and they were off. Before anyone could stop them, the ensemble was knee-deep in another tune. Bill Gaither—a little star-struck despite his own legendary status in the gospel music industry—certainly was not going to stop them. The tape rolled on. While the studio's ambient boom microphones captured most of the sound, eventually the singers began passing around a hand-held microphone so soloists could take passes at verses, breaking up the unison choruses of the performances. Occasionally, solo artists broke into emotional testimony— describing recent hardships, expressing how happy they were to be with old friends and fellow musicians. The circle was repaired, temporarily at least, in the ecstasy of the past-become-present. Through it all, the tape rolled on.

Having collected more than enough footage for the music video, the video crew gave Bill their piles of extra tape. In addition to the "official" music video, Bill cobbled together a longer program—one that captured the session's spon-taneity and spirit by broadcasting the sing-alongs, prayers, and testimonies. Fearful of losing the session's improvisational essence, Bill executed only a few sparse, remedial edits on the tapes. Most of the editing involved paring things down, since Bill had to condense the footage into a reasonable length for viewing. He showed his final, hour-long product to a team of Star Song executives. He gave the receptive executives permission to send the film to Norm Mintle, the network producer for the Family Channel, operated by the Christian Broadcasting Network. In the spring of 1991, Mintle aired the program as *The Gaither Vocal Band Homecoming Video Album*.

After the video's introductory piece, the "Where Could I Go?" music video, Bill appears standing in front of a mixing board. Dressed in a colorful sweater that recalled Bill Cosby's Heathcliff Huxtable, the grand benevolent patriarch of late eighties television, Bill prefaces the video with an apology: "this is not perfect by any stretch of the imagination because we didn't know any of the arrangements we were singing; we were just singing spontaneously. But the Lord kind of came in and visited that place in a very, very special way."[6] For the program's remainder, Bill is present primarily as a voiceover, setting up scenes and identifying songs and performers.

The first Homecoming resembles a home movie. The sound varies in quality; performers often sing while conversations between other performers are visibly and audibly prominent behind them. People walk in front of the camera; some unidentified, nonperforming figure partially might block a scene for several seconds. Only single, uninterrupted camera shots are used for the performances, prayers, and testimonies; jump cuts occur sparsely, at the transitions to new songs or to Bill narrating from his studio bunker. The scenes bounce and quiver, as crew members hustle through the room with their unwieldy equipment, trying to guess where the next opportune shot will occur. Boom microphone operators and singers appear on film with about the same frequency. Even the introductory, more overtly produced "Where Could I Go?" video views like a moving picture album, as it binds together, in sepia tones, a series of session clips with older footage and photos of the legendary gospel groups. *Homecoming* seems indeed like a private "video album"—a collection of loose, amateur footage bound together primarily for only an interested posterity.

The interested posterity turned out to include a sizable viewership. Immediately following *Homecoming*'s premier, the Family Channel received a barrage of requests for rebroadcasts. According to Bill, in but a few hours, over seven thousand people phoned the network to ask how they could purchase a copy of *Homecoming*. According to Bill, the Gaithers' Alexandria offices could not field all of the queries it received over the following weeks. Bill soon realized that his first Homecoming video—the musical harvest of a man preparing for his final curtain call—would not be his last.

Bill Gaither loves to tell this story of the first Gaither Homecoming. The story is a fiction—not necessarily a lie.[7] As a musician, I have experienced the euphoria of reuniting with musicians with whom I used to perform regularly—the thrill of taking up where all left off, the rush of collective recall and partial resynchronization. The errors, the gaps in memory when one is attempting to remember a tune, call to mind the natal stages of one's ensemble. Even rust is sepia-toned. Old spats and conflicts fade; the euphoria is a painkiller. Add emotive evangelical religion to such a reunion and the euphoria likely will amplify. I am disposed to believe Bill Gaither when he claims that the inaugural Homecoming session sincerely and profoundly moved him and the musicians present.

But it is as *fiction*—as a narrative, told and retold—that the first Homecoming resonates with most of the franchise's fans. Obviously, the fans were not present when the session occurred. None of the fans with whom I conversed two decades after *Homecoming*'s first airing recalled viewing that first airing—understandable, given that hardly any of these fans were following the GVB through the 1980s.[8] More conspicuously, only a few had seen *Homecoming* at all. Most of those who had seen it did so several years after the fact. This was after they had absorbed subsequent Homecoming programs, a number of which told the *story* of the first video—complete with Bill's stated motivation for organizing the session, vivid descriptions of the revivalistic transformation of the studio, and the narrative of the unexpected outpouring of interest. The fans to whom I spoke knew *Homecoming* through a Homecoming telling. No one I met had called the Family Channel or Alexandria in 1991.

Bill's Homecoming nativity story recapitulates a few of the apparently biblical motifs dear to American evangelicals: aging gospel patriarchs and matriarchs experience vocational rebirth, well after the assumed passing of their musical fecundity; a potentially unprofitable labor of love ends up resonating with millions of consumers, even though it was faithfulness to a call, not desire for market success, that motivated the laborers. Two years before the first Homecoming, Universal Pictures released *Field of Dreams*, a film version of W. P. Kinsella's 1982 novel *Shoeless Joe*. *Field of Dreams* tells the story of Ray Kinsella (Kevin Costner), an Iowa farmer who carves a baseball field into his cornfield on the instruction of an otherworldly voice that speaks privately to him. Ray's decision seems foolhardy; he acts only on his tenuous faith in the voice's promise: *if you build it, he will come*. Ray's act of faith leads to his connecting with the spirits of baseball legends and to his reconnecting with the ghost of his estranged, baseball-playing father. Baseball—the great American institution, as the film pronounces it—is the medium and content of Ray's reconciliation with his father. *If you build it, they will come* is the oft-misquoted version of the movie's tag line—misquoted for good reason: the ball field whose construction portended financial ruin for Ray ends up attracting countless pilgrims. Shortly after a stirring speech from Terrance Mann (James Earl Jones) about baseball's appeal to the American collective consciousness, the movie closes with a nighttime shot of the field and a band of automobile headlights stretching for miles—a visual indicator of the field's appeal, and the appeal of all it represents.

Field of Dreams's final shot possesses self-reflective and self-fulfilling edges. The "people who come" are the real and hoped-for moviegoers, flocking to a sort of mass baptism to be immersed in the enchanted waters of America's pastime. As in a number of biblical narratives, modern-day pilgrims must journey to the hinterlands—in this case, the wide open spaces of rural Iowa—for spiritual immersion. American pastoral and America's pastime co-sacralize each other. The motorists stretched across the screen at the movie's conclusion are the moviegoers lined up to watch (and rewatch) the movie; the film memorializes baseball and positions itself to become part of the memorialization. Universal Studios commissioned the building of the baseball field in a cornfield near Dyersville, Iowa, in order to use it for the film. It was built for fiction. After the movie appeared (and after it had been nominated for a Best Picture Oscar), the field itself became a tourist attraction. The fiction built the field on which the fiction was built: dreams delivered to dreams.[9]

Like *Field of Dreams*, the tale of the first Homecoming takes life at the close of the 1980s. The Reagan era of big business was also the era of the unapologetically synthetic, "space age" product: hair spray, new Coke, neon, electronic drums and keyboards—even the polyester-and-pastel Major League Baseball uniforms of the period testified to the lure of the lab-forged commodity. It was as if those wares that obviously were fashioned by human, corporate, or (better still) machine hands proved the power of unrestrained free-market capitalism and signaled its future possibilities. Even the GVB album covers of the 1980s trafficked in neon and pastel. The 1980s American fascination with the overtly synthetic product harked back to post-WWII America—the infancy of the nuclear age, and the flowering of what Lizabeth Cohen calls "a consumer's republic." As manifest in the sound and image of musical groups such as the Stray Cats and movies such as *Back to the Future*, 1980s popular culture frequently drew upon 1950s America. To the extent that 1980s popular culture looked backward, it looked backward to a decade that looked forward to a technologically sleek, efficient tomorrow—an era that held the future.[10]

Although the neon dreams of the 1980s were not proof of all Americans' purchase of Reagan's America, the dreams held great purchase in Reagan's America.[11] However, the grip slipped significantly in the sour notes of the 1980s coda: the S & L scandal, an economic recession that would result in the unseating of Reagan's presidential successor/former vice president, and a large-scale US military conflict launched against a Middle Eastern country whose military was fortified by US money and technology. Currency turned against itself; the dreamers had to reckon with the growing despair that occurred when Americans considered the catastrophic works of the nation's invisible hands. Despite the growing dissatisfaction with the results of the economic machine, in parts of the nation there remained a strong will to believe that the machine could yield better fruits. The machine had stalled but not failed. Surely the market—surely consumers—possessed more redemptive possibilities than had been manifest in the 1980s. In perhaps the greatest example of cognitive dissonance in post-Reagan pop music, the glam rock band Poison scored a major hit in 1990, when their front man (and later reality television show regular) Bret Michaels sang, adorned in spandex and doused in hairspray, "give me something to believe in."[12]

Between the stalling of various 1980s machines, the faint revving of *Homecoming* drew a number of American evangelicals—just as *Field of Dreams* was drawing moviegoers, just as the MTV network was swapping Poison music videos for the stripped-down *Unplugged* concert series, just as Hollywood hair bands were conceding *Rolling Stone* covers to the "raw" Seattle grunge bands. The accidence and spontaneity of the first *Homecoming*—qualities that the story of the first Homecoming highlights—bear witness to the video's authenticity. From a production standpoint, *Homecoming* is nearly unwatchable; at the end of the 1980s, that was what made it watchable. The low production quality also validates Bill Gaither's claim that the session was solely a labor of love. Family Channel and Star Song execs do not play major roles in the story; the story's power rests on the assumption that no "business people" in their right minds would have believed in the video's marketability. The enterprise's authenticity was directly proportionate to its foundation in extra-market or nonmarket values. Making the video was like cutting a baseball field into an Iowa cornfield; a voice from beyond the market must have called to the artifact's maker.

However, the Homecoming supersession of the market could not be narrated as total. The flood of consumer interest is as essential to the first Homecoming's narrative as are accident, spontaneity, and Bill Gaither's personal musical tastes. The nativity story happily ends with consumers' massive endorsement of the video. Bill built it, people came. The rest is history. When this story gets told later in the franchise's lifespan—after several Grammys, Dove Awards, platinum and gold product sales—both Bill Gaither and the early Homecoming fans appear prescient, like shepherds in the Galilean hinterlands, an unlikely first population to bear witness to the gospel born in the countryside. The predominantly white, southern, evangelical consumers knew best. The stone that most builders in the entertainment industry would have rejected became the cornerstone of the most lucrative enterprise in twentieth-century Christian music.

That this consumer republic's endorsement positively wraps up the Homecoming nativity story demonstrates a key free-market presupposition operant in the Homecoming world: (certain) consumers' desires and demands are trustworthy signifiers of authenticity. Thus the story of the first Homecoming is inscribed in a circle of mutual affirmations. If the market supports so obviously an authentic enterprise as Homecoming—"authentic" meaning built upon and manifesting market-transcending values—then the market must operate on trustworthy values. The market cannot help itself. If Homecoming and its nativity story garner such widespread interest in the market (a market composed of customers who for the most part possess supposedly trustworthy consumer desires), then Homecoming must be authentic—"authentic" meaning possessing widespread if not universal appeal. Presumed sanctified, Homecoming baptizes the market that contains its consumers. Presumed sanctified, the consumers in the market baptize Homecoming.

It is important to note how much the free-market presupposition resembles presuppositions that undergird evangelical soteriology and missiology—presuppositions regarding inclusion, exclusion, growth, and maintenance.[13] The evangelical Christ accepts every willing person and is acceptable to every willing person. Nothing better verifies this universally appealing Christ than having a large number of people—preferably people who come from a number of demographics—claim him as Savior. This evangelical Christ also proclaims, however, "strait is the gate, narrow the path." The universally appealing Christ also causes offense to the world. Not all are called—or, not all will answer the call. The notion of community narrowness sometimes tempers implicit and explicit evangelical celebrations over big assemblies at the altar and at Christian music concerts. If no one is being turned off by the proclamation—if everyone is buying the message—evangelicals might suspect that they have ceased proclaiming this Christ. During the Homecomings' heyday, this suspicion appeared most forthrightly in evangelicals' criticisms of evangelical megachurches, especially those that appear to preach a "health-and-wealth" gospel. Just about any popular evangelical person or movement, by virtue of their popularity, opened themselves to the criticism that they had sold out the gospel for a mess of pottage.[14] Related to this suspicion is the fact that the tenets and practices that comprise the sine qua non of evangelical identity become more difficult to define, monitor, and maintain as that dynamic, diffuse group called "evangelicals" expands. When evangelicals' gospel goes viral, they may take it as a sign of the promise, or as a sign that they have made some egregious concession—or possibly, anxiously, as a sign of both.

Judging by numbers and influence, the anxiety that results from being both a people set apart from a Christ-hostile world and a people called to bring that world into right relation with a world-loving Christ has been productive for American evangelicals. Sociologist Christian Smith's dyad, "embattled and thriving," sums up the American evangelical situation well.[15] With respect to *Homecoming* and its nativity story, the appealing and appalling "Gospel" of Christ is connected to an idea of a peculiar, permanent culture that cannot but move. This gospel has distinctive local colors, but the colors mix and mingle differently depending on the palette. *Homecoming* manifests and recommends a simultaneously sonic, visual, and textual aesthetic. This aesthetic is tied both to a particular (southern, rural, white) culture and to a particular evangelical gospel message. Few in the Homecoming world would insist that aesthetic, culture, and "the Gospel" must be wedded. For example, most fans whom I interviewed had a charitable (if occasionally condescending) attitude toward CCM. A typical refrain: *it's not for me, but, praise God, it's attracting the young people.* Evangelicals' will-to-growth—the desire to construct houses of prayer for *all* peoples—requires them to possess a bit of intraevangelical cosmopolitanism.[16]

The colors on the palette will mix, somehow, in use; aesthetic, culture, and "the Gospel" are closely connected. Because the Homecoming *tableau vivant* relies heavily upon all three, the Gaithers must be especially sensitive to all shades of compound colors the citizens of the Homecoming world make— more aware than the citizens who mix the colors. How do fans understand the relationship between aesthetic, culture, and gospel? Which sorts of disjunctions will they celebrate, tolerate, and reject? When is it acceptable for the Gaithers to play loose with the aesthetic or cultural boundaries manifest in the Homecomings in order to spread the gospel? What is the difference between expanding the necessarily expansive gospel and expanding *upon* the gospel? When must the gospel maintain a tight connection with the represented culture (for the gospel is necessarily incarnate—circumscribed, context-specific)? What happens when the Gaithers' own conception of the compound colors departs from that of their fans? These questions will become especially salient in chapter 4, when I discuss Gloria Gaither's Homecoming architecture. However, the questions surface at all periods in the Homecoming franchise, even in the first videos.

THE PERSISTENCE OF MEMORY:
THE EARLY HOMECOMING VIDEOS (1992–1994)

Even a perfunctory viewing of *Homecoming* leaves the impression that the 1991 project was built largely on accidence and spontaneity. Everything about *Homecoming* seemed accidental enough, thus authentic enough.[17] Bill Gaither was authentically excited about the substance of this "accident." He was eager to make a sequel.

On a practical level, Bill could conceive of a sequel because of viewer interest in the first video. After *Homecoming*, Bill needn't strain to prove to record executives that old-time southern gospel had a place in the market. Adding the fact that production costs for even a slightly more sophisticated program would be a pittance for Star Song, investment in a sequel was low-risk. Furthermore, Bill needn't strain to get performers interested in a follow-up. Most *Homecoming* participants jumped at the chance to participate in another taping, and a handful of additional musicians, having seen the first session, were ready to join the chorus.

The nuts and bolts of a sequel came easily. But how was Bill to recreate the immediate, unmediated spirit of *Homecoming*? On one level, Bill faced the continuity-versus-discontinuity dilemma endemic to all would-be media franchises. In *Homecoming*, Bill produced an "original" media object that reso-nated with viewers, performers, and himself. If he sought to produce another, similarly resonant object, it would have behooved him to attempt a formalis-tic reproduction of the original. But too exact a reproduction would turn the sequel into a mere repetition, potentially to be viewed as opportunistic and market-driven in a way that *Homecoming* was not.[18] This portended a prob-lem for Bill—a personal problem, apparently, for by his own account Bill was especially sensitive to the criticism that he only went into gospel music for the money.[19] A *Homecoming* sequel would prove all the more difficult because the original's power traced to its accidence and spontaneity. Could Bill *orchestrate* accidence and spontaneity in the sequel? If he could not, must he forfeit authenticity, since *Homecoming* authenticity seemed inversely proportionate to premeditation?

Bill navigated this dilemma in his second video: *Reunion: A Gospel Home-coming Celebration*, released in 1992. Looking back through the huge body of subsequent programs, *Reunion* seems a programmatic and stylistic transi-tion between the original video and the early 1990s videos that immediately followed it. Although it was edited more carefully, *Reunion* rehearsed much of *Homecoming*'s technological austerity. The cameramen sometimes walked into one anothers' shots, and the studio retained the unadorned, utilitarian air of a workshop. Viewers can see the wires.[20] *Reunion* also bore a famil-ial likeness to *Homecoming* because so many singers from the first session reappeared. At this point in Homecoming history, Bill Gaither reasonably could err on the side of over-accentuating this likeness. Despite the viewer interest in the first program, Bill could not count on all potentially inter-ested consumers having seen the original. He could not guess yet that he was starting a hundred-video, decades-spanning franchise. As he did in *Home-coming*, Bill was still gathering and memorializing musicians in *Reunion* as if each frame would be their last.

The most significant way in which *Reunion* anticipates the proceeding videos is its collapsing of two kinds of reunion. *Reunion* is both a reunion *like* the first video and a reunion *of* the previous video's participants. Bill gathered legends to memorialize gospel music and re-gathered legends to re-experi-ence and remember their recent gathering. Two kinds of reunion—two sorts of homecoming—converge. It is tough to distinguish in *Reunion* between remembering a pre-*Homecoming* southern gospel history and re-membering the previous Gaither video. This rolling over and compounding of memory is Bill Gaither's answer to the continuity-discontinuity conundrum. It is key to the franchise, as every video but the first is a Homecoming sequel.

The brief invocation of the Homecoming nativity story in *Reunion* signals how present and past Gaither projects will relate to one another. Before the main musical portion of the video commences, Bill speaks to singers Vestal Goodman and Eva Mae Lefevre—two of the aging "gospel legends" who appeared in the first video. He apparently talks to them before the recording session begins—pulling the smiling and laughing pair into the camera's field of vision as if they had been mulling about the studio, unprepared for a filmed interview. Standing on either side of Bill, the two southern gospel matriarchs frame him:

> BILL: We had so much fun back there in February when we did that other video, and that was kind of spur of the moment. And we said, "if God could bless that way, that just a spur of the moment, if we really kind of planned this thing and got some more people in here, we might really have a wonderful, wonderful time." And we had a good time.
>
> VESTAL GOODMAN: Oh, yes. It was wonderful.
>
> BILL: We had a . . .
>
> EVA MAE LEFEVRE: . . . I'll never forget that day, and I just have prayed that today would be another one just like it.[21]

Productive ambivalence concerning *Reunion*'s relationship to *Homecoming* is on full display in this exchange. Bill qualifies both the spontaneity that went into the first video and the premeditation that underwrote the second—a pre-meditation that Bill and the singers apparently have yet to execute (from the viewers' point of view, the session certainly has not been executed yet). *Home-coming* was "kind of" spur of the moment; *Reunion* was "kind of" planned. Bill's "we"—in this excerpt, the planners and the performers—hedges Bill's role as planner and improviser. He is a constituent of the administrative, premeditating *we* as well as the performing, spontaneous *we*. He declares that God blessed the spontaneous session but implies that such a blessing was more likely to fall on a better-planned project. Rather than concluding on this nod to premeditation, he routes the conversation back to *Homecoming* ("we had a good time"). Following Bill, Goodman offers a general, pleasant memory of the first project. The scene concludes when Lefevre interrupts Bill, her alto voice dropping lower, her gaze conspicuously serious and aimed directly at Bill. Lefevre names her personal act of memorialization. *She* remembers that day was wonderful. She will *always* remember. That day has become her standard. Lefevre hopefully expects the *Reunion* session to replicate the first (in the first video, Lefevre's speaking voice is the second voice that audiences hear, after Bill's).

As Bill's statement to Goodman and Lefevre suggests, the two significant dissimilarities between *Homecoming* and *Reunion* concern order and population. In contrast to the aimless, asymmetrical quality of the *Homecoming* space, Bill rigorously orders *Reunion's* space. Singers sit (or occasionally stand) in Gaither Studios in a semicircle, around a piano. Bill positions the primary camera opposite the performers; video viewers consequently occupy a position that would complete (or "unbreak") the circle, the camera's lateral swivel mimicking a turn of the head. Aside from the semicircle being only two rows deep at its deepest, and aside from the later addition of other cameras, the *Reunion* format forecasts that of subsequent Homecoming videos of the 1990s recorded at Gaither Studios. *Reunion's* song list has jointly sung choruses at its base. For these, the singers read music out of a few different hymnals—a marked contrast with *Homecoming*, in which participants shout out unrehearsed song requests, assuming everyone gathered will know the song.[22] *Reunion's* aural and visual orders compromise the first video's whimsy too much for the second video to possess *Homecoming's* appeal. *Reunion* does not appeal on *Homecoming's* grounds, precisely. In *Reunion*, Bill seemed to recognize that attempting to re-form *Homecoming's* formlessness would have made *Reunion* appear contrived, inauthentic. Ironically, in *Reunion's* case, blatant planning was more desirable—more honest—than trying to pass a planned program off as unscripted play.

But order and spontaneity are not mutually exclusive. *Reunion* still provided a forum for unexpected songs, testimonies, and jokes. The second item of departure in *Reunion*—that Bill "got some more people in here"—augmented this possibility. *Reunion* contains more participants than does *Homecoming*. Just as repeat performers lend continuity to the two programs, new personnel signals a promising discontinuity—one that suggests others have been (and might be) attracted to the fold. Since the new musicians bring with them different stories and different ways of responding to what takes place in the studio, Bill is able to renew *Homecoming's* implicit promise of improvisation and spontaneity.

"Getting more people in here" means more than merely assembling more live bodies. In *Reunion*, Bill adds a historical mass. Just prior to Bill's discussion with Goodman and Lefevre, *Reunion* begins with two black-and-white photographs of the Grand Ole Opry House in Nashville, Tennessee—first of the exterior, then of the empty interior of the Opry's Ryman Auditorium. As an unseen harmonica player warbles a legato rendition of "Amazing Grace," the interior photograph morphs into a color video, and Bill appears, moseying down an auditorium aisle. The monologue he delivers in this space is worth considering in its entirety:

Hi. My name is Bill Gaither, and this is the famous old Ryman Auditorium— the original home of the Grand Ole Opry [pauses to look around]. My, my . . . the music that has been made in this building by some of the greatest country singers of all time—Red Foley, Hank Williams, Hank Snow, Ernest Tubb, Roy Acuff . . . the list goes on and on and on.

But to me the building is very, very special, because it was in this very building—and, in fact, it was in this very seat; this is where I sat [points to seat]—that I heard my first gospel quartet concert. It was the original "Wally Fowler All-Night Singing," on the first Friday night in the month, back in 1949. I was in the eighth grade, and my parents brought me down, and life for me was never the same.

I can remember I wanted to hurry to get here before the whole thing started. And my dad said, "well for crying out loud, Bill, it's gonna go all night! It's an all-night singing!"

And I said, "I don't care. I gotta be there at eight o'clock, 'cause I wanna see how they get this thing started."

And so he said, "well, okay. But I tell you what: we're gonna get there, but you're gonna stay there until the last song is sung."

At 2:30 the next morning, when about everybody had left except me and a couple three hundred other folks, he wished he hadn't said that. Because the music so captivated my life. I had never heard such great four-part harmony singing, and those low basses and high tenors and piano players that could just play all over the place. It was called quartet music, and it captivated my soul.

The beautiful part about it is, later on I claimed as my personal savior the Christ they were singing about. At first, it was just fun music. But after I got listening to it for a while, I said "hey, they're singing about the Lord." And I loved it. And it pulled me into a saving grace with the Lord Jesus. So I thank God for gospel music.

Recently, we got together a bunch of our friends to just reminisce and sing some of the great old gospel songs of the past. We're going to go back into the studio, and then we'll come back here from time to time throughout the evening, to talk about this building, what this building means. But some of those singers that impacted my life in that very, very special way—we're gonna go back to the roots. We're going back to the old singing convention songs, Luther Presley's great old song, "I'd Rather Have Jesus." Listen to them sing [scene fades in to assembly at Gaither Studios].[23]

Before the singing begins, Bill already has gotten a lot more people in *here*. He calls out the names of five country music legends and indicates he could "go on and on and on." But the invocation of event organizer Wally Fowler and songwriter Luther Presley signal an alternative roll—a gospel roll that, judging by Bill's all-night obsession, Bill also could call out in its entirety if prompted. Bill is in *here*—as a starry-eyed youth and as an adult. He is *here* with his parents—particularly his father. He is *here* with the evangelical Son, his personal savior. He is *here* with the spirit of the Grand Ole Opry legends. Bill is *here* with some of the singers who played the Ryman at mid-century— singers he no longer calls simply heroes but friends. He is *here* with some ambiguous *we* that includes at least his partners in production, probably his bunch of gospel musicians, and perhaps all those deceased whom he names in the monologue. His final imperative, "listen to them sing," shows that he is also *here* with *you*, the viewer, and that you are here with all of *them*.

If you choose to view, you participate in this communion of the saints that requires and constitutes two locales: Ryman Auditorium and Gaither Studios. The former represents a broad music history and is the site of Bill's personal transformation. The latter is Bill's personal property, on this occasion arranged as a semicircle of singular persons who are protagonists in a broad music history. You the viewer complete the circle—you and the location of your viewing, most likely your home. In each location, made one location in the final edit, personal and collective histories overlap and fortify one another. Presences and pasts, broad and narrow bands, are here in the video, in communion. Nothing apparent separates Bill Gaither's Indiana from historic downtown Nashville, just as nothing apparently separates personal from collective memory, past from present, or recent past from distant past: "We'll come back here *from time to time* throughout the evening . . .

". . . to talk about this building, what this building *means*." Bill fills the Ryman with his hero-friends, who through their words and their sheer presence fill the space with meaning. They are the same people who fill the Gaither Studios. From the Ryman stage, Howard Goodman remembers joking on the Ryman stage years ago with his fellow southern gospel singers J. D. Sumner, James Blackwood, and Hovie Lister. Bill introduces the *Reunion* "talk about meaning" as descriptive. In at least two senses, it is. First, through the anecdote-sharing, Bill and his interlocutors describe what the building means to them personally. Second, these personal, gospel-inflected descriptions accord with the Ryman's institutional history. By most metrics, the Ryman, rightly described, is a house built on gospel. Saloon owner Thomas Ryman commissioned the building of the auditorium (first called the Union Gospel Tabernacle) in 1892 to host evangelist Samuel Porter Jones's revival services. It has hosted many Christian revival acts and services ever since. Still in operation as a concert hall but now also a National Historic Landmark—a museum unto itself—visitors cannot leave the self-monumentalizing concert hall without a strong sense of its gospel origins and connections.[24] Despite Bill's insinuating that his personal, gospel-inflected connection to the auditorium *departs* from the grand old narrative of the Ryman-as-country-music-cathedral—an insinuation that augments the urgency of reclaiming the "lost" gospel history—Bill offers his "counternarrative" on one of those famous Ryman benches that easily passes for a church pew.

The *Reunion* meaning-talk is also prescriptive. Aggregated, the personal stories in the video form an argument: that Nashville landmark that supposedly stands for country music, a distinctly American genre, has gospel music at its base. Country has gospel at its base. Beginning with Bill's anecdote of his first Ryman pilgrimage, the stories told by gospel music figures on *Reunion* fill the Ryman with gospel meaning. At the same time, the "country Ryman" enlarges the import of the gospel figures and their stories. Viewers may think the Ryman means country music. Indeed, Bill *needs* them to presume this meaning if he is to enlarge the import of the gospel heritage his video will celebrate—hence the importance of beginning his monologue with a country music roll call then supplementing it with a gospel roll call. The Ryman that stands for a distinctly American genre of popular music must be a glancing presence, just visible enough to render gospel music more visible. If one believes country music has a big, national meaning, one should be interested in the meaning of gospel music. One so interested should watch *Reunion*.

In the early 1990s, plenty of Americans were finding meaning in country music—the music of the common (white, rural) man and woman. No single country musician epitomized the synthesized authenticity of this moment better than Garth Brooks, whose sophomore 1990 album *No Fences* sold 17 million copies, spent twenty-three weeks on the top of *Billboard*'s list of country bestsellers, and ended up being the fourth best-selling music album of the 1990s. As his album title suggests, Brooks represented uncircumscribed country. Blue jeans and open-collared western shirts covered his slightly portly frame. His baby face was visible underneath a monochromatic cowboy hat. Like many songs in country music history, Brooks's songs were anthems for the simple and proud, the conspicuously indecorous lot who had friends in low places.[25] In concerts, he sang his songs through a wireless headset so that he could play guitar and walk the length and breadth of a gargantuan stage, rivaled in its high-tech fanfare only by those of rock behemoths the Rolling Stones and U2. Unlike U2, who during this same period overloaded its live "Zoo TV" stage with video screens and superfluous industrial objects in order to call attention to their medium's absurd excesses, Garth Brooks used his huge, blinking medium to deliver an ostensibly authentic picture of Americanness to a vast population of white midwesterners and southerners (and a number of other Americans). His popularity is partly explicable due to these populations' strong will to believe this picture. Brooks gave them something to believe in.

Bill Gaither gave them something to believe in, too—and it seemed to be roughly the same "them." Brooks and Gaither both represented and answered the longings for authenticity that one group of Americans had in an age of artifice—a group likely not drawn to the representations and answers provided by Seattle grunge or MTV's *Unplugged*. When I asked the Homecoming fans I interviewed what types of music they enjoyed aside from southern gospel, "country music" was the most common answer. Not only did they tend to prefer country over other Christian music genres; they sometimes listened to country *more* than they did southern gospel. Gaither's and Brooks's fans were in the same demographic ball park.

However, Gaither's 1990s projects also offered an alternative for country/gospel music fans who felt betrayed by Brooks's and other country megastars' spectacular employments of technological innovation. Brooks's country did not have enough fences. Like Bob Dylan or Miles Davis fans before them—and like many contemporaneous U2 fans puzzling over the band's early 1990s turn toward European industrial rock—some early 1990s country music fans felt the technological fanfare was an accommodating bridge too far.[26] To be sure, Bill Gaither made his own accommodations in order to expand his products' reach, even in the early videos (as I will discuss later, he will make more accommodations in the franchise's second decade). But no one could accuse the Bill Gaither of the early 1990s of overindulging in the available technology. The technological austerity set apart these early Homecomings—not only from genres like Christian and secular rock-and-roll but also from that other "Ryman genre." By Bill Gaither's hand, southern gospel became

more palpably continuous with historic country music than was contemporaneous country music. *Reunion* implicitly poses a question: where would Opry
country music legend Roy Acuff be more likely to know where he is—at the
Gaither Studios or at a Garth Brooks concert?

Notwithstanding Bill's tinkering with country music tropes, his priority
in the Homecomings of the 1990s was to showcase southern gospel music
rather narrowly conceived. Because Bill still was working out the programmatic kinks in the early videos, and because he still was establishing the
place of the Homecomings within the southern gospel narrative (a narrative that the early Homecomings themselves were discovering, creating, and
sustaining), he did not stray far from the primary preferences and references
of the primary fan base. At this stage, there was no guarantee that any given
video would be followed by another. The legends around whom Bill constructed the programs were getting older. A significant number were seriously ill—most notably the feeble Jake Hess, former lead singer of the famous
Statesmen quartet. It would have surprised no one if the full-framed Howard
and Vestal Goodman would have dropped dead from heart failure during
one of their exuberant performances. Even though Hess and the Goodmans
ended up living and performing for another decade, it was conceivable in
the early 1990s that each video could have been these singers' last. Recording memories with (and memories of) this population was Bill's most pressing concern. The new, younger acts participating in the programs he would
always have with him. He wanted to anoint the members of the old guard
while they were still alive.

In the early videos, when repetition was less risky, Bill anointed and
reanointed. Each of the early videos was a sort of homecoming. *Homecoming*
(1991), *Reunion* (1992), *Turn Your Radio On* (1993), and *Old Friends* (1993) all
contain footage of arrival and gathering—usually in the opening ten minutes
of the program. Viewers see the musicians stepping off of buses and airplanes.
In *Old Friends*, the video crew captures Eva Mae Lefevre and the Goodmans
in the Indianapolis airport terminal, talking about the importance of stable,
longtime friendships. The monumentalizing of arrival and gathering intensi-
fies the expectation that something special will occur in the ensuing session—
an expectation that is already high if viewers are familiar with the previous
gatherings' yield. Lefevre's remark on *Reunion* ("I will never forget that day,
and I have prayed that today will be another one just like it") effectively
returns in each of these videos—with compound interest. The Homecomings
gather both people and monumental momentum.[27]

Old friends and old legends gather. But "new friends" gather, too. The cast
is too numerous and too fluid to explore person-by-person, but it is helpful

to think of the new cast members in three categories: those who are drawn to the Homecomings and the culture they represent, those who are drawn *back* to this culture, and those whose presence (re)draws the boundaries and scope of the southern gospel host culture.

Gloria Gaither falls in the first category. Making her video debut in *Reunion*, Gloria is featured sparsely—once to recite the spoken portion of the Gaithers' "There's Something about That Name," and again to read a personal essay. The latter piece, which Gloria addresses to Bill, is a tribute to Bill and his musical passion. Through the vignettes she shares of their dating and marital relationship, Gloria simultaneously credentials Bill as a longtime southern gospel fan—a "walking encyclopedia of strange names, song titles, group personnel, and all-night singing tour schedules"—and marks herself as an outsider. Gloria, the Michigan-born minister's daughter, begins her narrative, "I don't come from a southern gospel background; I come from a northern evangelical background." It is Bill who introduces her to southern gospel: "I met this crazy world when I met this crazy man." The singers chuckle as she recounts some hilariously awkward first dates with Bill. She recalls "driving through the Indiana countryside, listening through the come-and-go reception to see if J. Bazzel Mull would play one of your songs on his gospel radio show" (more on the jokes about Bill's peddling in chapter 3). After her initial suspicion that Bill was fictionalizing all the gospel music knowledge he volunteered to her (unrequested), Gloria "was soon to learn that there really was someone named Burl Strevel, and Denver Crumpler." However, as the pair began to coauthor songs—through it all, they did share a general interest in music—Gloria became more intimate with southern gospel music and the people behind it. "Over the years these names I thought you made up came first to be real people to me and then precious friends."[28]

The essay moves from humorous anecdotes to more poignant expressions of the Gaither marriage itself. In an especially moving moment, having acknowledged the recent departure of their youngest child from home, a tearful Gloria says to Bill, "once again, it's just you and me, babe." Gloria signals the couple's primary allegiance to each other and their graduation into the same life stage as Bill's heroes (and a good many viewers). As things proceed in this emotive direction, the musical minutiae take a back seat to Bill and Gloria's union and to their faith. Gloria's final line uses musical terminology to turn from Bill's beloved music to his beloved Savior and beloved spouse: "These [old] songs, these are the ones that got your attention, captured your imagination, and showed you the way to Jesus. And the harmonies you loved became the seed of your dreams, dreams that we have together realized even more than even you could have imagined." A barely composed, wet-cheeked

Bill, who has been playing the piano lightly through the entire reading, leads the tearful assembly in a rendition of "Through It All."[29]

Strong heterosexual marriages between evangelicals certainly fit in southern gospel spaces, and judging by the essay's emotional impact on those gathered—everyone on camera is crying—few present seem to realize or care that Gloria masterfully has established her candidacy for inclusion in the southern gospel fold by appealing to her faith/marriage, even as she has avoided declaring her intent to be numbered among the southern gospel faithful. The piece's tear-jerking power essentially derives from its being about the Gaither relationship. Southern gospel is a part of the story only because Bill is a part of the story; never in the essay is southern gospel music (and culture?) anything but *Bill's* beloved. However, after *Reunion*, Gloria will be a permanent fixture in the videos. *Reunion's* front cover is the first to list Gloria's name with Bill's ("Bill & Gloria Gaither and Friends"), and the couple are pictured together on the back cover. Gloria's essay expresses her essential, ambivalent distance to a world to which she is related by marriage. In *Special Homecoming Moments*, a later compilation video, Bill recalls that it took some effort on his part to convince Gloria to appear on the video.[30] I will discuss Gloria's perpetual intimate distance with southern gospel in more detail in chapter 4.

Mylon Lefevre exemplifies the second category of new friends present in the early videos—the singers who once were in the southern gospel fold but departed from it. The son of Eva Mae and Urias Lefevre, Mylon was on the gospel music stage at an early age; his song "Without Him," written when he was twenty-two, was recorded by Elvis Presley. Lefevre left gospel music in the 1970s to pursue a career in rock-and-roll. The pursuit failed, and Lefevre ended up a heroin addict. By the early 1980s, Lefevre had returned to an evangelical Christian fold—even singing briefly with the CCM group 2nd Chapter of Acts.

In his 2004 essay on "ceremonial reinstatement" in the Homecomings, Michael Graves examines how the Gaithers deploy Lefevre's prodigal past. As Graves notes, despite the fact that Lefevre's evangelical return occurred over a decade prior to his Homecoming debut in *Reunion*, the first few Homecoming videos replay his fall and resurrection as if they were recent. The most striking aspect of this replay is that it occurs gradually, across videos. In *Reunion*, Lefevre's presence is muted. He wears dark glasses, an earring, and dark clothing (no suit coat), and his hair is tied in a loose ponytail that extends halfway down his back. During his solo, a split screen shows the present, vocal Lefevre alongside a photo of his former, clean-cut self. Graves accurately describes the slouching, laconic Lefevre as seeming "out of place, unsure of himself, even bored, at least initially."[31] By the *Turn Your Radio On*

/ *Old Friends* session, Lefevre has traded in his large, opaque sunglasses for smaller, translucent lenses (and sometimes they come off) and his dark garments for a shirt of many colors—one that resembles the sweaters and shirts Bill wears in the early videos. His hair extends just over his collar. He is much more animated in his performances and in his support for other solo and group acts. In the following *Precious Memories* / *Landmark* session, Lefevre's sunglasses have trim, circular frames, his hair is the shortest it has been thus far, and he wears a suit and tie. The final song selection on *Landmark* is the 1923 hymn, "Great Is Thy Faithfulness." Lefevre sings the verses solo as he stands in the middle of the circle; he and Bill jointly lead the others on the chorus between verses. Hardly has Lefevre begun the second verse ("Pardon for sin and a peace that endureth . . .") when his mother, seated behind him relative to the camera eye, begins to sob. By the second chorus she is crying so uncontrollably that she does not even attempt to sing. Mylon takes over Bill's role as choir leader for the song's conclusion. As Eva Mae dries her tears, Mylon leaves the center and retakes his seat in the choir. The wardrobe and the stage direction tell the story: Lefevre the prodigal travels via Bill Gaither back to his southern gospel roots, just as Gloria the outsider had arrived via Bill Gaither at southern gospel.

Graves focuses on Lefevre's rescheduled return to faith—on the fact that the Homecomings recount and replay a transformation that occurred a decade prior to the first Homecoming session. But Graves mentions in passing what I believe is a crucial point: Lefevre had not fully "returned" until he returned to southern gospel: "Arguably [. . .] there still remained the necessity for Lefevre to be welcomed back publicly to the quite different and basically separate cultural world of [southern gospel music]."[32] The physical transformation Lefevre undergoes from *Reunion* to *Landmark* loudly testifies to what is required of Lefevre for full inclusion. It is hardly arguable which Homecoming version of Lefevre seems fully present, fully at home—the cranky, long-haired adolescent whom Mom has dragged to Sunday meeting in *Reunion*, or the ecstatic, neatly coiffed leader of the choir in *Landmark*. In *Reunion*, when Lefevre finally performs a solo feature, Bill prefaces the song with a voiceover that overtly compares Lefevre to the prodigal son. "What a wonderful reunion this day with his mother—who is accompanying him on the piano, singing his great song, 'Without Him.' [. . .] It's so good to have you back home." Bill calls attention to the familial/cultural/genre reunion that is occurring *this* day—the day of Homecoming record. As Bill speaks, pictures of old southern gospel music albums (which invariably feature pictures of tidily dressed southern gospel groups) roll across the screen.

Despite the power of the returned prodigal motif, not all returning others in the Homecomings must return after a willed shunning of southern gospel for more lucrative or more profane endeavors. The Homecomings also offer a return for singers lost in the shuffle of younger acts, diminishing tour dates and album sales, and personal disabilities. In this sense, many if not most of the Homecomings' central figures seem to be "returning." I remember my family gospel band sometimes sharing venues in the 1980s rural Midwest with Homecoming legends Anthony Burger and J. D. Sumner. Our travel radius was relatively small, and the "love offerings" for which we typically played, typically at tiny rural churches, were barely enough to cover our costs. That we shared venues with the soon-to-be "Homecoming legends" testifies to the sluggish state of many southern gospel careers just prior to the Homecomings. Sumner had recorded with Elvis, and there he was on my family's stage. But for those Homecoming fans who knew that these musicians were performing actively when the Homecomings began, it was not the southern gospel musicians who were "returning" to the spotlight. Rather, the spotlight was returning to southern gospel musicians—via Bill Gaither. This was the return of the prodigal Christian music industry. Lefevre was its avatar, the southern gospel prodigal, returning from an acknowledged elsewhere, the counterpoint to the longsuffering southern gospel performers who faithfully stuck by their genre even when ticket sales were down. The son leaves his southern gospel family in search of brighter spotlights; brought low, he returns from the shadows to find his family bathed in the light he sought. *That* story promises a great return.

The Fairfield Four exemplifies a third type of new friends. Years before the all-male African American quintet (there were five members of the Four at the time of their Homecoming performance) gained wide recognition for their work in the film and on the soundtrack of *O Brother, Where Art Thou?*, Bill Gaither invited the seventy-year-old group to the *Turn Your Radio On / Old Friends* recording session. The videos include, respectively, the quintet's renditions of Kenneth Morris's 1947 "Dig a Little Deeper in God's Love" and the traditional "My God Called Me This Morning." They sing *a capella*, adorned in their "Tennessee tuxedos" (tuxedo coat and tie, white shirts, overalls). The Homecoming choir-turned-audience does not appear greatly moved at the beginning of "Dig." The younger members of the assembly are first to respond physically to the Four's calls, with nodding heads and shouts of encouragement. But the crescendo of the music, coupled with bass singer Isaac "Dickie" Freeman's rumbling solo breaks, eventually stirs all those gathered into clapping, joyful laughter, and even some vague iterations of dancing. By the end of "Dig," George Younce, the ecstatic sixty-three-year-old bass singer of the Cathedrals quartet, can barely compose himself.

All of the ambivalence of black musical performances before white audiences—in this case, heavily southern, Jim Crow-reared whites—is on display here. Drawn in to the Fairfield Four's songs, the white audience seems genuinely moved. Their clapping, calls, and caws reveal and establish cross-racial contact. As the Four's Reverend Willie Richardson takes Cynthia Clawson (a middle-aged white female musician) by the hand in the coda of "Dig" for a few seconds to dance, the contact becomes more than aural. Some variety of communion is unfolding.[33]

The white audience is genuinely moved—so far. This sort of communion is possible because it is temporary. Like many of the mid-century southern gospel stages, the Homecoming circle circumscribes this instance of inter-racial exchange.[34] The session provides a safe occasion for taboo-breaking because everyone knows that it will end—that it is not a performance norm, and it is certainly not a social norm. What happens occasionally in the circle remains in the circle—and remains only occasionally. The Fairfield Four move on out of the circle, and apparently out of the studio, after their feature concludes—unusual, since Homecoming solo performers typically melt into the big chorus before and after their features.[35] After "Dig," Bill's simplified, partially true narrative, via voiceover, honors black and white gospel as "great traditions" while also establishing their difference:

> Great traditions must be passed on to the next generation if they're going to survive the passage of time. Black gospel music has been preserved by mothers singing to their babies and teenagers hoping to sing in the church choir. In white gospel music, the singing convention style was passed on in schools where adolescents camped out for two or three weeks to learn to read shape notes and sing counterpart harmonies. These schools survive to this day.[36]

The scene switches to footage of Ben Speer leading a group of singing white children in a large classroom. It is the Stamps-Baxter School of Music—the long-running, most famous singing school of the variety Bill describes in the voiceover. Bill's intent seems to be to plug the school—he interviews Ben Speer about the curriculum—but his narrative rehearses the stereotypes of individually or culturally intuitive black musicianship versus trained white musicianship. Blacks learn in their domestic spaces (from women), whites in professional spaces (judging by Speer's directorship, from men).[37]

The Fairfield Four are not the only African American performers in the early videos. Gospel songwriter Doris Akers appears in the same session; in fact, *Old Friends* contains a lengthy tribute to the songwriter, which culminates in her playing piano and leading the ensemble as they sing her canonical hymn, "Sweet, Sweet Spirit." However, Akers's pale skin, and the absence in the tribute of any talk of her work with the foundational African American gospel group the Sallie Martin Singers, makes it easy for Akers to pass as white. Online commenters, on the Akers Homecoming clips on You-Tube, demonstrate how invisible was (and confusing is) Akers's racial identity to many fans.[38] Lillie Knauls is the most regular African American presence in the early Homecomings. A former member of the Grammy-winning gospel group the Edwin Hawkins Singers, Knauls is always visually prominent; she is usually seated in the front row, wearing one of her signature colorful hats that further signals her ties to southern African American church culture. But Knauls rarely occupies the center of the circle. She rarely performs solo, and she never soliloquizes. The Fairfield Four are present in the circle as African Americans singing in a traditional African American style—an all-male, counterpoint, harmonizing style that conspicuously resembles the putatively white southern gospel tradition. By including the Four, Bill is tugging at the veil that protects the implicit narrative of southern gospel racial purity. Because the Four are there but a moment, the risk is minimal. The lightness of Bill's tugging will certainly not tear the veil, but it does call attention to the veil, even momentarily pulls it open.[39]

The outsiders who problematize the boundaries can also shore them up. The "more people" who Bill Gaither "gets in here" in the early Homecoming videos are just present enough to allow southern gospel to know itself through exposure to what it is not. Moreover, the sharing of their space with black and contemporary Christian musicians allows southern gospel insiders to maintain a sense of both their intraevangelical cosmopolitanism and their southern hospitality. Never are they being more southern than when they are extending an invitation. Never are they being better "gospel people," broadly conceived, than when they put stylistic preferences aside and hear the gospel from other gospel people. Never are they being more evangelical than when they draw people—certain people, for certain tenures—into their fold. As video piles upon video over the years, the criteria for candidacy in any of these groups (and the criteria for candidacy in the permanent, insider group) will change. Indeed, the presence of the Fairfield Four in the *Turn Your Radio On / Old Friends* session demonstrates how the Homecoming project changed just a few years after the first video.

I will examine these changes as they are manifest in the Homecomings of the middle- to late 1990s. But first, I turn to the music of the early videos—specifically, three songs that represent and manifest the circumscriptions and subtle expansions of the early videos.

INTERLUDE: THE SOUNDS OF OLD-TIME GOSPEL

Looking for a City

Southern gospel music often deals in extremity and fanfare. Slow, sad ballads might bring the tears down, but speed and range tear the roofs off. Quartets often include tenors with a near-soprano range, bass singers whose lowest note is barely audible as a pitch.[40] As visitors to the annual National Quartet Convention know, quartets that have one or both of these weapons often use them *ad nauseum*.[41] Another weapon in the arsenal is the fast-paced, "tongue-twister" number—the song in which the lyrics fly by at a nearly inaudible clip. Adding to the busyness is the frequent usage of counterpoint; different singers will sing different lyrics, different melodies, at different paces, over and under the lead part. The immediate ancestors of this singing style are the "convention songs" of the late nineteenth and early twentieth centuries.[42] Typically, tenors, basses, and women simultaneously sing three different versions of the chorus—sung at different cadences, some repeating words or adding evangelical expletives like "glory, glory" and "praise Him." It takes some dexterity to perform and to listen.

Southern gospel ensembles also feature dexterous piano players—often as their only instrumental accompaniment. In the faster southern gospel songs, the bouncy eighth notes on the left hand and the frenetic, "tickling" right hand resemble Texas barrelhouse music (imagine the saloon pianist in a 1950s Hollywood western), and the early jazz, Harlem stride piano stylings of Fats Waller.[43]

In these senses, "Looking for a City" is an exemplary southern gospel song. Written by Marvin P. Daltin and W. Oliver Cooper in 1943, the song frequently appeared in mid-century singing convention songbooks.[44] The version that appears on *Turn Your Radio On* recalls this tradition. In true convention style, the ensemble sings the verses in unison then splits into counterpoint for the choruses. The video also features cutaway shots of the musical score written in shape notes, as it appeared in the convention songbooks. Sixty-seven-year-old Wally Varner—best known for his work with the Blackwood Brothers and the Homeland Harmony Quartet—leads the charge on piano, performing rapid-fire solo runs during the breaks between verses. The chromatic sixteenth-note runs Varner executes with his right hand nearly outpace the tempo; only Varner's left hand and a very understated, unseen drummer keeping time on a closed hi-hat keep the song from accelerating out of control.

The performance recalls another piece of southern gospel history. Vestal Goodman and tenor Johnny Cook are the two featured vocalists in the *Turn*

Your Radio On version of "Looking for a City." Goodman and Cook performed throughout the 1970s with the Goodman Family and used "Looking" as the occasion for a vocal duel. In the duel, the two would take turns singing the chorus—each successive pass a half-step higher than the last until someone forfeited, unable to sing any higher. In between their choruses, the two would feign exhaustion and disbelief that the other could keep going.[45] While the Goodman and Cook of *Turn Your Radio On* do not possess their old chops (they only sing through two key changes), for longtime southern gospel fans, this performance calls to mind the old fireworks.

Like a number of southern gospel songs, "Looking for a City" thematizes the afterlife. Borrowing from Book of Hebrews's gloss on the story of Abraham, Daltin and Cooper cast the story of Christians in peripatetic terms: as strangers, Christians merely pass through a world that is essentially hostile to Christians.[46] They do not belong "here among the shadows, in a lonely land." They are on their way to their true, heavenly home ("the city built above"), which will be a place of no suffering, where they will live with Jesus and the people for whom they cared in this world ("there we'll meet our savior and our loved ones, too").[47]

Like Mosie Lister's 1952 "Goodbye, World, Goodbye" and the oft-revamped gospel versions of Stuart Hamblen's 1954 "This Ole House,"[48]—both early Homecoming staples— "Looking for a City" offers a simultaneously joyous, morbid, and callous view of Christian purpose. In an upbeat major key and with Manichaean fervor, they declare an escape mission from the insufferable world. It borders on a death wish. If the "city" is heaven/the afterlife, to look for the city is to look for death. Granted, there are models of the heavenly city here on earth, and "Looking" is joyous because the community it celebrates in song represents a sneak peek of the city built above. But any celebration of the present, earthbound kingdom is minimized here among the shadows, where even "friends no longer share a word of love." Otherworldly union with Jesus and a fully sanctified (and perhaps quantitatively circumscribed) group of loved ones remains the goal. Although "Looking" does not shake this world's dust from its feet with the same glibness of "Goodbye, World, Goodbye," "Looking" inclines to the same "go to hell" posture. Christian responsibility to and for this world is absent.

I do not suspect many of the early Homecoming singers intend for songs like "Looking for a City" to sound so callous. In 2011, I attended Gloria's first "Songwriting Intensive" weekend of workshops at the Gaither headquarters in Indiana. Multi-instrumentalist Buddy Greene was one of the session leaders. A prolific songwriter (cowriter with GVB member Mark Lowry of "Mary, Did You Know?"—a song that likely rivals "O Holy Night" in its frequency of performance at evangelical Christmas services) Greene performed a short set of his songs one evening during the weekend. Among his selections was "I Don't Belong," a song I had seen him perform in several programs. Following the lead of the title/hook, I had always grouped it in the "callous escapist" category. At the workshop, Greene discussed "I Don't Belong," which he cowrote with Gloria (Gloria is credited with the lyrics). He explained that he intended the song as a reminder to Christians that they had commitments to higher orders than those that seemed to charge the vicious world around him ("Sojourner's Song" often appears in parentheses after the song title on album and video covers). As is often the case in Pauline evangelical rhetoric, Greene hoped "not belonging to the world" meant not being conformed to the sinful ways of the world. "I don't belong" is as much prescription as it is description (or, in theological terms, as much Hauerwasian as fundamentalist quietism).[49] The song calls its speaker back to the God to whom he rightly belongs and to the commitments that this belonging entails. While I remained skeptical that all Homecoming fans *would* hear Greene's intention in the song (not everyone had the luxury to hear his explanation), Greene convinced me that they *could* hear it, if they were listening against the right backdrop. "Looking for a City" held similar possibilities, though its pilgrims seemed steered toward the sky.

The Old Gospel Ship

Because Bill Gaither uses "Looking for a City" to exhibit a specific, historic style of music, Homecoming versions of the song do not depart significantly from mid-century arrangements. Bill believes in the quality of the old convention songs and the old quartet music. He believes that, if he simply exposes new audiences to this music in its most unaltered forms, the music often will bear its own witness. However, the Homecomings have other goals and other evangelistic modes. Not every "classic" song's value reduces to its "classic" execution. Some old songs, such as "The Old Gospel Ship"—written in the early twentieth century—are valuable *because* of their adaptability. Numerous variations of "Gospel Ship" exist. Rousing versions of the song have been recorded by country, bluegrass, and folk artists.[50] Paul Simon and Joan Baez each have performed the song. Over time, even the relatively small cadre of Homecoming artists built a diverse fleet of "old gospel ships"—from the Louis Armstrong-inspired version by singer-trumpeter Bob Cain to pianist Gordon Mote's grinding blues rendition.[51]

The first Homecoming video version of "Old Gospel Ship," on *Old Friends*, features Russ Taff, Vestal Goodman, and the GVB. Taff is a particularly important figure in this and other early Homecoming moments. He came to prominence in 1976 as the lead singer for the Imperials—an all-male singing group started by Jake Hess in 1964 that served as Elvis Presley's backup group from 1966 to 1972. The Imperials were the brainchild of Hess, southern gospel royalty, but the group turned southern gospel heads in the 1970s, experimenting with electronic instrumentation and adding African American singer Sherman Andrus to their core personnel in 1972. Taff's gravelly, soulful voice also made him anomalous in southern gospel. In his Homecoming debut in *Reunion*, his pierced ears and long hair meant his only rival in irregularity was Mylon Lefevre. By *Old Friends*, the hair was shorter, but the earrings and voice remained.

Bill's prefatory voiceover prepares listeners for the coming synthesis. Taff started young, but now he's "lived long enough to be gaining some perspective of his own [...] . But one of our dear old friends shows these kids how this song is really supposed to be sung." Vestal Goodman is poised to rise to the center of the circle.

Taff wails the first verse over light instrumental fills—tinkling cymbals, electric piano, harmonica, and a steel guitar. On the chorus, the drummer kicks into a straight rock pattern, and the GVB adds their four-part harmony to Taff's voice. For the second verse, the drums again recede, the song modulates a half-step higher, and GVB frontman Michael English sings over a light instrumentation similar to that of the first verse. The second chorus is like the first. A third key change, again one-half step higher, accompanies Vestal Goodman's third verse solo. Unlike the first two verses, the instruments now remain prominent. The ninety-five beats-per-minute song transitions into a double-time feel, led by the drummer's "boom-chick, boom-chick." The song remains in this mode through the final chorus.

Taff's and English's deliberately imprecise, undulating vocals resemble those of R & B singers. The instrumentation is decidedly 1990s Nashville: electric, twangy guitars, in-and-out harmonica, drums just prominent enough to signal the beat, bass guitar plunking subtly away on the first and third beats of the chorus, all instruments starkly differentiated in the mix. However, Goodman's double-time verse and the final chorus recalls older country, folk, and bluegrass versions of the song. Bill's preface encourages listeners to side with Goodman and her version; she sings the song as it "is really supposed to be sung." But Bill chose the song's arrangement (for *his* Vocal Band, no less), and he ushers viewers through all of the genres here represented. Bill's old friend Vestal and her version have the last word, but not before the ensemble has steered the gospel ship through a few different stylistic waters.

Thematically, "The Old Gospel Ship" is akin to "Looking for a City." Once again, Christians are gearing up to "sail through the air," to "leave this world behind." But "Gospel Ship" is less pessimistic than "Looking"—and more missionizing. The song is an invitation. Taff's first words: "I have good news to bring / and that is why I sing / all the joy with you I'd like to share." In contrast with "Looking," whose complicated counterpoint and larger quantity of lyrics requires some insider knowledge, "Gospel Ship" is vocally easy to share; it is a good sing-along tune for gospel music novices. Even the second verse's warning ("if too much fault you find / you'll sure be left behind / as I go sailing through the air") is aimed toward listeners' conversion and subsequent inclusion. Whatever "Gospel Ship" retains in the way of explicit and implicit domestications of the hereafter's social makeup, this ship seems built to hold a large group of people, not simply a small group of loved ones. The *Old Friends* version conspicuously omits a verse sometimes used in gospel musicians' renditions of the song:

> My loved ones gone before
> Now await me on that shore
> Soon I'll join them over there.
> For when my ship comes in,
> Then my voyage will begin.
> I'll go sailing through the air.[52]

Loved ones may be present, but the old gospel ship is a party boat—the more on board, the merrier. The glory of the ship seems less predicated upon the nastiness of the world from which it departs than is the glory of "Looking's" city built above. Indeed, "Gospel Ship" is not overly concerned with a destination. The trip itself, occurring between this world and heaven, is the site of the shouting and singing. In the *Old Friends* version, there is no shore in sight. You may as well enjoy the ride.

Old Friends

A song does not have to be old to be "old-timey." The Homecomings are filled with contemporary old-timey songs—one being the title track of the *Old Friends* video. Bill, Gloria, and J. D. Miller wrote "Old Friends" in 1993 with the *Old Friends* program in mind. The video begins and ends with two different studio recordings of "Old Friends." The first version is the longer of the two. As it plays, Bill appears seated on the floor in front of a living-room fireplace, holding a photo album and a handful of black-and-white photos of gospel singing groups. In the middle of the song, Gloria sits down next to him. In a scene reminiscent of Gloria's account of the pair's first dates, the two smile as Bill flips through the pictures, stopping to point out particular people.

The concluding, short version of "Old Friends" also includes a montage of old pictures. In this sequence, the shots of those who have died within a few years of the video have captions, providing singers' names as well as birth and death dates. The closing sequence also contains a number of still shots from the *Old Friends* session itself. Viewers see contemporary, aged versions of the people they saw pictured as young people in the opening "photo album" sequence. Moreover, they see a number of the younger Homecoming singers shuffled into the mix. Not only are the two "Old Friends" sequences some of the starkest Homecoming manifestations of new-and-old synthesis; they are also illustrative of the Gaithers' transformation of their own memorializing project into an object to be memorialized itself. *Old Friends* has not even concluded before photos from the session are filed alongside the black-and-white mid-century photos.

"Old Friends" is Homecoming at its most sentimental[53] and the Gaithers at their most derivative. The sluggish pace and instrumentation of the song recalls the clippity-clop, riding-into-the-sunset ballads of Roy Rogers. The song is uncharacteristically verbose for Gloria. Her most famous lyrics evince the primacy Gloria places on concise writing (a recurring theme at her 2011 songwriting workshop). Perhaps burdened with filling the song's cavernous spaces, Gloria employs copious amounts of worn, redundant imagery. "Old Friends" contains some of the worst lines in the Gaither catalogue ("I'm a rich millionaire in old friends"). Aside from the idiomatic "God must have known / there'd be days on our own / we would lose our will to go on / that's why He sent friends like you along," the song contains no overt theism. The friendship described in the song is free of interpersonal conflict—representative of a more systemic Homecoming absence that I will examine in chapter 3. Friends do not have conflicts with one another; unlike the friends of "Looking for a City," who "no longer share a word of love," "Old Friends" simply see each other through impersonal conflicts ("a phone call, a letter / a pat on the back or a 'hey, I just dropped by to say ...'"). The song's gooey, note-sliding sentimentality makes it the "Thanks for the Memory" of the early Homecomings.

However, the song accomplishes a number of goals central to Homecoming success. Because the song is so slow, singers can alternate not only verses but individual lines—a feature which, combined with the nostalgic content, eerily recalls "Those Were the Days," the theme song to the 1970s sitcom *All in the Family*. Therefore, a number of the major players in the Homecoming ensemble get featured in this song, and a number of singers testify in succession to the song's content. That "Old Friends" recalls "Thanks for the Memory" is an advantage; "Old Friends" not only sounds like a song from a bygone era but it sounds like a bygone song that is itself about bygone eras. "Old Friends" is doubly nostalgic. Trafficking in the old sonic tropes of sentimentality, the song calmly resolves the old southern gospel singers' careers—and lives. They are riding off into the sunset with one another, all of their elderly and long-time friends. Inasmuch as the early Homecoming videos place a premium on celebration of a past, this is no time for problematizing notions of friendship or history. There is also a moratorium on even the most common evangelical God-talk. Such talk may portend dissent and division.

"Old Friends" is a memorial(izing) song, but it is not a memorable song. It is not supposed to be memorable. Neither are the Homecoming versions of "Precious Memories," "The Old Landmark," or even the *Reunion* version of "Amazing Grace." Rather, these songs are Thomas Kinkade landscapes; the patina rather than the minutiae half-draws the ear. Songs like "Old Friends" put the sheen on the memories that will be available in the music, sights, and texts of the videos. The opening seconds of the first "Old Friends" sequence, with Bill grinning and thumbing through his old photo album, clarify what colors the Gaithers will use in the ensuing video to paint specific pictures of friendships.

BEFORE KNOWING REMEMBERS: HOMECOMING ADDITIONS, 1994–1999

Although "Old Friends" is emblematic of the Homecoming palette-setting songs of the early videos, it is somewhat rare as a Gaither-authored Home-coming song. Compared with twenty-first-century Homecoming projects, the early videos contain a small proportion of Gaither-penned tunes. One appears on the 1994 *Landmark* video. The *Landmark* session takes place on Brock and Faye Speer's forty-fifth wedding anniversary. Brock is the eldest son in the mid-century family band the Speer Family, to whom Bill had already paid extensive tribute in *Turn Your Radio On*, with old footage of a gray-haired George "Dad" Speer (Brock's father) tearfully leading a rendition of his song, "Never Grow Old."[54] In *Landmark*, Brock is the gray-haired patriarch; Faye is "Mom" Speer. The session includes the couple's daughter-in-law Allison and Brock's younger siblings, Ben and Mary Tom.

The *Landmark* tribute begins with Gloria's voiceover: "45 years of marriage to the same person is a real landmark. And Faye and Brock Speer were cele-brating this anniversary the very day we got together."[55] The ensemble then sings "Happy Anniversary" (to the tune of "Happy Birthday") as an assis-tant wheels in a two-tiered wedding cake. Faye receives a box of flowers, and

Gloria presents the pair with a plaque purchased by the current incarnation of the Speers' singing group.

At this moment, Bill says, "Isn't this great? Of all people they could have shared this day with, they shared it here with us." After Gloria thanks Faye and Brock for being an example to her and Bill of a traveling, gospel-singing, loving married couple, and after Brock offers a brief "thank-you," a crying Sue Dodge (who sang with the Speer Family) interrupts the proceedings to give what seems to be an unscripted tribute addressed to Brock. "I want to say thank you. I know Jeannie and Bob [Johnson, who also sang with the Speers] and all of us say, 'thank you,' for the example. When everything else is kind of unstable around us, you remained the same Brock Speer, and you remained a godly man who stood for the things we sing about. And I love you and I thank you." Bill, now seated at the piano, leads the ensemble in two choruses of the well-known Gaither song, "The Family of God." In between the choruses, Bill solos a verse that begins, "You will notice we say 'brother' and 'sister' 'round here / It's because we're a family and these folks are so near."[56]

As the video mediates it, the Speers are "the family of God": constellated around a lifelong marriage between a man and a woman; reproductively prolific; connected intimately to the generation before them (Mom and Dad Speer), the generation that follows (Allison and her spouse, Brian Speer), and the generation roughly coterminous with them (Mary Tom and Ben); represented by a "stable" patriarch who exemplifies Christian values. As this idea of "the family of God" has purchase in other quadrants of American evangelicalism (and perhaps beyond), _Landmark_'s Speer tribute strongly recommends southern gospel culture as a forum germane for the flourishing of such familial arrangements. If "family values Christians" are looking for a Christian subculture that best promotes and produces good Christian families, southern gospel, as represented by "The Speer Family," is it.

However, other material is seeping into the foundation of the landmark. Immediately preceding the Speer celebration is a two-song performance by Charles Johnson and the Revivers—an African American singing group. Unlike the Fairfield Four, the Revivers sing and literally _speak_ to the gathering. Charles Johnson expresses gratitude for being invited to the session. He also names the fact that he has shared stages with a number of those gathered, on numerous occasions. Performing piano-centered, moderately paced songs, the Revivers bear a greater similarity to the southern gospel groups of Jake Hess than they do to the Fairfield Four. While in one sense the stylistic similarity between the Revivers and, say, the Imperials, marks an erasure of black gospel distinctives, in another sense it is a riskier inclusion. There is little about the Revivers' sound or performance history to suggest that Johnson's group merely is *visiting* southern gospel acquaintances. These men reasonably can claim to be a part of the southern gospel family. Unlike the Fairfield Four, there is good reason to believe the Revivers will stick around for the rest of the session after their feature ends.[57]

And they do stick around. Before and after his *Landmark* performance, so does Larnelle Harris—African American member of one of the 1980s incarnations of the Gaither Vocal Band (from 1983 to 1985), frequent performer with white gospel diva Sandi Patty. Jessy Dixon also sticks around—Dixon, who wrote songs for James Cleveland and whose Jessy Dixon Singers sang on the *Saturday Night Live* stage with Paul Simon in the 1970s. Dixon will end up sticking around the Homecomings for some time long after *Landmark*. He will become a regular—and unlike Lillie Knauls, a frequent and regular soloist and song leader. These singers are all present at the Speer anniversary celebration. When Bill says "we" in "The Family of God," his "we" includes them.

In the mid-1990s, membership in the Homecoming "we" becomes more open. It remains a circumscribed "we"; there is still a conspicuously white, southern, and of course evangelical host culture at the center of the enterprise. However, during this period, the Gaithers can and do make bolder gestures away from southern gospel's visible core. Their early 1990s celebration of the older generation, coupled with their inscribing of their own memorial products into the story that they were memorializing in those products, earned them a great deal of trust, which came with a greater freedom to play at the celebrated culture's edges. They were fully in charge of every stage of Homecoming production and distribution by 1995. The videos went mass market during this period—the most significant coup being the 1997 deal that placed Homecoming products on the shelves at K-Mart and Wal-Mart.[58]

In late 1995, with the launching of the Homecoming Tour (and the tapings of the concerts), the Homecomings also become live, mobile events. For most of the 1990s, the Homecoming tour bus rolled predictably through southern gospel strongholds. Southern and midwestern venues prevailed, as is evident by a glance at the live concert videos released during this period: *Ryman Gospel Reunion* (1995); *Homecoming Texas Style* (1996); the GVB feature *Back Home in Indiana* (1997); *Atlanta Homecoming / All Day Singin' at the* [Georgia] *Dome* (1998); *Memphis Homecoming / Oh My Glory!* (2000, recorded 1999); *Mountain Homecoming / I'll Meet You on the Mountain* (1999, Blue Ridge Mountains).[59] The format and appearance of the concerts strayed little from the videos: the singers sat in a semicircle, once again situating the audience as completers of the circle, and soloists and ensembles performed one to three-song sets, interspersed with choruses that could also feature solo and ensemble performances. But the live shows placed the performers under more intense if implicit scrutiny. With the video screens that hung above the stages capturing and projecting particular visages—with all of the editing happening (or not) *in the moment*—live Homecoming performers had to assume they were always under massive watch. Live Homecoming musicians had to be model audience members, at all times. With the Gaithers' cameras and audiences watching them, the performers acquired the freedoms and restrictions of live acts.

All of these changes signaled and portended changes in the Homecomings. One was the possibility and burden of reaching an even broader audience demographic. On one hand, this was not new terrain; as early as *Reunion*, Bill Gaither had proven his skill at establishing southern gospel import via expanded narratives and their convergences. However, it had been no strain on the Gaithers' narrative loom to weave histories that, despite their divergences, occurred largely inside the Nashville beltline. Connecting Jake Hess to Roy Acuff through the Ryman was a relatively easy sell to an audience familiar with Nashville and its exports. How many more departures and connections were possible—or desirable?

* * *

Up until the mid-1990s, the Homecoming story was one of increasing expansion and inclusion. It would have been reasonable that the demographic would continue to expand primarily by ceding to younger audience sensibilities, and this likely would entail some shedding of the talk of the past. However, the Homecoming programs of the middle and late 1990s became *more* nostalgic. Why?

In her study of cultural memory in postcommunist Eastern Europe, Svetlana Boym offers a starting definition of nostalgia:

Nostalgia (from *nostos*—return home, and *algia*—longing) is a longing for a home that no longer exists or has never existed. Nostalgia is a sentiment of loss and displacement, but it is also romance with one's own fantasy. Nostalgic love can only survive in a long-distance relationship. A cinematic image of nostalgia is a double exposure, or a superimposition of two images—of home and abroad, past and present, dream and everyday life. The moment we try to force it into a single image, it breaks the frame or burns the surface.[60]

Boym's definition suggests reasons why the augmented nostalgia of the mid- to late 1990s Homecomings is not peculiar. Many of these videos are spatially distant from the early programs; Atlanta may be "southern," but the

Georgia Dome is a far cry from Gaither Studios. The temporal distance of the videos vis-à-vis their objects of nostalgia also increases—the objects being both the mid-twentieth-century heyday of southern gospel and the first few Homecoming programs.[61] The early Homecomings not only expressed and channeled nostalgia but also created a material version of a lost or imagined home. If nostalgia is "a romance with one's own fantasy," the Homecoming franchise is auto-romantic. The early videos not only executed their own romance but also provided filmy, fantastic flesh for the romance of the later videos. This was the future of Homecoming nostalgia.

Boym's distinction between *restorative* nostalgia and *reflective* nostalgia also sheds light on the changes in the Homecomings during the 1990s. Restorative nostalgia is a political project; Boym claims that it "takes itself dead seriously." Restoratively nostalgic people take some version of a past culture as their ideal, and they seek to (re)establish this ideal in the present. Restorative nostalgia seeks to "conquer and spatialize time." Reflectively nostalgic people view the past as truly passed. They look fondly upon former times, they do their share of idealizing, but they do not believe that the past can be (should be?) transplanted to the future: "*Re-flection* suggests new flexibility, not the reestablishment of stasis. The focus here is not on recovery of what is perceived to be an absolute truth but on the meditation on history and passage of time." Reflective nostalgia even can be "ironic and humorous."[62]

Boym's distinctions are helpful in organizing the possible motivations of nostalgia. But although she acknowledges that the two types of nostalgia may overlap in their deployment of symbols, Boym is incorrect when she claims that the aims of restorative and reflective nostalgia are mutually exclusive—that they "do not coincide in their narratives and plots of identity."[63] The Homecoming programs—and sometimes single performances—possess restorative *and* reflective characteristics. To deem the Homecoming programs as purely restorative would require one to ignore the changes that take place over time, to assume that performers and fans deny or resist all of the changes and the disruption of the imagined "old-time gospel" that those changes portend. Boym says restorative nostalgia insists on frozenness, that "the past is not a duration but a perfect snapshot." At the same time, to deem the Homecomings purely reflective would require one to ignore all of the programs' "snapshots"—normative recommendations of a golden era. For example, one would have to ignore the clear transformation of the "modern" Mylon Lefevre into his retro-redeemed self. Even in the early videos, the Homecomings were not simply memorials. They contained an argument.

In large, relatively diverse groups, and with respect to objects of nostalgia so vague as "old-time southern gospel culture," or "Christian society," or

"American evangelicalism," restorative and reflective nostalgia constantly overlap. It is not exactly reflective or restorative, but rather an *additive* nostalgia—not concerned simply with the rising and fallen homes, but also with the crumbling and expanding homes. The Homecoming community is constantly negotiating the blueprints of the home and its potential add-ons. Everyone in the community seems to agree that there is something about the old home place that can and should be preserved or restored. Everyone in the community seems to agree that some of the walls in the home, though they may be cherished, can and should be torn down. Everyone in the community seems to agree that some rooms can and should be added, some completely redesigned. Not everyone agrees on the specifics. In any case, additions to the structure, if they are to gain the approval of the maximum number of people in the community, must be added in such a way that people from a variety of backgrounds feel they have a room of their own (or *still* have such a room) in the old home place. Those who are inclined to resist the additions must be convinced that the base of the structure remains intact, that the additions are either merely auxiliary or that they are built in the essential spirit of the old home. If those who plan and perhaps inhabit the additions are to feel that they are true members of the household—not merely auxiliaries—they must be convinced that the additions are not merely decorative, but that they are grafted onto the foundation. One way to do this is to imagine the old home, the object of nostalgia, as much more expansive than it was in previous imaginings—perhaps to suggest that it was really always that expansive. If the construction is done carefully, the seams between the base and the superstructure will not show. It will seem as if the entire structure is of a piece. Ideally, it will give people of many walks of life a connecting point.

In the middle to late 1990s, the Gaithers have the phenomena of the early videos in their toolkit (and each new video adds to the toolkit). They are experiencing the first fruits of a mass market push that will reach full bloom in the first years of the new millennium. In the middle to late 1990s, the Gaithers are (re)constructing a massive home.

* * *

Some new beginnings: *Sunday Meetin' Time* (1996) begins with a scene of a flatbed, horse-drawn wagon arriving at a small country church. The attire of the couple driving the wagon (man in white shirt and flat-brimmed black hat, woman in bonnet) could place the scene in the nineteenth century, but there is an automobile of 1940s or 1950s vintage parked in the background, behind the church. Gospel songwriter Mosie Lister's lolling ballad, "Sunday Meetin' Time," sung by Jake Hess, plays in the background.

Revival (1995) opens with a shot of an open Bible, angled in the upper right-hand corner of the frame, on red velvet drapery. As Bill Gaither delivers a prefatory statement on revival spirit, the word *Reformation* fades in just below the Bible. Added to it, a fade-in of *Swiss Revival.* Then three at once: *Florentine Revival, Puritan Revival, The Great Awakening.* Then *Wesleyan Revival. Revival of 1857. Shanghai Revival.* Finally, *Asbury.*

All Day Singin' (1995), recorded during the same session that yielded *Revival,* opens with Gloria narrating over a reel of still photos. In an attempt to capture the interplay of sight and sounds, I transcribe a portion of this introduction below, describing the photos where they appear in Gloria's reading.

[A slow, piano-only version of the 1864 hymn, "Shall We Gather at the River?" plays. Opening shot of two wooden houses, then a covered bridge, then a forest. All photos are black and white unless otherwise indicated.]

Could you believe *[apparently Amish men painting a barn]* there was a time when life was simple and neighbors trusted one another? *[two white men in suit and hats, one with van dyke beard, and dog on porch]* A time when few people felt a need to lock their doors? *[white family, many children, posing on farm equipment; women and girls in white dresses]* Could you believe there was a time when farmers helped each other with the harvest? *[smokehouse]* When laborers gave their employers an honest day's work for an honest day's pay *[two white hands shaking, sleeves of suits showing]*, and a handshake was more binding than any contract? Could you believe *[schoolroom of white children, facing camera; shot scrolls over next two sentences so female teacher appears]* there was a time when learning was a treasured privilege? When children honored their parents and respected their teachers? *[white woman, man, and male child posing next to early twentieth-century automobile; dog sitting on side of hood]* When parents considered their children God's greatest gift? Could you believe *[group of white people, all ages, gathered outside a church]* there was a time when people went to church to stay all day and never got in a hurry to leave, *[musical ensemble, apparently male and female choirs divided, trombones visible]* a time when families met to sing together and pray for one another and then spread out a huge meal to eat together? *[early twentieth-century automobile, open top, full of white children]* Could you believe there was a time when no one went home empty in body or in spirit *[apparently camp meeting in semi-wooded area; white people seated, dressed up at picnic tables, one woman walking in front of*

chest-high tables, apparently serving tables] because there was always plenty—
plenty of laughter and music and fellowship and food to go around? *[white
people seated on flatbed wagon, one middle-aged, one elderly man, both in black;
many women and children in white]*

*[Music shifts to bouncy piano piece. Color still photos from the current Home-
coming session follow. Seven shots: (1) Bill at piano, laughing; prominent in
background, (black) Babbie Mason, also laughing; (2) Gloria and (white) Ann
Downing, smiling; (3) Wally Varner playing piano; (3) Jake Hess laughing; (4)
(white) Cynthia Clawson seated, singing with eyes closed, sitting next to (black)
Lillie Knauls, also with eyes closed; Hovie Lister looks on from back row, smiling;
(5) (white) the Talleys, with George Younce and Jake Hess, all singing; (6) Janet
Paschal singing; (7) the entire ensemble]*

Well, as you can see, there was such a time, and not so long ago *[narrative of the
recent event continues over more color photos of the current gathering].*[64]

In the black-and-white, "Shall We Gather" segment of the opening, each of
Gloria's questions gets answered in a photograph, and the sum of the answers
adds up to a view of the past that is disconcerting on a number of counts. The
deployment of the Amish as symbols of the past and of paragons of neighborliness both denies Amish communities' present-presence and erases some of
their more dubiously "neighborly" social practices.[65] According to the photos,
neighbors and churches are not only all white, but are also reproductively
prolific. The uniformity of clothing, which divides men and women in nearly
every picture, in nearly the same way, suggests that the virtues and the time
being celebrated had a value traceable to standardized gender roles. Gloria's
focus on the honesty of past laborers erases the villainous nature of bosses—
indeed, the suited hands shaking, though it appears after a comment about
laborers, points to white-collar virtue. The communities named and shown in
the segment are sonically linked, sanctified. These are they who "gather with
the saints at the river that flows by the throne of God."

The most disconcerting blow of this segment is its indictment of a
present and a particular group of present-absent bodies. Gloria asks viewers to imagine such a community because, presumably, it is either rare or
nonexistent in the present. You must *imagine* a time when doors could be
unlocked because *now* one must lock doors. Imagine tight church communities because now they do not exist. Given what the face of past virtue looks
like in each instance, it does not take much reading between the lines to distinguish the people whose absence occasions utopia. Could you imagine a

white population born or reared in the Jim Crow era, perhaps in the Jim Crow South, watching this video and not believing that they and they alone are the torch-bearers of a once-great society, a lost cause?[66]

However, the segment does not end in black and white. The most prominent figure in the first color photograph is an African American woman: Babbie Mason, singer-songwriter and instructor in songwriting at the Pentecostal Lee University, laughing along with Bill and the people seated behind her (she sits in the front row of the circle). The fourth photo shows Lillie Knauls, engaged in prayer or deep introspection, along with Cynthia Clawson, a middle-aged white woman who sits beside her. The picture contains its own veteran approval; sitting behind the two women, Statesmen pianist Hovie Lister smiles approvingly toward them (given Lister's known racism, which I will revisit in chapter 5, this is a significant visual endorsement). In contrast to the black-and-white photos, the great majority of the color photos show women with open mouths, often singing into a microphone. While a good many photos celebrate the elderly cast of the Homecomings, nine of the pictures that appear during Gloria's narrative show intergenerational combinations of people. The combinations sometimes capture differences not only in age but in gender and temperament—for example, the picture of the extroverted, less traditionally masculine Mark Lowry embracing the gruff, rumble-voiced J. D. Sumner, or the picture of the loquacious, high-pitched comedienne Chonda Pierce embracing the soft-spoken bass singer Brock Speer.

The final segment of the narrative by no means resolves the problems of the entire segment. The Homecoming circle remains overwhelmingly white, and nonwhite candidates for inclusion (as well as nonnormative others) still have to prove their worthiness according to the terms of the old circle. The omissions of historical conflict and difference suggest that white Christians alone have an (idealized) history. The color photos of the current Homecoming session remain an idealized picture of community. As long as it remains only an ideal, even a racially or sexually "improved" picture of the beloved Christian community provides at best a tiny step down the difficult path of reconciliation and mutual recognition. If the Gaithers value the latter, there is more work to do. But the Gaithers are making a step. Like *Turn Your Radio On, All Day Singin'* is an object of its own memorialization. The introductory still photos of the session render the videotaped session, *which viewers have yet to view*, as at least linked to the black-and-white precious memories, at most *already itself* a precious memory; fans are encouraged to long for an imminent but yet-to-be executed phenomenon. Idealized pasts, presences, and futures—real and imagined—converge. When viewers watch Cynthia

Clawson singing alongside Lillie Knauls in the *All Day Singin'* session, it will be a familiar sight. Viewers already will have experienced the scene in freeze-frame—as "such a time" of Christian goodwill and neighborliness as is emblematized for many Homecoming fans in Amish barns, horse-drawn wagons, and little country churches. A similar cross-generational collapsing of time occurs within the recording session itself. When Mark Lowry performs in the video, viewers will be able to recall him embracing the legendary J. D. Sumner. When Chonda Pierce performs, viewers can recall her embraced by the legendary Brock Speer. The embraces go both ways. In addition to being celebrated, the old southern gospel roll has a new role: to license the new roll, the emergent Homecoming beloved community.

This cross-generational licensing arrangement is extremely important in the mid-1990s Homecomings. At this point, Homecoming is a *bona fide* franchise. Business is booming. But death is still looming—not only for the core performers, but for many in the core fan base. The Gaithers do not want to cut short the trip, just when their gospel ship is hitting open water. There is more money to make. But there is also the Gaithers' desire to take southern gospel music out of its past and into the twenty-first century— out of its more troubling parochialisms, into cultural spaces where it can be transformed, where it is unknown, and where it might be an agent for positive change. Southern gospel is the leavening element that itself requires leavening.

By blurring the distinctions between generations and between epochs, the Gaithers expand the field of experience and memory that audiences regard as candidates for nostalgic reflection. For extant and potential fans who, due to youth or unfamiliarity with earlier southern gospel culture, might not be moved by the earliest videos, the late twentieth-century videos provide more access points into the narrow southern gospel world—points that, by virtue of their early Homecoming contact with the old guard, have the old guard's implicit blessing. At the same time, the old fans may continue to participate in the "old-timey gospel" once its heroes have passed away, but they must accept the condition that their Homecoming points of contact with the old-timey gospel also differ from it. The above-mentioned photo of J. D. Sumner and Mark Lowry serves as an apt analogy. Sumner died in 1998. Mark Lowry survived him. Lowry is different from Sumner, but he embraced and was embraced by Sumner. After 1998, old fans, who were drawn to the earlier Homecomings by Sumner, still have Lowry in the flesh. To the extent that the pair's embrace holds, they still have Sumner. After 1998, new fans who are (or might be) drawn to the Homecomings by Lowry do not have Sumner in the flesh. To the extent that the pair's embrace holds, they may still connect to Sumner—but only if they wish, for aside from their Homecoming history, little in Lowry's performative presence conjures up Sumner.

The Gaithers knew when and where such embraces needed to hold. Their ability to graft their versions of the new onto the old, such that the new becomes an object of nostalgia and the old becomes present, will require new techniques in the twenty-first-century Homecomings, after nearly all of their "original heroes" have died. But the ability was already on display in the 1990s. The catalogue would continue to grow because, to borrow from William Faulkner, the Gaithers successfully rendered the past as "not a diminishing road but, instead, a huge meadow which no winter ever quite touches."[67] In 1997—the same year some of the early videos achieved platinum-level sales— the Gaithers released *Special Homecoming Moments*, the first compilation of clips from previous videos. Even this compilation went platinum. The past was a renewable Homecoming resource.

COMPOSING THE UNCOMPOSED

It is barely captured on film. Approximately one minute and twenty seconds in to the "Where Could I Go?" music video, Buck Rambo's face flashes for three seconds on the screen, covered in sepia tones and tears. This was three years before his divorce from his wife, Dottie—one of the most celebrated (and, by most accounts, wiliest) southern gospel songwriters of the past decades. Buck and Dottie were well known for their rugged volatility and relative impiety in a southern gospel milieu that was (or pretended to be) prim and proper. As the *Homecoming* singers sing metadiegetically, "Needing a friend to help me to the end," Rambo, barely composed, wipes his damp eyes with his hands and mouths, as if to himself, *son of a bitch*.[68]

In 1991, Bill Gaither and his audience were well acquainted with the uncomposed gospel man. Gaither recorded the first *Homecoming* almost three years to the day after the television broadcast of Jimmy Swaggart's tearful confession, on the heels of the famous televangelist's liaison with a prostitute in a Louisiana motel. Swaggart's "I have sinned against you, my Lord," stuttered through a visage as moist and crumpled as a prayer hanky, punctuated an era of hard-fallen public gospel men. Swaggart's shoulders, heaving as he sobbed into the ceiling of his Baton Rouge Family Worship Center, bore the transgressions and the controversies of his fellow televangelists Jim Bakker and Oral Roberts. The 1980s were an age of artifice and mistrust in more ways than one.[69]

Like the falls and apologies it punctuated, Swaggart's iconic confession had multiple interpreters. For the Swaggart faithful, the fall was hard, but the apology was sincere, and forgiveness was possible; in fact, it was mandated by the Christian gospel. This was not the first time a man after God's own heart had fallen. And even if Swaggart was not as repentant as he professed—around the time of *Homecoming*'s first airing, Swaggart was pulled over with another prostitute in his car—there remained a gospel lesson in the episode: exalt no men save the Galilean carpenter. Whatever personality cult coagulated around Swaggart before his fall, the profound Christocentrism of a number of evangelicals within Swaggart's sphere kept Swaggart's Christ from being undermined with Swaggart himself.[70] After the fall, evangelical anti-Donatism kicked into high gear.

But skepticism outside Swaggart's religious sphere ran deeper. The confession marked not only the fallibility and hypocrisy of the public gospel man. It also marked the enterprise of televised ministry as essentially untrustworthy. Swaggart was caught in his transgression off camera. His confession was captured on—and for—television, on the very stage on which he had raged against the transgressions he was committing offstage. Who would believe his report? On what grounds would anyone believe the public gospel man's uncomposed confession was truly uncomposed? The genre of televangelism allowed and perhaps required ministers to put on contrition the same way they put on righteousness or makeup. A month after the first Homecoming session, in an episode of the Fox sketch comedy show *In Living Color*, comedian Jim Carrey introduced a shady televangelist character (the Reverend Doctor Carl Pathos), complete with baby-blue leisure suit and hyperbolic, Dixie-inflected praises to "Jah-hay-sus." In the many sketches in which Rev. Dr. Pathos appeared over the next two years, Carrey capriciously alternated between preaching and singing the gospel, soliciting sexual favors from contributors, and robbing his flock at gunpoint. The mercurial minister also changed moods on a dime. In one sketch, in an abrupt second, his gleeful, boisterous laughter morphed to a violent sob: "I have sinned against you, my Lord," Carey wails. The show resumes after the laughter has died down.[71]

The responses to Swaggart and the televised gospel republic for which he stood exhibited mistrust, though they varied in their depth and scope: do not trust even the holiest of men; do not trust any mere man to be holy; do not trust holy men *or* the religion they profess. The pervasive skepticism made televised ministries laughingstocks. No longer could televangelists conduct business as usual and expect large followings.

An end was beginning. But televised ministry was not dead. The pervasive hermeneutic of suspicion provided an auspicious climate for revisioning and rebranding the televised gospel. Bill Gaither was the man for the new old-time gospel hour. Speaking to me in 2010 of his early 1990s relationship to video, as we watched a rough edit of a soon-to-be-released DVD, Bill told me, "it took me three decades before I trusted this medium." Bill's confession provides a few clues to the Homecoming enterprise. First, Bill apparently had little trouble trusting *aural* media. Even if music also could play with listeners' emotions, the career gospel singer-songwriter did not think that music utterly could mislead—at least not to the catastrophic extent that visual media could. Bill's implicit trust in the positive power of gospel music is not solely the self-justification of a career musician; despite anxieties over the devilish potential of *specific* musical genres, evangelicals are a people of the songbook.

Second, Bill's doubts are hedges between himself, the Homecomings, and the viewers. In his published autobiographical writings, Bill describes himself as a persistent self-doubter—so much so that he writes of prolonged bouts of depression. Expressing his mistrust of the video medium to me, as we are viewing video clips that he and his staff have cropped and pasted, he is expressing a mistrust of himself. However, the admission makes him seem more trustworthy. Surely he is watching himself closely, isn't he? If he knows he is not above misusing this medium which invites misuse, he seems less likely to misuse it. He is a barely composed gospel man. In the next chapter, I will focus on another such man in the Homecomings—one of Bill's bare compositions.

2
BETWEEN JESUS AND JOHN WAYNE
CONSTRUCTING GUY PENROD

PUTTING ON THE NEW MAN

In September 1995, the Gaither Vocal Band teetered precariously between prosperity and decline. On one hand, the early Homecoming videos provided the GVB—revamped to accentuate its connections to traditional quartet music—a sizable audience it had not experienced in the 1980s.[1] The newly launched Homecoming concert tour was about to bring the GVB and others into contact with live audiences across the country. Despite losing some in-studio intimacy when they took to concert halls, the Homecomings gained a new sense of communion with live audiences.[2] Furthermore, most of the big-name Homecoming old-timers remained alive and kicking in 1995. Key musicians' deaths would not occur in quick succession for a few more years.

On the other hand, 1995 marked a time of transition, if not setback, for the GVB. Lead singer Michael English left the quartet in 1994 to focus on his CCM solo career—a career that already had begun with the release of his eponymous, Dove Award–winning solo album in 1992. A member of the GVB for nearly a decade, English's departure left a significant void in Bill Gaither's enterprise. With his slick hair and colorful attire, the tall, dashing English stood out in the aging Homecoming crowd. He gave the Homecomings a degree of CCM-style sex appeal. The early videotapes also tell the tale of a Michael English whose personal warmth and deference to his southern gospel roots endeared him to his Homecoming elders. English represented a

present and a future with which everyone could be comfortable. Bill Gaither
would have a difficult time filling his shoes.[3]

The controversy that surrounded Michael English shortly after his leaving
the GVB further complicated Gaither's quandary. In May 1994, a week after
collecting four more Dove Awards for his solo efforts, English announced
that he had been having an affair with Marabeth Jordan of First Call, a CCM
group with which he had toured since 1993. Shortly before the Dove Awards
ceremony, Jordan informed English that she was pregnant, apparently with his
child (both were married; Jordan later miscarried). The revelation prompted
English and Jordan to divorce their spouses, English to return his awards, his
record label to drop him, and Christian radio stations to pull his songs from
their playlists. English's CCM singing career seemed finished in a flash—one
of the most publicized flashes in Christian music history.[4]

Although the most immediately relevant details of English's transgression
took place away from the Homecoming stage, the proximity of the fallout to
English's GVB departure must have felt to Bill like a close call. Despite the
furor in the Christian entertainment community surrounding the English
affair, Bill did not get caught up in the controversy, and no one in the Christian
music industry expected him to do so.[5] But as he considered new lead singers
to fill the English void in the GVB, the consequences of his personnel choices
loomed especially large: how to replace and displace the broken English, his
sexy-and-dangerous persona?

In September 1995, at the Ryman Auditorium, Gaither trotted out his
answer: Guy Penrod.[6] Standing six feet three inches tall, Penrod had no problem catching audience members' eyes. Penrod's locks of wavy black-and-gray
hair, which cascaded to his shoulders, untied and slightly tangled, provided
the near antithesis to the pomaded, often-store-bought coifs of most Homecoming men. Sporting a full beard to boot, Penrod seemed suited for the lead
role in a Passion play, not for the lead part in a southern gospel quartet.

Guy-Pen-Rod: Freud himself could not have dreamed of a better name.
Bill Gaither's long, tall lead singer interrupted the symmetrical, minutely regulated tidiness typical in southern gospel male quartets. Like English, Penrod
broadcasted virility, relative youth, and a touch of macho untamability. But
where English's open-collared, multicolored shirts and bluesy, pentecosto-
gasmic moans could evoke a "darker" side of masculinity—dangerously
sexual; urban; black; even, ironically, foppish—Penrod's cowboy boots, bolo
ties, black-and-white attire, and slight twang evoked the Wild West. English
was a young hunk; Penrod was a young gun.

In contrast with the Penrod on display in his sixty-plus Homecoming video
appearances after *Ryman Gospel Reunion*, the Ryman Penrod sings soberly,

with little fanfare. He gestures only slightly, and only near the end of his feature song does he sheepishly smile. Only sporadically does Penrod's gaze fall on the front rows in the audience. His eyeline typically extends vaguely to the rear of the music hall. Penrod's nervous restraint even affects his singing, as he uncharacteristically slides flat several times on the song's choruses. The wild-haired cowboy is all business when he sings Joel and LaBreeska Hemphills' song, "When Jesus Says It's Enough." "I've had my share of troubles and trials. / Sometimes the going gets rough. / But when Jesus says it's enough, it'll be enough."[7]

Like the vigilante lawmen of Hollywood westerns, the Hemphills' Jesus will tolerate a few shenanigans. He will silently allow some rough patches in the lives of his faithful, a modicum of horseplay from wayfaring humans, and even some mischief from Satan himself. But at a certain point, Jesus's patience runs out. When this occurs, Jesus swings his authority and power down, absolutely. Jesus's "no" means "no." Looking part Wyatt Earp and part Son of God, singing on the heels of his predecessor's demise—a demise directly related to that singer's "misuse" of masculine heterosexuality—Guy Penrod is the vigilante who has come not to abolish the law of evangelical Christian manhood but to fulfill it.

From his cautious and awkward Ryman debut, Guy Penrod would evolve into one of the marquee faces of the Homecomings—perhaps only equaled by Howard and Vestal Goodman in recognizability, perhaps surpassing Bill Gaither himself. Penrod would remain with the Vocal Band for over thirteen years—the longest continuous tenure of any GVB singer not named Bill Gaither.[8] Penrod eventually became known for his expressive performances, in which he extends his wide wingspan skyward in praise, closes his eyes tightly as he mumbles apparent prayers and words of worship, pats affectionately the backs of his fellow GVB members, and grinningly works the front row of Homecoming crowds like a veteran Vegas act.

Nervousness and caution typically accompany first performances. To say of an established artist's early work, "she was still finding her voice," is to account for seeming discontinuities in the artist's corpus and to link the apogee of aesthetic achievement to the often-painstaking achievement of authentic selfhood.[9] In the Homecoming community, which so intimately connects virtuosity and expressivity to personal/spiritual authenticity in its valuation of artists, fans may interpret the tentative Guy Penrod of the 1995 Ryman show as at least underdeveloped, at best necessarily artificial—performing under duress, manacled by the immense implicit pressure of having to answer for his predecessor's trangressions and for his own otherness in an arena where familiarity reigns. The Guy Penrod of later videos is at once musically refined and liberated to "be himself" onstage—free to raise his hands, to smile and wave to the crowd as he sings, to act in all of those ways a good Christian man would act if he had nothing to hide and nothing to restrain him. Such an interpretation is understandable. The Homecoming corpus contains many more examples of the effusive Penrod than it does of the staid Penrod. And the improvements in Penrod's vocal tone and pitch in later videos suggest that he did become more at ease on the Homecoming stage. Singers who relax— who are "just themselves"—typically sing better.

However, one cannot so definitively separate self-actualization, adaptation, and assimilation. The Homecomings became a concert tour around the same time Penrod joined the GVB, meaning the live Homecomings and the live Penrod developed nearly in tandem. For at least two nights per weekend for large portions of the year, from the mid-1990s to 2008, these two live entities learned to live with each other—to live *as* each other. The restrained Penrod is rendered nearly invisible, along with his decade of working as a backup singer in Nashville studios and on The Nashville Network's *Music City Tonight*—gigs which do not require, encourage, or cultivate physical expressivity. Penrod wears Homecoming makeup—makeup that hides, reframes, or steers audiences away from some of Penrod's less usable features and renders prominent other, more usable features.

Usable features are always usable to some end(s). And consistency is one prevalent end in the Homecoming community. Fans need to know that the man onstage bears an acceptable resemblance to the man offstage; this is another measure of Homecoming authenticity. Even if Penrod always wears makeup, fans want confirmation that at the very least he chooses the same shades of makeup on all occasions—or, that he gives his staged body over to handlers who presumably know him well offstage and who are adroit makeup artists, people who know best how to bring out his "natural tones." In any case, consistency is Penrod's foundation.

To bring out the natural: the solipsistic promise of the cosmetic industry. Also the promise of the Homecomings. And Guy Penrod represents one of the Gaithers' most successful efforts at promise-keeping. In this chapter, I will demonstrate that the persuasiveness of the Homecoming Penrod rides upon the Gaithers' play between artifice and authenticity. Just as usability requires an end, authenticity and artificiality require referents. One can only be an authentic or artificial . . . *something*. I also examine which authenticities Guy Penrod projects and which authenticities Homecoming fans expect and receive from him, paying special attention to Penrod as a "real man." Masculinity provides the node of my analysis of Penrod's filmed and staged biography; of Homecoming fans' acceptance of him; of the American evangelical culture of manhood out of which, and in which, he rises to fame; and of a few of his "signature" songs. However, a node is but a point of intersection—a tangle of numerous threads and streams of identity. While masculinity serves as my interpretive center, it will become clear that charting of Penrod's masculinity necessitates investigating a number of other Penrods—among them the southern/western Penrod and the rural, white Penrod. These identities often mutually reinforce one another as they converge. However, the multiplicity also yields ambivalence and paradox— the same ambivalence and paradox charging discourses of white, evangelical, American manhood during the era of Penrod's staging. Guy Penrod occupies a Homecoming space between order and disorder, freedom and determinism, individuality and conformity, soft patriarchy and rugged manliness, Jesus and John Wayne.

CONTINGENCY, YEOMANRY, AND SOLIDARITY

When the Gaithers search for musicians to fill the long-term, "tentpole" positions in the Homecoming troupe, they seem to look for people who possess a baseline of serviceable characteristics that the Homecoming cameras, stagelights, and song catalogue can augment. Musical ability ranks high on their list of criteria. However, as evident in Mark Lowry's Homecoming career, the Gaithers will take chances on an adequate musician if they think he has other desirable skills, and if they think he will improve musically (Lowry did). Like their fans, the Gaithers attend to more than musicianship when they look for musicians; they look for personalities, biographies ("testimonies"), and faces. As a matter of course, candidates submit their personalities, testimonies, and faces to the Homecoming refinement process.[10]

In the 2005 *Best of Guy Penrod* DVD, Bill Gaither and Guy Penrod talk about this very process. The lengthy conversation between Bill and Penrod— which Bill breaks up into segments and splices in between the compilation of Penrod's greatest Homecoming moments—begins with Bill asking, "what's the deal with the cowboy image?" The question prompts Penrod to narrate his regional and familial cowboy heritage. First highlighting his Texas birth ("all Texans have to be a cowboy at some level, I guess"), Penrod then invokes his grandfather (an "honest to goodness" cowboy) who lived in New Mexico. By casting himself as the latest in a chain that extends deep into the past and deep into the American Southwest, Penrod makes a case for his bona fide, unaffected cowboy identity. His bolo ties and cowboy boots are not charades; they are a familial inheritance.[11]

However, immediately after this exchange, Penrod calls attention to the constructed nature of his cowboy image. Speaking directly to Bill, Penrod reminds his boss, "you gave me the advice, that I kind of needed to have some kind of look that was different. You remember that? And we ran across some . . . those coats . . . those real long coats, and you said, 'hey, that would look. . . .' That was your idea." Here, Penrod not only undermines the continuity of his current look with a familial cowboy legacy; he incriminates Bill as the impetus behind the fabrication. The latter's original query suddenly appears obviously scripted. Bill knows very well "what the deal is" with Penrod's cowboy image. Bill recommended it.[12]

Bill answers Penrod's comment with a story about the latter's audition: "You know the real story on that was when we tried you out. We said, 'the voice is fantastic.' And Gloria was there. I said, 'what are we going to do about his hair?' [Guy laughs, repeats 'his hair'] And Gloria said, the exact words were, '*don't touch his hair*.'" Bill's prefatory claim to the "real story" (whose veracity he bolsters by repeating Gloria's "exact words") suggests that he is about to offer a corrective or addendum to Penrod's "cowboy coat" anecdote. Instead, he recounts another episode involving the shaping of Penrod's image.

This exchange illustrates Bill Gaither's skill at stage-setting. Penrod's account highlights externality and supplementarity. Bill, rather than Penrod himself, came up with the "long coat idea," and the coats are *added* accessories to Penrod's wardrobe. The focus on Bill's agency and Penrod's relative passivity portends an interpretation of Bill as a conniving, perhaps autocratic bandleader. But Bill reorients the conversation. He follows Penrod's story, not by denying that he built the "Homecoming Penrod," but with another story of Penrod-building. The Bill of this story also constructs Penrod, but he does so in conversation with a partner (Gloria), and the construction appears to respect the "real" Penrod by permitting him to retain the hairdo with which he entered the Homecoming world. The *laissez-faire* nature of this executive decision makes it hardly seem an executive decision at all. The decision not to touch Penrod's hair testifies to the Gaithers' authority over their employees' images, for the *permitted* retention of a haircut is as much an image-constructing maneuver as is the addition of a long coat. But the story of a *preserved*, pre-GVB Penrod recommends Gaither image-building as an exercise in transparency. The account of Penrod's audition depicts the arc of Gaither autocracy as bending toward respect for individual musicians' self-determination. In light of Bill's anecdote, the advice regarding the long coat seems simply that: advice, given to one man by an employer who really wants his employee to "be himself." Bill recommended the coat because it fit Penrod's frame.

That the Gaithers bring their marketing tales to market—that these tales are told, taped, and sold—demonstrates the Gaithers' deft navigation of the paradox of projecting authenticity. By pointing their audience to the backstage workings and marketing strategies of the Homecomings, they portray themselves as being completely available to scrutiny. They invite fans into the strategy room; suddenly, everything seems less calculated. The Gaithers masterfully blur the boundary between the stage, the conference room, and the green room.

Bill's anecdote of Penrod's audition exemplifies such a staged deliberation and the benefits that accrue to the Gaithers by sharing it. Bill's apprehension regarding Penrod's hair not only makes visible his practical business concerns (will Homecoming fans accept a male lead singer with such hair?). It also suggests his cognizance of, and perhaps his sympathy with, his conservative fans' concepts of proper male grooming. It is as if he is saying to such fans, *I understand your hesitations over Penrod; I had hesitations, too.* Bill *almost* refers Penrod to a barber, when his spouse/business partner convinces him to leave the young man's head alone. His incorrect assessment of Guy's image— "incorrect" because either Bill was wrongly preoccupied with appearances or he underestimated his audience's willingness to embrace a long-haired Penrod—nearly led him to make a mistake. In comes Gloria—the risk-taking, power-wielding Homecoming sage—to pull Bill from the precipice of superficiality. The rest is history. The long-haired Penrod becomes a Homecoming icon, in part *because* of his long hair. Either the fans never cared about the hair, or they learned the lessons Bill supposedly learned—and the lessons the Gaithers had set them up to learn: appearances should not matter; individual style should be respected; and, not insignificantly, wives often know better than husbands on matters of appearance.

Obviously, the man (and woman) behind the curtain to whom the Gaither wizards direct their audience's gaze is as constructed as any other aspect of the Homecomings. But as a result of nothing seeming off-limits in a Homecoming script, nothing seems scripted. On-camera accounts of image-building, onstage tales of incontinence (there are strangely many of these) and Bill's absent-mindedness, live comedic banter with the microphone-wielding soundman Rory (whose booth is usually fully visible, stage right, at Homecoming concerts)—all build the case for Homecoming authenticity. The payoff for the apparent transparency occurs when the Gaithers justify their employment of an apparent outsider.

And the depiction of the Homecomings' backstage workings does not stop at the audition room. As *The Best of Guy Penrod* illustrates, it reaches to their employees' hearths.

* * *

We are sitting in the middle of the backseat of Guy Penrod's big pickup truck. Penrod is driving. Bill Gaither sits in the front seat. The two men respectively comprise the left and right frames of our gaze, which the camera centers on the windshield. Through the windshield, we look out onto a rainy summer day, to a narrow ribbon of road that is pocked with divots and standing water—a dirt-and-gravel soup of a trail that cuts through trees and fields, likely impossible to navigate with less robust vehicles.

The truck approaches a particularly profound, flooded dip in the path. Someone—apparently the cameraman—speaks from behind the camera, which jumps and sways with every bump and turn in the road: "you sure you can get through here?" Penrod answers flatly as he accelerates into the rough: "No." We are edited ahead a few seconds in the trip. As the truck bucks over the bumps in the road, Penrod mumbles, as if to himself, "if I can just keep from hitting this pipe here." Evidently, he hits the pipe, for no sooner does he stop speaking that the camera pops suddenly and violently, nearly hitting the roof of the cab. The flailing cameraman manages to film Bill grabbing the dashboard to steady himself and Penrod lurching forward, gripping tightly the wheel and the stick shift. Another jump-cut occurs. Guy, half-laughing, asks Bill: "You all right? How about it?" He slaps Bill on the leg. "Was that fun?" (Bill: "That's fun.") "We came through." (Bill, chuckling uneasily: "It's fun.") "We're safe." In the ensuing seconds of silence, the background music, which has been playing throughout the scene, becomes slightly louder. It is Penrod, singing, "you think it's a dream but it ain't / I'll be singing with the saints."[13]

Thus we arrive at Penrod's farm in rural Tennessee. The camera follows Penrod as he hefts huge bags of feed out of his barn into his truck, into his cows' feeding troughs, chocolate labrador retriever in tow. We see the saddles, the bridles, the tractor—all housed in a refurbished barn that "has been here for 120 years," according to Penrod. We ride past the two small, one-level homes of Penrod's parents and in-laws, both of whom occupy portions of this vast estate. We see the deer stands and little wooden shacks that some Penrod or Penrod in-law has built in the woods. With a southern drawl slightly more pronounced than his Homecoming stage voice, Penrod tells us stories of animal traps he and his family have placed throughout the woods. As the tour concludes, the video fades into a clip of the GVB performing "On the Authority." It is Penrod, singing, "on the authority of the Holy Word / I rise up and take my stand."[14]

Here, on the brim of Dixie, Penrod takes his stand. If he is to command authority in the Homecoming community, he cannot do otherwise. Here, class, gender, regional, and religious identities orbit around one another in mutually authorizing circles. Viewers learn that Penrod owns land—some of it farmland, which bears all of the marks of human cultivation and care; some of it woodland, which contains many of the contingencies of an "untamed" wilderness. The dual sense of agrarian order and wildness that this tract of land exemplifies also is embodied in Penrod.[15] Penrod drives his big pickup truck headlong into the uncertainty of the nasty roadway—acknowledging the dubiousness of the venture with an indubitable "no" that betrays neither fear nor foolhardiness. After the conquest of the road, he is boyishly gleeful, seemingly anxious to try the whole thing again. Penrod is a risk-taker, but he is also trustworthy enough to lead his company through the storm.

But Penrod is more than guts and games. The cattle-feeding sequence gives viewers a glimpse of Penrod's physical strength, as we see him (and him alone) toss the bag of feed. Multiple bags of feed already lie stacked in the truck. We do not see who created this stack, but as a grunting Penrod swings the last bag onto the pile, we are led to believe that he piled them all—or, he *could* have piled them all. At the same time, we hear him murmuring in nurturing tones to his cows as he performs his chore. Penrod's dog—a member of the "sporting group"—walks behind Penrod and carries a big stick in his mouth.

The Guy Penrod we see in this sequence confirms and denies a number of narratives operant in Homecoming circles. Bill Gaither is chopping away at his fans' possible suspicions using the ax of their probable assumptions. He returns the blade to them sharper than he found it. The probable assumptions get affirmed, strengthened, and corrected. Does long hair signal effeminacy, studio softness? No. Watch Penrod drive his truck, haul his feed. Does long hair mark Penrod as a Nashville city slicker? No. Look around at his blessed plot; see how this man moves on it. Does long hair portend disorderly living, or a disregard for responsibility? No. Penrod's is a productive, managed disorder. This is a man at home in nature, with all of its contingencies. Yes, it takes a wild man to tame nature. But look at the pristine barn. Watch how dutifully Penrod feeds his cows. Does long hair suggest nonconformity and individuality? Not in their pernicious forms. It is a nonconformity that attaches itself to tradition. It is a rugged individualism that sustains the old homestead.[16] Penrod has provided for his parents and in-laws. The barn is 120 years old. If the reeled Penrod is to reveal that there is no one-to-one relationship between Penrod's unique appearance and a pernicious antinomianism, he has to be shown reeling in the prevailing tropes of an acceptable manhood—country roads, livestock, woods.

And family. No aspect of Penrod's biography receives more attention on Homecoming stages and videos than his spouse, Angie, and his eight children, six of whom were born after Penrod joined the GVB. At the time of *The Best of Guy Penrod*'s recording and release, the Penrods had seven sons. Introduced playfully as "Father Abraham" at many live shows, the mood is often as lighthearted around Penrod's big brood as it is around his hair. Mark Lowry regularly jokes onstage that Penrod grows two things on his farm: hair and kids. This playful juxtaposition is efficacious. Whereas Penrod's hair may be the variable in his profile that gets him stopped and frisked at the southern gospel gate, his family is his golden ticket. Wife and kids are both standard biographical features for southern gospel male performers. They are not completely necessary for success, but those who cannot lay claim to this "family" (e.g., Mark Lowry) must gain the benefit of the doubt, and chip away at the questions regarding their sexual and marital situations, in other ways. When Lowry rhetorically combs the Penrod offspring into Penrod's dubious locks, there is a new sheen to both. Moreover, Penrod's unorthodox hair augments the sense that this "family" to which he belongs is normative; what better proof of the universality of a familial arrangement than to show that many supposedly different people are thus arranged? Even long-haired guys get married (to women) and have children.

To the extent that Penrod is the ideal southern gospel man, Angie Penrod (*née* Clark) and the Penrod children represent "the best" of Guy Penrod. Without them, Penrod's estate is but a farm. With them, it is a fully operational Christian homestead. The compilation video drives this point home, with numerous shots of the Penrods in full domestic mode—clips that taken together are intended to approximate a typical day in their lives. Standing five feet nine inches tall, slender but strong, Angie seems physically up to the task of homesteading (she led Liberty University women's basketball team in total points and rebounds the one year she played for them). In the video, she first appears in the kitchen, vigorously turning the wheel on a nonelectric, Country Living–brand grain mill. It is no painless task; neither is making bread from scratch. Viewers see some of the boys helping her prepare breakfast in the kitchen. Just before they eat, the parents, children, one set of grandparents, and Bill Gaither gather around the table as the children and parents sing "O Worship the King" and "The Doxology," complete with harmonies and slickly delivered key modulations. Either they did this every morning, or they were well rehearsed. While the camera captures some of the boisterousness endemic to spaces with such high concentrations of children (children whose home has been invaded by a camera crew, no less), order abounds. The order extends to the dress code; all Penrods sport something denim, something blue.

One of the major orders of the day include the children's schooling, which occurs primarily in a separate structure on the property whose façade resembles the rustic schoolhouses of Lancaster County, Pennsylvania. Angie does nearly all of the teaching—with the exception of the "Bible instruction," which falls to Guy (on the video, Angie makes this point). Among the footage of the school day captured on film is art class—which on that day involves recreating Warner Sallman's famous *Head of Christ*.[17]

The Penrods may have a well-ordered house, but the story of its conception redounds with apparent improvisation. Lounging with Guy and Angie on their front porch, Bill asks Guy, "Did you and Angie sit down somewhere and begin your marriage philosophically and say we want to have a whole bunch of kids?"

> GUY: Bill, Bill, Bill, there's never been a moment we've sat down and planned anything. [Bill laughs] I mean, that's the truth, and I don't say that . . .
> BILL: Because you were married for how many years before you had kids?
> GUY: Seven . . .
> BILL: . . . seven years . . .
> GUY: . . . before we started having kids, yeah, and you know there wasn't any planning that . . . we didn't plan anything. We just, we just started living life, we fell in love and got married, like a movie, you know, and just went off on our own, just started doing stuff. And God has been such a . . . gracious father in our lives. We just are blessed, that's the only thing I can say. And kids . . . I never thought I would have a bunch. I just didn't foresee it. I have one sister and I didn't grow up in a house with a bunch of kids. And as we started having 'em, she [indicating Angie] was just such a great mama. She feels like that's what she's put on earth to do, is be a mama.

Guy's reply crackles with fuzziness—from unspecified divine blessing to vague, desexualized plot points regarding the Penrods' marital and reproductive life. This inexactitude parallels the unscheduled, spontaneous nature of the Penrod family. According to Guy, the future was always unsettled. Although Guy's offhand reference to the movie-like quality of his relationship with Angie signals an awareness of a cultural script to which they conformed, and although the pair's immersion in an evangelical discourse in which motherhood is all but deified surely informs Angie's "call" to be a mother of many children (the pair met in the 1980s at Liberty, around the time its founder, Jerry Falwell, was at the height of his influence), Guy explains the Penrod familial arrangement as something the pair happened upon unexpectedly. He didn't foresee anything. He didn't imagine kids. They didn't plan. Things "just" happened. Naturally.

In this case, the Penrod contingency has an evident sexual and theological upshot. That the lack of planning would yield so many offspring underscores the Penrods' fecundity and sexual virility. Certainly, the childless first seven years of marriage qualifies either the accidental nature of the conceptions or the rampant fertility. But read alongside Guy's reference to God's blessing, the seven childless years appear as a sort of preordained holding period. In retrospect, while the Penrods were "just [. . .] doing stuff," their gracious Father was planning to bless them with offspring. Their openness to contingency prepared them to receive the blessing. Penrod's jocular introduction on Homecoming stages drives home the typology: Father Abraham, indeed.

The self-contained familial setup may seem suspicious—especially as it is a domestic cloister inflected with conservative evangelical religiosity. Guy arrives authoritatively (and exclusively) in the curriculum the moment the Bible falls open. Guy is the primary respondent in the joint Guy-Angie interview, even on matters concerning Angie. Moreover, this ideal domestic arrangement is distinctly, if not uniquely, the privilege of the well financed. The housing of several generations on a single tract of land and the homeschooling of many children—primarily by a stay-at-home mother, who has abundant resources at her disposal (tangible and intangible: Angie holds a master's degree in health promotion education from Vanderbilt)—are options only for families in which the husband's income is relatively high and the resources are plentiful. These "good family values" cost something. Furthermore, the Penrod homestead seems an attempt to recuse one's family absolutely from the world beyond the property line. It appears deserving of the moniker Americans reserve for the impossibly removed, perniciously out of touch: it is less a homestead, more a "compound," where the discourse can be circumscribed, and substantive differences between citizens do not or cannot exist. It seems a project predicated upon the myth of independence, of absolute control over fully isolatable variables.[18]

But not absolutely. While the Penrod homestead stands as a bulwark against a potentially hostile world, it also represents a refuge for those in the world. If it is a fortress, the Penrods desire it to be a fortress with an open gate. The Penrod parents understand their home as a place where proper virtue and right relation with others can be cultivated—first among themselves, their children, and their grandparents, then extended as an invitation to others. Once again pointing to the Gaithers' influence on his choices, Guy explains:

GUY: We learned something from you guys, educators. You would always tell me to build the fire warm enough at home so that they would always bring all of their friends over, you know, like you do with your kids. So we've tried to build a place where everyone wants to come to.

BILL: I just believe in that philosophy. If it's built warm enough, if it's just like, I mean, even if they stray some, they will come back, you know?

This approach presupposes a good deal regarding the superiority of "the family." The "fire" analogy presumes the world beyond the home is a cold or fraudulently heated place. Bill and Guy do not entertain the possibility that the Penrod children might find a sustaining warmth outside the Penrod hearth. Concomitantly, Bill and Guy assume that they should gather others to *their* fires. Here, Bill operates at full evangelical, market-savvy steam; the test of the fire will be its retention (or reclamation) of old clients and the attraction of new ones. However, Bill and Guy do not suppose that the family should barricade itself in a completely closed compound. The difficult question for them is how to make one's home(coming) sufficiently closed to provide safety yet sufficiently open to allow as many people as possible to be nurtured in that safety. While everyone who has been charged with the care and growth of dependents has faced such a difficulty, this is an especially sticky conundrum for a religious people bound simultaneously to "go make disciples" and to be "a people set apart."

Among the corollaries of this struggle is the relationship between Christian practice(s) and the Christian ideal. Are there institutions and structures so essential to the cultivation of Christian faith and practice that they become indispensable—such that when one recommends Jesus, one must recommend those institutions and practices as well? As I will show later in my discussion of Penrod's songs, the relationship between internal salvation and external witness is tricky to define for evangelicals, especially evangelical entertainers. Penrod's final "family-laced" comments on the video illustrate this conundrum. Directly addressing the camera/viewing audience, Penrod delivers one of those explicit invitations to conversion that occurs so frequently in evangelical churches but so rarely in Gaither videos:

I would pray that every one of you join our family. And what I mean by that is, if you've watched these things down through the years and there's a warmness that you feel, or a connection that you feel, or love . . . you feel loved because . . . what we're singing or saying, I would hope that you know that there is a way to get in the family, and that is just to give Jesus your heart and soul and trust him.

Ask him to forgive you for your sins and to come into the family. We'd love to have you be a part.

The video closes with the Gaither song, "Loving God, Loving Each Other," as photos and video clips of the Penrod family flash across the screen.

Penrod's language illustrates the centrality of "joining the family" as both analogue and ideal—and the tension that its dual deployment creates.[19] Penrod encourages listeners to imagine the family in the metaphorical sense. If his family—or any particular "family," including the family of musicians in the Homecomings—has any merit, it is as a sign of the broader kingdom of God. To the extent that the Homecoming videos have created warmth and love, they have given viewers a glimpse of "the family of God." The way into this family is not through marriage and child-bearing, but through evangelical conversion—which, Penrod assumes, is a live option for anyone. "Actual" families such as Penrod's serve only metaphorically.[20]

However, the content of the video—summed up in the closing photo montage—leaves little doubt that a family of the Penrod variety at least closely approximates the Christian ideal. When Penrod invites viewers to conversion, he also is recommending some version of his family as at least a very rich site for godly living—a site where conversion is likely to happen and a place where the converted are likely to grow in faith. Having this sort of familial setup in one's own life may not be prerequisite for membership in God's big family, but the power of Penrod's testimony relies heavily on viewers extrapolating that warmth and love are endemic both to Penrod's unfilmed home and to similarly arranged domestic spaces. If the reasons fans give for liking Penrod are any indication, the Gaithers were wise to count on this extrapolation.

TO THE RED COUNTRY

ROY: Guy Penrod, when he first came, you know, with the long hair . . . I've always had a little problem with that, you know, not, not [points at my head; we three laugh] . . .

JEN: He really did. I think God has shown him some things.

ROY: I don't know, you know. But my tendency, because of . . .

JEN: . . . the way we were raised . . .

ROY: . . . I was raised. Why don't the guy cut his hair? He'd look a lot better. [Jen laughs]

ROY: And I'm okay with it now, and that's took me a few years to work up to that.

RYAN: What happened with Guy? How did you come to that?

JEN: He got to listening to him, and on his testimony.

ROY: I saw his ... have you seen his personal story?

RYAN: *The Best of Guy Penrod*?

ROY: Yeah, the farm and all that, and his family.

RYAN: Yeah.

JEN: [whispering] Awesome.

ROY: Things like that. I think, this guy's for real. He's genuine. And hear people talk about him in their little interchanges, you know, with each other and ... like I say, I'm not judging the man ... I wouldn't judge him because that's God. ... Yeah, I accept Guy Penrod.

JEN: I really couldn't see this man [indicating Roy] in long hair.

[we three laugh]

I met Roy and Jen in 2009—at their church, after a Sunday morning service. The pair addressed me jointly. Over forty years of marriage had made them sensitive to the rhythmic rudiments of each other's narrative style. Roy spoke with the casual, spacious lilt of a wind-blown saloon door; every time it swung open, Jen filled the space. Together they grooved.

This particular groove contains riffs I found in a number of my conversations with Homecoming fans. The connection Roy makes between Penrod and me, the relatively hirsute ethnographer sitting before him, prefaces everything he says about Penrod (while not of the epic length of Penrod's, my hair was sufficiently long and unmanaged during most of my fieldwork to invite comparisons). This informs the confessional tone of Roy's stated aversion to long hair on men. His culturally specific stylistic preference once was tantamount to a presumptuous moral judgment—and perhaps, despite his efforts, still is. Roy's lament, "why don't the guy cut his hair?" expresses a formerly held opinion but has a fluster to it that betrays some extant desire. It may well have been addressed to me. There may have been a time when Roy would have been reluctant to sit down with a guy like me. There was a time, after all, when he was reluctant about a guy like Guy.

But "God had shown him some things." Or had *Jen* shown him some things? It is Jen who elucidates Roy's seeing of the light. "[Roy] got to listening to [Guy], and on his testimony." Roy's deliberate speech allows room for his longtime spouse to fill in the gaps—with playful, God-laced digs.[21] Although Jen attaches herself to the same tradition that shapes Roy's prejudice—"the way *we* were raised"—Jen gives little indication that she struggled as Roy did to overcome the prejudice. Roy finishes the thought by implicating only himself: "the way ... *I* was raised." It is as if Jen has waited for Roy to learn lessons that she either learned long ago or never needed to learn. Her knowing smiles and gentle jabs at her spouse make Jen appear as the one in the relationship most capable of seeing through, or looking beyond, appearances.

This gendered division of authentic perception mirrors that which Bill Gaither expresses in his story of Penrod's audition: Bill had reservations, Gloria did not; Bill had to learn, Gloria had to teach. Roy and Jen also manifest a division I found in all of my interviews with Homecoming fans: fans who admitted having initial reservations regarding Penrod due to his appearance were invariably men, never women. Rather, women who commented on Penrod's appearance expressed approval—variously expressed, but usually tinged with physical attraction. Sometimes, women affirmed Penrod-as-cowboy, as evidenced in this comment from Susan, a late middle-aged midwestern fan: "Since I'm a cowgirl at heart, I love that cowboy look, you know. And [Penrod] glows. I love his smile." On some occasions, women explicitly noted Penrod's good looks. After learning that I had been backstage at Homecoming concerts, one woman jokingly asked me if I could introduce her to Penrod ("he's gorgeous"). No one is throwing underwear onstage at Gaither concerts, but the grizzled family man—who looks conspicuously like many evangelical renderings of Jesus—definitely releases erotic energy.[22]

Roy's and Jen's highlighting of Penrod's "personal story"—specifically the rural and familial aspects of the story—encapsulates the single most-emphasized aspect of the singer's appeal among all fans I interviewed. What sold people on Penrod was his life as a husband (in all senses) and father. In Roy's and Jen's case, the site of our interview is worth noting. The church in which we met was a self-described "cowboy church"—located within sight of acres of farmland and one of middle America's major interstates. The high-tech utilitarianism evident in the church's warehouse exterior, stadium seating, state-of-the-art sound equipment, and kitchen/coffee bar (continuous with the sanctuary) seemed straight out of the playbook of many American evangelical churches fewer than twenty years old.[23] But this church possessed distinct iconography: a massive horse and buggy in the lobby; sepia-toned pictures of tractors and antiquated rusty farm tools on the walls; a *faux*-barn facade for a stage backdrop. That morning's service featured a baptism; the pastor—a smiley white man in boots, cowboy hat, and blue jeans, with a thick, stammer-free southern drawl—dunked his fully clothed candidate in a tin feeding trough located at the side of the stage. While any Christian rock group could have waded in the wattage of the massive sound system, this church's "praise team" used it to pump up the volume on their fiddle, mandolin, and steel guitar.

But the most profound icons were the people. Nearly every man—and a substantial number of women—donned either a ten-gallon cowboy hat or cowboy boots (often both). Flannels, hunting jackets, overalls, and starched button-up shirts tucked into tight navy blue jeans dominated the congregation.[24] While I received smiles and polite tips of the hat from the congregants, I felt out of place. I wanted either to make for the mandolin and prove my country-bluegrass mettle, or to make for the parking lot, where my Honda Civic hid somewhere in the gravel between the broad-shouldered pickups. I was white. I was midwestern by upbringing. I knew the discourse. I knew the music (making for the mandolin was in this sense a live option; I was a decent mandolin player). Absent one of these variables, my discomfort would have been greater.

Sporting their own flannels and boots, Roy and Jen initially struck me as reasonable candidates for founding members of this cowboy church. They both grew up in rural areas. They spoke with thick southern accents. But such was not their account. As they told it, their attendance in this casual congregation required adjustment, especially for Roy, because their previous churches were "traditional"—formal in attire, which seemed to signal a cultural stodginess that the pair came to regard as out of keeping with good Christian practice.

RYAN: Now would you think Guy would be the type of guy . . . he's also . . . he's got the long hair thing. He's kind of got this cowboy image going.

JEN: Yeah! He does, doesn't he?

RYAN: And we're here at this cowboy church talking . . .

ROY: See, that was a problem when I came here.

JEN: Oh my.

ROY: Over three years ago, you know . . . traditional things, you didn't bring in here.

JEN: It was a transition.

ROY: I went to church all my life. We came from a church we attended thirteen years.

JEN: Baptist church.

ROY: And I wore a suit and a tie and . . .

JEN: Dressed up.

ROY: . . . I was on the board . . .

JEN: I *never* wore slacks to church. [laughs; she was wearing jeans that day]

ROY: . . . and I taught Sunday School. Young women, they wouldn't let you on the platform if you didn't have a dress or a skirt.

JEN: Right.

ROY: Anyway these things, you just kind of go along and accept it without really analyzing it, I think.

JEN: Or what does the *Word* teach about it?

ROY: I came here . . .

JEN: You know, it's men's ideas.

ROY: . . . and I saw this, you know, we were . . . we felt we needed to go somewhere to church other than where we were at because . . . personal things happened. Anyway, I had a problem . . . not really bad . . . but just, I don't know if I could be around this.

JEN: It was kind of a culture shock.

ROY: But the first day I heard [pastor] preach . . .

JEN: Oh my.

ROY: . . . it was on January 1, 2006, and I told her going home, I said, "I could drive and listen to that guy any time."

JEN: He is awesome.

ROY: And we came back and . . . occasionally someone will bring a dog to church here, you know, a pet, and stuff like that, and they wear shorts and everything, which that's all right. But we were taught, you ain't gonna do that in church.

JEN: But it's the heart.

ROY: You dress up because you're going to God's house. But anyway, it caused me to look at a lot of things that had been ingrained in me . . . traditional . . . even music, you know? And you know God, he's not that way. I mean, I understand that now.

Again, Roy seems to be warring with his stylistic tastes. He balks at shorts and dogs in church (a few canines were present during that day's service), but he feels he should not do so. He feels these things should not be important, but he must exert some effort to convince himself of their unimportance.

Roy's hesitation regarding these matters is significant, despite their seeming triviality. How much could long hair really matter? Guy Penrod went to Liberty University; he talks the evangelical talk—fluently. For all intents and purposes, he is thus already "in the family." Isn't the long hair but a straw man? Doesn't the narration of an erstwhile prejudice over hairstyle help one imagine oneself as having opened one's heart, mind, and church, in full inclusion, to "all kinds"—even if one still shuts a number of others out?

Yes and no. To some extent, when Bill Gaither hands Penrod to his audience, he is handing them to themselves, repackaged as an "other." The Gaithers never would have auditioned Penrod had his hiring and acceptance been *thoroughly* unimaginable—had Bill had to ask Gloria, for example, "what are we going to do about Guy's same-sex partner?" Furthermore, I find it very probable that Bill's narration of his own apprehension over Penrod's appearance informed Roy and other men who expressed to me reservation regarding Penrod. Many fans to whom I spoke identified the biographical *The Best of Guy Penrod* as the moment of their "conversion" to Penrod-sympathy, though this did not always chronologically match their positive encounters with Penrod prior to 2005. Because Penrod's follicles, family, and farm pervaded pre-2005 Homecoming narratives, it seems likely that *The Best of* program punctuated and finalized a decade of successful biography-pitching—thus, conversion to Penrod-sympathy was not quite so dramatic or instantaneous.

But dismissing men's concern over male appearance as a retroactive centralization of an ever-marginal issue among evangelicals ignores the historical and present-day evidence of this issue's salience. Appealing to the same sorts of "natural law" arguments used against homosexuals in the late twentieth and early twenty-first century—using as their textual centerpiece I Corinthians 11:14 ("Does not nature itself teach you that if a man wears long hair, it is degrading to him?")—many twentieth-century evangelicals came down hard against long hair on men, and some still do.[25] The poster-visages of southern gospel's major event and magazine—the National Quartet Convention and *Singing News*, respectively—reveal that the unspoken rules governing southern gospel men's appearance still skew quite conservative.[26] Two decades after Guy Penrod's GVB debut, his hair—and, to a lesser extent, his cowboy getup—remain anomalous.

In light of this legacy, the "culture shock" that Jen describes upon her and Roy's initial attendance of their cowboy church makes sense, despite the fact that both grew up in a rural, "cowboy culture" of sorts. While Roy still seems to harbor misgivings that extend beyond the church regarding appearance and behavior, his more pressing struggle pertains to what transpires *within* a designated sacred space. In former times, one may have dressed casually all week, but one dressed up when one went to "God's house." Roy does not obey this rule anymore, nor does Jen. Although Roy has accepted and adopted the attire common to the community at hand—flannels, boots, jeans (even for Jen)—he sees this less as a redefinition of what constitutes "dressing up" and more an abandoning of a rule he once considered more binding. That he can cite a "noncowboy" clothing article such as shorts as an example of fellow congregants' boundary-pushing—and that he can acknowledge this, too, as morally acceptable, despite its grinding against his tastes—demonstrates something more than a new sartorial dogmatism is in place. It is not just that flannels count as church clothing nowadays; it is that he has abandoned or seriously undercut "church clothing" as a moral category.

In the case of both Penrod and the cowboy church, Roy's overcoming of his "culture shock" would not have been likely had he not been shocked with a familiar, direct current. "Cowboy gear" and the symbols of American rurality were supremely familiar accoutrements to Roy outside of church, which lessened the shock of adapting them inside church. Provided it remained "Christian," the church could be adorned in the cowboy way. In the case of Penrod, the rugged rural regalia served not as the variable to which Roy adjusted, but rather as Roy's point of connection that facilitated further adjustment with the long-haired vocalist. Provided the long-haired artist adorned himself in the cowboy way, he became an acceptable Christian entertainer.

Given Jen's and Roy's cultural location, Penrod's cowboy image makes sense. Indeed, a large proportion of the Gaither audience is rural or identifies with what they perceive as "country culture" (the many pristinely waxed pickup trucks I saw at the cowboy church—a couple with golf carts in the back—suggested to me that it wasn't simply, or even mostly, farmhands in attendance). But the appeal of Cowboy Penrod does not reduce merely to geographical and vocational affinity. The muscular, multivalent motion of manhood in American evangelicalism, from the 1995 addition of Penrod to the GVB to the 2005 *Best of Guy Penrod* video, serves as a broader cultural horizon against which the Homecoming buckaroo cuts his silhouette.

MEN IN FULL

When Penrod boarded the Gaither ship, University of Colorado football coach Bill McCartney was steering his own vessel of Christian manhood across the nation. Started in 1990, McCartney's Promise Keepers (PK) was by mid-decade one of the country's largest parachurch organizations. Its massive all-male gatherings—the largest of which was the 1997 "Stand in the Gap" event on the National Mall in Washington, DC—perpetually garnered the attention of journalists. One of the PK movement's stated motivations was that Christian men had abdicated social and familial responsibility. They had been negligent fathers, bad churchmen, and subpar leaders in their communities. The PK movement reminded Christian men of their Christian calling as men: to take on the burden of leadership at home, at church, and in their communities. The PK rallies drew ire from many women's advocacy groups. To many, these men-only events were little more than testosterone-driven recruitment meetings for an army—an army that sought to retake territory won by women's rights movements. The National Organization for Women led the anti-PK counteroffensive, warning, "this group is not about hugs and tears in stadiums but is, instead, a dangerous continuation of the anti-woman, extreme agenda of the religious right."[27] When feminists engaged the content of PK rallies and literature, they had their pick of potentially insidious patriarchies to dispute. Those familiar with earlier Christian men's movements would have recognized some Teddy Roosevelt–era "Muscular Christianity" in the PK narrative.[28] But the PK message also represented something new. From the outset, racial reconciliation formed one pillar of the PK platform, which marked its departure from the eugenicist and imperialistic project that underwrote Muscular Christianity in its prevailing Anglo-Saxon forms.[29] Furthermore, the PK movement borrowed from feminism even as it seemed to undermine it. Despite the assumptions regarding "innate" gender identities at play in PK rallies and literature, the performative gender language of the PK movement oddly recalled Simone de Beauvoir as much as it did Teddy Roosevelt. One *became* a "real" man—by *doing* something. Behavior defined Christian manhood. Boys had to learn it. Fathers had to teach it. Males had to put away childish things and become men. To this end, Promise Keepers practiced a broad array of "manly" activities. They cried and hugged one another a lot. They talked openly about their sins—often very private sins. They apologized to everyone—white men to black men, especially. They promised to make themselves emotionally available to their families (and, of course, as their popular slogan suggested, "real men keep their promises"). They talked about the pitfalls of various "Hollywood" images of manhood—the "tough guy," the "strong, silent type," to name a few—and how their Christianity called them to a different sort of manhood.

The PK movement shaped and was shaped by a wide array of evangelical men (and in some cases, women). Bill Gaither was among them. In fact, a Gaither song became one of the movement's anthems: the title track of the 1990 GVB album, *A Few Good Men*. Suzanne Jennings—the Gaithers' oldest daughter—cowrote the song with her spouse, Barry. The pair borrows the title from the then-famous US Marine Corps recruitment slogan: "we're looking for a few good men." In the song, God is the recruitment officer, looking for a "few good men" to enlist for Divine service. The chorus elucidates what sort of men God calls:

> Men full of compassion, who laugh and love and cry,
> men who'll face eternity and aren't afraid to die,
> men who'll fight for freedom and honor once again,
> He just needs a few good men.[30]

The song couches the male Christian life in militaristic terms. God's need for men who will "fight for freedom and honor" suggest that God is looking for the same sort of man as is the US military—a loaded comparison, given the 1990–1991 Operation Desert Storm campaign. In a first verse that riffs on Ephesians 6, God's desired man will "raise the shield of Faith, protecting what is pure"—a defensive gesture, but militaristic nonetheless. However, the song is not merely an articulation of an essentially bellicose religiosity. The song deploys its tropes more ambivalently. The first qualities on this recruitment sheet are decidedly not warlike. God needs compassionate men who will "laugh and love and cry." While the second line could call to listeners' minds the soldier who willingly dies on the battlefield, the nonresistant overtones (death and eternity are "faced") also evokes the martyr—the man who stands with his chin up in the middle of the coliseum as the lions are released. The second verse contains the song's strongest qualification of the military imagery: "[God] doesn't need an army to guarantee a win." Whatever God's assembly is, it is not an army in the conventional sense.

The song played well in PK rallies. PK speakers also employed qualified, cautious warfare language to describe men's ostensibly spiritual struggle with powers and principalities. Promise Keepers regarded gender identity as fundamental and natural; in "A Few Good Men," God calls to men who *already* possess a set of characteristics; their predispositions determine the conditions of the call. However, manhood remains performative; in the song, God wants men who act—or who *will* act—a certain way.

The Promise Keepers lost momentum after 1997—partly due to financial miscues, as McCartney tried to maintain a free admission policy even as the cost of the growing PK rallies increased. However, American evangelical fascination with manhood did not lose momentum. The beginning of the twenty-first century witnessed a surge in the number of evangelical authors and speakers who explicated Christian manhood to Christian men. While a number of the new apologists for this manhood had institutional roots in the PK movement, and while all were indebted to the movement for identifying and creating a massive, self-conscious evangelical men's market, the early twenty-first-century evangelical man exercised a different sort of muscle—something more like an iron claw. Turn-of-the-century evangelical men received a testosterone injection. While the essentially otherworldly, spiritual component of the war talk remained, authors and speakers began to proclaim a physically aggressive, battle-ready masculinity inherent to all males—a deep, untamed will-to-wildness, a hawkish instinct to display power that a feminized culture (and church) sought to undermine but could not eradicate.

The leader in this San Juan charge was another Coloradan: John Eldredge, a former employee of James Dobson's Colorado Springs–based Focus on the Family. In the opening pages of his best-selling 2001 book *Wild at Heart: Discovering the Secret of a Man's Soul*, Eldredge effectively pronounces the end of the reign of rule-following, duty-defined, responsibility-driven (in short, promise-keeping) evangelical men:

> Christianity, as it currently exists, had done some terrible things to men. When all is said and done, I think most men in the church believe that God put them on the earth to be a good boy. The problem with men, we are told, is that they don't know how to keep their promises, be spiritual leaders, talk to their wives, or raise their children. But, if they will try real hard they can reach the lofty summit of becoming . . . a nice guy. That's what we hold up as models of Christian maturity: Really Nice Guys. We don't smoke, drink, or swear; that's what makes us *men*.[31]

With his patricidal jab at McCartney's men's movement, Eldredge was marking his territory. Too many preachers and authors defined manhood prescriptively; men became "real men" insofar as they fulfilled some list of duties and requirements. Conversely, Eldredge showed men their *a priori*, masculine selves. As the book's subtitle suggested, Eldredge viewed his project as descriptive—a voyage of discovery, not a manners manual. *Wild at Heart's* three-pronged thesis—all men desire a battle to fight, an adventure to live, and a beauty to rescue—were, according to Eldredge, not suggestions *for* men but observations *of* men. His primary evidence—the rowdy behavior of little boys and males' overwhelming attraction to "shoot 'em up" Hollywood films—signaled the profundity of his departure from a PK movement that tended to look upon boyhood as in need of supersession and Hollywood as productive of pernicious male stereotypes.

While the great masculine adventure in Eldredge's best-selling book turns out to be spiritual in nature, as it is in the PK movement, *Wild at Heart* more consistently depends upon and more forcefully recommends displays of male physical power. The ideal Christian man does not exhibit simply inner fortitude. Eldredge makes this clear when he criticizes the feminized church's feminized version of Jesus: "[these images] leave me with the impression that [Jesus] was the world's nicest guy. Mister Rogers with a beard. Telling me to be like him feels like telling me to go limp and passive. Be nice. Be swell. Be like Mother Teresa. I'd much rather be told to be like William Wallace."[32] Eldredge's preference for *Braveheart* over Mother Teresa—and his implication that the latter's work among the sick and poor was mawkish and demanded little physical resilience—is not an opinion that PK preachers would have been likely to articulate.

Eldredge wrote a few follow-up books to *Wild at Heart*, cowrote a women's companion piece with his wife, Stasi, and published a "Field Manual" workbook for *Wild at Heart* small groups.[33] The *Wild at Heart* franchise achieved unparalleled success, but Eldredge was not a lone evangelical wolf howling in the wilderness in the early twenty-first century. In the first years of the century, macho Reformed pastor Mark Driscoll, writers Erwin McManus and Eric Ludy, radio personality James Dobson, and others sounded their divinely ordained barbaric yawps over the roofs of a mincing, hyper-feminized American culture.[34]

And none too soon. For manhood—and concomitantly Western, supposedly Christian civilization—faced a crisis. In 1999, just up the interstate from Eldredge's and Dobson's Colorado Springs, two teenage boys, armed to the hilt, killed twelve of their fellow students and one teacher at Columbine High School, precipitating the question in secular and religious media: what was wrong with American boys (or, what was wrong with what America was doing to its boys)?[35] Later, the events of September 11, 2001, marked America as vulnerable in a new kind of way to enemies who used new kinds of warfare. The nation's response, under the presidency of cowboy-hat-wearing Texan George W. Bush, was to strain its military muscle on multiple fronts. The times demanded it. It was also becoming apparent to many that the times demanded some "official" answers to the question of homosexuals' place in American society.

For a number of evangelicals, all of the era's problems were explicable in terms of manhood. Columbine demonstrated that America's schools and churches had given naturally rowdy boys no proper outlet. September 11 and America's actual and possible responses to it were cause and effect of a "clash of civilizations" between East and West, the forces of light and darkness. If the right (light, white) side was to prevail, a few good men would have to answer the war call. Public discussion around homosexuality—particularly pertaining to gay men—changed a good deal over the years. Evangelicals found it increasingly difficult to dismiss homosexuality simply as a willful transgression. Social conditioning became a more acceptable and pervasive evangelical explanation of the fact of gay men and women. Architects of evangelical "ex-gay" programs understood sexual identity as relational—the result of a social process. Their moderate form of behaviorism joined with the traditional, essentialist constructs of gender identity long prevalent in evangelical discourse, yielding a new, urgent call for "manly" (heterosexual) role models and relationships, and for properly masculine environments for all males—especially young boys. Masculinity was innate, but it needed activation and appropriate encouragement lest it become suppressed or misdirected. Something or someone had to bring out the "natural" tones in men.[36]

Guy Penrod premiered on the Homecoming stage about the same time that Bill McCartney's Promise Keepers had already gained its most significant yardage. In January 2002, shortly after the September 11 attacks, Penrod sang "A Few Good Men" with an ensemble of singers at the patriotic Homecoming concert at Carnegie Hall—performing the improvised wails on the coda that Michael English had performed on the original GVB recording.[37] Like the Homecomings themselves, Penrod continued to rise in popularity as the PK movement receded, giving way to Eldredge-style evangelical masculinities. Penrod and Eldredge were offering almost exactly the same product:

—"I think every little boy has a desire to be a cowboy at some level." —Guy Penrod
—"There's a reason the American cowboy has taken on mythic proportions. He embodies a yearning every man knows from very young—to 'go West,' to find a place where he can be all he was meant to be." —John Eldredge
—"I had a real, honest-to-goodness cowboy for a grand-dad. My mom's dad grew up in New Mexico." —Guy Penrod
—"My grandfather, my father's father, was a cowboy. He worked his own cattle ranch in Eastern Oregon, between the desert sage and the Snake River." —John Eldredge[38]

There is good reason to believe the similarity is no accident. In Bill's filmed interview with the Penrod parents, at the precise moment when Angie mentions that Guy "teaches Bible" to their children, the video cuts to a scene of Penrod sitting at the dining-room table, raising his fist (and apparently his voice) as he reads to his captivated sons. A quick pause and zoom of the scene reveals he is not reading from the Bible. He is reading from *Wild at Heart*.

STRONG MELODIOUS SONGS

Penrod sings southern gospel music—a genre in which several regionally and religiously inflected masculinities have abounded and intersected for decades. On one hand, southern gospel music, like much of white southern culture, promotes the rugged, untamed, even iconoclastic rural white male. Proficiency with plows, horses, guns; preference for the contingency of open air over central air-conditioning; fluency in a folksy, no-nonsense southern idiom; indifference or half-hearted, provisional resignation toward human institutions (religious institutions included) in favor of authentic, unmediated relations with friends, family, and God—these are marks of a southern gospel man in full.[39]

But the rugged southern man usually has had a partner: the southern dandy.[40] Southern gospel is nearly synonymous with this masculinity. The all-male quartet historically is a scrupulously ordered, well-groomed, uniform entity. Typically, all hairs on singers' heads are numbered, swathed with some viscous embarrassment of product. As I previously noted, clean-shaven faces and suits abound. If the men's suits do not match, at least they coordinate with one another. The quartet is visually flush, like four manicured fingernails. Historically, leisure suits and seersucker abound. The stage shows possess symmetry and stability. Even the term "close harmony" points to enforced musical cohesion. The contrapuntal mixed-part tunes many groups borrow from traditional singing conventions demand clockwork precision; if individual singers do not hit the proper beats and pitches in their assigned parts, the tapestry of a convention song unravels. The arrangements allow little in the way of individual improvisation. Southern gospel artists do not scat-sing.

Over the past twenty years, this curious collusion of disorder and domestication, of frontier virility and foppish vanity, has occurred on a physically expressive homosocial stage. While mutual affection between members of quartets always has been a selling point in a milieu that so highly values geniality, mid-century groups like the Statesmen Quartet and the Blackwood Brothers did not hug and rub so frequently as the Gaither Vocal Band, Ernie Haase and Signature Sound, even the Cathedrals lineups of the late 1980s onward. Lengthy embraces, hearty backslaps, shoulder rubs, and knowing gazes into one another's eyes during solos and duets have become regular fare in quartet performances—the stuff that marks performers as earnest, loving, possessed of good Christian hearts. If the expressive emotionality of white men might signal to audiences a worrisome effeminacy—or a worrisome "passion" not appropriate to *white* gospel singers—it also may signal healthy transgression and spontaneity, a wild-at-heart disregard for the social fetters that imprison males within themselves.[41]

Never is Penrod's dexterous combination of these masculinities on such full display as when the GVB performs one of the Gaithers' many epic, crucicentric anthems. Songs like "I Believe in a Hill Called Mount Calvary" and "Then Came the Morning" narrate the story of Jesus from death to the empty tomb—and coterminously tell the story of a convert's transition from despair to victory in Jesus. These songs begin subdued, even lachrymose, then crescendo to gigantic, celebratory orchestrations of eschatological proportions. They demand that singers exhibit a wide spectrum of emotions and decorum in a four-to-five-minute performance.

Penrod's many performances of the Gaithers' "It Is Finished" illustrate the man's range. Depending on the personnel with whom he sings, Penrod takes center stage in different portions of the song. The 1998 *Singin' with the Saints* version of the song features Penrod almost exclusively, as he performs with the Bill Gaither Trio (Bill, Gloria, and Bill's brother Danny).[42]

The song starts soberly at Golgotha, which the first verse identifies as the site of the great battle of the ages. As Penrod surveys the cross, he sings softly and gestures little. The instrumentation is sparse; no other vocalist sings. This is a solitary moment that demands sobriety. If his eyes are not closed, he is gazing skyward or absently ahead. The Trio joins him, singing a subdued version of the chorus, which forecasts the result of the battle: "It is finished, the battle is over / it is finished, there'll be no more war."[43]

Then, the second verse pushes back against the chorus's finality. The narrator has not fully embraced the outcome the chorus predicts: "yet in my heart, the battle was still raging." Penrod becomes slightly more animated as he sings the first-person verse of the song. He is now looking all around the Homecoming circle as he sings. With increasing fervor, leaning into the faces of those sitting in front of him, he slaps at his chest ("these were battlefields of my own making / I didn't know that the war had been won"). He sings slightly louder. The orchestra is growing. The other singers are nodding, mouthing "yes" as Penrod inclines toward them.

Oh, but then I heard the king of the ages / had fought all the battles for me. "Ages" and "fought" are high, sustained notes, which Penrod sings with his right hand stretched to the sky. His eyebrows raise; he grins briefly. In the background, Bill begins to smile, looking eagerly around at the gathering. *And that victory was mine for the claiming.* Penrod nearly snarls as he sings "victory." He fervently beats his chest. In the background, Gloria lifts her hand, as do a number of other singers. *And now, praise his name, I am free.* On "now," he stabs at the ground with his index finger. A male singer behind him is mirroring his motions. On "I am free," he extends his right arm fully to the sky. Now, everyone is standing, raising their arms. Everyone is singing on the final chorus. *IT*—Penrod stabs the air with his index finger—*IS*—another stab—*FINISHED*—Penrod slams his finger down toward the ground, his brow furrowing for an instant as he flashes a belligerent sneer, before the smile sets in. When Jesus says it's enough, it's enough.

* * *

Penrod uses his full palette of masculine propriety and passion in the big Gaither anthems. However, another subset of songs in Penrod's

Homecoming playlist speaks more literally to his role as male lodestar: his "country gospel" songs. With increasing frequency over the course of Penrod's tenure, Bill Gaither featured Penrod on tunes written by or cowritten with country artists.[44] Because these pieces ride on the "rugged frontier man" trope, they initially seem plucked from John Eldredge's playbook. But by no means were the songs unequivocal celebrations of Eldredge's holy cowboy; indeed, they often seemed to undermine him. A careful look at two of Penrod's most famous country gospel songs, and fans' reception of them, reveals them to be replete with ambivalence and contradiction vis-à-vis good country Christian manhood.

One of Penrod's staple songs during his stint with the GVB—"The Baptism of Jesse Taylor," written in 1972 by Dallas Frazier—spells out one of the kinds of men Penrod is meant to call to mind. For those who know country and southern gospel history, and for those who know the history of "Jesse Taylor," the GVB's version of the song encapsulates the enduring (if sometimes uneasy) mingling of the genres. "Jesse Taylor" is the GVB "going country," which had long ago gone southern gospel, which had long ago gone country . . .[45]

The lyrics tell the story of a standard country music character: the hard-livin' male rounder. As the title suggests, however, this version of the character does not drown in his beer:

> Among the local taverns they'll be a slack in business
> 'Cause Jesse's drinkin' came before the groceries and the rent
> Among the local women they'll be a slack in cheatin'
> 'Cause Jesse won't be steppin' out again.

> *chorus:*
> *They baptized Jesse Taylor in Cedar Creek last Sunday*
> *Jesus gained a soul and Satan lost a good right arm*
> *They all cried "Hallelujah" as Jesse's head went under*
> *'Cause this time he went under for the Lord.*

> The scars on Jesse's knuckles were more than just respected
> The county courthouse records tell all there is to tell
> The pockets of the gamblers will soon miss Jesse's money
> And the black eye of the law will soon be well. (*chorus*)

> From now on Nancy Taylor can proudly speak to neighbors
> Tell how much Jesse took up with little Jim

Now Jimmy's got a daddy and Jesse's got a family
And Franklin County's got a lot more man. (*chorus*)[46]

"Jesse Taylor" is a character sketch of a protagonist who hides beneath, or above, the sketch. The putatively pivotal moment in Jesse's life hardly appears at all. Only the chorus describes the baptism, in rather general terms. Listeners only have access to the sinful Jesse Taylor of the narrative past. The post-baptism Taylor only appears late, in the third verse, as a vague reverse negative of the old man who was "put away" in baptism. We do not know how the baptized Taylor behaves; we only know how he *no longer* behaves.

The presences and absences, and the active and passive characters in "The Baptism of Jesse Taylor," communicate much to listeners regarding the effects of sin, the scope of redemption, and the boundaries of personal guilt. Although all of Taylor's sins involve the exploitation and harm of other people, the song draws us away from the human parties chiefly offended—an ironic steerage, as Frazier *does* highlight the sinful people and institutions adversely affected by Jesse's conversion. Jesse is the entity most damaged by Jesse's sins—Jesse, coupled with the general (divinely instituted) moral order he transgresses. We hear of Jesse's scars. We hear of the "black eye of the law." We hear of no other scars, no other black eyes. Even Jesse's long-suffering spouse and son only appear in the song's third verse epilogue—bearing no wounds from previous wrongs, just happy to have "a lot more man" around, at last.

The earthly hell that Jesse's transgressions create for his family and community remain implicit throughout the song. The true concern is the state of Jesse's soul before God. For Jesse's soul, the wages of sin are eternal death. Evangelical conversion seeks to redress this death; conversion changes the orientation of the individual soul toward the God who issued the law that the individual violated. Whereas once the individual, in a state of sin, was held perpetually and totally guilty, conversion covers the sinner's soul through Jesus's saving grace. The violations and the fate that the sins portend are gone, for all eternal intents and purposes. It is finished; the battle is over. In most articulations—even in those strands of evangelicalism that call sinners to personally, willfully decide to "come to Jesus"—the essential benefits of conversion accrue to a passive subject, because Jesus is the active agent. Although Frazier's song does not wade deeply into soteriological waters, the chorus tells a specific redemption story. "Jesus gained a soul." Jesus did not gain the "good right arm" that Satan had lost. That Jesse had been the arm of Satan speaks both to the pre-baptism Jesse's passivity and to his activity—to his instrumental usage by a larger evil force and to his complicity with that force. Although they appear merely as memories, the sins of the pre-baptism Jesse are his only detailed "actions." In sin, Jesse is personally, fatally active. In his transformation to sainthood, he is passive. *Jesus* gained a soul. *They* baptized Jesse Taylor.

Those who endorse this model of conversion expect measurable changes in the converted person's behavior (even though the prevalent Pauline subject—the "not I but Christ in me" who acts virtuously—still locates agency outside of the born-again). Still, better behavior is the byproduct, not the meat, of the matter. Sins still occur. But they are aberrations in a life cleaned by grace through faith, and God no longer holds these sins against the guilty party's eternal soul. In the eternal scheme of things, there is no longer a guilty party.

"The Baptism of Jesse Taylor" makes evident how this supernatural, eternal guiltlessness can effect an erasure of this-worldly, societal guilt and accountability. Frazier relegates Jesse's past wrongs to a past that has become inconsequential. To introduce characters wronged by Jesse—characters who live on both sides of the baptism, characters whose scars and defensive wounds did not get washed away when Jesse's offenses did—would be to undermine the baptism's transcendent efficacy, to remind everyone that some of Jesse's debts remain outstanding. In this light, Nancy and Jim Taylor's appearance in the final verse is vital. Of all of Jesse's acquaintances, his family members are most likely to bear deep wounds from systematic neglect and mistreatment. If *they*, of all people, appear unscathed, surely the past has passed, indeed, and there is no reason further to address or redress Jesse's wrongs.

Of course, the sins and guilt of the past do not vanish. There is no "Baptism of Jesse Taylor" without the voiced recollection of the sins placed underwater and under erasure. Is this a case of evangelical voyeurism—the sort of which allows the righteous some vicarious participation in titillating and taboo lifestyles?[47] Or is this simply a case of the breadth of grace being proven by the depth of sin? If Jesus can save someone like Jesse, can't Jesus save anybody? The song probably feeds multiple hungers. The narrative salience of a supposedly nullified past gives listeners a good deal of freedom to construct for themselves a particularly converted—and at the same time particularly masculinized—Jesse Taylor. "Franklin County's got a lot more man" is the song's punchline. Frazier (and music-writer Sanger Shafer) strengthens this punch by having the singer suddenly jump a full octave on "and Franklin County's," and deliver the remainder of the line at a great tonal height above the rest of the song. This vocal climax seems to punctuate the song, but the line actually invites further listener speculation. Did Jesse Taylor become a "lot more man" because he rejected his erstwhile, fraudulent manhood—the "popular" (worldly, bellicose, womanizing) manhood operant in the taverns? Or did Franklin County gain "a lot more man" because Jesse Taylor carried some of that "wild man" with him into Christendom—and Christendom was the better for it because it gained a warrior? And if the latter is the case, in what conflicts will Jesse Taylor, the presumably southern, white Christian male, acquire his *new* scars? In 1972? In 1998?

Since country and gospel songwriters often employ ironic reversals of clichés, the former conclusion has precedent: Frazier's song argues that liberally exercised sexual virility and physical prowess have nothing to do with "true manhood." Real men love their wives and keep their promises. But Frazier's indulgence in Taylor's rugged "mangressions" suggests Frazier is not simply setting up a straw man for quick and ironic destruction in the third verse. This song would not work as a country or southern gospel song were Jesse Taylor a different articulation of "bad" male—say, a sedentary banker consumed by his career. And there is a reason Bill Gaither assigns his resident six-foot-three, reproductively prolific, holy cowboy to take the lead on the GVB version of the song. When *Guy Penrod* performs the song, Homecoming fans are watching Jesse Taylor testify—his manliness purified by the refiner's fire.

* * *

A decade after Penrod first performed "The Baptism of Jesse Taylor" for Homecoming audiences, the GVB added a new "Guy song" to their setlist— "Jesus and John Wayne," written by Bill and Gloria Gaither, their son Benjy, Doug Johnson, and Kim Williams. Johnson and Williams already had successful solo and collaborative careers as writers of country and gospel songs (and "country-gospel" songs). Randy Travis's version of their "Three Wooden Crosses" won the pair the Country Music Association's Song of the Year award in 2003. The award-winning cast of songwriters wrote "Jesus and John Wayne" for the GVB's 2008 album *Lovin' Life*. There was no doubt who would sing lead.

I witnessed firsthand Bill Gaither's exhilaration over the song backstage after a show in Pennsylvania in 2007. He shuffled me out to the GVB tour bus specifically to listen to an unmixed version of the song before its release. I knew from previous listening sessions that, when Bill got excited about a song around me, he got excited primarily about lyrics, about the *message*. Typically, I offered constructive (usually positive) comments about the mix, the instrumentation, the harmonies. Attending to the musical minutiae allowed me to prove my musical mettle, to engage Bill on a level I figured he could not engage many of his listeners, and to avoid committing myself to hasty affirmations of the songs' messages. The latter was difficult, for Bill typically countered my "sophisticated" stylistic notes with "yeah, yeah . . . now listen to this line here; listen to these words Gloria wrote." More than the music, the lyrics were the gems.

Before examining fans' appraisal of the Gaithers' John Wayne gem, it is worth looking at the gem itself:

> Daddy was a cowboy, hard as a rock
> Momma, she was quiet as a prayer
> Daddy'd always tell me, "son you gotta be tough"
> Momma'd kiss my cheek and say, "play fair"
> I did my best to make them proud of me
> But it's never been an easy place to be
>
> *chorus:*
> *Somewhere between Jesus and John Wayne*
> *A cowboy and a saint, crossing the open range*
> *I try to be more like you, Lord, but most days I know I ain't*
> *I'm somewhere between Jesus and John Wayne*
>
> Momma's love was tender
> Daddy's love was strong
> But both of them were there to help the weak
> They taught me to stand up and fight for what is right
> Showed me how to turn the other cheek
> Since there's a bit of both of them in me
> Then maybe that's the best that I can ever hope to be (*2x chorus*)[48]

Both "Jesse Taylor" and "John Wayne" possess a casual swagger reminiscent of the Hollywood frontiersman riding his horse through long shadows after a long day on the prairie. "John Wayne" trots a little faster—nine beats per minute faster than "Jesse Taylor"—but it does not gallop. As in "Jesse Taylor," the chorus of "John Wayne" is written for four parts, and the melody line is higher on the scale than the solo-voice verses. The power of collective singing in the chorus, added to its repetition, enhances the chorus's broad thematic punch. Following the relatively subdued solitary voice of the verses, the several male voices speaking univocally as the chorus's "I" transpose the predicament from lonesome cowboy to Every Man. Individual testimony and male solidarity resonate.

Judging solely by the verses, "Jesus and John Wayne" articulates a predictable view regarding gender and the Christian ideal. Both country and gospel music abound with tender, soft-spoken mothers and stern, gruff fathers. If gospel music ever dares to render God, or the Christian ideal, as anything but exclusively male, the Divine Masculine typically stands for those ostensibly hard, unflinching attributes (He is just, all-powerful, inviolable), the Divine Feminine for the "softer" qualities (She is compassionate, merciful, gracious). Moreover, the essences of manhood and womanhood usually manifest themselves fully in parenthood. *Feminine* means "motherly"; *masculine* means "fatherly."

Daddy was tough and strong; Momma was quiet and tender. Daddy instructs his child how to take a stand and fight (when necessary); Momma teaches how to absorb blows. The speaker (who seems to be a son, since the song features Penrod and a male quartet) concludes, at the end of the second verse, that he embodies some quasi-Mendelian combination of his parents' traits. However, his resignation suggests that the tired gender constructs upon which the verses rest are not operating at full justificatory steam. *Maybe that's the best that I can ever hope to be*—the speaker does not sound satisfied with the way the Christian Punnett square has worked out for him.

In the chorus, the speaker more severely undermines the commendability of the gender constructs—or, more specifically, the desirability of their combination. It is safe to assume that, when a gospel song explicitly invokes Jesus, it is recommending an ideal for emulation. No Homecoming song—no song in gospel music history of which I am aware—ever has cast Jesus as one ingredient in a cocktail for right relation with God and neighbor—an ingredient that requires a chaser. Even Jesus's more presumably singular acts (dying on the cross to save humanity from sin) get translated into a species of exemplary behavior (Jesus took up his cross; Christians should take up their crosses daily). Unless "Jesus and John Wayne" relegates Jesus to an extreme, nonideal behavioral pole—an unprecedented relegation in gospel music—Jesus remains the Christian ideal in the song.

If Jesus indeed plays his old role in this song, and if the writers position him at one end of a spectrum, it would follow that the figure who occupies the other end represents his opposite—an antihero, an example of how Christians should *not* behave. Jesus is perfection, is pure good. John Wayne is . . . imperfection? Pure evil? Even a charitable interpretation of this John Wayne—that he represents not the thoroughly evil pole on the spectrum, just a fault-ridden and dangerously alluring type of male—places John Wayne as the outer boundary of ideal Christian masculinity. The song's narrator is decidedly closer to Jesus when he moves away from John Wayne. And this is what he desires, though the desire cannot be fulfilled: "I try to be more like you, Lord / but most days I know I ain't." The narrator's plotting of himself between Jesus and John Wayne represents not a struggle to find the virtue that lies in the mean, but a hang-dogged confession that he is caught between virtue and vice. The archetypal male who sits at the other end of the bar, six-shooters at his side, calls the speaker away from his true Lord.

Not only does the song undermine the value of the John Wayne version of manhood; the song divinizes its version of femininity. If the parallel structure runs consistently through chorus and verse, the speaker identifies Jesus with femininity/Momma and John Wayne with masculinity/Daddy. That Momma repeats Jesus's teaching verbatim ("turn the other cheek"), and that Daddy imparts some vague, vernacular wisdom that is at best Christian in spirit, suggests that these are the intended associations. If the chorus establishes the interpretive terms for the song—if the "particularities" of the verses are to be understood in light of the general, and generally true, claims of the chorus—Momma and her femininity stand in for the (male speaker's) Christian ideal. Daddy is the flawed John Wayne. Momma is the Son of God. Momma is Lord.

"Jesus and John Wayne" presents a remarkable predicament—especially as the Homecoming vessel for this song is a tall Tennessee cowboy with seven sons. If *Penrod* is a combination of mother and father, and if *he* is trying to be more like mother/Jesus, what happens to the spiritual Punnett square? What gendered identities are *his* sons going to inherit? Whereas "The Baptism of Jesse Taylor" suggests ambivalence toward rough-and-tumble masculinity— a masculinity that takes shape according to listeners' filling in of the song's narrative gaps—"Jesus and John Wayne" forcefully shunts listeners away from this masculinity. The song's lyrics make it difficult for listeners to come away from the song with a positive view of the "John Wayne male."

Difficult, but not impossible. Songs communicate through more than lyrical content. When Penrod honky-tonks the opening line, "Daddy was a cowboy," over the clippity-clop instrumentation, the GVB is trafficking in a distinctly "pro-cowboy" musical genre. It matters little what the song says about cowboys; it has cowboys in it, and it sounds like something a cowboy would sing, so it must be celebrating cowboyhood. In fact, the notion that "the cowboy way" is not commendable paradoxically makes it more appealing (when Willie Nelson and Waylon Jennings famously sang in 1978, "mammas, don't let your babies grow up to be cowboys," no one took their valedictions seriously). As with "Jesse Taylor," "John Wayne" indulges in that trope that it seems to reject—though in the latter case, the lyrics more forcefully state the rejection, and the indulgence is more exclusively sonic.[49]

Performances and comments of the song available on YouTube provide a window into how fans select and negotiate the song's meaning. The first result in my 2010 search of "Jesus and John Wayne" was the GVB's 2008 performance on the video *Country Bluegrass Homecoming, Volume 2*. However, a number of results were recordings of amateur and smaller-venue musicians performing the song in church services. Jeff Dugan's recorded performance of the song at "Cowboy Church of Ellis County"—a church styled like the one at which I interviewed Roy and Jen—demonstrates this song's country appeal. It did not appear to matter to the ten-gallon-hat-donning Dugan that he looked a lot like the song's antihero.[50]

The *Country Bluegrass* GVB performance of the song was the most viewed and most commented-upon YouTube version. As is the case with all Gaither videos on YouTube, many viewers make general references to the song "speaking to them"—reminding them of their own faith struggles. However, a few commenters stall at what they perceive as the song's unholy *likening* of its two main characters: "i love southern gospel but seriously whats so good about John Wayne? NOTHING! Half the movies he was in & himself he had a very dirty mouth . . . I don't see ONE connection between Jesus and John Wayne!" A comment from a self-identifying African viewer adds Guy to the mix:

> I have a question . . . I couldn't understand why Guy is comparing him self with John wayne. I thought John Wayne was not a born againe christian. U guys know the stories behind because you'r from same place. As I am from a country that is very far from ur culture and all (Ethiopia), I would appreciate if someone explain these song for me. God bless.[51]

The song causes puzzlement for a Christian who identifies herself or himself outside American country culture. Why is John Wayne invoked at all?

To such criticisms—which more than the above two commenters express—a number of viewers respond by encouraging a closer reading. In direct response to the first criticism above, another viewer writes, "there is no connection. seriously before people comment they need to listen to the words first. they are not comparing jesus and john wayne. they are saying that no matter how we try on this side of heaven we will never be exactly like God because we are imperfect." A responder to the "Ethiopian" viewer writes,

> Hi Ethiopia! In American movies, John Wayne was a bit of a tough guy, lived on his own, not thought of as a Christian, drank a lot of booze (well—only in the movies). This song is more about how we can never really live up to Jesus' standards. Christians hope to be like Jesus, and we try to act like him, but we all fall short of the mark—most times, we act more like John Wayne's characters in movies—we just go back to being bad, as John Wayne's movie characters tended to be.[52]

Both responses are reasonable given the song's apparent message. The song-writers are not likening John Wayne to Jesus, and any invocation of the former signals either an opposition to or a falling short of the Christian ideal. While these responders exercise a dubious charity in softening John Wayne from thoroughgoing antagonist to merely imperfect archetype—they recognize that the chorus is not arguing on behalf of John Wayne.

But none of the song's defenders wrestles with the full consequences of his or her conclusions. What does this rendering of the song's chorus mean when one considers the song's *verses*? In a series of threads so committed to a "proper" reading of the song, the absence of a single direct reference to the verses is stark. While one commenter's hesitation over the Jesus-John Wayne dichotomy ("personally I would've used Lucifer myself. .Somewhere between Jesus and Lucifer . . . that's pretty much more accurate, but it don't sound as good. .lol!") hints that he or she may have anticipated such problematic consequences, this listener does not explore in detail this hesitation, and eventually resigns him/herself to the fact that the song sounds better employing the figures it does. If the matter of Jesus and John Wayne gets settled by dichotomizing the two, what does this say about Mommas and Daddies? Only a single, pithy comment hints at some awareness of the upshot: "I love both Jesus and John Wayne!"[53]

Were this omission of the verses limited to the comments of anonymous, perhaps casual YouTube viewers, it might be feasible to dismiss the oversight as resulting from half-hearted fans' cursory engagement with the song. After all, this is YouTube, not gaither.com. But the same controversy and the same interpretive issues emerge among the southern gospel faithful. In March 2009, Joy FM radio in Winston-Salem, North Carolina (one of the premier southern gospel radio stations in the country), pulled "Jesus and John Wayne" from its playlist after many complaints from listeners. Joy FM deejay Daniel Britt—a southern gospel aficionado and a friend of Bill Gaither—explained to me, "two things were brought up by the public: comparing Jesus to John Wayne and saying it's 'ok' to have sin in your life . . . or resigning to the fact that you might not get any better in this life." Britt pulled the song, but not before posting online an explication and defense of the song's theology—a document that rehearses (in more articulate form) the song's YouTube justifications.[54]

Justification: if *that* had been the central issue, "Jesus and John Wayne" would not have generated such theological controversy among southern gospel fans. Be they Wesleyan, Reformed, Baptist, or Pentecostal, most of the evangelicals who follow the Gaithers prioritize the Pauline "justification by faith" as the linchpin moment of a soul's salvation. There may be disagreement about what acts of human and God will or *must* follow logically or chronologically from justification, but whatever happens is predicated upon a justificatory event. Justification is a sufficiently malleable, sufficiently abstract notion for there to be sufficient consensus regarding its centrality.

Evangelical consensus begins to unravel, however, when *sanctification* enters the equation. For any examination of how a Christian comes to be holy *in character and action* requires a discussion of particular behaviors, specific motions of the Holy Spirit as they are manifest in the elect, here and now. And the here and now does not reduce easily to creedal summary, to inspired utterances of the tongue.

Between Jesse Taylor and John Wayne, the Homecoming community demonstrates this unraveling. Jesse Taylor is man justified. The song's vague venture into the post-baptism life only snatches the relatively low-hanging fruit of evangelical (and country-western) American morality: no more heavy drinkin', gamblin', runnin' around with women. The justified man changed in these ways. He also changed in other ways which listeners can only imagine. No argument there. "The Baptism of Jesse Taylor" generated no widespread controversy.

"Jesus and John Wayne" is Jesse Taylor's sequel, in ways aside from chronological order. The narrator is man (being) sanctified—or not. It is Jesse Taylor speaking on the other side of his baptism. While this man does not seem to doubt his salvation, it is clear to him that his salvation has not created in him a clean heart or renewed in him a right spirit. While he still strives for the Christian ideal, he seems to resign himself to the inevitability of his failings— failings that are his inheritances as the product and carrier of the masculine/ Daddy's and feminine/Mother's tendencies. Here, there is argument. The song forces those in the Homecoming community to speak more specifically about the effects of salvation. What is to be expected of this man, the man (being) sanctified? At what point do his failings become so ubiquitous and perpetual that it becomes reasonable to push doubt as to his membership in the "family of God" back one step further—to his justification? Stated differently, how much more like Jesus than John Wayne must Jesse Taylor be in order to be counted among the righteous? And how is that similarity specifically made manifest in the life of one who has given Franklin County "a lot more man?"

PAINTING THE PHENOMENAL WORLD

Such questions perpetually confronted the Gaithers and Guy Penrod during the latter's career on the Homecoming stage. If the Gaithers, Penrod, or Homecoming fans were to make a compelling case for Penrod's inclusion in the community, they had to search out and employ material manifestations of the man's "righteousness" (signs of grace, signs of marketability) around which consensus existed in the Homecoming community. The black coats, the big belt buckles, the farm, the family, the varied carols of American Christian manhood—all built the case.

Bill Gaither invested a lot in the plausibility of Penrod's case. No Home-coming artist's private life was placed putatively on display more than Penrod's. Unless Bill truly believed in the consistency between Penrod's private and staged selves, it is unlikely he would have so "exposed" the man behind the curtain—for certainly the highly public fall of English, Penrod's GVB predecessor, reminded Gaither of the risk in such an investment.

But Bill believed. As he says to the Penrods on the *Best of* DVD: "One of the reasons we wanted to do this video . . . a lot of people say, 'is that real? I mean, is this whole thing real?' They all need to come—not all at once [laughs]—but it is real. You are here . . . and when I walk into this house . . . I have to pinch myself and say, I can't believe this. But God bless you." This comes from a man who once told me that it took him three decades before he "trusted" the medium of film, due to its tendency to mislead and manipulate viewers, whose first video was as roughly edited as a home movie.

Home movies have frames, too. Even if Bill does not consciously crop his portrait of Penrod—or, even if he believes his editing of Penrod nonetheless captures the *essence* of the man's life—his cameras, like his eyes, exclude mate-rial. As a producer and authorizer of Homecoming artists' public, "authentic" selves, Bill Gaither must be confident that the unused crumbs that fall from his editing table cannot be reassembled to produce a biography that contra-dicts or problematizes his edition. If Penrod were to have "fallen" in a similarly jarring way as did Michael English, or if his life had been revealed to contain moments that undermined his Homecoming biography, the Gaithers would have faced a more precarious situation than they did in English's case—for they wedded tightly Penrod's witness to the witness of the Homecomings.

Bill Gaither did not face such a predicament. Along with Marshall Hall, Guy Penrod officially left the GVB in January 2009. Both planned to pursue solo ventures, but the publicized reason for Penrod's departure also included his desire to scale back his touring.[55] Penrod's mother died in January 2007. If the testimony of *The Best of Guy Penrod* is accurate, she played a signifi-cant role in keeping the Penrod homestead running smoothly. It is likely that the Penrod homestead had to reorder itself. Still, the southern gospel rumor mill grinded out explanation after explanation of Penrod's departure—that he mismanaged money, the farm was in trouble, he had a drinking problem. Separating truth from fiction is difficult in the southern gospel world, and I have yet to find hard evidence to verify these rumors. I call attention to them because the fact of their circulation demonstrates the southern gospel world's anxiety over questions of correspondence, of authenticity: do artists' private and public pieties align? *Is that real—I mean, is this whole thing real?* Recalling Michael English, fans have been soured before, and their teeth are set on edge. The only thing Bill said to me after Penrod and Hall left the GVB, after he had begun to assemble a new lineup, was nearly impermeable: "you don't make changes because you want to; you make them because you have to." As in 1995, in 2009 Bill had to reorder the GVB.

He did reorder. When Bill published the departures of Hall and Penrod, he also announced he would be putting old makeup on the empty space, in a sort of GVB Homecoming. The new "quintet" version of the GVB released their first album, *Reunited*, in 2009. Only Gaither-penned songs appeared on it—all "Gaither classics," only one written as late as the 1990s. Former GVB member Mark Lowry returned. Former GVB member David Phelps returned. Singing lead: Michael English.

3

LET'S JUST PRAISE THE LORD

(A)POLITICS OF THE HOMECOMINGS

UNWARRANTABLE JURISDICTION

Sarah Palin's appearance on the podium of the National Quartet Convention (NQC) in September 2010 received little attention from major media outlets. Everyone reasonably might have expected Palin, then-darling of the American politico-religious right, to perform well before southern gospel fans, with her folksy mic manners and perpetual paeans to God and country. There was no juicy scoop in the Palin-southern gospel pairing—only Palin being Palin, rallying the base.

Although the convention crowd apparently received Palin warmly, her occupation of the main stage during a peak evening of the program sparked some debate. In the spring of 2010, the NQC had announced Palin's upcoming appearance, and southern gospel loyals hit the blogosphere expressing their concern. One fan wrote,

> I am very conservative and have no problems with her in that area [political arena]. I have a HUGE problem with her at nqc. She does not represent sg music and her stump speeches do not promote jesus (even though she is a christian). Nqc is way off base here and will damage itself in the process. Preach Jesus, not politics. Political parties didn't hang on the cross and die for me![1]

Reservations hardly waned after Palin's speech. Many fans balked at Palin's apparently feigned knowledge of southern gospel music. Posting after Palin's convention address, blogger and gospel musician Sue Smith said, "She really doesn't know anything about southern gospel music. That became apparent when she more or less equated it with country music (and that got some nervous laughter from the so-go [southern gospel] crowd) and then called the [famous southern gospel family group] "Neelons" the "Nehlons."[2] For other fans, Palin's adorning herself as a southern gospel fan was an expectable, unfortunate outcome of the combination of religion, music, and politics. One poster on a blog, who self-identified as a "Conservative Bapticostal" spouse of a Southern Baptist minister, remarked,

> Christians run around all the time trying to look "pious", "religious", "knowledgeable" and "with it", and they end up losing their credibility. In my opinion, the NQC has lost their credibility for inviting ANY political candidate to be on the stage. Obviously, Palin didn't have a clue about SG music. And obviously, the NQC is no longer JUST ABOUT music. The NQC has now made a political statement, and it's a shame that this has been mixed in with a Southern Gospel musical showcase.
>
> Can music just ever be music? Can the church just ever be the church?[3]

The backlash by no means represented the feelings of all fans; plenty of convention attendees had no problems with Palin's appearance or speech. But the amount and the substance of the criticism warrant attention. Of particular note is the frequency with which those who expressed reservations claimed sympathy with Palin's politics. Few questioned the content of Palin's political views or the sincerity of her Christianity. Rather, the problem emerged when convention planners opened a space designated for gospel musical performers to a performing politician. Palin may have been the politician for the national hour, but the NQC was not the hour for the national politician. By buddying up to such a political superstar—even a Christian superstar—the NQC organizers had gone too rogue.

Sociologists have noted the tendency across twentieth- and twenty-first-century American populations to balk at politics—to partition those activities and values they hold dear from the political sphere, to deploy the terms *political* and *politicized* to signal the tainting of a once-pure or otherwise pure phenomenon.[4] Most of us have heard someone (perhaps ourselves) invoke politics with a sigh: *That organization is too political for me—I love that musical group, but I don't like it when they get political—I used to participate in that conference, but it's become so political.* In everyday apolitical speech, *political* might possess one of the following three meanings, or some combination of the three: a phenomenon is *political* if it (1) clearly expresses allegiance to a political party; (2) manifests or promotes a general philosophy of, or programs for, governance and/or legislation; (3) involves groups or individuals in the wielding and grasping for power, with and against each other, so that they can protect specific interests or achieve specific goals. I will refer to these senses of politics as (1) party politics, (2) policy politics, and (3) community politics.

In a discursive environment in which two major political parties often dictate the terms, *party* and *policy* politics tend to overlap; some policy becomes codified as coterminous with a Democratic or Republican agenda. At the same time, *Democratic* and *Republican* serve as shorthand for a set of policies or a general philosophy of governance on which all specific policy decisions are based. If I write on a southern gospel blog that I am a Republican, I am signaling a set of policies that I endorse. Conversely, if I use the space to promote "political issues" like disallowing legalized abortion or gay marriage, my fellow bloggers might make a reasonable guess concerning which of the two parties usually gets my vote. Readers may not receive my signals completely to my liking, and my signals will be incomplete. I may be strongly against abortion but strongly in favor of universal health care; I may be a Republican for whom "small government" means no restrictions on gay marriage. But if I know the work that certain terms and statements perform in my discursive space, I will be able to approximate my mark when I state my commitments or party affiliations. Unless I intend to cause doubletakes in the southern gospel world, I would not declare [then expect my readers to hear], "I am a conservative Republican [so of course I favor gay marriage]."

The NQC planners could not avoid *party* and *policy* politics altogether, even if they so desired, because thousands of people attended the convention; therefore, there were many circulating notions of what constituted a "political" phenomenon. Did Palin's sheer presence constitute a *clear* expression of the NQC planners' party allegiance? Would a different NQC speaker have been manifesting or promoting a program for governance or legislation if she endorsed a "culture of life" or "social justice" from the podium? What is the difference, exactly, between *manifesting* and *promoting* an agenda? That Palin's presence generated a variety of opinions demonstrates that *party* and *policy* politics were unsettled concepts. However, it seemed that many in the debate over Palin tacitly agreed: if it could be established that Palin's presence was, in fact, *political* in one or both of these senses, then the NQC planners facilitated some desecration of the NQC. *Politics* is that which defiles this sacred space.

The desire to convey apoliticism is understandable—and arguably essential to the integrity of a gospel music gathering. The rules governing the annual national singing convention resemble those of a big Thanksgiving family dinner. If the participants' party and policy politics are diverse and divisive, it behooves a gathering whose participants seek unity in their variety to bracket off politics provisionally, to traffic only in those topics and terms that foster unity. For "music just to be music," and "the church just to be the church," politics cannot appear. To be sure, there are intended and unintended violations of the prescriptions; given the conservative bent of the NQC faithful, Palin's violations likely posed fewer clear and present dangers to group unity than, say, a keynote address from Ralph Nader or Bernie Sanders. But with astounding success, almost everyone learns and uses the sorts of language that will keep everyone seated politely at the table—for a little while, at least.

Conflict avoidance is sometimes prudent, sometimes neurotic. If the sopophoric pleasantness of a Thanksgiving dinner without incident becomes the standard for quality interpersonal communication, the erasure of politics in *some* circumstances becomes a normative expectation in *all* circumstances. If party and policy politics always portend conflict, and the measure of any group's worth is its liberation from conflict, then *politics* rears its head on penalty of implicit or explicit censure. Here, *community* politics—pertaining to the motions and imbrications of power and interest inside a social body—becomes relevant and vexatious. Provided the worrisome aspect of party and policy politics reduces to concerns about particular senators or bills before the House, well enough; although one might challenge the desirability of a democratic citizenry's divorcing of governmental concerns from its other concerns, one might concede that not every social moment could or should entail a discussion of politics so understood. However, if party and policy politics are to be avoided because they involve *community* politics—if the nasty aspect of the political milieu is the *inevitably* tangled, conflict-laden motions of power and interest—more is at stake. In this case, the items discursively disallowed from the social body are the conditions and considerations necessary for the sustenance of *any* social body—for wherever two or more are gathered, community politics are at play. Denying community politics either cuts off all discussion of the powers and interests operant in a social body, or pronounces the social body in which the denial is in effect as actually exempt from the rules governing social life. In both cases, politics-denying members of the social body are not likely to name, much less to contest openly, whatever powers and interests prevail in the group (even their own). To deny community politics, then, is not merely to keep people seated politely at the table; it is to deny the table historical and cultural mass. Through the denial, the mass gathered at the table assumes a kind of transpersonal divinity. It is a kingdom without conflict, populated by humans without interests, wrought through the ministrations of bodies without contexts.

It is not possible to say with perfect precision which senses of *political*, in which degrees and combinations, southern gospel fans mean when they seek to cleanse their temples of politics. But the Gaithers and their Homecomings provide a fruitful site for investigation. The Gaithers have sustained their celebrity over a long period of time—from Nixon-era Billy Graham Crusades to Clinton-era Homecoming videos and beyond. That gospel audiences have entrusted the Gaithers with the microphones from age to age bespeaks the Gaithers' ability to follow and adapt to evangelical rules of engagement. As proprietors of the stage, they stand to gain or lose the most by violating or confirming audience norms. Their record has been mostly one of gain. That the microphones have lifted Gaither voices from age to age, *over* these audiences, signals the pair's determinative power over the rules of engagement. As proprietors of the stage, they influence community norms. They have played the game well, and their playing has affected the game itself.

Unbelievable though it seems, given the popularity of the Homecomings, the Gaithers became the standard-bearers of *southern* gospel relatively late. While Bill is a lifelong fan of the middle-twentieth-century music that came to be known as "southern gospel," and while musical groups of these varieties performed Gaither songs long before the Homecomings existed, only after the Homecomings did the Gaither name become broadly attached to a gospel called *southern*. Consequently, the Gaithers' achievement and maintenance of southern gospel insider status—not to mention their status as southern gospel royalty—requires some degree of deliberate work on their part. In contrast with many "native" southern gospel performers—those who grew up swimming in the doxic waters of southern gospel and who seem to intuit, rather than consciously to obey, the rules of engagement—the Gaithers are strongly conscious of the southern gospel community as a circumscribed entity, possessing unique, specific characteristics. Even as it is "their" world, the Gaithers have had to render the southern gospel world to themselves as *other*—as an object of conscious investigation and monitoring.[5] Despite their being baptized into the fold, their immersion is not full. As a result, they have to be strategic—especially in their approach to politics.

On the stage and in personal interactions, the Gaithers pride themselves on their spaces being "apolitical." To make sense of Homecoming apoliticism in this chapter, I will use the three senses of *politics* I list above. I will show that, when the Gaithers speak of the Homecomings being "apolitical," they have in mind primarily party politics, secondarily policy politics. Cleansing their spaces of party politics is their highest self-conscious goal, and they are fairly successful at meeting it. However, partly through the very strategy by which they achieve party apoliticism, they tip their hand on policy politics. I examine Gaither policy politics, focusing on the "Give It Away" epoch of the Gaither programs and on the Gaithers' biographies and community commitments. Finally, I examine the Homecomings' eschewing of community politics—a less deliberate but nonetheless essential apoliticism. This apoliticism becomes salient in fans' comparative ecclesiology vis-à-vis the Homecomings and in the nonconflictual drama of community played out in Homecoming programs. The community apoliticism to which the Gaithers respond and for which they are responsible ends up working at cross-purposes with their communitarian values—the very values that charge their policy politics. At the heart of the Homecoming apoliticism, there is a tragic irony, one which accounts for the often-touted, ever-deferred communitarian dreams of American evangelicalism—and, more broadly, American democracy.

MEET JOHN DOE: THE GAITHERS AND PARTY POLITICS

"I'm Bill Gaither and I'm running for President."

Cheers and laughter erupt through the arena. Kevin Williams, the guitarist, general stage director, and occasional funny man of the Homecomings, answers Bill with a sigh: "Everyone else has, I guess you should." Williams continues. "Well, what's your platform? What do you promise to do?"

Bill, straight-faced and stately, pauses to think. "Everything."

More laughter. Bill remains somber until Williams delivers the final punchline: "Then how are you any different from the rest of them?"

As if a dam had broken inside him, Bill lets loose a torrent of chuckles. The night resumes what seems its natural flow—on to the music, on with the show.

From 2006 to 2008—the heart of a presidential campaign season that culminated in Barack Obama's election—I heard some version of this exchange at nearly every Homecoming concert I attended, always near the show's beginning. Every audience laughed heartily.

I laughed, too. It was silly; Bill Gaither did not take himself seriously enough to embark upon a career in politics. The bit worked because Bill's self-important posture contrasted so profoundly from his typical personae. Bill's onstage lapses in memory and frequent stuttering—not utter fabrications, but certainly hyperbolic renderings of offstage idiosyncrasies—constantly reminded audiences of the gospel legend's mere mortality. Typically, the staged humbling of Bill assumed the form of jabs from musician-comedians, particularly Williams and Mark Lowry. The perpetual roasting of Bill could border on mean-spirited—even ageist—as Bill's unorthodox hair and apparently false teeth provided regular targets for comic assault. Some fans balked at this (in one oft-narrated case, a woman cornered Mark Lowry after a concert to chide him, saying, "how dare you make fun of Mr. Gaither like that!"). But most fans with whom I spoke realized that Bill exercises at least some control over the Homecoming scripts (the oft-narrated case concludes with Lowry answering the woman, "Ma'am, I'll have you know Mr. Gaither pays me good money to make fun of him like that"). Since the stage belongs to Bill, the jokes are, in a sense, playful self-mockery, which translates easily to humility, to authenticity.

Naming the synthetic accoutrements Bill dons to minimize aging's physical cost is hardly tantamount to advertising more personal character faults. Admitting to having fake teeth is not the same as admitting to having, say, a mistress, or even a bad temper. However, the creaks that accompany the aging process, and the attempts to dam up the process, are familiar to many in the aging Homecoming crowd but largely unnamed in more youth-oriented popular culture—which, like American culture more broadly, is well practiced at denying aging and the elderly. Bill's candor about "senior" matters casts him as but a fellow (senior) citizen of the Homecoming world. In an evangelical milieu that places a premium on humility so cast—in which the first must be last—the celebrity who knocks himself off his pedestal reinforces his right to stand on the pedestal.

The obvious artificiality of "Candidate Gaither" communicates a few (a)political messages. First, it makes the "normal" Bill Gaither and his Homecoming stage seem authentic by contrast. When Bill ends his presidential charade by bursting into laughter, he breaks character and becomes a man of character again. The scene has ended, and we return to a scene that feels presently less put on, to the "real" Bill, who sings and directs gospel music on a stage of his own beloved design. Bill's laughter escorts us back into the realm of given knowledge. We leave the silly pomp of professional politics to sit back and watch the program for which we paid the admission price. Second, the presidential joke depends upon and reinforces the notion that professional politics is essentially a mendacious endeavor. It is not just that Candidate Gaither is playing a role out of keeping with the "real" Bill Gaither; it is that *anyone* who would be a candidate for office must wear a mask. In their attempt to be all things to all voters, professional politicians must make promises that they will not, and perhaps cannot, keep. No real man, no keeper of promises, would run for office.[6] Related to this second point, lest one imagine that the Gaithers primarily target "secularist" Democrats, and that those Republican politicians who espouse conservative evangelical values get cast as the defenders of truth, the Gaithers pride themselves on equal-opportunity hazing of both major political parties. No party is the party of God. Another of Bill's favorite onstage jokes (not original to the Gaither stage)[7] involves a conversation between two senators, one Democrat and one Republican. The Republican tells the Democrat, "the problem with the Democratic Party, you all don't know anything about religion. In fact, I'll bet you twenty dollars that you can't recite the Lord's Prayer." The Democrat takes the bet. He begins to pray the wrong prayer: *Now I lay me down to sleep....* The Republican shakes his head, hands the twenty dollars to his colleague, and says, "You showed me. I didn't think you could do it." The message is clear: just because politicians of any party claim deep religious commitments, it does not mean they actually possess them. The first time I heard Bill tell this joke occurred right before a concert intermission. When I saw him backstage during the break, the first thing he asked me was if I liked that politician joke. I told him I thought it was funny. He replied, "we really stick it to both sides, don't we?"

That no political party is the party of God is on first blush a platitude—one that most people accept intellectually but easily transpose to a politicized key. "No party is the party of God" can come to mean, "even Democrats can be against gay marriage if they wish." But however safe seems an evangelical's prophesying unto God's nonpartisan nature, it is important not to overlook both the personal and broader historical backdrop against which the Gaithers issue this claim, nor to underestimate the challenge it poses to a number of Homecoming fans. Over the course of their careers, the Gaithers have witnessed firsthand the overwrought synonymizing of God's will and the will of one political party—typically the Republican Party. Bill and Gloria sang on Billy Graham's stages throughout the 1970s and 1980s. They watched the great evangelist publicly commit himself to specific (Republican) politicians like Richard Nixon, who espoused "good Christian values" (and, earlier, to commit himself far less evenly to Martin Luther King Jr.). They watched as Nixon fell from grace, as a burned Graham retreated from Washington's fires.[8] The Gaithers were singing before, during, and after the heyday of the Moral Majority. They watched many of their friends and colleagues in public ministry—Jerry Falwell, Pat Robertson, and James and Shirley Dobson—become key players in (or lackeys of) the Republican Party. Partly by luck, partly by design, the Gaithers managed to emerge from the frays of these evangelical-political epochs—frays that narrowly defined and sometimes destroyed the careers of other public evangelicals.

It requires but a perfunctory glance at a Homecoming video to conclude that the Gaithers espouse many sociopolitical causes of ultraconservative evangelicalism. The Homecomings' lionizing of the heterosexual, monogamous, reproductively prolific family unit bespeaks, at the very least, the

Gaithers' unwillingness to disrupt publicly the social model most conservative evangelicals deem normative.[9] But the Gaithers do not simply check all of
the boxes on the Religious Right's agenda card. They have never held exclusive
fellowship with right-wing evangelicals. Gloria served on the board of Ron
Sider's *Prism* magazine—a moderate to left-leaning evangelical publication
that focuses on issues such as global and domestic socioeconomic injustice
and racial reconciliation. Gloria also served on the board of directors of the
Council for Christian Colleges and Universities (CCCU) and later became a
trustee of the Council's United Christian College Fund—a minority scholarship program. The Gaithers are close friends with Tony and Peggy Campolo,
two Philadelphia-based evangelicals who have been key figures of the late
twentieth- and early twenty-first-century evangelical left. Peggy Campolo has
gained notoriety for being an outspoken advocate of gay rights.[10]

   A stark departure the Gaithers make from the Religious Right is evident in
the formers' brand of patriotism. The Homecoming paeans to America, when
they occur, conspicuously downplay American military prowess. "Because
He Lives," probably their best-known song, was written in 1971, during the
Vietnam War. When the Gaithers publicly tell the story of the song's inception, they invariably highlight the unrest of the 1960s through which they
had lived. Gloria's staging of "Because He Lives" in her 2007 book *Something
Beautiful* is worth examining at length:

> Racial tensions had torn the country apart [. . .] Civil rights activists had suf-
> fered and some had been killed as our country was forced to look at the gaping
> chasm between the celebrated American promise of freedom and the reality for
> many of its citizens.
>
> The Vietnam Conflict (we refused to call it a war) would drag on through
> three administrations and eighteen years, taking fifty-seven thousand Ameri-
> can lives. It would be the first war in our history in which there would be no
> winners. Young men had fled the country to avoid the draft. Many who stayed
> to serve were uncertain of America's objectives and would feel deserted them-
> selves by the very citizens they marched off to defend.
>
> A young generation of Americans felt disillusioned and unable to find
> answers to insistent questions few had previously dared to ask aloud. Many
> asked good questions about the materialistic lifestyle their Depression-era
> parents had relentlessly pursued, but few went to the right source for answers.
> "What's It All About?" was more than the name of a song; it was an unanswered
> question this generation drowned in alcohol and obliterated with drugs [. . .]
>
> The hippy generation felt increasingly estranged from society. While some
> took daring risks to get involved and make a difference, others chose to "get

high" and "drop out." They called themselves flower children and advocated free love, yet all too often what they experienced was not so much love as deep disappointment and burned-out minds.[11]

From the exclusive focus on American casualties in Vietnam to the sweeping censure of the drug-addicted hippy generation, the passage certainly contains several motifs one would find in the literature of the Christian Right (though it is striking to note the similarities between Gloria's critique of the "checked out" flower children and James Baldwin's critique of them in *No Name in the Street*—in 1972, the year "Because He Lives" truly hit the gospel music world).[12] Furthermore, Gloria is writing from the vantage of the present; it is easier for her to be both critical and charitable. However, Gloria refuses to tell the simple stories of American greatness that remain central to many conservative Americans' understanding of their "Christian" country. She renders the American dream of freedom as but an empty slogan for many. Her hesitations regarding Vietnam are clear. She sides with the "young generation" in their questioning of their "materialistic" parents—choosing the rebellious 1960s over the prosperous 1950s to which members of the Christian Right often point as a golden era.

Nor is Gloria's aim to narrate tumult, even reformative tumult, as located exclusively in the past. Gloria focuses on the 1960s because she wants readers to understand the age in which she and Bill conceived their third child. The 1960s' particular instability caused the Gaithers anxiety about introducing a new life into the world. But the upshot of her account is the recognition that instability is endemic to history:

> It isn't because the world is stable that we have the courage to live our lives or start marriages or have children. The world has never been stable. Jesus Himself was born into the cruelest and most unstable of worlds. No, we have babies and keep trusting and risk living because the Resurrection is true! The Resurrection was not just a onetime event in history; it is a principle built into the very fabric of our beings, a fact reverberating from every cell in creation: Life wins! Life wins![13]

Again, conservative Christians would find much to "amen" in this passage, from its "focus on the family" to its triumphalistic conclusion. But Gloria also issues a challenge to a Christianity that prioritizes security and stability (again, James Baldwin might "amen" Gloria on some counts). Likewise, Gloria's rendering of the Resurrection as a universal "principle," while not a denial of Christ's literal resurrection, routes the discussion away from the empty tomb in first-century Palestine toward the empty, contingent future that the faithful hopefully fill in. In "Because He Lives," Gloria concludes that her newborn child is able to "face uncertain days" because Jesus is alive, now. The calm assurance provided by the principle of resurrection does not erase uncertainty; it gives one the strength to confront uncertainty. In "Because He Lives," Gloria sounds more like Rudolph Bultmann—or Pete Seeger—than Jerry Falwell. "Because He Lives" proclaims that we shall overcome.

Gaither patriotism appears most overtly in the January 2002 Homecoming concert at Carnegie Hall, which yielded the DVDs *Let Freedom Ring* and *God Bless America*. Taking the stage in New York City a few months after the terrorist attacks of September 11, 2001, the Gaithers could have tapped the American evangelical tradition of championing America's indefatigible military might; in that national moment, they would have found plenty of fellow saber rattlers, evangelical and nonevangelical alike. But the videos tell a different story. While they contain a number of "God and country" moments that redound with moments one might find in Religious Right programs (Gloria leads the crowd in a recitation of the Pledge of Allegiance, complete with "under God"), the videos' patriotism does not glow with the rockets' red glare. *Let Freedom Ring* opens with Woody Guthrie's "This Land Is Your Land." Near its opening, *God Bless America* includes a rendition of Pete Seeger's "If I Had a Hammer."[14] Two songs about community and justice written by well-known leftists of the early and middle twentieth century foreshadow some of the themes that will be developed in the programs.

The America of which the Gaithers proudly sing and speak (in narrative interludes, which are staged throughout New York City) is rich in diversity—racially, religiously, and otherwise. In this event, the Homecoming franchise that so often idealizes rural America casts the Big Apple as containing the nation at its best. Reading Gloria's script, Mark Lowry says in *God Bless America*, "Perhaps more than any other American city, this city, confined to an island, has modeled the experiment of diversity, *e pluribus unum*, from many one. This is New York." At its best, America was and is a place where concern for justice translates not merely to police and military protection against aggression from criminals and the state's enemies, but also to concern for the disadvantaged and those who are low on the socioeconomic ladder. When uniformed representatives of the NYC police force appear onstage as the Homecoming chorus sings "A Few Good Men," they appear shoulder-to-shoulder with another set of uniformed men: soldiers in the Salvation Army. To be sure, no forthright problematizing of the nation's many atrocities, often executed by its security forces, occurs on this occasion. But the Gaithers seem aware that the history is not spotless. In *Let Freedom Ring*, Gloria again names diversity as an ideal, but also points to the nation's failings to measure up: "Sometimes that golden door has been tarnished by fear and prejudice. Sometimes we who came here from immigrant heritage ourselves have been selfish with the opportunity this land once freely afforded those who passed the chance to make a life onto us." Singer and Seventh-Day Adventist minister Wintley Phipps's narration and rendition of "Amazing Grace" on *God Bless America* reminds the audience that the song's author John Newton was a British slave trader. Phipps argues that the song's melody emerged from the melodic groans issuing from the bowels of his slave ship; as Phipps demonstrates on the piano, the song can be played entirely "on the black keys." Through Phipps's performance, both American slavery and the people who survived it are rendered central to the nation's story. Reflecting on the Carnegie Hall concert and videos in 2009, Bill told me that he, Gloria, and their team were especially careful about the scripts and setlists for these programs.[15]

Claiming that no party is the party of God, narrating American greatness without centralizing success on the battlefield, parenthetically nodding to gross national miscarriages of racial justice between celebrations of American diversity—the Gaither challenges to their audience may appear mild. But it is important to bear in mind the world in which many of their aging, white, evangelical, largely southern and midwestern constituency lived and live. A substantial number of Homecoming fans did not attend a racially integrated high school. A large number were married and raising children during the rise of the Religious Right. A large number of these fans probably do not regularly engage left-of-center evangelicals such as Jim Wallis, Ron Sider, Peggy and Tony Campolo, much less nonevangelical liberal Christians. One need only watch some of the programs that run before and after the Homecomings on religious television networks to recognize the Homecomings might be the one occasion when a number of these fans hear the conjunction of right-wing ideology and Christianity complicated, even slightly. To claim that Democratic and Republican politicians alike are not necessarily "Christian" is no radical prophetic act, but it still chisels away at the ossified bond between evangelical piety and red-state party politics.

WHICH GOVERNS LEAST:
THE GAITHERS AND POLICY POLITICS

Angelic Relations to Men

The Gaithers use their stage to advertise their noncommitment to political parties and candidates as such. This apoliticism is in many respects admirable—not simply because it contrasts with how many of the Gaithers' evangelical media peers have built and used their platforms, but also because the Gaithers actually have more legal leeway to "be political" than do some of their confreres. Although the Gaithers believe the Homecomings are a "ministry" in the sense that they provide soul sustenance, they are quick to point out that the Homecoming franchise is a business. By intention, the Homecomings are not "ministries" in the 501c3, nonprofit sense. This means the Homecomings are not subject to the regulations governing political advocacy that other evangelical "ministries" face. The Homecomings could be the machines of party politics. The Gaithers choose not to run them that way.

However, the Gaithers do not so diligently sweep their stages clean of *policy* politics—*politics* pertaining to some general philosophy of or program for governance. In fact, the very means by which they eschew party politics reveals their policy politics. Their problematizing of the presumed monopoly the Republican Party claims over evangelical Christianity takes the form of equal-opportunity hazing. Both Democrats and Republicans wear politically expedient masks, make lavish promises to garner votes, are not necessarily as religious as they sometimes claim. Homecoming fans should beware of these wolves in sheeps' clothing—even the red wolves. But because Democrats and Republicans together hold a near monopoly in national and state legislatures and executive bodies, a cynicism toward the very project of governance resides at the heart of the Gaithers' apoliticism. If government is comprised overwhelmingly of wolves in sheeps' clothing, Homecoming fans should want as little to do with government—indeed, they should want as little government—as possible.

However, Homecoming overtures to policy politics do not occur through forthrightly political language. The Gaithers do not speak for or against particular legislation. Rather, the Gaithers' particular policy politics becomes manifest through a dialect of the Gaithers' primary tongue: the language of evangelical piety, particularly as it pertains to charity, personal responsibility, and plight.

When I first met the Gaithers in 2006, the GVB was about to release a new album. *Give It Away* would be the first album to feature the lineup of Bill, Guy Penrod, Marshall Hall, and Wes Hampton. Lynn and I were privy to a sneak preview of the album in the summer of 2006. In the Gaithers' living room, we, along with Gloria, sat as Bill stood fidgeting with a remote control until he found the album's title track and sent it thumping through his massive speakers. Fresh off having a stent put in a major artery, he nevertheless was bursting with energy, punctuating our listening with reminders that we should be listening: *now, listen to this . . . listen to this part here.*

More than the tight vocal blend, stylistic playfulness, and high-quality production of *Give It Away*—by all these criteria the GVB's best album—it was the message of the title track that stirred Bill. The title track's title leaves little to the imagination; the song encourages listeners to exercise Christian charity, to share one's bounty with others:

(Chorus)
If you want more happy than your heart will hold
If you want to stand taller if the truth were told
Take whatever you have, and give it away
If you want less lonely and a lot more fun
And deep satisfaction when the day is done
Then throw your heart wide open and give it away.[16]

While the song still couches its appeal for charity in slightly egotistical terms—giving will result in happiness for the giver—the song represents the Gaithers' effort to get their fans to disassociate accumulation from joy, to detach themselves from their material possessions. The Gaithers' son Benjy—also a gospel songwriter and occasional collaborator with his parents—sets Gloria's lyrics to an upbeat 6/8 shuffle that gives the song a pulsing, forward momentum. The song gains steam—giving it away causes (sonic) accumulation and growth—which makes it effective as a climax at live shows. When "Give It Away" first hit the Homecoming stage, it typically concluded the first set of the evening—with everyone on their feet, yelling the refrain: *give it away!*

In the ensuing years, another audience participation activity prefaced "Give It Away." Before the big number, Bill would announce the names of two concertgoers who had been chosen at random to receive $500 apiece from the Gaithers. Reminiscent of the giving sprees in which Oprah Winfrey occasionally indulged vis-à-vis her live audiences (though not nearly as lavish), Bill was simply going to "give it away." There was but one condition to the gift: what they got, they had to give to another, however they saw fit. Bill gave no further instructions and noted that no one would be following the money trail, but as shows passed and Bill gave more money away, he gleefully recounted some of the letters he had received that described the ways recipients had put the money to use. The stories often demonstrated the ingenuity of recipients' charity. Exemplary recipients typically did not simply give the money away; they did so in a way that maximized the money's use in meeting specific, concrete needs, and/or in a way that facilitated the money's "growth." Good givers were enterprising givers. Although the recipients received the most tangible charge and the most blatantly unmerited "blessing" of sudden wealth, the lesson was for the entire audience. Bill encouraged everyone to think about the Christian duty they had to be good stewards of whatever blessings they had received. "Imagine what this country would be like if Christians would do their duty," Bill said at a Maryland concert. "We wouldn't even need a government if Christians would take up this responsibility."

This subjunctive mood dominates all Homecoming talk of charity. *If* Christians would give more radically, faithfully, freely—in short, *if* they would be truer to their Christian calling—*then* things would be better. Among the improvements: a reduction of government social welfare programs—which tend toward inefficiency, needless bureaucracy, and ultimately lackluster delivery of the assistance they promise. Bill bases his philosophy on his observation that, *when* Christians historically have taken up the cross of charity, they have proven themselves better at responding to human need than have government agencies. His favorite example pertains to 2005: Hurricane Katrina. A prominent secular musician who was involved on the ground in the months after Katrina informed Bill of the overwhelming support of churches and parachurch organizations. Very shortly after the disaster, these religious groups mobilized. They brought financial and human resources to the Gulf region from across the nation. They worked tirelessly over the next year to rebuild, to feed the hungry, to clothe the naked—all while the Federal Emergency Management Agency fumbled its way through its ill-organized channels to alleviate the suffering.

This conception of social responsibility is neither original nor exclusive to the Gaithers. It is based on at least two presuppositions that extend deep into Christian practice and thought, past and present. The first is that social responsibility is measured under the rubric of charity. The Christian injunctions to love one's neighbor as oneself, and to care for "the least of these," primarily means giving one's own (usually surplus) resources away—money, goods, perhaps time. The ideal "socially concerned" Christian is the philanthropist.[17] Since the first light of mass industrialization and the rise of private and municipal bureaucracies, a number of writers have noted—and complained about—the connection between a morally central notion of charity and industrial capitalism. Henry David Thoreau complained that philanthropy was "almost the only virtue which is sufficiently appreciated by mankind. Nay, it is greatly overrated." Conceding that philanthropists were due some praise, Thoreau worried that inordinate focus on charity kept people from addressing the deeper issues that resulted in societal ills. Philanthropists were "hacking at the branches of evil," and the magnitude of social ills (for Thoreau, epitomized in the slave industry) required "striking at the root."[18] Max Weber saw the Protestant call to maximize one's capacity for charity as a key justification for maximizing wealth. Weber cites a passage from John Wesley that he claims might sum up his "Protestant ethic" thesis: *"We must exhort all Christians to gain all they can, and to save all they can; that is, in effect, to grow rich."* Weber further states, "there follows the advice that those who gain all they can and save all they can should also give all they can, so that they will grow in grace and lay up treasure in heaven."[19] Decades after Weber, Raymond Williams offered a more pointed indictment of Christian charity as a cloak for exploitation. Williams splits the concept of charity in two: the charity of production and the charity of consumption. The former posits a basic equality of laborers seeking to procure goods from nature; it entails "loving relations between men actually working and producing what is ultimately, in whatever proportions, to be shared." The latter is not concerned with conditions of production; it assumes any inequalities in work are nullified, even redeemed, by a subsequent, collective consumption of goods. According to Williams, the Christian tradition of charity tends heavily, and disastrously, toward a charity of consumption. Using the communion feast as his example, Williams argues that the consumables on the communion table, which in actuality laborers procure from nature, are imagined by the landowner as a "natural bounty," bestowed graciously by God/nature upon the landowner and his table. The notion of a "natural bounty" renders invisible the laborers and their labor. Therefore, when the Christian landowner invites the "lower-class" laborers to join the feast—to consume that which they procured—the invitation appears charitable, as an act of sharing with "the poor" that which is not "naturally" theirs.[20]

Thoreau, Weber, and Williams rightly highlight some of the problems with Christian charity. However, they do not investigate how a narrow, centralized notion of charity undermines the very capacity of charity's recipients for ethical action. They do not examine a second presupposition, related to the first, that underwrites the reduction of social responsibility to charity. This presupposition I call *tourniquet ethics*.

According to the logic of tourniquet ethics, the apogee of Christian social duty occurs when Christians respond to some great catastrophe—for example, Hurricane Katrina or the AIDS crisis in Africa. Christians who respond quickly and passionately, with seemingly instinctual concern for people in dire need, demonstrate that Christian churches (at their best) are willing and able to do good in this world as well or better than any other group—certainly better than any cold, bureaucratic government agency. Provided "acting ethically" is synonymous with stopping gaping wounds from bleeding—providing tourniquets—Christians who promote and celebrate Christianity as ethically exemplary have some solid ground on which to stand. Bill Gaither is right; for a time, American churches did come in power and passion to the Katrina-ravaged Gulf Coast.

However, such a conception of ethics leaves little room to discuss (a) the social conditions that lead to and exacerbate the effects of a crisis, (b) the individuals and institutions that exacerbate and intend to capitalize on a crisis, (c) the possible systemic, long-term solutions to a crisis, and (d) the extent to which such solutions are authored, endorsed, and instituted by the citizens of the affected communities.[21] The failure to think systematically about unjust social conditions—conditions that sudden disasters can render visible to outsiders and more horrific for insiders—both assumes and perpetuates the notion that "objects of charity" are just that: objects. They are acted upon; they do not act. They are a problem to be addressed. They have no power to address.

Tourniquet ethics has an ironic and damning effect for those in need of tourniquets. When Christians elide the broad, systemic view in favor of the immediate, they ensure a nearly perpetual supply of human emergencies around which the charitable may cinch their tourniquets, heroically and temporarily. Because tourniquets neither heal nor endure—because they only stop the immediate flood of blood, and they must constantly be replaced if the wound is not (re)dressed—the upshot of tourniquet ethics is a population in perpetual need of emergency care and another population that can congratulate itself for providing such care. Because only those who control the resources—only those who possess tourniquets—are in a position to act ethically in such a discursive formulation, those who need the tourniquets are not only objects of pity but also persons of questionable character. It is impossible for them to act ethically because they are not in a position to perform what has been codified as the supreme ethical act: to give out of their abundance. They are at best nonethical, at worst unethical. The final verse of "Give It Away" suggests the latter:

> There are two kinds of folks—takers and givers
> There's gripers and complainers and big hearted livers
> It depends on how we choose to spend our days
> We can hoard up all we've got, or give it all away.[22]

When tourniquet ethics become *the* ethic, good only flows into the ward. Indeed, the ward sucks it in. But good never flows out. Those in need—and those who do not have money or time to hoard—stand thus condemned. As objects of charity, they are necessary—necessarily—takers. Because they are takers and not givers, they are unethical.

Like most Christians who adopt the tourniquet ethics model, the Gaithers either do not intend or do not realize the upshot of the "taker/giver" dichotomy for people in need. I do not sense that the Gaithers cling to the taker/giver dichotomy as dogmatically as the matter-of-fact formulation in "Give It Away" suggests. In 2011, Bill brought me into his office and played for me another new song: "Do You Want to Be Well?" written by his children Benjy and Suzanne. The song is based on the "pool at Bethseda" episode in the Gospel of John. In the story, Jesus approaches a crippled man who is reclining at some distance from the pool, which supposedly possesses healing powers. Complaining that he is always slow to arrive at the pool—thus it is always packed with people by the time he gets there—the man asks Jesus to carry him to the pool. Jesus then poses the question, "do you want to be well?" A lifetime of hearing evangelical sermons on this passage prepared me for the song's not-so-veiled suggestion: if your life is bad, it is up to you to take the steps to make it better.

True to form, Bill fidgeted with excitement as the new song played and as I read the lyrics. However, skepticism flavored Bill's typical antsiness in the ensuing conversation. "Is that too harsh?" Bill asked. "I mean, the guy in the story is paralyzed." As we talked, it became evident that Bill was trying to reconcile two strongly held beliefs. On one hand, he felt that American society suffered from a deficit of personal responsibility. People felt entitled to having their miseries alleviated by external forces. People did not want to be well—at least, not if wellness required effort on their part. On the other hand, Bill seemed aware that healing was not simply a matter of "sucking it up." Either oppressive circumstances or profound personal brokenness (or both) made it unlikely, if not impossible, for many even to reach a point where they willfully could pursue their own healing. Even individuals who wanted to be well could not simply will themselves well.

Bill's quandary has much to do with Homecoming demographics. Who is listening to the Gaithers? What do they want to hear? What do they need to hear? On one end of the spectrum, the Homecoming world contains citizens of some means, some mobility, and a relatively large number of life options. Comfortably retired, they have the money to pay for Homecoming products and the time and means to travel to concerts. A good many of these fans likely could stand to use their resources more charitably, to quit "hoarding up" all they have. Bill's onstage narrations of how previous recipients of his five-hundred-dollar grant had "given it away" were parables of people who lifted their gaze from their televisions, hoisted themselves from their living-room sofas, and met needs in their community. The lesson remained under the consuming rubric of tourniquet ethics, but Bill intended it to turn people toward their neighbors. Homecoming fans who had ears to hear, and who had the means, were to listen to these parables, then go and do likewise. I met fans like these during my fieldwork.

On the other end of the spectrum, the Homecoming world contains many citizens of limited means, mobility, and options. A large proportion of their money comes from Medicare or social security, and they must spend it on items like dialysis machines and drugs that make it possible to get through a day with relatively little pain. Or, Homecoming fans may be caregivers for a similarly situated loved one. Of necessity, these fans experience the Homecoming programs on television—from their living-room sofas, or their wheelchairs, or their beds. They are not a live audience; Bill cannot return their gaze. I met fans like this as well.

Even those fans who manage to attend live shows often exhibit symptoms of moribund hard living—not simply the pangs of aging, but serious debilitation. In May 2007, I drove to a Homecoming concert in State College, Pennsylvania—one of the first concerts I attended. Suspecting that a college town in the Pennsylvania hills would provide some nice bicycling environs, I packed my bike, planning to pedal the few miles from my hotel to the concert and back. Before and after the show, I sat beside the bike rack located near a handicapped parking area, which was filled to capacity, outside the Bryce Jordan Center. I watched numerous elderly and middle-aged fans slowly make their way into and out of the arena, with the help of shaky crutches, crooked canes, and wheelchairs that looked like they dated back to the Roosevelt administration. Many fans simply hobbled in and out on weak legs that supported soft and weighty torsos—not, I deduced, soft and weighty merely due to age. Many took advantage of the golf cart shuttles that ran from the lot to the doors and back. More than their frames, their visages were heavy—sagging under some invisible weight on entry and exit, before and after having heard the gospel show. Their gazes seemed to fall . . . nowhere. They looked defeated and empty. What were these people supposed to "give away?" If they had nothing to give, were they then takers—gripers and complainers?

Standing beside my bike, feeling quite good about myself and what I considered my life choices, I was surprised how easy it was for me to narrate this population into the dichotomy. Yes, these were the takers. Here was the drain on society—the population who was costing my nation so much. Although I was a partial product of the social sciences—trained to set my eye on systems and broader cultural conditions when I rendered accounts of individuals—my first instinct was to think in terms of individual choice. I had seen these people (and all Homecoming crowds) shovel concession-stand grease and soda in to their frames at concert intermission. I had watched them flag down the golf cart shuttles not one hundred paces from the arena door. They were in such a terrible state simply because they were lazy, ate badly, and so on. And the rest of us who made better choices were stuck funding their willful incapacity. Punctuating my frustration, this population had the audacity to narrate itself (I assumed) as the "real" (hard-working, values-possessing) America, in opposition to the lazy, entitled, resource-draining, usually dark-skinned, pseudo-America. I was ready to return to Princeton, where I would purchase vegetables from one of the city's many organic vendors, where I would bike carefree down the trail the citizens had decided to fund before I was born. I was not like the people in this lot; I was well, because I wanted to be well.

How frightfully easy it was for me—a son of the rural Midwest, of a population of similar carriage, now a graduate student at a prestigious East Coast university—to diagnose disease and to write general scripts. I could see this population's falls; surely I knew their wrestling.

What did this population look like from the Gaithers' Indiana home?

The Unsettling of Anderson

It is impossible to tell if it is a machine in the garden or a garden in the machine.

One need not venture far afield of Indianapolis to realize why *Indiana* means *farming* in the public imagination. Drive northeast from Indianapolis on Interstate 69 and witness the corn and wheat stubbling the horizon in all directions, the combines shaving clean and brown the flush cheeks of the Hoosier State. Then, about thirty miles from the Indianapolis beltway, the agri-gauntlet yields to a sprout of fast-food billboards and gas station signs, all propped on tall, thin metal stalks. The farm fields give way to a sprawling, concrete gray area—nearly as flush as the fields but for the signs and handful of chain hotels squatting thick just off exit 26. This is the interstate commuter's introduction to the city of Anderson.

The drive north through Anderson on Highway 9 (called the business route) is another gauntlet—a shallow cavity of bulky, abandoned or semi-abandoned structures setting slightly off the road, behind the chain restaurants and strip malls. Signs along this road point to Hoosier Park, the horseracing track—which lies at an invisible distance off the business route, which in 2008 added nearly two thousand electronic gambling machines.

While Hoosier Park was adding games and amusements, Anderson had been losing citizens for some time. As of the 2000 census, Anderson had 57,021 residents—about 13,000 fewer than it had in 1970. Most of the ghostly structures that loomed in the background of the business route once housed General Motors operations. At its operational peak in the 1970s, GM owned twelve factories in the city. One in three Anderson residents worked in one of these plants. Only in Flint, Michigan, did GM employ a greater proportion of a small city's residents during the American auto boom.[23]

Partly due to the documentary work of its native son Michael Moore, Flint's demise is well known. But the fall of the auto industry hit Anderson nearly as hard. Starting in the early 1980s, GM's Anderson plants began closing their doors. The closings caused a gradual exodus from Anderson. As members of the United Auto Workers (UAW), Anderson's numerous factory workers were the beneficiaries of, by most accounts, one of the best blue-collar pension plans in American industry. When the closings began, a number of Andersonians were persuaded to accept buyouts and early retirement packages. Meanwhile, the city built on a dying industry had difficulty attracting new residents. In a city where the median age already skewed old, Anderson became a city comprised in large part of elderly people who relied heavily on GM pensions for their livelihoods—particularly for their medical expenses. In 2006, GM retirees outnumbered employed auto workers in Anderson four-to-one.[24]

The Gaithers live in the 6,000-person town of Alexandria, about ten miles north of Anderson on Highway 9. I recognized the arrangement, having grown up in 7,000-person Jackson, Missouri, about eight miles away from Cape Girardeau—a 30,000-person town with two hospitals, a university, and a shopping mall. Friendly and unfriendly rivalries between the towns aside, it was no secret where many Jacksonians went to work, where we all went to shop. Alexandria and Anderson are equally yoked. Properly speaking, the Gaithers call two towns "home."

Many wide-open spaces surround Anderson and Alexandria, and one might expect Madison County's best-known gospel couple to occupy some gated mansion on a hill, to cloister themselves in the middle of a massive tract of land, far from what counts as a population center in the rural Midwest, even one so small as downtown Alexandria. Maximizing acreage (and privacy), getting more land for less buck—this is Midwestern Real Estate 101, a major reason midwestern towns of almost any size have "suburbs." Since the Gaithers have a lot of bucks and some understandable reasons to hide away from ambitious gospel singer-songwriters, the lure of unincorporated property would be especially strong in their case. However, the Gaithers live basically in the middle of Alexandria, in the only home in which they have ever lived as a couple, which they built in the middle 1960s. While far from being a Luddite shack—it sports a high-tech kitchen and, as might be expected, a formidable home entertainment system—the Gaithers certainly could afford more (and a more modern) house. I have been inside numerous larger, newer, and more garish homes in the Midwest—homes of doctors, lawyers, even schoolteachers.

The minimal extravagance does not mean that Gaither wealth is thoroughly invisible, or that they do not possess significant luxuries. The Gaither backyard contains a small swimming pool and tennis court. The Gaithers own properties in and around Alexandria aside from their home—notably three little cottages that often serve as guest accommodations for Gaither visitors. One of these is the tiny farmhouse in which Bill grew up. On top of the four buildings that house the administrative offices, recording studio, warehouse and distribution center, and the Gaither Family Resources store and café, a significant slice of Madison County belongs to the Gaithers.

At the same time, the Gaithers believe they and their family resources belong to Madison County. Every time I rode through the county with one or both of them, I was reminded how well they know the place, how much they love it, and how much it sometimes frustrates them—the sort of stubborn, active frustration that only loving relationships yield. They are especially committed citizens of the Anderson University community. Bill has served as a trustee for the school for three decades. The campus's massive, state-of-the-art performing arts center has significant Gaither money in its foundation, as does the university Wellness Center. From time to time, the Gaithers use their properties to provide transitional, affordable housing for low-income or struggling students. A number of the employees in the Gaither offices have worked for the Gaithers for decades—a fact that Bill believes attests to his and Gloria's integrity as bosses. On top of the many longtime regulars, Gloria regularly employs a number of young people in Gaither Family Resources—specifically young women who are college students, struggling to make ends meet.

The Gaithers' Madison County pride is not limited to projects of their own design. On my first drive through the county with the Gaithers, we passed the newly built public elementary school. Bill beamed as he pointed it out, but he explained with some irritation that it had taken a serious battle to get voters to approve the tax increase to fund the construction. Conceding that he was no fan of tax increases, he lamented that many citizens' dogmatic antipathy toward taxation of any sort made them resistant to considering tax increases to fund even much-needed local projects. "I mean, we're talking about *your own town*, for crying out loud," he said.

Attending church with the Gaithers provided me a different kind of glimpse into the Gaithers' life inside Madison County. As we mingled with the crowd that gathered after Sunday School and before the worship service at Park Place Church of God, on the Anderson University campus, some of the extended gazes that fell on us testified to the Gaithers' celebrity stature. However, clearly Bill and Gloria were not absentee celebrities. We were not peculiar spectacles. Gloria dropped two of the Gaither grandchildren off for "children's church" before the service; many congregants knew the children by name. Bill bantered with a number of congregants. The conversations were just banal enough, just replete enough with mutual personal trivia and midwestern easiness, to suggest that Bill actually knew many of these people, and that they knew him. The fawning, I-just-want-to-tell-you-you're-great encounters I had witnessed when fans cornered Bill and Gloria at a concert did not occur here. People wanted to say "hello" to them because they were the Gaithers, their great gospel neighbors.

I was impressed by all of this. ASCAP's Gospel Songwriters of the Century seemed to wear their fame and fortune like a light cloak. It called to my mind stories of Jimmy Carter, who during and after his presidency taught Sunday School in his home church in Georgia. People in the Christian music industry with Gaither-level notoriety and money (there were not many) who did not end up living on the Nashville beltline must have possessed some deep commitments to their hometown.[25]

While Bill's father worked to keep up the small family farm, he also had worked for GM and was one of the beneficiaries of the UAW deals. Gloria Gaither was the daughter of auto-boom-era Michigan—daughter of a Church of God minister, erstwhile employee of the Battle-Creek-based Kellogg Company (which has its own interesting religious story). These two children of the post–World War II, industrial-rural Midwest wrote gospel music on the side while they taught in public schools. In their obscurity, they tirelessly shopped their products to gospel singers and publishers. They had the good sense to retain their copyrights—a decision that paid huge dividends by the time the songs reached the likes of Johnny Cash and Elvis Presley. Their family trio began performing in community centers and ended up on Billy Graham's stages. While every plant in Madison County was withering, the Gaithers were yielding bumper crops of gospel music. After Presley, Graham, and others helped to certify the Gaither name, the Gaithers planted and grew the Homecomings—during a season of life when many people with similar or lesser means begin the decrescendo on their public careers. Into their seventies, they hardly have slowed down. They hardly will slow down. They are the working rich.

Superimpose the Gaithers' career trajectory over that of Madison County, over the same period, and it would be nearly inverse. When the Gaithers step out of their front door, they meet few in their community who possess either vocational or civic passion. When the Gaithers consider the works of their own hands, they see the result of hard work, personal drive—much of it undertaken after their fiftieth birthdays. When they consider their community, they are pained over the rampant economic, psychological, cultural, and spiritual barrenness. How might one account for the fact that the Gaithers "made it" in the very same landscape that consumes the wills of so many of their neighbors? Isn't the simplest explanation that they wanted to be well?

My sympathies are not with the Gaithers on most matters of labor and industry. I believe the failures in Madison County were largely the result of failures of corporate imagination, an unwillingness to share capital (and, to be sure, an unwillingness on the part of big labor to demand it), and a lack of long-term concern *for the region* on the part of the absentee owners of capital. I also believe the Gaithers' determination is exceptional, though perhaps their sincere humility and the maddeningly contradictory demands of midwestern evangelicalism (all are uniquely called, but no one should "get above their raisin'") prevents them from owning their exceptionality and inscribing it into the palm of their politics. Bill was determined to be a gospel singer-songwriter. But the determined will is rare. And one ever will be frustrated if one expects everyone to be exceptional.

I understand, though, how the Gaithers' biographies inform their visions. Like all of our biographies, they are fictions, not utter lies; the storm and stress of the narrative fall on the historical items that makes the Gaithers coherent to themselves and helps them to see coherence, and to account for the incoherence, around them. Bill and Gloria truly have worked hard. Truly, they are well in large part because they have wanted to be well. Truly, a lot of laborers and bosses could learn from them.

Truly, the Gaithers want their community—and all communities—to be well, too. Their policy politics are aimed toward this end. Herein lies the tragic irony of Homecoming apoliticism. It may be the tragedy of American evangelicalism.

COME SUNDAY: THE GAITHERS AND COMMUNITY POLITICS

When I was drafting discussion prompts for my interviews with Homecoming fans, I decided to play by the apolitical rules of the game. I would not bring up *politics*. Because the Homecomings deliberately avoided politics, I worried that introducing the term would tilt the conversations too profoundly away from fans' lexicons. Furthermore, most of my conversation partners were white southerners or midwesterners. I spent a good deal of my life in this demographic, and I was fluent in the primary public tongue: "apolitical niceness," as St. Louis native Jonathan Franzen terms it.[26] Be polite, be smiley, be light, avoid contentious issues—in other words, be apolitical. This choice came with a cost. It is possible that some fans were quite attuned to the political dimensions of the Homecomings and wanted to discuss them; they merely awaited a cue from me, permission to place a moratorium on "apolitical niceness." By refusing to steer the conversation, I steered the conversation.[27] As always, politics required compromise; I sacrificed some candor on one topic hoping that I could cultivate a spirit of candor on other topics. One such topic was church.

In her study of "everyday" religious practice among Christian African American women in rural North Carolina, Marla Frederick spends a good deal of space examining women's experiences of televangelists. At the heart of Frederick's inquiry lay questions about community:

> Do televangelists encourage people to engage society or do they merely encourage listeners to contribute to their individual social and spiritual advancement? With televangelists coming from various social and denominational backgrounds, what influence is such a medium having on the particular faith experience of black parishioners given the black church's historic (even if overly idealized) role as a place of both spiritual and social uplift?[28]

As with most scholars who recognize "laypeople" as more than passive recipients of pulpiteering but at the same time as seriously affected by media and message, Frederick does not believe there are simple answers to her questions. But despite finding that viewers selectively interpret televangelist messages, Frederick concludes that a message of individual, rather than community, uplift dominates the ministries and their reception. The "triumph of individualism," as she calls it, dictates even what she regards as the more encouraging manifestations of everyday religious life.[29]

Due to the black church's presumed emphasis on social engagement (an emphasis which has import even if it is, as Frederick notes, sometimes overestimated), Frederick frames her inquiry primarily as an investigation of *televangelist-viewer* as (or versus) *churchgoer*. The (black) church is the touchstone for society—not synonymous with society, but actively constitutive and critical of it. Therefore, the televangelist's intrusion in the individual's relationship with her local church is tantamount to an intrusion into her relationship with her broader community. I share Frederick's interest in televised ministries' impact on viewers' sense of community. But the case of the Homecomings requires taking a step back from some of Frederick's socio-ecclesiological assumptions.[30]

One of my primary concerns is the relationship of Homecoming viewer to wider community-*as*-church—not community-*through*-church. The church so conceived is not a touchstone of broader civic engagement but is itself a political, public entity—a site of community politics, *inside which* individuals and groups must grasp for and wield power, negotiate competing interests, and protect and achieve specific goals. Whereas Frederick wonders how televangelism affects viewers' willingness and ability to critique their community—critiques that black churches, in some forms, enable and execute—I wonder how the Homecomings affect viewers' willingness and ability to be a part of a local congregation at all—even a church community that is "apolitical" in the "party" or "policy" senses of the term.[31]

I asked all my interviewees to reflect on the ways in which the Homecoming concerts and/or videos were like and unlike church. I tried to bring up the question when conversation drifted toward personal appeal—when interviewees explained what drew them to the Homecomings, what emotions they felt, what sorts of response the programs elicited from them. I knew the Gaithers had strong opinions regarding Homecoming ecclesiology. As indicated by their insistence on being a (non-tax-exempt) ministry/business, they did not want people to replace involvement in local congregations with regular Homecoming viewings. I also had in mind the multitude of people who informed me in casual conversation that they knew someone who would not set foot in a church but who watched the Homecomings religiously. Although I cannot be certain about the existence of this ubiquitous, antinomian gospel fan (I do not think I have met such a person; he usually gets cast as a cantankerous male relative), his very ubiquity in the discourse demonstrates that Homecoming fans assume that the programs provide something *like* church. Perhaps old Uncle Bob would roll out of bed for Sunday meeting someday, but until then, at least he was hearing the gospel somewhere.

To answer how the Homecomings did or did not resemble church required that fans articulate what *church* was. Judging by the answers I received, *church* was essentially a worship service. With near unanimity, the question of the Homecomings' churchiness primarily revolved around its recapitulation of Sunday morning in the sanctuary. Typically, the Homecomings resembled church because of the music and the atmosphere the singing created: a body of believers gathered to lift their voices in praise. Concerning the live concerts, Cathy—a southern, middle-aged, Baptist fan—said,

> It was like church, my church experience, when people worshipped. Their hands were up, their eyes were closed. The emotions of worship affect people. I grew up seeing that and so I can see that when I watch them so that's how it's

like church to me, because I lean more musical—the worship part, the musical worship part of church has always been the part that draws me.

Concerning the taped performances, the answers also likened the Homecomings to song-saturated worship services, though fans occasionally emphasized the meditation-inducing aspect of the programs. Lewis, also a southerner, had similar things to say about the live shows as Cathy, but he made distinctions about the videos:

> As far as watching [a Homecoming] at home, it reminds me of church in a different way. But especially if I'm watching it by myself, and depending on what my emotional state is at the time, I can become very reflective and get a lot of meaning from it—feel the spirit just talk to me in a way that maybe I don't find in church sometimes. Maybe sometimes I do, but like something—a line in the song or just how pleasing it is to my ear, whatever it may be—just sometimes it just makes me really just sit there and be still. Not just listen to the music, but listen to what God's saying to me. So I've had some very, very good moments with God just listening to a Gaither tape or watching a Gaither tape.

As with many fans, Lewis explains the private experience of a taped Homecoming in language that redounds with "devotional time"—eliciting inner peace or contemplation of the sort he rarely experiences at church (though his longing sighs suggested that he would like to have this experience in church more often).

Lewis's and Cathy's comments point to a "community conundrum" in Homecoming concerts, in Homecoming recordings, and in church. In all cases, there is no clear delineation between worship-as-participation and worship-as-observation. Cathy's eyes are wide open to her worshipping neighbors' closed eyes; by using the third-person, she positions herself as an observer, somewhat outside or above those gathered. However, she is also inside that worshipping body; it is *her* church experience, even if she is not necessarily one of those with closed eyes. Is corporate worship for Cathy about being moved to participate in such an embodied fashion—alongside others so moved—or is it about the feeling one gets watching others so moved? The taped Homecomings prompt Lewis to experience intense devotional moments in the privacy of his home. Yet they are the result of his observation of a corporate recorded performance. Is Lewis participating in these Homecomings, or is he observing them? Of course, hard distinctions between observers and participants often do not exist (as many ethnographers know). However, because the Homecomings and church are kindred in structure and content—dissimilar yet related, mutually defining events, wherein the experience of one colors the expectation audiences bring to the other—it remains necessary to attend to the specific kinds of participating and observing that transpire in both venues.

It is understandable that fans would refer so invariably to worship services in their reflections on the Homecomings. The Homecomings have a stage. There are songs—many that fans know from their Sunday worship services. The audience behaves like some congregations. There is a (roughly) circumscribed time for the programs. It would be presumptuous to expect fans to compare the Homecomings to, say, a small group Bible study or a church business meeting. The Homecomings literally look and sound like Sunday morning.

However, when fans considered how the Homecomings were *dissimilar* to church, I expected that they would point to extra-worship-service aspects of church: for example, there were no Bible studies or business meetings. But when the fans I interviewed contrasted the Homecomings with church, the emphasis tended to remain on worship service. Those aspects of the Homecomings that departed from church did so because they did not include some key component of a Sunday morning service. My conversation with Chris was typical: "[The Homecomings have] always been like an uplifting, entertaining type of thing. I've never tried to associate it with actual church." Chris's humorous implication that church was neither uplifting nor entertaining led me to believe that he was about to articulate an ecclesiology that expanded beyond Sunday morning in the sanctuary. He did not. "It's lacking, obviously in ... I mean, people, I think, share testimonies or stories, encouraging stories, but it is lacking kind of expository preaching of the word." Chris's contrasting of the Homecomings with church kept intact the "Sunday worship" view of church. He was not alone. "No preaching" was by far the most common feature of the Homecomings to which fans pointed when they structurally contrasted the Gaither programs with church. Fans also tended to offer qualitative contrasts between the Homecomings and church. The Homecomings were not so much different from church as they were like church at its best. "Best" sometimes referred to talent; the Homecomings were like a church with a top-notch choir and music leaders. More often than not, some combination of musical quality, mutual love between all those onstage, and the overall pietistic temperature of the event made the Homecomings an ideal church. Otherworldly comparisons abounded. Jacob—a worship leader at a large nondenominational church in the Midwest—said,

> I think [the Homecomings are] a lot like a church service, a worship service ... kind of gives me an inkling of what it might be like when we're in heaven, and

all the saints are just gathered around and worshipping the Lord—except this time instead of having Bill and Gloria onstage, it's going to be Jesus, and we're going to be focused upon him.

Jacob qualifies his substitution of Jesus for Bill and Gloria; Jesus apparently will be the *object* of saints' heavenly praise in a way that Bill and Gloria are not in the here and now. Nevertheless, that Jacob takes Bill and Gloria to be holding a place that will be occupied by Jesus points to the idealized nature of the Homecoming stage.

Fans did not always idealize the Homecomings by extrapolating from the end of history backward. Especially in the case of fans sixty years of age and older, the Homecomings represented a great lost church tradition. The "best of church" is the church of the past. According to Judy, a midwestern woman in her eighties, the Gaither programs are "like it used to be at church. I think, you know, they really get into it, and there seems to be such a spirit present when they do these Homecomings. I mean it's not just show." Invoking abstract gestures and moods—which presumably one could find in younger, contemporary-style churches that "get into it"—Judy locates spiritual authenticity in a bygone church that the Homecomings resurrect. Few fans reflected on their own idealization in my interviews, but a handful did. Dwight, a southern-born, retired professor of the humanities, said,

> As you look at [the Homecomings], it brings back your image now of what that day was like. It reminds you of the best of those days. Now we may fantasize and exaggerate, what the best *was* at the time, but I think it does for most people . . . it brings back that good feeling. It took me several years to figure out that worship, for most people, is reliving the feelings that you've had with God in the past. That's why there's such a battle over music in today's churches. Young people music: praise songs. Old people music: old traditional songs. Um, for us, those, that new stuff, contemporary, does not bring back any memories. It's just kind of void for us. It's a . . . you don't feel anything. But you hear one of those old songs, "Amazing Grace," and something kicks in.

Dwight was willing and able to discuss the editorial work that any construction of the "ideal past" entailed. His explanation of the memory-contingent emotional appeal of various types of sacred music helps shed light on Judy's comments. Dwight was in the minority in naming the "fantasizing and exaggerating" endemic to remembering. But even historically conscious fans like Dwight accepted the content of the fantasy; the Homecomings *did* capture what was, apparently, "the best of those days." Dwight may have recognized the Gaithers' selective memory, but he believed the Gaithers selected the appropriately ideal items.

Claiming the Homecomings were church at its best was another way of saying that church, on those ideal occasions, looked and sounded like the Homecomings. The very reduction of church to a worship service was a sort of idealization, for fans typically described worship services as ideally univocal occasions: the faithful sang in one accord, bowed their heads in prayer together, and perhaps read the same scripture passages together, and a preacher expounded on the one true Word of God.[32] Unity seemed to determine the ideal, and unity seemed synonymous with consensus. In Homecomings and in (ideal) worship services, all of the participants seemed thoroughly united—musically and spiritually. They were spaces where substantive conflict was absent or invisible. The community of God, at its best, satisfies the Pauline injunction, "that all of you be in agreement and that there be no divisions among you."

Given the great diversity of institutions and individuals in Protestantism, and that further division seems ever imminent, it seems odd that consensus would be such a high priority. It may be that evangelicals so value consensus, and so love naming it, because it so eludes them. If Pauline nondividedness is the mark of the beloved community, everyone will be anxious to apprehend signs of it in their social bodies. The Homecomings offer evidence that this-worldly communities can in fact achieve oneness—that Christians are capable of setting aside differences and lifting up their voices in one accord. While any single Homecoming concert or recording maintains this conflict-free unity only for a few hours, the shows' repeatability masquerades as sustainability. The Homecomings are always on. Fans can go to multiple concerts. In many regions, fans can watch the Homecomings daily on television. If they own recordings, fans can imbibe the Homecoming communion about as frequently as they wish. Furthermore, the Homecoming franchise is over twenty years old; few public ministries, and even fewer gospel music ministries, can boast of such unbroken success. There is apparently no end to—and no serious conflict within—Homecoming consensus.

The profundity of fans' eschewing of conflict became clearer on those few occasions when talk of church turned away from Sunday morning. When I prefaced my question, "how are the Homecomings like/unlike church?" with a nod to a broader, extra-Sunday morning ecclesiology, fans were more likely to respond with an expanded definition of church. Occasionally, I used the archetypal, non-churchgoing Homecoming fan as my preface. My conversation with Steve and Susan, a married couple from the Midwest, illustrates the common alterations in ecclesiology:

RYAN: I've talked to some people who say they know someone who doesn't like church or go to church, but they like this Gaither stuff on TV. What would you say to someone like that?

SUSAN: Well, I personally feel like we need to be connected to a local body of believers that's always going to be there. Bill comes and goes [laughs], I guess, you know, and he provides a great ministry, but we need to be connected with a group of believers that we have support from and can work together. So I don't think Bill needs to be a substitute for church. Yes, you can worship but . . . it's not the same.

STEVE: I'd probably ask [the fan] what they like about the Gaither Homecoming shows and what don't they like about church. Maybe talk about the need for service as well as to worship. And just to get individual—to plug in individually . . . if there becomes individual needs, or I'm not sure what else in your life, Bill Gaither's not going to come into your home and sit down and talk to you.

When I presented Susan and Steve a hypothetical person who had decided to ditch church for the Homecomings, the pair highlighted key facets of church life that extended beyond Sunday morning. Yes, Susan implied, the Homecomings might substitute adequately for corporate worship services, but church also involved interpersonal relationships—receiving support from and working together with "a group of believers." The readiness with which Susan and Steve articulated a broader ecclesiology when I provided the appropriate entrée suggested that Homecoming fans might not simplistically equate church with the Sunday morning collective.

However, those interpersonal elements with which Steve and Susan distinguished local congregations from Homecomings had a distinctly (pre) scripted flavor. When they spoke of Homecoming dissimilarity to church, they issued a qualification:

STEVE: There's not preaching, though lots of time the message is proclaimed clearly—either through the songs, or it seems like . . . somebody's giving testimony . . .

SUSAN: . . . scripture is quoted . . .

STEVE: . . . about something that's gone on in their lives, the Lord's been there, met a need there or provided.

There was, indeed, a personal element to the Homecomings that made it like church—even church more broadly conceived than worship. Steve refers to "meeting needs" and "things going on in one's life" both in his description of the Homecomings and in his description of what congregational life provides and requires of its members. Later in the conversation, Susan explains that the Homecomings appeal to her because she feels like she knows the people personally.

It is difficult to detect differences between the interpersonal dimensions of the local congregation and the intimacy the Homecomings offer. If Steve's and Susan's language is any indication, personal knowledge has distinct parameters in both cases. Susan's interjection, "scripture is quoted," unintentionally highlights the script(ur)ed nature of personal testimony in the Homecomings—and, by comparison, church. In each case, the testimonies must accord with a congregational narrative that supports and employs the devices, assumptions, and principles of the congregation. Getting to know members of the body of believers occurs coterminously with receiving affirmation, or reaffirmation, that the body is sufficiently of one mind.

In any community seeking oneness, personal testimony is risky but enormously advantageous. Particular people, speaking their particular stories, can subvert community norms; there is a chance that an individual voice will fire in a heterodox direction. However, the risk is minimized because the speakers forge their testimonies within the community itself, using its norms. Then again, the sheer quantity of testimonies minimizes the minimization. Hosting many speakers creates the impression of difference and contingency. When many supposedly different speakers—say, a hirsute white southerner like Guy Penrod and an urban-born, African American woman like Lynda Randle, whom I will discuss later—tell their unique stories yet testify to the same articles of faith, seemingly independently of one another, the payoff is immense. The vast quantity of qualitatively similar voices makes consensus on the "important" matters seem not only a possibility, but a reality. The unified kingdom of God seems at hand.

In the case of the Homecomings, the rhetoric of death and disease illustrates how this process works. Because to know someone intimately is, among other things, to know them in situations of vulnerability, a truly pathos-inducing testimony requires some degree of conflict and struggle. Death and disease work well because they are at once universal and particular vulnerabilities (everyone generally knows they come with particular struggles, and everyone will face them) and because they involve conflicts that are not *primarily* interpersonal. Given the age of many of the staple Homecoming performers, death is perpetually being narrated—and sometimes, sadly enacted. Pianist and Homecoming regular Anthony Burger died onstage during a Homecoming cruise. Rex Nelon died suddenly in his London hotel room, shortly before the taping of the *London Homecoming*; his death was acknowledged and mourned onstage. During my fieldwork, Homecoming regular Janet Paschal was just emerging from a long series of treatments for breast cancer. At the same time, Sheri Easter, the matriarch of the Easters family singing group, had just been diagnosed with breast cancer; she sang in a wig for several concerts—a fact that she publicly acknowledged. Both of these women's sagas were regular parts of their Homecomings scripts.

A number of fans with whom I spoke mentioned the testimonies of Paschal and Easter. Luke said,

> A way [the Homecomings] are not like church is, I never heard anybody preach at a Homecoming. But there has been testimony given, and you know that testimony does mean a lot—giving thanks to God for what they have in their life and things. The Janet Paschal testimony she gives since her bout with cancer. Jeff and Sheri Easter . . . and it's great to see them to be able to give a testimony and a praise onstage in front of that many people.

The conflict and struggle concomitant with death and cancer are, of course, very real. That Paschal and Easter let fans in on this trial is a strong gesture toward intimacy. But as Luke's comments highlight, the stories have a predictable arc. Recalling Steve's comments about "how the Lord met a need," testimony "means a lot" to Luke when there is gratitude and triumphant resolution. Cancer is instrumental. The presumed emergence on the other side of struggle—a presumption that is easy to make, as neither woman would be alive to give testimony had they not emerged "triumphant"—sets up the expression of gratitude. In Luke's words, Paschal gives a testimony "*since* her bout with cancer." The victory is already won. Notably, in narrating the Easters' case, Luke trails off; he does not voice Sheri's conflict (at the time of our interview, Easter was still being treated). But even in her case, thankfulness and triumph are necessary ingredients to Sheri's narrative. "A testimony and a praise" occur *necessarily* at the same time. These two women's surnames tell the story: Homecoming fans are an Easter people, and they expect the staged members of the gathering to be an Easter people. That is how fans feel like they know artists. At the concerts I attended, Paschal's testimony prefaced what became her staple song, the Gaither-penned "It Won't Rain Always."

"I feel like I know them"—no phrase was more common in my conversations with Homecoming fans vis-à-vis Homecoming performers. And the Gaithers create this expectation. Fans are privy to performers' stories of illness. They witness—sometimes literally—performers' deaths. When a singer or a singer's spouse has a child, fans get a glimpse into the delivery room—sometimes literally, via the postdelivery photos that appear on the huge video screens at the concerts. The Homecoming website is filled with biographical information about the performers. Even Rory, the chief soundman at concerts, is a known, visible personality; the "backstage" personnel is part of the family, available for fans' gazes. *Homecoming Magazine* is filled with even more "intimate" details. Appropriating teeny-bop magazine strategies, the publication gives lists of singers' favorite books, pet peeves, favorite foods, and more. As a subscriber to the publication, I received a complimentary copy of *Homecoming Kitchen*—a little cookbook filled with singers' (and their spouses') favorite recipes. I can now whip up a batch of Vestal Goodman's "famous coconut cake." Alongside the ingredients and instructions is a picture of a singing Vestal and an excerpt from her "personal note to Gloria": "This is my most requested and celebrated cake recipe. I've changed it slightly, but believe me, the results are the same (Ask Bill: The last time he had it, it was from this recipe)."[33] This feels like communion.

THE WORK OF COMMUNION IN AN AGE OF MECHANICAL REPRODUCTION

To the extent that fans believe church is ideally conflict free or conflict resistant—that is, there are no community politics—and to the extent that the Homecomings seem to achieve this apolitical ideal—that is, they cultivate the sense that the interpersonal knowledge endemic to local congregations can exist without the interpersonal conflicts that exist in local congregations—it is hard to tell why fans would not prefer the Homecomings to church. The Gaithers say they do not want fans to substitute the Homecomings for church. But why *wouldn't* fans make such a substitution?

Steve's quip that "Bill Gaither's not going to come into your home and sit down and talk to you" suggests one possible answer: Homecomings are not like church because the personal sharing and intimacy in the Homecomings is not reciprocal. Fans do not get to volunteer their personal information to others in the Homecoming community. But if fans do not *get* to volunteer themselves, neither do they *have* to volunteer themselves; if they do not get to *share*, neither are they forced to *withhold*, to shape their biographies to fit the community norms. If the implicit and explicit circumscriptions of local congregations too tightly strangle individuals and their narratives in order to preserve the aura of apolitical consensus (in order "that there be no divisions"), there comes a point when the disadvantages of involvement in the local body outweigh the advantages. If the content of "personal sharing" in local congregations can only include non-interpersonal conflicts, and if

personal testimony in the apolitical community must follow the triumphalistic "thanks and praise" model, those individuals who cannot or will not adjust
their narratives to conform to this model cannot become intimate. Of course,
neither can they become intimate if they do *not* conform.

So why should individuals try? Why not reap all of the benefits of the apolitical community by watching the Homecomings at home, without having
to risk judgment by narrating oneself in public? *Bill Gaither will not come
into your living room and sit down and talk to you*—this is precisely what Bill
Gaither does.[34] If Bill is offering the same circumscribed, apolitical spiritual
counsel and consolations that one would hear from one's pastor or one's fellow congregants, if a fan "knows" Bill just as well as she can possibly know
anyone in a local congregation that anathematizes interpersonal conflict
and apotheosizes consensus, and if Bill, unlike "locally known" people, asks
for no accountability and renders no judgment, why not stay at home, turn
one's television on, and tune one's ears to the music of the beloved, unified
community?

After spending time with the Gaithers in their own backyard, and because
I believe the Gaithers intend their paeans to *church, family*, and *community*
to be more than empty platitudes, I do not believe the Gaithers want Homecoming fans to turn on, tune in, and drop out. And perhaps fans will not and
do not draw such a stark conclusion. After all, could one reasonably expect
the Homecomings to operate like a local congregation? A Homecoming show
rolls into town for an evening (or two), then leaves. Even the recorded performances are circumscribed in time and space. In this light, the Homecomings
are more like revival services than "church." Like the historical rural-church
"homecomings" I described in the introduction, the Gaither Homecomings
are built upon ephemerality as much as stasis. A homecoming is not a "home
norm." It is a special irruption into ordinary time.

If the Homecomings are so cast, it does not seem reasonable to expect
the Gaithers to stage, say, a theological debate, or to hold a business meeting in order to highlight the reality of interpersonal conflict in communities.
To insist that a community must undermine all suggestions of consensus at
all times would be to undermine the community itself. Even if healthy communities house dissent, they also have rituals that express and create a sense
of common purpose. Herbert Anderson and Edward Foley call such rituals
"mythic." Borrowing from biblical scholar John Dominic Crossan's myth/
parable distinction, Anderson and Foley define mythic rituals as those that
ignore dissonance and contradiction in order to affirm a community's self-
understanding as continuous, coherent, and singular of mind and purpose.
Conversely, parabolic rituals highlight dissonance—"embrace the discordant

and admit the painful." Anderson and Foley point to the national presidential inauguration as a mythic ritual; the regularity of the ritual, regardless of the particular politicians entering or leaving office, conveys the sense that "we are one undivided nation moving toward a common goal."[35]

Revivals can be one such mythic ritual—which helps to make sense of the ubiquity of the term *just* in evangelical prayers and praise songs, to mean "nothing but [this singular, essential, unifying act]." The chorus of one famous Gaither song advises, "Let's just praise the Lord! Praise the Lord! / Let's just lift our hands to heaven and praise the Lord!" The message is clear: *in this performative moment, WE will do nothing but lift OUR hands collectively in praise. WE are of one purpose.*[36] If this seems troublingly simplistic and conformist, it is worth noting how much a gathering that followed this injunction would resemble a U2 or Bruce Springsteen concert. No one expects even politically charged music concerts like these to problematize the fevered univocality that they create and affirm. All of these "revivals" are occasions where problematizing and qualifying get "bracketed," to be dealt with another time. Stated in the terms of Anderson and Foley, the Homecomings seem all myth, no parable. This is not necessarily a problem, if citizens of the Homecoming world take the Homecomings to be one ritual among many, like a revival.[37]

But there is a serious problem if church members—and citizens of a democracy—take the Homecomings to *be* the community, or to be the achieved/achievable communitarian ideal. The exhaustive social sweep of the Homecomings makes this view possible, if not probable. Unlike Bruce Springsteen concerts, the Homecomings make it seem as if there is not "another time" where the bracketed problematizing and qualifying of the gathering get "unbracketed." The bracketed bits seem bracketed for good, because in the Homecomings it seems as if *everything* happens onstage. Homecomings traffic in the intimate and the quotidian. The singers appear singing on the same video screens that show them in the natal unit of hospitals, their newborn infants still slick with afterbirth. The Gaithers plot the deaths, the cancers, the recipes, and the book recommendations in a wide, public domain that is also, apparently, a local and private domain. What is discursively absent—namely, the interpersonal conflict—seems truly absent, since it appears in neither the public nor private realms that the Homecomings conjoin. In the first verse of "Let's Just Praise the Lord," Gloria writes, "We've been sharing all the *good* things the fam'ly can afford" [emphasis mine]. This qualification should suggest to listeners that there are some other, "not-so-good things" Gloria and Company could share—that the Gaithers should not be taken to be offering a holistic view of "the fam'ly." But it is easy to lose track of this qualification in the Homecoming onslaught of familial intimacies.

The Gaithers did not start this. Southern gospel fans and performers were co-conspiring to create the expectation of performer intimacy long before the Homecomings. Fans wanted to know performers were "real," performers learned that "personal sharing" in public worked well toward this end, fans consequently bought and demanded more intimacy with performers, and the cycle continued. As a result, southern gospel is a notoriously gossipy genre. Speculations abound among fans regarding performers' personal lives because they feel like they have been invited into these lives.[38] But the well-funded Homecoming machine—birthed and nurtured during the age of home entertainment systems, then the Internet, then YouTube, then online social networks—could stage (intentionally and unintentionally) a simulacrum of intimate, localized community unprecedented in its apparent holism. The Homecoming machine is an inverted audio-video panopticon—the fan at its center, pixilated and amplified members of the Homecoming pantheon surrounding her. For willing fans, this is more than a revival; this is a southern gospel Second Life, a virtual beloved community. And the Gaithers are partially responsible for creating it.

* * *

Can music just ever be music? Can the church just ever be the church?—the blog respondent's Palin-prompted questions in 2010 strike at the heart of the matter. Like a number of her fellow fans, the respondent wants the answers to be "yes." That her questions sound like an exhausted plea suggests that she knows "yes" is not the answer—that Palin's NQC invitation is the latest in an interminable series of "no's." But if music has never been just music, or if the church has never been just the church, whence the expectancy? And whence the disappointment?

This gospel fan appears peculiarly quixotic about "music just being music" only if one fails to register how widespread is the belief that art can extricate itself from the ideological messiness of communities. If ever there was a scholar attuned to and concerned about social fragmentation, surely Robert Putnam is he. Yet in *Bowling Alone*, even Putnam treats music as a bypass around social conflict: "Singing together (like bowling together) does not require shared ideology or shared social or ethnic provenance." Claiming that art is "especially useful at transcending social barriers," Putnam issues a call to America's artists "as well as ordinary Americans":

Let us find ways to ensure that by 2010 significantly more Americans will participate in (not merely consume or "appreciate") cultural activities from group

*dancing to songfests to community theater to rap festivals. Let us discover new
ways to use the arts as a vehicle for convening diverse groups of fellow citizens.*[39]

Putnam may be forgiven some generalizing. In this passage, which occurs
near the end of *Bowling Alone*, he is not concerned so much with offering a
well-wrought aesthetic claim as he is with imagining possible sites for building "bridging social capital"—that is, connections and networks between distant and ideologically dissimilar individuals and groups. If Putnam is suggesting
that participation in (rather than mere consumption of) musical activities might
lead individuals to set aside potentially divisive ideological commitments and to
make tangible connections with people different from them, he may be correct.
But I cannot imagine a concrete example of any of Putnam's named activities
that would not have serious ideological overtones; the content, the setting, the
very act of gathering to participate expresses and presupposes particular ideological commitments. To use Putnam's terminology, even activities that yield
bridging social capital presume and yield *bonding* social capital—that is, they
affirm tight community bonds and (re)define who belongs to the group.

Certainly, the act of singing *southern gospel music* together requires—or
at least presupposes—a good deal of shared ideology and social and ethnic
provenance. Aside from the particular theological and cultural commitments
expressed in the songs, the music occurs in communities that see themselves
as "one," and in settings where, to borrow the title of Bill Gaither's autobiography, "more than the music" unifies participants. However, the (re)affirmation of
bonds that occurs in collective singing would be unnecessary were the community boundaries truly stable and discernible, and/or tightly controlled by a
recognized hierarchy. Because it is difficult to discern where this particular community begins and ends, the (re)affirmation of bonds is difficult to distinguish
from the (re)building of bridges. Moreover, the larger the community that imagines itself as "one"—a four-hundred-person local congregation, an arena full of
Homecoming fans, the Homecoming fanscape writ large, American evangelicalism writ large, Christendom writ large—the blurrier the distinction becomes.
Bonding and bridging are not helpful explanatory concepts in such cases.

Understanding individuals as "imagining" their communities helps shed
light on how and why bonding and bridging occur coterminously. In his positing of the modern nation as an "imagined community," Benedict Anderson
makes three observations that are relevant to the Homecomings:

1. "[The nation] is *imagined* because the members of even the smallest nation
   will never know most of their fellow-members, meet them, or even hear of
   them, yet in the minds of each lives the image of their communion"

2. "The nation is imagined as limited because even the largest of them, encompassing perhaps a billion living human beings, has finite, if elastic, boundaries, beyond which lie other nations. No nation imagines itself as coterminous with mankind"

3. "Finally, it is imagined as a community, because, regardless of the actual inequality and exploitation that may prevail in each, the nation is always conceived as a deep, horizontal comradeship"[40]

Transposing the Homecomings into Anderson's key helps to account for the Homecoming harmonies and dissonances. The Homecoming world is comprised of people who for the most part do not know one another but who imagine that they do (and they participate in rituals to give imaged flesh to this imagining). Its boundaries are finite (there are only so many Christians, and even smaller a population fluent in the discourse of Homecoming theater) yet elastic (no hierarchy enforces the boundaries, and the theater and the audience can and do change, albeit slowly, over time). Any social disparities that exist between members are counted as secondary issues, for all equally are members of "the family of God."

With imagined communities, what, precisely, is being imagined? To reply, "a community is being imagined" does not advance the discussion very far. What, after all, is a community? When Anderson imagines what his subjects imagine as a community, he employs the phrase, *deep, horizontal comradeship*. While Anderson offers little in the way of specific definition, the words *deep* and *comradeship* suggest intimacy. His contrasting of this sort of relationship with relationships involving parties who possess and wield power unevenly and unjustly ("actual inequality and exploitation") suggests that he intends *horizontal* to signal a sort of egalitarian situation. Individuals are on the same social level, or they live in such a way as to cancel out unjust or arbitrary social disparities. They do not exploit one another. In fact, if exploitation requires arbitrary, uneven distribution of power, they *cannot* exploit one another. If this is the case, what Anderson imagines being imagined as a community is an intimate network of relationships between essential equals whose essential equality precludes them from desiring or achieving power over their comrades. It is the same sort of apolitical community toward which those in the Homecoming world aspire—a kingdom without substantive interpersonal conflict, populated by humans without potentially different and divisive interests, wrought through the ministrations of bodies without determinative contexts.

When the tide of this utopian vision becomes so strong as to nullify all crosscurrents—when the mythic utterly sweeps away the parabolic—communities

become imperiled. When a group of people take such an imagined community to be actualizable, the actual forging of a healthy community suffers a serious obstacle: no one has developed the desire, let alone the skills,
to reckon with the interpersonal conflicts that inevitably arise. In the life of
the Christian church, the idealization of the undivided beloved community
produces Christians who head for the exits at every sign of conflict—off to
find a church that is "just being the church"—only to be disappointed and
to repeat the departure when they find their new congregation divided.[41] Or,
if the Christians in question wield significant power, the idealization produces Christians who draw and redraw circles around their communities
ever tighter so as to exclude dissenters, in an effort to make their community
one. In the twenty-first century, television and Internet ministries, which can
expand conversation and promote exchanges across difference, also ensure
that Christians seeking unity will ever have an escape route out of local
groups when unity falls apart. One finds conflict in the local church; one stays
home and watches televangelists. If the dream of the unified church prevails,
it should come as no surprise to find more American evangelicals staying at
home, holy-rolling alone.

American evangelicals are not only church citizens. They are citizens of
a democracy as well. Their imagining of the community/communities of
which they are (and would like to be) citizens has consequences outside of the
church. In her 2004 book *Talking to Strangers: Anxieties of Citizenship since
Brown v. Board of Education*, Danielle Allen points to the idealization of oneness and unanimity as two primary sources of "our bad habits of citizenship"
in the United States. After offering a compelling interpretation of the 1957
desegregation of Little Rock's Central High School—specifically, the famous
photo of white student Hazel Bryan shouting down black student Elizabeth
Eckford as the latter proceeded to class—Allen names an old "myth of oneness" that charges American culture: that "out of many, a democratic people
should become one" (the motto Mark Lowry invokes in the *God Bless America*
video). The photo, Allen argues, shows that the two women had radically different experiences living in the "one" American democracy—experiences that
made them well practiced at different forms of citizenship (Bryan at domi-
nation, Eckford at acquiescence). The photo exposes the fictitiousness of the
oneness myth: "the metaphor of 'oneness' could not capture both Elizabeth's
and Hazel's experiences of citizenship, for they lived radically different versions of democratic life."[42]

In a later chapter, Allen addresses the issue that she believes underwrites
the oneness myth: "the philosophical tradition that idealizes unanimity."[43]
Taking Jürgen Habermas to be the most recent, trenchant proponent of this

tradition, Allen critiques Habermas's call for interest-free discourse that seeks "consensus through speech rather than relying on majority vote." Allen is particularly critical of Habermas's belief that individuals can bracket off interests from public deliberation. She believes Habermas fails to account for how sufficient trust is generated between citizens so that they are inclined to enter into "mutually well-intentioned," interest-bracketed deliberation at all. "When ordinary citizens commit themselves to the aspiration of perfect agreement, they lose sight of the complex contributions that human interaction, broadly understood, makes to communal decisions."[44] Allen is concerned because she believes that more than "neutral rhetoric" mediates between speakers and auditors—already-related citizens who have different experiences of citizenship.

In order to form a less perfectionistic union, Allen recommends that citizens replace oneness and unanimity with "imperfect ideals," concepts and aspirations that account for the inevitably irreconcilable aspects of community life. In place of oneness, which presumes (and, in its more worrisome forms, enforces) singularity of experience and vision in a population, Allen recommends *wholeness*—which accounts for difference and the complications involved in relationships between different people:

> A speaker cannot use the word "one" to mean multiplicity, but the word "whole" entails just that. The effort to make the people "one" cultivates in the citizenry a desire for homogeneity, for that is the aspiration taught to citizens by the meaning of the word "one" itself. In contrast, an effort to make the people "whole" might cultivate an aspiration to the coherence and integrity of a consolidated but complex, intricate, and differentiated body.[45]

Similarly, Allen advocates turning away from "idealizing unanimity to idealizing the proper treatment of disagreement." Drawing on a medical analogy, Allen believes citizens' deliberations with one another to define and achieve specific goals should not seek totally to *cure* the population of dis-ease through the (seeming) eradication of dissent and defeat, but rather endeavor to *care* for the total social body, which requires acknowledging, treating, and hopefully palliating ever-present dis-ease. Allen's imperfect ideal of a democratic rhetoric is one that "seeks not perfect consensus but maximal agreement coupled with satisfactory treatment of residual disagreement and those emotions in which it is often registered: anger, disappointment, and resentment."[46]

I find Allen's account of bad citizenship extremely compelling, yet I believe that her proposed (imperfect) remedies are open to the same charge she levels at Habermas: if the turn away from the myths of oneness and unanimity are to be more than gradual, unconscious shifts in the discourse—if the shifts

require at least some significant body of citizens to make these turns consciously—such citizens already will have to be predisposed to value wholeness
and the "proper treatment of disagreement." How do *these* predispositions get
generated? If Allen were to respond that the social fact of multiplicity and
dissent forces citizens eventually to confront the failures of oneness and unanimity myths (e.g., the case of Hazel Bryan and Elizabeth Eckford), Allen
nonetheless must recognize that the plastic attraction of these myths often
completely elides their failures and the "reality on the ground"—especially
for those citizens who benefit most from the myths. Hazel Bryan, Elizabeth
Eckford, and their ancestors lived inside a ridiculous myth long before 1957.
These myths have a self-fulfilling edge to them; populations who idealize oneness will enforce oneness, consciously and unconsciously. Not all stories of
enforcement end with integration.

In her attentiveness to historical narrative(s) and the multivalence of
material and etymological artifacts, Allen executes what Richard Rorty might
term a powerful "redescription."[47] By historicizing the oneness and unanimity myths, Allen says, in effect, "it has not always been so; it need not always
be so." By (re)describing Bryan, Eckford (and Aristotle, and Ralph Ellison,
and others who appear in her work), she points readers to moments where
her recommendations and the predispositions that generate them were/are
already present. It is not so much about generating new habits and practices
of citizenship *ex nihilo* as it is about showing where these habits and practices did and do exist. One might still ask Allen, "for your redescription to be
compelling, would not readers already have to possess an inclination to your
narrative details—indeed, to the type of narrative you tell—to be persuaded?"
Perhaps there is no answer to this cycle of challenge. I take Allen to be writing
out of the hope that her (re)description will hit some mark.

Homecoming apoliticism is founded on some of the troubling premises,
and fosters similarly troubling habits, to which Allen points—premises and
habits that threaten not only the small, local communities that the Gaithers
purport to value but also threaten vibrant congregations and broader democratic societies. The threats require description. So too do the counternar-
ratives available inside the Homecomings—narratives whose terms and
characters reveal latent possibilities and alternatives. One Gaither wrote, in
1972, "I then shall live as one who's learned compassion. / I've been so loved,
that I'll risk loving, too. / I know how fear builds walls instead of bridges; / I'll
dare to see another's point of view. / And when relationships demand commitment, / then I'll be there to care and follow through."[48] In the next chapter, I look at the complex world of this Gaither, the Homecomings' principal
narrator.

4
PREACHING TO THE CHOIR
GLORIA GAITHER AND HOMECOMING
INTRAEVANGELICALISM

DIVINEST SENSE

In 1945, Lionel Trilling published "Art and Neuroses" in *Partisan Review*, one of the major publishing venues of the mid-century "New York Intellectuals." Like many critical essays published shortly after Freud's death, the noted Columbia professor's piece takes up the question of artistry and mental disorder. Trilling wondered who benefited from the "myth of the sick artist"— the portrait of the artist as mentally unstable and by virtue of that instability capable of producing great art.[1]

Always quick to grant charity, slow to offer unequivocal praise, Trilling identified three types of individuals for whom the sick artist myth provides vocational, practical, and moral advantages. First, artists themselves benefit; the myth both explains and justifies an artist's distance from "respectable" society. The artist who believes in the myth of her own sickness carves for herself a solitude akin to that of a desert prophet or a Shakespearean seer/fool—a vantage outside of "normal" society from which she can critique that society and its norms. It is a circular situation: the sick artist possesses distance because of her sickness; the distance augments her sense of her prophetic vision; the society from which she is quarantined (or quarantines herself) recognizes her eccentricity as evidence of her sickness, the cause of her distance.

Trilling identifies "the philistine" as the second type that benefits from the myth. Trilling's philistine is not merely a boorish anti-aesthete. True, the sick artist myth allows the philistine to dismiss the artist's work and social critique as the product of a neurotic, untrustworthy mind. However, as Trilling points out, the very sickness that makes the artist dismissible also grants the philistine access to a viewpoint that simultaneously puzzles him, repulses him, and resonates in him. "By supposing that the artist has an interesting but not always reliable relation to reality, [the philistine] is able to contain (in a military sense) what the artist tells him [. . .] . He listens when he chooses."[2] The philistine may take medicine from the quarantined artist that he would reject from licensed doctors.

The third beneficiaries of the sick artist myth are "sensitive people." Although they are not artists themselves, sensitive people reject the philistine's tendency to dismiss or contain artists whose work grinds too coarsely against societal norms. Aware of their own "neuroses"—of their emotional, spiritual, and moral uncertainty regarding themselves and others—sensitive people see in the sick artist and her work a manifestation, perhaps a magnification, of their own condition. "To these people the myth of the sick artist is the institutional sanction of their situation," Trilling says. "They seek to approximate or acquire the character of the artist, sometimes by planning to work or even attempting to work as the artist does, always by making a connection between their own powers of mind and their consciousness of 'difference' and neurotic illness." Sympathetic with the artists' presumed mental distress, sensitive people find in the sick artist a cloistered companion.

It is difficult to imagine that Trilling, who regarded struggle as the key constituent and mechanism of culture, would regard the Homecomings as art—at least, as the sort of critical art that typically leads to speculations about its maker's "sickness."[3] As I demonstrated in the previous chapter, the Homecomings will not plumb some kinds of human dissonance. Bill Gaither's articulation of his project as a prophetic unity-affirmation in the midst of an all-too-divided-and-divisive Christian community suggests that certain dissonances are not merely incidentally absent; they are positively prohibited. In the Homecoming world, the neurotic artist trope seems neither possible nor necessary because, physical ailments aside, no Homecoming artists seem availably, psychologically "sick" when they are *on* the Homecoming stage.

However, some internal symptoms and environmental factors suggest that a permutated strand of the sick artist myth lodges itself in the Homecoming breast—and yields benefits akin to those Trilling identifies. It is necessary to understand how the Homecomings as *musical* phenomena fit into the larger landscape of American evangelicalism. Music has been a centerpiece of American evangelical culture for nearly as long as "American evangelical culture" has signified anything intelligible. Behind (or before) most popular

American preachers, there usually has been a popular music leader and song-writer—Sankey-Moody, Rodeheaver-Sunday, Shea-Graham. The centrality of music is nowhere more evident than in the schismatic ire it produces. While late twentieth- and early twenty-first-century Mainline Protestant churches may have split over, say, issues surrounding gender and sexuality, conservative evangelical churches tended to split over electric guitars and hymnals. Notwithstanding the common practice of defining evangelicals according to articulable beliefs regarding the Bible, the cross, salvation, and personal witness, the power of music in evangelical circles supports the conclusion of a number of twenty-first-century scholars of evangelicalism: nonrational, or supra-rational, experiences are the marrow of evangelical identity—experiences that defy communicability in expository language, that do not reduce to propositional doctrinal content, that involve participants in actions not aimed at the fortification of "higher" (textual/doctrinal) principles but are themselves defining moments of religious life. To borrow from Kierkegaard, a knight of evangelical faith may not need to make herself reasonably intelligible.[4]

It is important to acknowledge that evangelicals' identities do not reduce to theological formulations and disembodied "statements of faith" that float in the Internet ether from church website to church website. However, scholars should also resist the temptation to enforce an opposite reduction: to cleanse the evangelical temples of theological thought. Evangelicals remain largely a people of the book and pulpit—expository and propositional people, whose worship services often hinge on the nominally exegetical sermon, who identify their homes, small groups, churches, and denominations as "biblical" or "Bible-based." True, this "bibliolalia" is often rhetorical sleight of hand; as Susan Friend Harding has ably argued, Bible-basted speech does not so much signal biblical literacy or actual concern with "biblical" doctrine as it grants imprimatur to evangelical insiders. By this reckoning, "biblical" evangelicals are not so much people of the book as they are people of the adjective *biblical*. But this is not how many evangelicals see things. To evangelicals, the Bible is not a talisman but a text containing authoritative, propositional truths essential to salvation and right conduct. The fact that insiders see things this way affects whatever talismanic effects the iterations *Bible/biblical* possess.[5]

Reducing away doctrinal matters is also ill-advised in the case of gospel music, which is driven in part by propositional content. Southern gospel fans listen doctrinally; they do not always like a gospel song just because it has a good beat and they can worship to it. Even when explanations relate to lyrics in loose or difficult-to-anticipate fashions (as in the "Jesus and John Wayne" debate of chapter 2), listeners forge moral-theological interpretations. At the same time, evangelical debates over song lyrics rarely achieve the fever or scope that debates over books (and authors) and sermons (and preachers) achieve. Debates over "Jesus and John Wayne" cause no huge schisms; rarely do they lead to judgments about where the Gaithers will stand on Judgment Day. To the extent that music is central to evangelical faith, it is central because it is officially decentralized. If not the work of "sick" or "neurotic" minds, music making is largely imaginative, intuitive, nonexpository, possibly eccentric human activity. As such, it has measured value to evangelicals.[6] While there are limits to the doctrinal (and stylistic) eccentricities evangelical singer-songwriters can manifest in their music (it would be tough imagining a song that exalts the teachings of Buddha winning a Dove Award), the theological watchdogs of American evangelicalism typically salivate over "heterodox" sermons and books, not songs or music albums. During the span of my research, I witnessed major public evangelical spats surrounding Rachel Held Evans's vagina monologue, *A Year of Biblical Womanhood* (2012), Rob Bell's hell-bent *Love Wins* (2011), and William Paul Young's *The Shack* (2007; I will discuss Young's book below). All of these occurred over the white noise of evangelicals bashing the "prosperity gospel."[7] If evangelical musicians garner major criticism, it has less to do with their music than with their offstage words or deeds. Moreover, evangelicals are often eager to adopt and adapt any secular musicians if those musicians' creations gesture even slightly to "the Christian [evangelical] worldview." U2, Sufjan Stevens, Mumford and Sons, the Arcade Fire, and even Radiohead are evangelical darlings.[8] If any of these were authors for, say, Zondervan Publishing—if they were propositional insiders rather than "creative" outsiders—a different sort of critical evangelical eye would fall on them.

The first words of Gloria Gaither's 2007 book *Something Beautiful*, her collection of reflections on a number of Gaither songs, belong to Charles Colson—former Nixon advisor, famous evangelical author, and preacher. In other words, a "propositional content" man grants imprimatur on the story of the music. Colson makes this clear in the first words of the book: "Preaching can reach the mind—at least those of us who spend our lives preaching hope that is true. But music reaches the imagination, which is often far more powerful. C. S. Lewis said, 'Reason is the natural organ of truth, and imagination is the organ of understanding.'"[9] This sideways compliment suggests that the "imaginative" Gaithers and their music are both central and incidental to the larger American evangelical landscape. This is an auspicious arrangement for a musical franchise that is "more than the music," by the Gaithers' design—one that possesses didactic, expository elements. Not only through the lyrical content and the spoken interludes between songs in the programs, but also through such venues as the Homecoming website, the magazine, and *The*

Gaither Homecoming Bible (Nashville, TN: Thomas Nelson, 2012), the two former schoolteachers do plenty of explaining and proposing. The Gaithers' *fame*
as artists gives them a forum from which they can disseminate their theological reasons and truths broadly; their fame *as artists* means the consequences
of theological missteps are minimal. If there are "evangelical philistines" in
the Gaithers' audience—people who do not trust or stake much on artists and
their views, but who are drawn to the music nonetheless—those listeners can
shut their ears, or listen as they choose. As I will show later in this chapter,
Homecoming fans are quite willing and able to listen selectively.

The Gaithers-as-artists and the Homecomings-as-art have the benefit of
being taken halfway seriously in a loosely organized, noninstitutionally hier-
archical evangelical population that is perpetually anxious over sound belief.
But the picture remains incomplete without revisiting the peculiarly gendered
characteristic of the Homecomings' context. Notwithstanding the observable
discord between lay practice and the pronouncements of self-styled power-
brokers, men overwhelmingly occupy the positions of expository-proposi-
tional power in American evangelical culture—in charge of forging official,
normative evangelical theologies.[10] With varying degrees of intentionality,
evangelicals tend to recapitulate the old equation of maleness with intellec-
tual-theological sophistication—and, conversely, femaleness with emotion,
expressivity, and "intuition."

The evangelical gender divide is stark, but it is neither total nor static.
"Expository" evangelical women span the theological, educational, and pedagogical spectrums (for example, Beth Moore, Joyce Meyer, and Rachel Held
Evans). Moreover, prevailing ideas and practices of manhood in contemporary
evangelicalism preclude simple gender dichotomies. While emotion, expressivity, and intuition are *primarily* the province of evangelical women—and
rationality is officially or unofficially *not* their province—it does not follow that
evangelical men have no responsibility to cultivate their "nonrational" qualities. As the men's movements in which Guy Penrod became a Homecoming
celebrity demonstrate, the evangelical charge for men to man the theological-
rational helm in their homes and churches does not exonerate them from being
men after God's own *heart*—from embracing and expressing their emotions.
American evangelical men have fretted a good deal about being emotionally
unavailable to their families, to one another, and to God. Evangelical male normativity does not simply entail privileging male tastes and predispositions;
it also means men must contain (in all senses of the term) the full range of
humanity. Following the logic of the gendered dichotomy of mind and heart,
one might say that evangelical women are expected to be women, but evangelical men are called to be omni-gendered—all things in all men.

From the cowboy tears of Guy Penrod, to the James Brown knee-drop convulsions of southern gospel heir-apparent Ernie Haase, to the arm-in-arm crooning of singers George Younce and Glen Payne, the Homecomings feature and encourage men's emotional expression. Homecoming women are not so effusive. Homecoming women shed their share of tears and embrace their share of others (usually other women or male family members), but they operate within a more rigorously circumscribed field of expression than do men. No Homecoming woman would gyrate like Ernie Haase.

The rules that proscribe women's emotions are unspoken and thus difficult to pin down. They are partly the result of worries over sexualized female bodies—bodies whose sexuality supposedly becomes augmented in moments of even pious enthusiasm (I will revisit this issue in chapter 5). Judging by fans' reactions to Lynda Randle, which I will discuss in chapter 6, the rules have something to do with southern gospel notions of "respectful" women's behavior (in Randle's case, respectful *African American* women's behavior). If the pioneer/agrarian (often Amish-themed) fiction that proliferated in Christian book catalogues during the years of the Homecoming's full blossom is any indication, the rules are traceable to the myth of the strong, pioneering rural woman—the matriarch, or matriarch in training, whose domestic responsibilities require a kind of fierce, matronly stolidity.[11] Women must be emotional and intuitive, but not to the extent that the evangelical domestic sphere falls apart.

Therefore, the Homecomings stage a strange and complicated confluence of expectations and sometimes-conflicting norms. Evangelicals self-consciously prioritize the rational, expository, propositional provinces of religious life. Men tend to dominate these provinces. As an art space, the Homecomings reside outside these provinces—in the nonrational, emotional, expressive vicinities that evangelicals also highly value. However, by the Gaithers' design, the Homecoming as a supra-musical franchise retains expository and propositional elements; these elements simply do not get first billing. As exemplified in the marquee all-male quartets (especially the GVB), men hold Homecoming dominion—not as rational expositors (as in broader evangelical culture), but as emotional, expressive performers. While women are key presences in the Homecomings, they are less animated; even the Pentecostal Vestal Goodman cannot express the same full-bodied panoply of emotions as her male counterparts. Women find themselves decorously aglow in the penumbra of the Homecoming spotlight. In the case of the Homecomings-as-musical-phenomenon, women have a peculiar companion in their partial illumination: not "feminine" emotionality, but "masculine" rationality.

Here resides Gloria Gaither, the partially illuminated legislator of the Homecoming world. While her extroverted spouse works every social space like a presidential candidate, shaking hands with friends and strangers, and poking fun at himself on and off stage, Gloria prefers either backstage darkness or the approximate anonymity of the Homecoming chorus. When she appears in concerts, she only takes center stage in order to recite one of her poems, her short essays, her video-specific narratives, or the spoken section of a Gaither song.[12] The brevity and growing infrequency of her performances over the life of the franchise enhance the expectation that her offerings will be intellectually heavy.[13] The arc of her presence follows that of the unassuming "Zen-philosopher-warrior" of popular film: first, silent, self-possessed, and unattached as she observes the action from behind; then purposeful as she slowly limps into the action on bad knees—a step that usually follows and extends a particularly quiet, meditative portion of the program; then utterly composed, without so much as a stuttered syllable as she pours her three-to-five-minute oratory (from memory) into the arena, employing a lexicon just elevated enough to signal her residence over the common discourse, just cognate enough with everything sung and said thus far onstage to seem a culmination, a synthesis of the action; finally, steady and absorbed as she limps back into the penumbra, reabsorbed into the chorus.[14] The music resumes. The Homecoming stage has been transfigured: its labors dignified, its quest blessed. This is no woman to take lightly.

And no one does. While most Homecoming programs contain dozens of jabs at Bill's old age or unorthodox hair, Gloria is never the object of such jokes. When I asked Homecoming fans to describe Gloria Gaither in a few words, "dignity" and "wisdom" came up repeatedly. Those who either explained these terms further or offered more verbose descriptions of Gloria pointed to her quiet power. One woman noted appreciatively that Gloria "doesn't have to be in the limelight. She seems very happy for [Bill] to be more in the limelight." Even those who professed little knowledge of Gloria spoke about Gloria's projected authority in their conjectures: "I don't know much about Gloria, but I have a feeling she is really involved behind the scenes, she's really a part of this thing." The mystery that surrounds Gloria Gaither enables her to be all things—all things potentially feminine—to all Homecoming fans. Those Homecoming fans who warm to the idea of women as visible spiritual leaders can read Gloria as exemplary of quiet *power*. She writes most of the scripts for the Homecoming videos.[15] She has authored and coauthored numerous books, before and after the Homecomings began. She is the editor-in-chief of *Homecoming Magazine*. She has her own merchandise table at those live concerts she attends; they are invariably among the most crowded (particularly when she is present, signing books). And then there is the songwriting. With the possible exception of Fanny Crosby, no female lyricist has put more words on more American Christians' lips more frequently.[16] But because Gloria is primarily present through her texts, and because she appears only sparsely on Homecoming stages, those fans who might fret over her usurping her husband's authority can interpret her as exemplary of *quiet* power. One of my interviewees told me he liked Gloria because "she stands *behind* Bill all the way" (emphasis *resoundingly* audible in the original). Both models—help-meet and authority—are available to Homecoming fans. Those who reject the dichotomy have a model, too: Gloria can be *quiet power*. To borrow a line from her famous children's song, Gloria is a promise; she is a possibility.[17]

Gloria's extractability arises in part from political necessity. The Gaithers hold together a fan base that includes the enterprising, funky-dressing Anne Beiler (founder and CEO of Auntie Anne's Pretzels, whom I've seen backstage at numerous Pennsylvania shows), Mennonite and Pentecostal women who come to Homecoming concerts with their heads covered, Catholic women religious, and women Lutheran pastors. However, Gloria's "in-betweenness" is not merely market-savvy waffling. To assume so is to believe there must be a "real" Gloria whom the public does not see—a Gloria who in actuality resides on one side of the presumably linear spectrum of gender politics, because no woman could hold in tension this feminism, this patriarchalism. Likewise, reducing Gloria's appeal to her chartability onto a number of polarized narratives of womanhood and feminism presumes that Homecoming fans themselves map easily onto one side of the spectrum. Some do. Some do not.

I feel this dismissal and these assumptions tugging at me every time I read Gloria's books and hear her speak. If Gloria sounded like Mary Daly, Beverly Lahaye, Gloria Steinem, Phylis Schlafly, or whomever I imagine to represent one of the "stable" poles on the spectrum of feminism, I could pretend to comprehend her. But onstage and at her dining-room table, Gloria eludes my taxonomies. It may be true that I have not found the "real" Gloria Gaither until I find *Gloria Steinem* or *Beverly Lahaye* in her. I find it more likely that the real Gloria Gaither, insofar as one is available to an ethnographer or anyone else, reveals the limitations of the idea of a "culture war," being waged between two unchanging, monolithic teams, respectively anchored by an idea of *Gloria Steinem* and of *Beverly Lahaye*. Gloria Gaither is in the perceived middle—the site of intense identity contestation. That people try to appropriate Gloria to fit into their own overtly gendered cultural and theological categories speaks to the power that the perceived middle affords her. Every Homecoming pawn and bishop defends the Homecoming queen; everyone wants to hear echoes of themselves in Gloria. Certainly, Gloria's apparent "in-betweenness" allows fans to graft her onto theological and cultural roots and branches that are not necessarily her own. However, this grafting also means that Gloria attaches herself to roots and branches that may not recognize the full import or direction of the appropriations. It is not always clear who is being grafted onto whom.

This chapter focuses on the Gloria Gaither behind and within the Homecoming scripts.[18] First, I examine Gloria's contribution to the Homecomings as she understands and expresses it. Intentionally and unintentionally, Gloria's self-expositions reveal one of the key productive tensions of the Gaithers' project: the struggle between their parochial, "southern" gospel and their cosmopolitan, world-bent and world-bending "Gospel." I then turn from "Gloria in her own words" to her visible and audible Homecoming effects, starting with a guest speaker at the Gaithers' annual Family Fest and proceeding to one of Gloria's most explicit and vexing soteriological statements in the Homecoming corpus. These cases illustrate that, although the apolitical Homecomings minimize occasions for interpersonal friction, the Gaithers' (particularly Gloria's) pedagogical impulses lead them occasionally to push the boundaries of evangelical theologies.[19] I term this the Gaithers' *intraevangelical* impulse: missionary zeal that takes the converted as its object, that the Gaithers consciously design for the conversion (and reconversion) of their audience to an inclusivistic but still-contained evangelical worldview.[20] Audience members perceive this intraevangelical push as a nudge, a shove, or sometimes do not perceive it at all. As the two fans whom I introduce at the end of the chapter demonstrate, Homecoming viewers are willing and able to channel Homecoming theologies into their own and to duck and dodge the messages and metaphors that do not resonate with them. The jangle of the voluminous viewership meets the clangor of Gloria's expansive legislation; the ring of Homecoming symbols swells exponentially.

TIDAL POOLS TO STARS

Gloria Gaither's face has no middle ground. This makes her a bit intimidating. When she is not donning her big, squinty, cheeky smile, her eyes—already wrung small under thick mascara frames—become as certain and pointed as the end of a rifle barrel. Her smile is summery, but when she is not smiling, her mouth defaults into a slight frown, and the uncompromising winters of her Michigan childhood prevail on her. The first time Lynn and I rolled onto the Gaither properties, a be-sunglassed Gloria trailed Bill by a few steps as they walked toward our car in the July sun to tell us where to park. She said nothing. Per Bill's instructions, we parked and walked to the back porch, where Bill was waiting for us, shortly before Gloria emerged with glasses of lemonade and sat with us. We told the Gaithers a bit about ourselves. Bill was quickly gregarious. Gloria quietly observed from behind her sunglasses. Coming as I do from southern-midwestern stock that preempts potential social awkwardness with chattiness, and not being entirely happy with these tendencies in myself, I both puzzled over and appreciated Gloria's spacious and discomfiting hospitality. Obliged to concede no more artificial yellow glow than was contained in the Country Time, she insisted that we—not her—make ourselves feel at home. The following day, after we had braved her winter, Lynn and I would spend about two hours talking with Gloria in the Gaither Family Resources café.

Gloria's in-residence hospitality is like and unlike the hospitality she attempts to create and sustain in the Homecomings—a duty that, she explained to me in 2008, she regards as one of her most important:

> I think my role has been to give focus, and to do it not in verbiage that makes outsiders. If there's anything about the Gospel, it is "whosever will may come." And if we have any flaw in the Christian community, I think it is that we love to stamp pieces of universal truth with our own personal stamp and call it ours. And I don't think that is pleasing to God. I think God wants us to keep our arms open.[21]

Gloria proceeded to offer her reading of Jesus's driving out the moneychangers from the Jerusalem temple. She theorized that the chief sin of the moneychangers was not their usage of sacred space as a place for business (though that was also a problem) but their arrogation of the outer courts, the space intended for outsiders:

> [The moneychangers] had taken the space for the many and filled it with their own selfish interests. And we still do that, with this "us/them" mentality. I think, you know, if there's any place that should be open . . . it's the place for the stranger, the outsider, and Christ was angry because this place to enter was usurped. It's my job to make sure the outer court is empty and welcoming for everyone who tunes in or walks in and has no clue what this is all about. I think as quickly as possible they should feel like they are insiders. They are in the circle.

Gloria's concept of hospitality involves creating a clearing, vacating the premises. To the extent that creating a clearing often means refusing to fill spaces with one's own opinions, this concept of hospitality accords with how I personally experienced Gloria. It also jives with a few of the stories I heard about

Gloria outside the Homecoming sphere. Attending a conference on faith and art a few years after I first met Gloria, I struck up conversation with a Christian poet—an openly gay southern man, a member of that small guild of Christian aesthetes sometimes called "post-evangelical." When conversation turned to my research, the man recalled fondly the time that Gloria had invited him to speak in Alexandria. He also recalled overhearing her talking with a person who questioned the wisdom of her inviting a homosexual writer to speak. "Aren't you worried about how this will look? Isn't he gay?" The poet remembers hearing Gloria responding, "so?" Then silence. Gloria did not fill the space further. Whether or not Gloria's *inquisitor* construed her reticence as hospitality (according to the poet, there was no reply to Gloria's "so?"), Gloria's clearing of the air made *the poet* feel welcomed, if not quite affirmed.

The Gloria Gaither of Alexandria, Indiana, does not play fast and loose with affirmations of anything or anyone. The room she makes for you is an open challenge as much as an open invitation. You must speak: who do *you* say that you are? She seems willing to accept your becoming thought, to establish no walls (I experienced more of Gloria's pressing hospitality after she had read a draft of this manuscript). The Gloria Gaither of the Homecomings possesses a slightly different charge. This Gloria assumes more responsibility for the positive maintenance of the outer court's character. Maintaining the outer courts as a peculiarly open space requires maintaining it *as a peculiar space*—identifiable, a space with walls. With no partitions, the outer court would bleed out—either into the streets, or into the holy of holies. The former would mean a loss of Christianity's singular witness (Christ is *distinguished* as an inviter, a space-maker); the latter would portend idolatry ("if we have any flaw . . . I think it is that we love to stamp pieces of universal truth with our own personal stamp").[22]

The scripts of Gloria that I have read suggest that she holds these truths to be self-evident: (1) there is a universal, essential truth; (2) that truth uniquely resides in the body of Christ; (3) Christians usually mistake accidental features of the body for universal essences; (4) the universal is identifiable and accessible via the accidental. By clearing the space of personal interest, calling out idolatry by noting all of the "personal stamps," Gloria does justice to (1) and (3). But doing justice to (2) and (4) requires positing a specificity—articulating *particular* actions and annunciations that are conduits of the divine. How to do justice to all four might be the key riddle of any Christianity that wrestles with the implications of the Incarnation. It is certainly the riddle of order-enlarging evangelicals like Gloria Gaither.[23] In any case, being the Homecoming wordsmith necessitates some positive articulations.

Gloria writes the narrative scripts, and she wields the narrative microphone; to speak is to fill the space—with something. Despite her worries over "personal stamps," Gloria believes in the power of personal testimony—or, the power of an aggregate of testimonies—to convey universal truths. She is fond of noting that Jesus was a parable-teller—a maker of stories. Talking about "bad" gospel songwriting, Gloria told me in 2008, "I think the mistaken idea that novice writers have—and sermons, too, and in all kinds of literature—is, if you want to appeal to a lot of people, then be very general. Say all of these generalities about your truth, your idea. The opposite is really the case. The more specific you can get, the more details you can give, the more universally it's understood." Gloria aspires to focus, specificity, and conciseness in all of her writing. In the same 2008 conversation, she described to me her approach to Homecoming scriptwriting:

To experience everything that's going on in the room—to distill that into some kind of statement that can actually find expression—I think that's kind of what I do in all of our traveling life. It's to give focus, I guess is a better term: to give focus to a smattering of true things that are happening theologically, emotionally, spiritually, biblically, or just as a community, and to be the sort of fly on the wall that is experiencing it.

But I'm also saying, "What is going on here? What is really happening? What is the core of the truth here?" And then saying that as succinctly as possible. And I do that in several ways. I do that sometimes live, in the room, introducing the final song or making a statement about some truth that has come up—let's say, "doubt." And there's a smattering of people saying, "well, this happened to me, this happened to me, this happened to me. . . ." But how do I distill this down and say, "Well, this is universal—this is what always happens?"

And, of course, story is the best way. These people are all walking stories—all stories. And we, together, as a community, are a story. So to basically tell our story so that people who are not in the circle physically are drawn into the circle and experience truly through a camera what we are experiencing, and make it as true and as poignant as possible . . . I also do that writing scripts. By that . . . I say, the thing is never scripted from the front; it's scripted from the back. So part of that is, Bill will say, "I need you to come in and connect this piece of the edited, final version to this piece." And so that, again, what I do, I say, "Ok, here is what's happening." I write the hinge, the turnaround; "this truth is connected to this truth, or this piece of history" (sometimes it's just more like a PBS special) [laughs] "this piece of history is tied to this piece of history, and what you're seeing here is the outcome of this heritage, the spawning of this future."

Perhaps conceding to a version of the sick artist myth myself, I have learned not to expect too much in the way of systematic, internally consistent methodology from Gloria. This passage provides no such methodology. However, it provides a glimpse into a number of Gloria's values and struggles. Her prioritizing of stories over didactic theologizing is conscious. She believes the particular testimonies and performances of Homecoming musicians fund her eventual distillations. At the same time, the distillations themselves she regards as (ideally) precise and specific; "what is really happening" can be named "as succinctly as possible" without any significant damage to the reality happening. She understands herself to be an aesthetic Baconian—*discovering* the ties that bind, not *preemptively* forcing the realities into precepts. She starts by collecting data. Based on that data, she draws broader conclusions about the general program. Finally she spins the data out as a story that, in the final edit, is both filament and web: a particular testimony, built from testimonies, that shows the underlying order. To be true to this process is to be what Gloria calls a *communicator*—a title she often bestows on her favorite singers, speakers, and authors.

One of these authors is John Steinbeck—the subject of her master's thesis (a lyrical drama of Steinbeck's novel *To a God Unknown*) and the handful of essays she has published in academic journals. Gloria is particularly interested in Steinbeck's concept of the "connectedness" of all natural entities, and his insistence upon observing the particulars of nature without teleological presumption. In a 1992 essay published in the *Steinbeck Quarterly*, she says,

> An important link between his first important concept—connectedness—and the next is Steinbeck's recognition of the inconsistencies and contradictions that are found in nature and in human nature. The discovery led him to be suspicious of simplistic systems, rigid dogmas, or even "scientific" cataloguing. He developed a healthy cynicism that caused him to reject stereotypical categorizing or any kind of reasoning that begins with an "answer" or an assumption of what "should be." He believed that to suspend such reasoning, though it offers a "safer" harbor, and only believe *what is* makes way for the discovery of new truth. To begin with the general assumption and force the specifics into ready-made systems often too hastily ignores the contradictions and tends to reject the paradoxes.[24]

As with John Steinbeck—the believer in "connectedness" who thought it "advisable to look from the tide pool to the stars and then back to the tide pools again"—the overall "view from the stars" attracts Gloria.[25] Powerful though particular Homecoming stories and experiences as such may be, they still possess an instrumental property. Gloria operates with the self-assurance that something in the particular, seemingly disparate songs, images, and spoken testimonies of the Homecoming programs can, will, (and must?) transcend their particularity—that making a start from the particulars, rolling up the sum, she will reveal and proclaim some general, generally sufficient truth. Things will connect. Gloria's answer to the question, "what is really going on here?" resides in the presumed connectedness, the universality manifest in the compilation of testimonies. "What is really happening" is not Michael English's return to the Gaither stage or Janet Paschal's cancer; "what is really happening" is the power of forgiveness and redemption, or the fragility of human health. Personal stories remain the "best way" to get at "what is going on," but the stories do not make this big reality sufficiently available to Gloria's audience; otherwise, there would be no need to distill and focus. The medium is not quite the message. The grand narrative passes through particular stories, but eventually the stories fall away like husks, and we all are left with the hard, phantasmic kernels of the universal truth. This truth has to be dictated—presumably by what Ralph Waldo Emerson (who will figure in shortly) calls an "eternal," not a "plainly a contemporary," soul.[26] Even in the cleared outer courts, the premises cannot be totally vacated.

The books seem cooked from the outset. If Gloria enters into her project presuming the latent presence of some larger truth, of course she will attend to those elements of the Homecomings that are conducive to being subsumed into that truth. Likewise, she will render salient those artifacts that are consonant and continuous with other artifacts. This unity depends on the winnowing out of difference: dissonance, divergence, and discontinuity, if they appear at all, are by definition incidental properties that prove the fact of manyness but do not disprove the singularity of the universal truth. Homecomings may be "scripted from the back," but there appear to be some prescriptions operant from the front.[27]

At first glance, this prefatory verdict on reality makes Gloria appear at best naïve, at worst disingenuous—especially so to the twenty-first-century humanities scholar trained to furrow his brow at all attempts to condense particular stories into some general entity, especially some antediluvian entity called a "universal truth." As will become clearer later in the chapter, there are good reasons to furrow one's brow at Gloria's space-clearing claims and the "personal stamps" visible in the Homecomings.

But second and third glances are first in order. This situation is not unique to Gloria Gaither, or to American evangelicals struggling to open themselves partially to contingency—to expand their cultural horizons yet keep their horizon fixed according to supposedly transcultural standards. The humanities are filled with people who purport to start from particulars but privilege precept over realities. As I write this passage, Lynn is working on an essay that has led her to the life and work of artist Mark Rothko. She reads me two sentences from his 1943 manifesto to the *New York Times*, written with fellow artist Adolph Gottlieb: "There is no such thing as good painting about nothing. We assert that the subject is crucial and only that subject matter is valid which is tragic and timeless."[28] I find myself composing this passage barely cognizant of a set of questions—inside and outside of me, before and behind my field of vision: *A fine tale you've told about the Homecomings; but what does your book contribute to the field? What do the Homecomings tell us about . . . evangelicalism . . . religion and music . . . American religion? What is really happening here? Ethnography? Cultural history? Alongside what titles shall we shelve your project?* I have trained myself to disdain generalities, but I am constantly justifying my work according to its fruitfulness for more general examinations. My story—call it my *profession*—must play a role in some larger narrative. Situating my account according to this kind of narrative leads to the account having purchase, being sold, being shelved. Gloria-the-academic knows this, too. Describing her work to me, she compared us: "that's my background research-wise, too. I mean, any academic writing I've done is to take all the voices—it's what you're doing [points to me]—take all of the voices you hear and the information you hear and say, 'so what is the central truth?'" Looking back at Gloria's methods from my own, in time my brow unwrinkles.

Another of Gloria's strongest conscious literary influences shares her particularity-affirming partiality for grand, unifying truths: Episcopalian Madeleine L'Engle. Although L'Engle is most famous for her many works of children's and young adult fiction, Gloria's primary point of contact with L'Engle is the 1980 collection of essays, *Walking on Water: Reflections on Faith and Art. Walking on Water* reads like a chess match between a prophet of the (Christian) Universal and a prophet of the low, the particular—a match that teeters on stalemate but seem to favor the former. The match is especially even and vexing in *Walking on Water*'s second essay, "Icons of the True." Part defense of religious iconography, part criticism of the 1979 revisions to the Anglican Book of Common Prayer, the piece displays L'Engle's generality-particularity vascillations. Although she sympathizes with some monotheistic restrictions on artistic depictions of God and some of God's prophets, ultimately she sides with what she identifies as an Eastern Orthodox theory of icons—one that admits the inability of artwork to capture the full essence of Jesus or an apostle but insists that even an errant particularity in art can shed light on important aspects of God and God's people: "the orthodox painter feels, Jesus of Nazareth did not walk around Galilee faceless. The icon of Jesus may not look like the man Jesus two thousand years ago, but it represents some quality of Jesus, or his mother, or his followers, and so becomes an open window through which we can be given a new glimpse of the love of God."[29] Representations of Jesus should not be abstracted from a particular, historical Jesus, but neither should an artist be too consumed with historical precision.

It is unclear if by "some quality" of Jesus, Mary, and the disciples L'Engle means something historical or transhistorical. But whatever particularity the icon represents is instrumental, pointing to the larger truth ("the love of God"). Some general truths precede and determine what L'Engle deems acceptable particularities, even as particularity is necessary to communicate these truths. Her criticism of "bad" representations of Jesus a few sentences earlier reveals a similar tension: "soppy pictures of Jesus, looking like a tubercular, fair-haired, blue-eyed goy, are far more secular than a Picasso mother and child. The Lord Jesus who rules my life is not a sentimental, self-pitying weakling. He was a Jew, a carpenter, and strong." Historical accuracy is one litmus test for "Jesus art"—no "non-Jewish" renderings of Jesus. But alongside this historical complaint resides a constellation of assumptions regarding what "qualities," translatable from first-century Palestine to L'Engle's own soul, this "Lord Jesus" manifests. If L'Engle cannot detect a transhistorical quality in an icon, the icon is a failure. That these qualities are L'Engle's ultimate concern is suggested by the fact that L'Engle not only exempts Picasso from the criterion of correspondence (even Picasso's most "representational" mother-and-child paintings are not obviously *more* accurate representations of the *material* mother and child than many sappy representations of Jesus and Mary) but celebrates Picasso's work as substantially expressive of the sacred. Picasso's work seems less "secular" not because it better re-presents material/historical particularity, but because it traffics in essence.[30] Picasso knows "what is really going on."

L'Engle and Gloria Gaither imagine themselves writing against similar groups of "philistines": reductionistic rationalists. Art and faith give and require wonder, imagination, some privileging of the "probable impossible" over the "possible improbable"—all essential to human existence.[31] Whereas L'Engle seems to have in mind some naturalistic group of "rationalists"—either non-Christians or "liberal" Christians who have excised miracles from their faith—Gloria has in mind the rationalism of hyper-conservative evangelicalism—particularly as it is manifest in the more stringent forms of biblical literalism. Gloria's predisposition for the big picture simultaneously provides her a defense against such biblical literalists and gives her an audience with them. Again indebted to L'Engle, Gloria frequently makes distinctions between *fact* and *truth*—the former signifying the material particulars of an event (the "Who? What? Where? When?"), the latter signifying those verities that transcend all material facts and by which one may measure and assemble those facts into a coherent narrative. Like L'Engle, Gloria believes that, while Christianity often will concern itself with matters of fact (Gloria is not flippant about Jesus's actual historical existence), matters of truth should be Christians' priority. During our conversation about bad songwriting, Gloria said that aspiring songwriters often believe their songs are good because they are true ("true," in these songwriters' usage, meaning something more like "fact" above: *it really happened*): "I see a lot of bad songs. People send us a lot of songs and they say, 'well, you know it's true!' Yeah, it's true; the encyclopedia's true . . . for the most part [laughs]!"[32] A song's power does not reside in journalistic reportage. Gloria's prioritizing of truth over fact cuts deeper than her songwriting. During the first lengthy conversation Lynn and I had with Gloria in her coffee shop, Gloria received a call from an excited grandchild. After leaving to field the call, she returned to our table and informed us that her grandson had seen on television that some archaeologists believed they had discovered traces of Noah's ark in Turkey (I supposed this to be related to the Durupinar site, a favorite among some evangelicals). After a few-seconds pause (I did not know what to say to this), Gloria told us that she found it best to encourage her grandson's curiosity and sense of wonder about the world. She said she did not think it helpful to tell this six-year-old that Noah's ark might never have existed. She said this so matter-of-factly that I had to confirm with Lynn later that Gloria had indeed said it. After all, I was just getting to know Gloria.

This approach to faith may seem risky in Gloria's Homecoming context, where biblical literalists abound (but are neither unanimous nor monolithic). However, Gloria's faith remains highly, recognizably Christocentric. To borrow a phrase from Gaither friend and sometime-collaborating songster Andraé Crouch, Gloria still views Jesus as "the answer for the world today." In fact, one might say that Gloria is *supra-christological*; for her, everything, including the Bible, is scripted forward, from the truth of Christ. This supra-christological, text-qualifying hermeneutic has many precedents—from Paul's typological reading of the Hebrew scriptures, to Augustine's allegorical scriptural readings, to Reformed Barthians' reading of scripture through the revelation of Jesus, to (closest to home for Gloria) the Wesleyan insistence upon reason and experience as gaging (even as they are gaged by) tradition and scripture.[33] In Gloria's American context, this approach to reality connects her to a strand of American poetic thought that runs back to Ralph Waldo Emerson—whose influence, notably, Gloria perceives in John Steinbeck's thought.[34] Emerson identified the poet as "a beholder of ideas, and an utterer of the necessary and causal"—the figure who regarded all nature as symbolic ("nature certifying the super-natural"), and every fact as carrying "the whole sense of nature."[35] Aspiring to comprehend her relations from the heaven of "truth"—to look to the tide pool from the stars—Gloria positions herself above the opaque airs of biblical literalism. She does not get bogged down in the same biblical particulars (the "facts") that fund the obsessions of some dogmatic biblical literalists. But because Gloria's heaven of truth contains, assumes, and recapitulates a number of the same key characters and beliefs that the biblical literalists claim to value (Jesus is still the answer), it would be difficult for such literalists to dismiss her as rootless, perhaps heretically so. She claims to be a steward of the same particular mystery as they do.[36]

But what does it mean to be the steward of a *particular* mystery? For evangelicals, who stake so much on the "gloriously impossible" mystery of transcendence-and-immanence, the question is not whether or not they will get bogged down in particulars, but which particulars are sinking sand and which particular is the generally solid rock.

The Homecomings I had witnessed struck me as broadcasting and recommending a particular southern culture. As I mentioned in the first chapter, the early Homecomings styled Gloria as an approximate outsider vis-à-vis southern gospel.[37] However, in my lengthiest recorded interview with Gloria, she conceded very little to me in the way of her distinctiveness from southern gospel culture and in the way of Homecoming regionalisms. Granted, as Gloria reminded me, the woman who married her southern-gospel-super-fan-spouse when she was twenty years old literally had spent "more time in [her] life in [southern gospel] than out of it." Granted, this conversation took place in 2008, nearly two decades from those early, roughly edited tribute/reunions in which she played less visible roles. Moreover, the Homecomings had changed. If the Homecomings of the aughts were "southern," to some degree they were only as southern as their scriptwriter—and how southern was that? I wanted to talk about particularity and difference. Gloria wanted to talk about the big picture:

> It isn't really about southern, northern. It's not about style. If you're really paying attention, Ryan, very little of the Homecoming is, truly is, what has now come to be known as southern gospel. There's contemporary, there's bluegrass, I mean um, Larry Wayne Morbitt that starred for eight years on Broadway was on the *Hymns* video and fit there perfectly, nobody said, "Oh, what's he doing here? He's not southern gospel." We have Alabama. There are all kinds of styles.

The community of it is what is happening, and the shared love for this gospel message. What makes gospel gospel is the lyric. This pattern is country music, this pattern is bluegrass, this pattern is lots of songs that you sing in church that have outlived any style—it's not about style. It's about community. And maybe "southern," the reason that has grabbed people, is that we still think that in the South, there is community, as opposed to the urban North. And anybody who lives in the urban North knows that there's also community in Manhattan. But when you think of going back home, you tend to think about going to a more agrarian sort of place—some farmish community, where life doesn't move at quite such a pace, and where you have time.

In but a few sentences, Gloria reveals a central tension of the Homecoming franchise, especially as it looked to Gloria in 2008: how "southern" are they? How "culture-specific" are they? Initially using "southern" as a descriptor for a musical genre (her first two invocations of this term seem to mean "southern gospel music"), Gloria reprises a chorus I heard from a surprisingly large minority of Homecoming fans: the Homecomings are not "truly" southern gospel music, or they are not "what has come to be known" as such—the implication being that either southern gospel music has changed (presumably outside Homecoming influence), or that the Homecomings are not containable within the agreed-upon parameters of southern gospel music. At most, the Homecomings incidentally include some southern gospel; at least, they are not southern gospel venues.

Were Gloria only using "southern" to signal a musical genre, the items of evidence she uses to establish the Homecomings' cosmopolitanism would be more persuasive—though southern gospel, bluegrass, Alabama, and even the often-Nashvillean contemporary Christian entities she names certainly do not come from vastly different cultures.[38] If Doug Harrison is correct about southern gospel theatricality, even a Broadway star is well within the genre's parameters.[39] However, Gloria comes to use "southern" to signal a particular way of life—one that she is recommending as a norm. "Southern" means "agrarian," and "agrarian" means authentic "community." This community is predicated upon and conducive to a slower pace of life. Gloria's nearly inevitable positing of the agrarian South's regional opposite (the "urban North") as its *normative* opposite seems an endorsement of the "real America" narrative that was especially prominent when we spoke in 2008, as Sarah Palin and others were defining the stakes in the upcoming presidential election in just such unqualified terms.[40]

But Gloria qualifies herself. She believes, or she wants to believe, that the "community" she advocates is a transregional, and therefore a transcultural, value and possibility—realizable for Manhattanites and rural Georgians alike (what goes on in Atlanta, or rural Vermont, she does not discuss). As Gloria continued to talk to me, she clarified what she meant by community. The stakes of the struggle became clearer; the struggle did not resolve. "I think our society right now is in a stage of isolation, alienation—at the same time so much stimulation," she said. To illustrate this point, she again invoked an urban space, this time with more subtlety: "You think of isolation, you're alone; but you can be isolated worse, much more, in a crowd, when you don't belong." She provided one example of isolation: "I mean, who even invites people to their house for dinner anymore? Because our crazy life— you meet somebody at a restaurant; that's how people have community, and everybody else is watching. You're not in an intimate setting." Having community required walking the fine line between intimacy and isolation. Community was necessarily plural, but to have *true* community, people had to recuse themselves from gatherings in which individuals were legion and on display but essentially unknown to, and uninvested in, one another. This problem was not exclusively metropolitan, but metropolitans seemed especially susceptible. Gloria believed it was difficult for the urban soul to select her own society.

Gloria's true community is related closely to her hospitality: she wants community and hospitality, and she recommends what she sees as open, inclusive versions of both. But both require boundaries—and boundary keepers. Gloria's language in the quotation above includes and excludes. Much rides on her pronouns and common-noun-subjects. If the "we" of "we still think . . ." means "Bill and Gloria Gaither," and the "people" of " . . . grabbed people . . ." signifies the demographic who responds positively to the Homecomings, the whole Homecoming ship appears steered toward a very particular audience with very particular attitudes about the values that American southernness-and/as-rurality represent—and, conversely, that northernness-and/as-urbanity do not represent. It seems that the "anybody" living in the urban North whose experience belies the equation of southernness, rurality, and community are unlikely to be the "people grabbed" by Homecoming southernness. If "you" are not among the population who, "when *you* think about going home," think about "farmish" communities, it is an open question whether or not the Homecomings will resonate with you. Gloria claims she would like to bring you into the circle. She wants to make you feel at home, whoever *you* are. Whosoever will may come. But who will have the will?

By some metrics, citizens of the unincorporated zones of Gloria's America—the places where there is no assumed affinity between community, rurality, and southernness—rarely have the will. Despite the national and international appeal of the Homecomings, the franchise has never spent much time in New York City, or Vermont, or the Pacific Northwest, or Paris. If it did, perhaps its members would see things differently. I did not live in New Jersey or New York City very long before I became aware of the rooted-ness—the sense of community—that many residents of these places feel. The pride and involvement Princeton residents take in their public library and their farmers' market, the neighborhood block parties, the children walking to their neighborhood schools (schools that garner a great deal of pride)—rare was the occasion when I saw this kind of communal dynamism during my years in the South and Midwest. I have witnessed residents' nostalgia for Central Park at Christmas, for specific neighborhoods in Brooklyn, for the Brunswicks, the Amboys, and especially for the Jersey shore. Nostalgia may not be tantamount to "true" community. But if, as Svetlana Boym suggests, one definition of nostalgia is a longing for a once-real or an imagined home (a definition that matches well with Gloria's "when you *think* of *going* home"), and if, as Benedict Anderson suggests, imagination is a key constituent of communities, these other American nostalgias are telling. Not all people of all pasts are "grabbed" by southernness, rurality, home, and community all at once.

Bracketing Gloria's precision regarding Americans' realities, her assess-ment of the Homecomings' trans-southern appeal contains some truth. The Homecomings may roll through New York City less frequently than the Caro-linas, but there are Homecoming fans in these and other regions outside the rural South. Three phenomena may explain this broad appeal. The first is the phenomenon upon which Gloria herself insists when she speaks in her full anti-parochial mode: Homecoming viewers are drawn primarily to the "big picture"—the Homecoming manifestation and recommendation of "commu-nity"—not some specific "southernness." The multitude of Souths that per-meate fans' sensibilities, coupled with my limited contact with northern and urban fans, makes it difficult for me to assess precisely the extent to which Homecoming "southernness" is incidental to fans. But when all fans identi-fied the Homecomings' redeeming extra-musical elements, they discussed performers' familiarity with and love of one another. Almost none explicitly named these as essentially southern qualities. As Rebecca, a northern fan I will introduce shortly, demonstrates, fans can resonate with the sweet Home-coming spirit without wishing they were in Dixie.

A second phenomenon is American mobility. In addition to the movement of populations *into* America, Americans are on the move *within* America.[41] Even if an American is not mobile, she is increasingly likely to have friends and family who live in different regions. Social networking websites and the erasure of "long-distance plans" via cell phones, texting, and Skype have

increased the ease of contact between distant friends and family. It creates
the conditions whereby people who do not *presently* reside in the South or in
agrarian regions can feel some connection to these cultures. The connections
are real in the sense that they are felt, even if they involve idealization of the
region in question.

A third, related phenomenon is the nationalization of "the South" via popular media. Even if Gloria's equations of southernness, agrarian living, and
community do not map onto many Americans' experience, they map onto
many Americans' maps of American experience. John Egerton's 1974 work,
The Americanization of Dixie: The Southernization of America, was the first
substantial treatment of the cross-pollination between American and southern identity, and it continues to be the jumping-off point for social scientists
and cultural historians.[42] Media promulgations of southern living encourage
people to develop felt connections with a region and culture with which they
may have no on-the-ground contact. One can adopt a culture. If the culture
in question is imagined to be synonymous with "hospitality," it is even easier
for one to feel permitted to execute the adoption, for one is being adopted in
turn (country singer Lyle Lovett sums it up well in one of his most popular
songs: "That's right, you're not from Texas, but Texas wants you anyway").[43]
Recall the golf carts in the pickups parked at Roy's and Jen's "cowboy church"
in chapter 2. The reason a cowboy church can be a near-megachurch in a
region where actual farmland is giving way to subdivisions and golf courses
is that citizens adopt and adapt rurality and much that goes with it (Gloria's
term, "farm-*ish*," is appropriate). It is "country" because it so adorns itself. It is
"country" because it *used to be* country. Although it may require more acro-
batic autobiographical maneuvers, it is possible to imagine Brooklynites making similar appropriations; when they think of going home, they might think
of some farmish community, even if they grew up in a brownstone adjacent
to Prospect Park. Some of the best bluegrass music I have ever heard was
played in Prospect Park.[44] Is this native music, made by and for native listeners? Whose nativity, which musicality?

Gloria is partially correct: the Homecomings are about community, and
since a large group of people associate the South with rurality and with community, when people are "grabbed" by Homecoming community they just
so happen to grab Homecoming southernness, too. However, these associations are *made*—not simply, incidentally begotten. And they are *remade*, as
Gloria (re)cultivates viewers' habits and tastes, to the Gaithers' benefit. Gloria
preaches to the choir.

At the same time, Gloria's Homecoming role does not reduce to deference to and recapitulation of viewer tastes. She also produces scripts that

she intends to challenge the sensibilities of some in her audience. If Gloria is preaching to the choir, it is a choir that is not necessarily always singing in close harmony with her or with itself.

RISKING THE SUPREME FICTION

"Our audiences are always so warm, so receptive. I know this year will be no different. I promise that if you all stay where you are and listen, you're going to hear something special."

Never in previous shows had I heard Bill so deferentially massage ticketholders to remain attentive and in their seats. Sounding every bit the former schoolteacher in the Gatlinburg, Tennessee, auditorium, Bill seemed concerned that his "class" might embarrass him in front of their guest speaker that morning.

The guest was William Paul Young. Starting in 2007, the Oregon janitor-minister rose to fame through his novel *The Shack*. Self-published by Young with two friends, *The Shack* eventually found its way to the *New York Times* best-seller list.[45] The book tells the story of Mack, a father of three whose youngest daughter is kidnapped, apparently sexually tortured, and killed in a shack deep in the Oregon woods. Most of the novel takes place in these woods, where Mack meets the members of the Christian Trinity: Papa, a large African American woman; Jesus, a dark-featured handyman (he "appeared Middle Eastern"); and Sarayu, the mystically translucent East Asian Holy Spirit-gardener. More theological treatise than work of fiction, *The Shack* revolves around Mack's working out his theodicy in conversation with these three.

The Shack garnered widespread approval, but, it also fomented controversy in many evangelical circles. Passages such as the one in which "Papa" remarks, "I don't need to punish people for sin," caused some to complain that Young was too soft on atonement. Critics of Young's Trinity typically insisted that he did not distinguish sufficiently between the Three Persons—citing the fact that Papa bore Jesus's nail scars in Her hand as the mark of a pernicious patripassianism. The most common complaint pertained to *The Shack's* creeping universalism—most manifest in Young's carefully crafted, vague statement regarding the members of the kingdom of God: [Jesus speaking] "Those who love me come from every system that exists. They were Buddhists or Mormons, Baptists or Muslims, Democrats, Republicans and many who don't vote or are not part of any Sunday morning or religious institutions." Young's playful pairings read like an iconoclastic overreach into universal reconciliation to many evangelicals (among them, Southern Baptist Theological Seminary president Al Mohler, whose ilk got paired with Muslims). The past tense "They *were* Buddhists . . ." could vaguely refer to this-worldly conversion or post-death (and Christocentric) reconciliation. This last possibility elicited no small amount of howling from evangelicalism's most active heresy hounds.[46]

Bill Gaither seemed concerned. Fans trusted the Gaithers to provide a quality product. By the sheer fact of his presence on the Gaithers' stage, Young should have secured at least a bit of sympathy from the audience. But Bill apparently thought his guest required a more forthright endorsement.

Whence this risk? The Gaithers did not stand to expand their fan base by inviting Young. Devotees of *The Shack* who had no Homecoming ties were unlikely to attend a three-day gospel music event in eastern Tennessee over Memorial Day weekend just to hear Young. This was a *Homecoming* event, first and foremost. And Family Fest was a musical event at its root; the Gaithers hardly needed the presence of a potentially controversial speaker to bolster ticket sales (Bill later informed me that a small number of people returned their tickets after they heard Young was speaking). Rehearsing the possible explanations for Young's appearance, I kept returning to the summer prior to this Family Fest, when I paid the Gaithers a week-long visit in Alexandria. The Gaithers and I were all writers and readers, so we often discussed writing, books, and authors over meals. Astonished that I had never heard of *The Shack*, they praised it effusively. Gloria all but insisted that I read it as soon as possible, plucking for me a complimentary copy from the shelves of Gaither Family Resources. The Gaithers believed in the book's message, as they understood it, and they believed in sharing it. The Gaithers had delivered *The Shack* to me. In Gatlinburg, they were delivering William Paul Young to their Homecoming faithful. They were evangelizing all of us.

In Gatlinburg, Young developed Bill's risk-management prelude into a masterful oratorio. Moseying the circular center stage in jeans—no podium, no script—the avuncular author spun his story into a homecoming story. He began by recounting *The Shack*'s inauspicious inception—written for family members, never intended to be a best seller, rejected by twenty-six commercial publishers, self-published through a press Young started with some friends. He told of his mother's initial reaction to *The Shack*: upon finishing it, she called Young's sister and informed the latter that her brother had written a "heretical book." It was not until a kindly Episcopal priest, a distant friend of the family, discussed the book with Young's mother that she changed her mind and theologically reconciled with her son.

In a seeming *non sequitur*, Young then flashed back decades, to tell the story of a premature birth. A medical necessity had required a pregnant woman

to give birth to her baby several weeks early—so early that it was more surgery than "giving birth" (though Young chose the latter term). Since this happened before technological advances made fetal viability nearly redundant,
this fragile entity, small enough to be held within one hand, seemed destined
not to survive. The woman's doctor took the tiny being, handed it to his nurse,
and said, "dispose of it." (Young rehearses the doctor's words mechanisti-
cally; the Family Fest audience lets out a collective gasp.) Instead of dispos-
ing it, the nurse wrapped it in a warm cloth and hid it behind some medical
equipment—a makeshift incubator. Unbeknown to the doctor, for weeks she
nursed the infant to reasonable health. Despite early medical complications,
the baby survived. When Young finished the story, he revealed that it was told
to him by the same priest who had talked to Young's mother. The priest knew
the story because *he* was the infant. For the rest of the weekend, I could barely
access Young's merchandise table due to all of the people gathered.

Young's extroverted, affable nature helped to endear him to the Family Fest
crowd (when Bill introduced him to me backstage, he gave me the biggest
hug any stranger has ever given me). His onstage narrative all but guaranteed
him a hospitable reception. Like the Homecoming nativity story, Young's tale
riffed on biblical stories: Moses in the bulrushes, Hagar and Ishmael, Joseph's
reconciliation with his persecutor-family, even the Holy Family's exile into
Egypt. He counts on and plays on the pro-life leanings of the crowd. The doctor is the cold instrument of contemporary secular medicine—privileging
statistical probability over the probable impossible; the compassionate female
nurse bets against the house of technocratic rationality. Out of this Egypt
God called a son—an Episcopal priest—and that son facilitated a mother-
child reunion: a sort of homecoming. The saga pairs well with the story it
follows: *The Shack* almost did not see the light of day. It was rejected—in at
least one case by someone whom Young may have hoped would have cared
for it. It took a faithful remnant of people willing to bet against the odds to
see it through to the full light of the marketplace. Homecoming fans may note
another harmony: William Paul Young and Bill Gaither both turned what
started as labors of love, meant for their inner circles, into best sellers. In both
cases, market success was unexpected and inadvertent. The products' nativity
stories move the products.

Young probably did not mollify all audience members who balked at *The
Shack*'s "heresies." However, the immediate audience reaction and weekend-
long attraction to Young (and to his merchandise table) suggested that Young
had won at least some charitable witnesses, if not some converts. The character and economy of his Trinity, the non-retributive nature of his divine
justice, his sidelong Christocentric universalism—all of those doctrinal

"content matters" that so many evangelical apologists identify as the integral stake around which intraevangelical solidarity is constructed—were shunted to the penumbra of the spotlight. Young knew that he and the members of his audience were walking stories, not walking creeds; on the Homecoming stage, he related to people through stories. Relating to and through stories requires identifying (and perhaps identifying *with*) audience habits of feeling and seeing. It means knowing how and why a story about a nearly terminated premature baby will elicit usable horror, praise, and trust. If there was any possibility of audience members endorsing *The Shack*'s unsettling doctrinal matters, those audience members needed to understand that the author had settled *some* matters the same way they did. In this instance, Bible-suggestive narratives of danger and deliverance mattered more than the "inerrant" facticity of Moses's life story. *Roe v. Wade* mattered more than the Council of Nicaea or "the sinner's prayer." Upon these barely visible foundations, Young built and accomplished his mission. It was clear why Gloria Gaither had extended her invitation.

TELLING THE GOSPEL SLANT

"Why don't you all do altar calls at your concerts?"

"Because we don't leave still-borns on doorsteps."

I asked the question over my lemonade on the Gaither back porch, to any Gaither who would reply. Gloria gave the answer, then looked at me long and directly, drilling the point into my head with her steady, unsmiling gaze. I did not expect Gloria to slap down such an unnerving image, with such finality, like an ace in the hole.

Gloria had the ace ready because she was accustomed to the Gaither hand being called on this issue. Why don't the Gaithers offer that moment, near the end of their program, where audience members have an opportunity to accept Jesus Christ as their personal savior? So many other ministries on the Christian networks that air Gaither programs contain such a moment. Even Houston megachurch minister Joel Osteen—accused by so many evangelical Christians of "softening" the faith—closes his programs by leading all willing viewers in a truncated "sinner's prayer," which, if recited sincerely, means the one who prays has been "born again." The altar call even constitutes a regular part of Christian music concerts, particularly those many southern gospel concerts that occur in arenas and churches across the country. Why don't the Gaithers squeeze their eyes shut, reach toward the cameras with outstretched hands, and lead lost souls in their viewership to eternal salvation? Why not that moment at Homecoming concerts, when with every head bowed and every eye closed, lost audience members may raise anonymous hands to the sky, admit under their breaths that they are sinners, affirm the efficacy of Christ's salvific, atoning work on the cross, and ask Jesus to dwell within their hearts?

The Gaithers and their employees do not presume that they are singing to the unconverted—as is evidenced by their onstage usage of the first-person plural when they talk about Christians. While Christian rockers might assume that lots of lost souls bang bodies with the elect in the moshpits of Christian rock concerts, Homecoming performers assume that most southern gospel fans are among the elect—or, at the very least, that fans know the language of evangelical conversion.[47] The many jokes that Mark Lowry and other Homecoming funnymen tell about heaven and "getting saved" only work because everyone present assumes such matters are settled. Bill and Mark Lowry could not wonder jocularly whether or not Pentecostals would get to heaven (punchline: "yes, if they don't run right past it") if the multitude of ticket-holding Pentecostals did not appear in every other ticketholder's Book of Life.[48]

But the redundancy of a Homecoming altar call only partially accounts for the Gaither aversion to the practice. Gloria referred to "still-borns," not "prematurely-borns." The latter possesses life, the former does not. Following Gloria's metaphor, conversion, construed as a singular response to an altar call or as a onetime recitation of "the sinner's prayer," does not yield salvation, a life eternal. This is a bold claim for an evangelical to make, even implicitly.

In conversation and in her Homecoming scripts, Gloria has convinced me that she would not follow her metaphor to this end. She remains wedded to a conversionistic soteriology—of sorts. Gloria understands the Christian life of faith as irreducible to an identifiable moment—either of total capitulation to a set of doctrinal propositions or of heart-mind-and-soul surrender to Jesus. Without negating the potential import of such a moment, Gloria's lyrics and Homecoming scripts slide listeners away from a soteriology that plots conversion on a calendar and into a soteriology that constructs conversion as perpetual and experiential—a maneuver traceable to the Gaithers' Wesleyan/Holiness roots; one works out one's salvation in fear and trembling. At the same time, the Homecomings' portrayal of God's grace and love as superabundant nudges all Homecoming talk of salvation toward a sort of provisional, Christocentric universalism akin to Young's—one that maintains Jesus's death and resurrection as necessary for human salvation but one that leaves room for Jesus's sacrifice to cover those who do not respond to altar calls.[49]

The ninety-plus Homecoming videos that the Gaithers released between 1991 and 2009 are almost entirely free of "altar call moments." In addition to the Guy Penrod invitation I discussed in chapter 2, a notable exception occurs on *A Billy Graham Musical Homecoming* (recorded February 2001, released the following October), a two-volume set that includes not only Homecoming regulars but also a number of big-name Christian musicians who at some point in their careers graced a Graham Crusade stage: Ray Boltz, Andraé Crouch, George Beverly Shea, Michael W. Smith, and CeCe Winans. Filmed at Graham's retreat center in western North Carolina, the videos pay homage not only to Graham Crusade music but also to the iconic minister himself. As no Graham Crusade is complete without an invitation for lost souls to come forward to the stage and "accept Christ," the Gaithers close the videos with the nearest approximation to an altar call that they offer in their entire video catalogue. This moratorium on their "no-altar-call" policy is important, for in this instant viewers get a rare look at how Gaither soteriology fits into a Graham frame.

At the conclusion of the second Graham Homecoming video, Gloria reads her "invitation" as video footage of Graham Crusades (and footage from the just-ended program) rolls on the screen (italics and commas added to indicate emphasis and pauses):

> God *loved* this *world* he *made so much*, that he *came* as his *own son*, so that *all* who would *dare* to *recognize him* for *who* he *is*, and em*brace* that *revelation*, would *not self*-destruct, but *have life—life* that be*gins* with that *great* discovery and is *never snuffed out*, even by *death* it*self*.[50]

Anyone conversant with Billy Graham sermons would recognize immediately the biblical text Gloria appropriates: John 3:16. Those listening for this keystone Bible verse of evangelical soteriology will hear it—not only in the content of Gloria's words, but in her cadence. Gloria's reading follows the heavily iambic and anapestic rhythm and caesuras of John 3:16 as it often sounds in spoken-word liturgies (for *God* so *loved* the *world*—that he *gave* his *only* be*gotten son*—that *whosoever* be*lieve*th in *him*—would *not* pe*rish*—but *have* ever*lasting life*).[51]

However, Gloria gives herself room for improvisation. By not offering a chapter-and-verse citation of the passage, she preemptively exonerates herself from charges that she is changing or appropriating the biblical text—potentially pejorative charges in a hermeneutical milieu in which meaning typically is conceived as stable and extractable from a stable, authoritative text. Gloria clearly authors this passage. Even so, its close resemblance to the biblical text gives the passage the air of biblical authority—a sort of canonization-by-similitude. If one has a problem with Gloria's words, perhaps one should take it up with the "Author" of John 3:16.

What does Gloria 3:16 teach? First, Gloria 3:16 stresses God's creative work. John 3:16's "the world" becomes the more pointed "this world he made." The highlighting of God's intimate involvement with creation in these first eight words sets up the proceeding claim about Jesus. Neither a gift (sacrificial or otherwise) bestowed by a Heavenly Father, neither a "begotten" (eternally or otherwise) Son, Jesus *is* God come to earth. Only in the paradoxical "he came as his own son" does Gloria retain the Father-Son distinction. Because Gloria renders God and Jesus as *nearly* synonymous, all subsequent first-person masculine pronouns are vague (Gloria uses "he" for God before she introduces "the son"). For the remainder of the passage, "he" could mean God (the First Person of the Trinity), Jesus, or both. As a result, the "all who would dare to accept him for who he is" could include a number of populations. In Homecoming circles, one probable interpretation would follow evangelical conventions: "all" means those who accept Jesus as God Incarnate (i.e., "who he is"). But because "that revelation" has a number of possible antecedents—it could refer to God's deep love of the world, to God's creation of the world, to Jesus's divinity as a manifestation of God's love, or to all three—it is possible to read Jesus's divinity as *illustrative* of a broader truth, rather than as the truth itself, to be comprehended and accepted precisely, in all its particulars, like a proposition. The broader, essential truth is that God is involved in a loving way in the world God created.

Since the passage implies that the Incarnation is *the* illustration of God's loving involvement, Jesus remains significant. But the Christocentrism of Gloria 3:16 is not crucicentrism. Beginning with her replacement of "*gave* his only begotten son" with "*came* as his own son," Gloria downplays the notion of Jesus as sacrificial gift. Gloria renders Jesus's existence as God incarnate, not his death and resurrection, as the most pertinent reality. While Homecoming fans can attach the cross and empty tomb to the Incarnation—since Gloria's words occur after a program replete with songs about blood atonement, the Gaithers facilitate such an attachment—these supposedly fundamental evangelical aspects of Jesus's life are conspicuously absent from the final altar call. Gloria 3:16 is a Christmas verse—not a Good Friday verse, not an Easter verse.

The heightened sense of believers' agency also sets Gloria's passage apart from its biblical counterpart. Whereas the "whosoever" of the King James John 3:16 only acts once ("whosoever *believeth*") Gloria 3:16's "all who" act repeatedly. First, they must "dare to recognize" and "embrace" the revelation. Gloria later collapses these two actions into one "great discovery," a phrase that connotes a discovery *by* the self and/or a discovery *about* the self, and in any case highlights the self's agency. Failure to so act leads the self to "self-destruct"—in contrast to "perish," the common English-usage verb in John 3:16, which leaves unspecified the agent behind the self's destruction. The primacy of the individual will again demonstrates Gloria's Wesleyan/Holiness proclivities—proclivities about which both Bill and Gloria were consistently self-conscious and vocal throughout my fieldwork, onstage and off.[52] Granted, Gloria 3:16 could be amenable to Calvinist-leaning Christians, who typically cede less to human agency. God's revelation precedes human action. "Recognition" and "embrace" of revelation do not necessarily connote self-conscious acts of a will that precedes God's grace. "Self-destruction" is not necessarily self-conscious (Bill and Gloria are equally self-conscious about actual and potential Calvinist challenges to their theology, and intentional about crafting as well as they can a conciliatory, "big-tent" evangelical theology). Nevertheless, in Gloria 3:16, humans' responses to the revelation of divine love take center stage.

Another of Gloria's subtle but significant glosses on John 3:16 concerns what Gloria's born-again believer is saved *unto*. Like the biblical text, Gloria 3:16 nods to eternal life. But it is decentralized and vague. Rather than rehearsing the syntax of the typical English translation—verb and object separated by an adjective ("have everlasting life")—Gloria trims the phrase to verb-object ("have life") and follows it with an explanatory clause. She only notes the everlasting nature of this "life"—or, more ambiguously, the impotence of death to "snuff out" whatever this life is—at the very end of the clause. Gloria's Holiness roots show again, for sanctification looms behind this conclusion.[53] Being "saved" certainly can mean being *eternally* "saved," but the stress lies on the possession of "life" on this earth—a life whose lack of adjectival qualifications suggests that it is *the* life that God intends for humans to live.

Immediately after the 3:16 riff, Gloria concludes the program with the following words:

I guess in spite of our blustering denials, in our bones we know it: there is a God. And if this God is anything he is love so pure and powerful that we are recreated when we are touched by it. If a lifetime of trying to say that one simple truth makes even one of us embrace life that is life, Billy Graham and all who work and sing with him will have accomplished what God put them in our lifespan to do. His voice has been strong and true for over half a century. The rest is up to us.[54]

Regarding agency in conversion, Gloria equivocates a good deal more in these final words than she does in Gloria 3:16. The final six words—the most forthright cue that this is a sort of "altar call"—point to the responsibility of the individual in conversion. But the passage emphasizes the irresistibility of the recognition of God; our "blustering denials" are powerless to gainsay the universal, hard-wired human knowledge of God's existence. While Gloria's repetition of the injunction to "embrace life" (not "revelation" this time around) calls individuals to action, humans possess far less agency in this conclusion. It is "we" who "are recreated," "are touched" by God's love. God does most of the acting (as well as Graham and his ministerial cohort—filling a mediating role between God and potential converts).[55]

Thus ends the Gaither altar call. It is an altar call in which no Bible verse is quoted (directly), in which Jesus is never mentioned by name and only once mentioned as God's son, in which references to eternal life, sin, or substitutionary atonement are at most passing—a peculiar evangelical altar call, indeed.

The peculiarity and rarity of the Homecoming altar call does not prove that Gloria intends to overturn the entire evangelical scheme of conversion. One of the reasons she can render Jesus and the Bible in such a translucent manner in these few sentences is that Jesus and the Bible permeate the entire space. Jesus, the Bible, the cross, and eternal life all appear time and again in the ministry of the man to whom this particular Homecoming video pays tribute. One does not watch any Homecoming video from any period and wonder whether or not Jesus, the cross, and eternal life are key Homecoming entities. Gloria takes this all for granted when she delivers her altered call to Homecoming fans. Still, the peculiar altar call shows that there is an immense amount of room for improvisation within evangelical rhetoric and theology. Gloria and her Homecoming scripts illustrate how evangelical rhetoric can be altered from within—how evangelicals who are willing and able to operate within evangelical communities can make evangelicalism more inclusive without alienating those evangelicals who are committed to its more exclusivistic claims. The genius of Gloria's altar call—and the Gaither Homecomings themselves—is that, despite the absence of several of evangelicalism's usual rhetorical suspects (the Bible, sin, blood atonement), those who listen for evangelical conventions will hear them. Those who do not listen for them need not hear them—or, at the very least, need not centralize them.

* * *

I met John at a coffee shop. He was in his eighties, recovering from a recent illness that still manifested itself in his speech and mobility. He spoke loudly and gruffly, and it was hard for me to discern if his stridence was a consequence of passion, the effort it took to speak, or both. A lifelong fan and regional

performer of southern gospel, John had very specific ideas about what constituted quality southern gospel music—ideas that pertained more to content
than to style, as was evident in his criticism of the "new" Christian music: the
CCM and "praise and worship" music prevalent in his own church:

> JOHN: I don't think they sing enough about the cross. They don't sing enough
> about the blood. I don't like that.
> RYAN: So there's different thematic issues.
> JOHN: Yes.
> RYAN: How about the style of the music? Is there anything . . .
> JOHN: If they don't sing and talk about the blood of Jesus Christ and the cross,
> for me it's no good. That's me speaking.
> RYAN: But it sounds like you still tolerate it. You're still at the church.
> JOHN: Oh yes.
> RYAN: Is there anything redeeming about it at all?
> JOHN: [pauses three seconds] My wife likes it. [both laugh] Fifty-three years [of
> marriage], so we go ahead.

Given John's adamant crucicentrism, I expected him to have some problems
with some aspects of Homecoming theology.

> RYAN: If I'm watching a Gaither Homecoming video, what are the key ideas I'm
> getting?
> JOHN: What you wanna know that . . . the end of their songs, they tell you how
> you can be saved, what you can do about getting saved.
> RYAN: Okay, so there's a salvation aspect . . .
> JOHN: That's right. That's what salvation is all about, is people telling you all
> about his word and what's gonna happen.

As I spoke to John, Gloria's firm refusal to "leave still-borns at doorsteps" rang
in my head. At the time of John's interview, I had watched over half of the
ninety Homecoming programs (programs from every era of the series). I had
attended eight live shows—including the Sunday morning program at Family
Fest, which more closely resembled an evangelical church service than any
other show I had attended. With the exceptions I have noted, I never witnessed any moment like the one John was describing—the "altar call" moment
when the Gaithers or some other performer would tell listeners how to get
saved. If John meant that "the gospel" was embedded in the music, as was
an implicit invitation to accept Christ as one's personal savior, I could follow him. But John's commitment to the Gaithers' "direct" communication of

a salvation narrative—one that proceeded the singing—baffled me. Were we even talking about the same phenomenon?

In a way, no. This became clearer to me as I considered John's claim against the backdrop of the rest of our conversation. John has been singing gospel music since the age of four. His "phenomenon" extended back nearly eight decades—into small-town concerts, revivals, church "homecomings," into performances that likely preceded sermons, or altar calls, or both. Whereas scholarly necessity, relative youth, and a fascination with Gaither dissimilarity from other southern gospel musicians caused me to circumscribe the Homecomings as an isolatable entity for investigation, John drew no such boundaries. To him, the Homecomings were one current manifestation of southern gospel—the *quintessential* manifestation, the best the southern gospel industry had to offer, but still *one* manifestation. To again recall William Faulkner, southern gospel was to John not a diminishing road but a huge meadow, where long-gone and recent stages were divided only slightly, by the narrow bottleneck of the most recent years.[56]

John was unique among the fans I interviewed, both in the length of his involvement with southern gospel music and in his insistence on the presence of specific and prominent soteriological moments in the Homecomings. However, he was one of many fans I interviewed who told me that people who see a Homecoming will "hear the gospel." He also typified a large proportion of interviewees in his melding of the Homecomings with other southern gospel entities. Most of the Homecomings fans I interviewed had significant knowledge of southern gospel music outside of the Homecomings. Several had attended the National Quartet Convention, many numerous times. Many were musicians themselves—singing or playing in family bands and with groups in their church. A few traveled regionally and nationally as performers. After hearing interviewees ask themselves and me numerous confused questions regarding Homecoming personnel (*Are [southern gospel group] in the Homecomings? I'm trying to remember if I saw [artist] in concert before [he/ she] joined the Homecomings*), I realized that I was in the minority in my strict demarcation of the Homecoming stage.

I was in an even smaller minority in my knowledge of the Gaithers' "non-southern-gospel" endeavors. As I mentioned previously, almost none of my interviewees followed the Gaither Vocal Band in the 1980s. Most fans had pre-Homecoming familiarity with the famous Gaither songs written in the 1960s and early 1970s, but never did it come up that Gloria cowrote with Richard Smallwood "Jesus, You're the Center of My Joy"—that "contemporary classic" in black gospel that garnered a fresh audience in 2004 when *American Idol* star Ruben Studdard included it on his gospel album. Only one person

mentioned the Gaithers' decades-spanning, pre-Homecoming Praise Gatherings—annual festivals of Christian music (of all varieties) that, from an
organizational and structural standpoint, foreshadowed and informed the
Homecomings.[57]

The perceived porousness of the Homecoming stage vis-à-vis other southern gospel musical acts, coupled with the relative lack of familiarity with the
Gaithers' extra-Homecoming enterprises, made it easy for fans to import
whatever they regarded as standard southern gospel theology and practice
into the Homecoming space. The Homecomings facilitate the importation
by featuring longtime southern gospel groups singing the songs that made
them popular. All the while, new acts slide into the Homecomings space—
some who perform their own work, but many who cut their teeth on southern gospel standards. Only occasionally does one hear a Gaither-authored
tune—even so canonical a song as "Because He Lives"—in the early videos.
As time passes, members of the older groups die. By 2004, the Homecoming pool of performers is skewing noticeably younger. Gaither-penned songs
appear in greater proportions. "Homecoming classics" such as "Goodbye,
World, Goodbye," "I'll Fly Away," and "Your First Day in Heaven" make room
for the Gaithers' "Loving God, Loving Each Other," "Something Beautiful,"
and "I Then Shall Live." As these titles suggest, the Homecomings undergo a
gradual thematic as well as stylistic reorientation ("I Then Shall Live" takes its
title from evangelical apologist Francis Schaeffer's documentary film series
How Should We Then Live? and is set to the music of Jean Sibelius's *Finlandia
Hymn*). Songs about getting to heaven and getting away from "the world" still
appear in the later programs, but they no longer comprise the undisputed
center of the Homecoming corpus. But John's experience shows that fans still
can hear the "old-time gospel" in the Homecomings—and hear it loudly—if
they so desire.

However, this is not the only possibility.

* * *

I met Rebecca when she led an interfaith music program near the New Jersey
shore, at which I was performing. A vivacious Roman Catholic laywoman in
her fifties—office manager during the week, music leader for a few Catholic
and Protestant gatherings on weekends—Rebecca demonstrated an encyclopedic knowledge of psalm-singing and hymnody in her portion of the program. I judged by some of Rebecca's more transparent theological statements
(snarky comments about the church's stodginess, gender-bending God-talk)
that she leaned away from the strict orthodoxy of the church. I also surmised,

by her uninhibited singing and clapping during my bluegrass ensemble's performance, that she knew and enjoyed low-church Protestant music. Talking with her after the service, I learned that she loved the Gaither Homecomings. We set up a time to talk more.

Further conversation revealed that Rebecca grew up in the North, in the Hungarian Reformed church. In college, she majored in music. After graduating, she began assisting in the music life of several Roman Catholic groups as leader and teacher. One of her projects was helping tone-challenged and vocally skittish priests to sing better and more confidently during Mass. Somewhere in the middle of this thirty-five-year vocation, Rebecca "realized that [she] had in fact become a Catholic and just needed to do the paperwork." Although Rebecca described herself as a "card-carrying Roman Catholic," she traced much of her love for music to her Protestant background—singing in church, even performing in a few of Billy Graham's mass choirs: "I'm not sure if I had been raised a cradle Catholic . . . I'd be doing what I'm doing today."[58]

Rebecca was drawn to the form, the sound of music—"anything that makes music, or if we're talking, we'll take it right out of scripture, if it makes a joyful noise, particularly in harmony." However, when she began describing what she liked about the Homecomings, conversation turned from structural to social and theological aspects of music:

> There's something also very warm and embracing because, to me one of my theological principles is, "who hasn't been included," you know? And you look at the Gaithers and their intentionality of . . . first of all, putting out that this is a family, whether we're all related by blood, that doesn't matter. This is a family, you know? Catholics might call it, "this is the body of Christ." But there's something that really, again, is appealing to me, if you look at them on television or you go to a concert and there's couches all over the stage and they're all sitting around just being kin, you know? And that, that is the kingdom. That's the *kin*-dom [emphasis in original].

While Rebecca connected it to a "theological principle" more deliberately than did most of my interlocutors, she was like nearly all Homecoming fans I interviewed in believing that Homecoming performers genuinely, intimately loved one another. And like most fans, she suspected that she could tell if the Homecoming artists were merely putting on a show ("I have a skeptic meter that goes off, and it's pretty accurate, and I can't say that I have felt like this is just for the camera"). Despite the many heterosexual, reproductively prolific couples (and grandparents) that graced the Homecoming stage, Rebecca, a lifelong single woman, saw an extended family onstage. She felt like all people—or, failing that, many, many people—were included. This was just as Gloria intended.

Following her kinship/kingship statement, I tried to push Rebecca to name some aspects of the Homecomings she did not find "authentic" or edifying. The exchange warrants full quotation.

REBECCA: I didn't grow up in a monarchy, so it's not, you know . . . inclusive language or any of that kind . . . I don't have an experience of a king. I *have* experience of kin, so . . . and when I look at . . . that what's I . . . it's easy for me to sing, "Soon and very soon, we are going to see the King," but when you see that experience, or you have even experiences like [the psalm-singing she had just led], what pulled us really together, solid, quickly, was the song, you know? And everybody gave it their best, and it came together. God was praised, and you can't fake that, so that's where I'm thinking that [Homecoming "kinship"] is not just for the cameras.

RYAN: So I'm hearing the positive, but . . . the skeptic meter. There's gotta be . . . is there some stuff there . . .

REBECCA: Well, and I'm not slamming . . . it's not the Gaithers. There's some theology, the older I get . . . I would probably say my first *naïveté* was hymns, you know? Because there's some theology that's set forth in them that, you know, I have trouble wrapping my head around now as a fifty-five-year-old woman. So sometimes that will . . . I will hear a line in a song, and I have to work hard to right myself because . . . I can have a tendency to throw the baby out with the bath, you know, and say, "oh God, well forget it; if they're saying X, Y, Z, then how can . . ." you know . . . No, I can't do that. God's love is for all of us, and the world's big enough for all of us to operate, and if we do it, you know, with a genuine love and integrity and . . . I'll listen for the line or the idea that will be off-putting to me, then there will be a turn of phrase that just nailed it for me—that says, "yeah that's exactly what I felt like this week." You know, when we were singing before [in the psalm service], "my God! my God! Why have you abandoned me?" There isn't a person in the room, in the building, I'm sure, that hasn't said that in some language. Maybe not church language but . . . so it's . . . you know, you'll find what you need to hear. That's a little Buddhist, but, you know, you will definitely find what you need to hear when you're listening.

RYAN: So obviously, you're being waaay charitable [laughs] and I want you to get specific, though, like . . . is there a line or a particular theme that . . .

REBECCA: Truly? I can say that into the [points to tape recorder]?

RYAN: Yeah.

REBECCA: I don't want to hear that Jesus died for my sins.

RYAN: Okay.

REBECCA: I don't want to hear that.

RYAN: So that's the place where it requires more work for you as a listener?

REBECCA: Yeah, 'cause, you know, I'll just say, "No." [laughs] "Not really." [laughs] "But go on, keep singing." [both laugh]

RYAN: But something's going to come . . .

REBECCA: Yeah, yeah. My preference is always to recognize our worthiness, not our unworthiness. There's a line every week in the Catholic Mass that I just don't say out loud: "O Lord, I am not worthy, but only say the word and I shall be healed." That word [Word?] was incarnated, and I'm done. It's done for me, you know? It doesn't mean I can go out and be a real idiot, but I don't have to ask every week, or I don't have to . . . so it's in my faith, too. So there's all kinds of places—little hot buttons, let's just say—that I'll hear, and as I say . . . I grew up *absolutely* singing that Jesus died for my sins, and believing every word of it, and came to a different place, you know? So it's that kind of stuff.[59]

Only five words into her criticism, Rebecca exonerated the Gaithers for the faults she was about to identify in their programs ("it's not the Gaithers"). This statement could have meant, "it's not *simply* the Gaithers"—the theological problem was bigger than two people, or their franchise. But her earlier reference to the "intentionality" of the Gaithers in constructing what she regarded as the central communal feature of the Homecomings suggested that Rebecca believed the Gaithers' priorities—and, for the most part, their execution— were sound (I sensed, too, the sick [religious] artist myth at work here: the Gaithers were artists, not theologians, thus not to blame). Like John, Rebecca preemptively placed the Gaithers in her theological corner—or, at least she did not place them in the corner opposing hers. Like John, she connected the Homecomings to larger narratives and practices. When she identified the "kinship" manifest on the Homecoming stage, she connected it to her understanding of Catholic theology ("Catholics might call it, 'this is the body of Christ'"), her life experience of kin, and her musical endeavors (e.g., the psalm service that had just ended).

Also like John, Rebecca had an understanding of what sacred music could be, at its best, and she worked to harmonize the Homecomings with that understanding. However, Rebecca's naming of the "work" involved in her harmonizing set her experience of the Homecomings apart from John's. Unlike John, Rebecca expressed full awareness of a theology extant in the Homecomings that did not jive with her own. Faced with such a theology, she had to "work hard" to "right" herself. That Rebecca admitted to having to "work hard" testified not only to her discernment and self-awareness as a listener, but also to the heavy visibility in the Homecomings of a theology she eschewed. Something in the Homecomings cued her to fortify her theological defenses—defenses likely built up over decades of "unbecoming" one type of Protestant and becoming another type of Catholic. Certainly, her refusal to recite a portion of the invitation to Eucharist is of a piece with her selective approach to Homecoming theology. Rebecca's matter-of-fact statement of defiance ("I don't want to hear that Jesus died for my sins") seemed quivering in her holster, easily and bluntly wielded once the ethnographer who was digging for criticism reassured her that criticism was acceptable. Ironically, John *wanted* to hear in the Homecomings that Jesus died for his sins; he *did* hear it, and he did not say he had to dodge what he understood as inconsequential or subpar theologies to do so. Rebecca detected more obstacles in her way as she searched for her usable Homecoming. It was her self-described "Buddhist" hermeneutical mantra ("you'll find what you need to hear") that enabled her to conduct a successful search. Rebecca was looking for a broad communion in her Christianity; she would find it or she would make it—in the Homecomings as she did in Mass. At the same time, Rebecca had no bad blood for the "orthodox" in her communions. The hedges, she felt, were sufficiently wide and permeable to allow her to say amiably to her dissenters, "No, not really. But go on. Keep singing."

* * *

The apparent ease with which theologically conservative fans like John find what they are looking for in the Homecomings does not mean that fans simply "find" a meaning—or *the* meaning—inherent in the Homecomings, and fans like Rebecca simply project meanings onto them. Rebecca may "work" more strenuously and self-consciously than does John to discover her theology, but that does not mean that John and other Homecoming fans are not also filling in narrative gaps.[60] Just as Rebecca's experience, and her presupposition that inclusive communalism is a central principle of Christianity, shapes what she is looking for, what she finds, and what she must dismiss in the Homecomings (and Mass), so too does John's experience shape what he is looking for, what he finds, and what he must disregard in the Homecomings (and his home congregation; the theological transgressions of his church's contemporary worship music apparently do not override his wife's tastes). In fact, by some metrics, the chief Homecoming scriptwriter's theology may align *better* with Rebecca's than John's. Consider Gloria 3:16. The centralization of the Incarnation, the absence of the cross, and the downplaying of Christ's atoning work are common to Rebecca and Gloria. John would have to labor to make Gloria 3:16 fit his soteriology. The Homecomings facilitate John's kind of theological importations more frequently than Rebecca's largely because the Homecomings tend to be experienced by evangelical southern gospel fans against the discursive backdrop of a larger evangelical southern gospel world. Rebecca, the ex-Hungarian Reformed Christian, the erstwhile singer in Billy Graham choirs, brings a fluency in the evangelical Protestant tongue to her experience that affects her interpretive work. But she brings more.

Gloria Gaither makes it possible for fans to hear the commonest evangelical theology in the Homecomings. Given many fans' contexts, such a hearing is likely. As is the case with Homecoming "southernness" and "community," there are too many signs pointing the way to conventional concordances to deny that Gloria endorses at least some aspects of the concordances. But Gloria posts detour signs, too. Her Homecomings do not *insist* on the conventional paths. John and Rebecca *both* manage to find and centralize disparate (to some extent opposing) theologies. Gloria 3:16 has been variously translated; it remains open to interpretation.

THE UNACKNOWLEDGED LEGISLATOR

Authors matter. Even conceding that Homecoming meaning rides heavily on audience interpretation, the question of what *Gloria* believes and intends remains inescapable. A ship's actual course depends on the weather, the crew, and many other variables, but the captain wields significant directive power. If I am a passenger, it is reasonable for me to inquire about the captain's sobriety.

As I looked at Gloria's varied private and public scripts—all I had was scripts, and that is all she had with me—I wondered at the possibility of contradictions between them. What if Gloria concealed a more open-armed pluralism than some of her scripts let on? What if, were it not for having to appease the large, conservative portions of her fan base, Gloria would push even harder against the outer court's walls, extending unconditional invitations not just to theologically liberal Roman Catholics like Rebecca, but also to Unitarians, Muslims, or atheists? Conversely, what if Gloria harbored a tighter exclusivism than some of her scripts let on? What if, were it not for her having to court those potential customers just beyond the outer courts (one of whom was a university ethnographer), Gloria would honor the thick old fortifications, and Roman Catholics and other outsiders would be granted entry only on explicit, concrete conditions? In either case, if the scripts were too dissimilar from one another, Gloria would be guilty of an egregious kind of disingenuousness.

Further complicating matters was Gloria's fractured awareness of some of her exclusions and inclusions. Neither consciousness of intent nor control in execution are either/or states; Gloria's consciousness and control were partial. This was especially evident on the topic of southernness, rurality, and community. Her dismissal of the significance of Homecoming southernness and her gestures toward "communal Manhattan" suggest that she was throwing the Homecoming doors open. Like Bill, Gloria loved telling stories about Roman Catholics, Norwegians, and homosexual Jewish New Yorkers in their fan base; she delighted in the expanse.[61] However, her strong, persistent associations between community and the rural South suggest that she was not throwing the doors open as widely as she thought. Gloria seemed to regard her claims about "farmish communities" as universal truths, but to those actual and potential viewers whose universe did not testify to Gloria's, the truths were particular, disputable claims. Such viewers either had to accept Gloria's particular universals or explain them away as incidental to the Homecomings' essential meaning. They had to position themselves to say, like Rebecca, "no, not really. But go on. Keep singing." The further viewers perceived themselves to be from the visible cultural and theological core—the inner courts—of the Homecomings, the more self-conscious interpretive agility was required of them.

John, Rebecca, and nearly all of the Homecoming fans I encountered were drawn to the *authenticity* of Homecoming performers, epitomized in the Gaithers themselves. The Gaithers are so real. If "real" meant that all of one's scripts, public and private, presented a unified version of oneself, Gloria was "authentic" in a complicated sense: the same unresolved tensions between the universal and the particular, the same fluxional theologies, the same partial illuminations, appeared in all of her scripts. Her partialities are of a piece. There are eddies of meaning all over her work. They swirl and pool around some of the usual issues of American evangelical culture. Their motion is nearly imperceptible, but it is there—expanding and contracting the ranges of possibility. Hers in marginal work in reality and myth. She conducts it in the fluxional landscape often designated to artists, women, mystics, and philosophers—a seemingly simple landscape, one full of hidden meanings, partially understandable.

5

SOME WORK OF NOBLE NOTE

THE HOMECOMINGS IN THE
TWENTY-FIRST CENTURY

AMERICAN GOSPEL

In August 1998, the Homecoming ship docked on the banks of the Potomac River for a concert in Washington, DC's John F. Kennedy Center for the Performing Arts. Although the Gaithers had played on the center's stages off and on for decades, the Homecoming's booking in the main concert hall was a new landmark. The center's three main stages usually were reserved for ballet companies, symphonies, or musicians who contributed significantly to American culture. Although they may not necessarily have achieved the status of those awarded Kennedy Center Honors, main-stage performers often are representative of, or on their way to becoming, "American institutions."[1] This national stage implicitly requires musicians to showcase their particular contributions that, due to their particularity, typically manifest a culture or genre contained by, but less unwieldy than, "America" or "American music." It is a place for delivering signatures, not forging new ground. Willie Nelson likely would not perform a hip-hop set if he played the center. The Kennedy Center's cosmopolitan program is a national tapestry woven out of localized threads, and the threads become nationalized via the Kennedy Center loom.

It was somewhat predictable that the Homecoming ship would land in the Kennedy Center in 1998. The southern gospel music that the Gaithers had spotlighted since 1991 was distinctly *American*: born and reared in America.

In 1998, the Gaithers and the particular genre and culture they represented, with great success, loomed large enough to occupy the center's center stage. But what did the Gaithers understand themselves to be representing in 1998? The relative, intraevangelical cosmopolitanism that was subtly manifest in the early Homecomings was becoming increasingly salient (and increasingly cosmopolitan) as time progressed. Like the Kennedy Center, the Homecomings showcased varieties that formed a whole (recall Gloria's insistence that many styles were represented in the Homecomings). However, the Homecoming tapestry was not as variegated as the Kennedy Center tapestry. The former was a tapestry of synoptic gospels, and it would be but a thread in the Kennedy Center's American story.

But in *Kennedy Center Homecoming* (video released in 1999), the Gaithers lay claim to a larger American inheritance. The video implicitly argues, not so much that the Homecoming and its gospel are distinctly *American*, but that there is something distinctly *Homecoming*, and *gospel*, about America. In his opening voiceover on the video, Bill says that the program will explore "the roots of our country and our country's firm heritage in the foundation of faith."[2] In the middle of the video, Gloria appears in the center's Grand Foyer, its iconic bronze bust of John F. Kennedy visible over her right shoulder. She says,

> History has a way of sifting through our human choices and the ideas of the human mind, putting them to the test of time and leaving us with only those things on which it is worth building the lives of a new and precious generation. Fads and product and ideology may come and go, but the principles of the commandments given by God and virtues that allow us to live in honor, preferring one another, never change: love, peace, forgiveness, kindness, gentleness, joy, compassion, humility, faithfulness, integrity, truth, honor. These never go out of style. These endure forever. May these true qualities always be the definition of America and of those who bear the name of our Master.[3]

Speaking in this outer court, Gloria juxtaposes a number of big concepts and in so doing facilitates a number of interpretations. By asserting that the *principles behind* the commandments of God, rather than the commandments themselves, are timeless, Gloria gestures toward a moral universe founded on something other than, or higher than, some particular sectarian religion, Christianity included. People who hold to the timeless principles need not agree about the particular commandments, or about their procession from some particular deity. If they are truly the right principles, they will succeed; one cannot wrong the universe. When Bill talked to me in 2008 about the Gaithers' goals in the Kennedy Center program, he offered a slightly less general view: "I think you get a sense of the historical perspective and the importance that faith has played in our country from the beginning. I mean, obviously, there was a lot of effort made to separate church and state, but at the same time, there were a lot of people—not all of them but a lot of them— who were . . . you know, most of our laws on the book come out of *some* kind of faith, based *somewhere*. You can't kill people. You can't steal." Bill's comments rang with Protestant-Catholic-Jew-leaning theism: *some* vaguely Judeo-Christian faith undergirded the American experiment.

However, the principles and virtues that Gloria lists (in her rendering, "principles" and "virtues" appear interchangeable) would sound particularly Christian to evangelicals. Gloria's principles and virtues combine a number of New Testament texts, most evidently Galatians 5:22–23 ("But the fruit of the Spirit is love, peace, forbearance, kindness, goodness, faithfulness, gentle-ness and self-control," NIV) and Colossians 3:12 ("as God's chosen people, holy and dearly loved, clothe yourselves with compassion, kindness, humility, gentleness and patience," NIV).[4] As with Gloria 3:16, her verse is not a direct transcription of a single Bible passage, but Bible-literate Christians would rec-ognize her sources. Like her list, Gloria's final sentence may be read as a dec-laration of the conjunction of American and Christian identities (these "true qualities" define America and/as followers of the "Master"); it may express a hope for the eventual conjunction (these "true qualities" might come to define America and/as Christians); and it may signal complementary, mutu-ally informing, but not necessarily synonymous identities (why distinguish between definitions of America and Christianity, and why add virtues like *truth* and *honor* to the lists, if Americans and followers of the Master were identical?). As the blonde-bronze heads of Gloria and JFK share the camera, viewers are watching two universalizing entities attempting to subsume each other into their respective wholes. It is not clear if it is Christians, or Ameri-cans, or both together, who are "God's chosen people," clothing themselves in timeless virtues, in each other.

If the Gaithers are to have a compelling claim to this large share in the American inheritance (at least its principled parts), the Christianity they pro-mulgate in Homecoming speech and song must be large. The more particular Homecoming Christianity seems—the more it is narrowly white, rural, and southern—the more it risks forfeiting the persuasiveness of its claim vis-à-vis outsiders. However, the Gaithers also hope to promulgate a neglected particu-larity—to place some iteration of *southern* gospel, epitomized in the figures of "legends" like Howard and Vestal Goodman, Jake Hess, and J. D. Sumner, on the larger national consciousness. Too broad a gospel showcase would over-whelm the particular, particularly *southern* gospel present.

It is difficult for the Gaithers to be all things to all people in the nation's capital. But they try. *Kennedy Center Homecoming* bears the mark of the early Homecoming versions of old-time southern gospel. The semicircle of Homecoming regulars is as full as it is in any program. The Goodmans still occupy their front-row plush chairs. Bill still paces from end to end as he directs the ensemble. The setlist features southern gospel acts old and new, singing southern gospel standards further standardized by (and standardizing of) the Homecoming videos of the past seven years. The video begins and ends with "Old Friends."[5] But there are changes. The massive pipe organ in the background and the decorative flora in the foreground makes *this* Homecoming stage resemble a televangelist's church—an amalgam of James Kennedy's Coral Ridge Presbyterian Church and Robert Schuller's Crystal Cathedral. Below the organ pipes and above the Homecoming regulars is a massive choir. Their director is Geron Davis, writer of several contemporary praise-and-worship songs. Added to the live orchestral accompaniment, the choir makes *Kennedy Center Homecoming* "full gospel" indeed.

This Homecoming's stage is filled with gospel musicians and music outside of the southern gospel fold but within the Gaithers' wider gospel orbit. Larnelle Harris is present—performing a waltz-shuffle version of "America, the Beautiful" that recalls Ray Charles's popular 1972 rendition. Harris also performs with Sandi Patty their signature duet: the epic, Broadway-esque "I've Just Seen Jesus." Gospel music's Barbra Streisand (discovered by the Gaithers in the early 1980s), Patty had been a subdued, background guest in previous Homecoming choruses, but she was fully present as *herself* at the Kennedy Center.[6] Patty also performed the Gaither song, "Right Place, Right Time," a big-band-backed evangelical swing tune reminiscent of Kurt Weill's and Bertolt Brecht's "Mack the Knife." The Katinas, a DC-based, all-male family singing group from American Samoa, sing *a capella*. Looking and sounding like a contemporaneous boy band, the Katinas perform their own song, "One More Time." Addressed to a vague but apparently divine "You," the song could easily pass for a secular love song on another stage (the melody actually resembles The Captain and Tennille's 1980 single "Do That to Me One More Time"). However, Bill's introductory remarks situate the group in the musical and cultural tradition exalted in the Homecomings; noting they are from a large family ("eight boys, four girls"), Bill says the group "epitomizes family harmony at its best."

Kennedy Center Homecoming also contains a lengthy tribute to African American gospel singer-songwriter Andraé Crouch. Known outside gospel music circles for his frequent arrangement and direction of gospel-inflected pop recordings (Michael Jackson's 1987 number-one single, "Man in the Mirror," is the most famous example), Crouch rivaled the Gaithers in his prolific mid- to late-twentieth-century gospel songwriting—composing songs that, like the Gaithers', often crossed racial boundaries.[7] Bill introduces Crouch, who is seated in the second row of the Homecoming chorus, to the live audience as a living legend of gospel music. After receiving a standing ovation from the singers onstage (the audience is not shown), Crouch sits down at the piano and leads the gathering in his two staple songs: "Soon and Very Soon" and "The Blood Will Never Lose Its Power." The video contains an offstage dialogue between Bill and Crouch, during which Bill reiterates how Crouch is included in a "heritage" with (white) gospel songwriters Fanny Crosby, Stuart Hamblen, and Mosie Lister. For some (southern gospel fans?), association with Hamblen and Lister would validate Crouch. For some (fans of black gospel, or wider gospel music?), association with Crouch would validate Hamblen and Lister. For some, association with Crosby may well validate all three—or vice-versa. For some, Bill Gaither validates all four—or vice-versa. The members of *this* firm heritage are joined in a cross-credentialing sphere.

Kennedy Center Homecoming contains crossings of the sort that will occur in the Homecoming franchise through the first decade of the twenty-first century. In the six years that follow the video's release, the Gaithers will record Homecoming concerts in London, Jerusalem, Sydney, and Ireland. By the end of this period, the Homecomings will have made a splash in popular music unprecedented for a gospel group. In 2004, the Gaithers will appear on *Rolling Stone*'s "fifty wealthiest musicians" list, and the Homecoming road show will be among the nation's top-grossing music tours. During this period, they will begin hosting two "Homecoming Cruises" per year: one in Alaska, one in the Caribbean.[8] Benjy Gaither will produce four computer-animated children's videos, the "Gaither's Pond" series, which feature anthropomorphized water animals rendered to look like Homecoming cast members, who provide the voices.[9] During the same period, a number of the old "legends" will die: J. D. Sumner, November 1998, age seventy-three; Brock Speer, March 1999, seventy-eight; Glen Payne, October 1999, seventy-two; Rex Nelon, January 2000, sixty-eight; Hovie Lister, December 2001, seventy-five; Howard Goodman, November 2002, eighty-one; Vestal Goodman, December 2003, seventy-four; Jake Hess, January 2004, seventy-six; George Younce, April 2005, seventy-five. A number of younger, newer acts will edge into the Homecoming spotlight. I already have examined the changes in style, personnel, and form that the Homecomings underwent during the 1990s. The first decade of the twenty-first century will witness and require more stark changes.

In this chapter, I will use three Homecoming events to examine these changes. The first two are Homecoming concerts and videos set outside typical southern gospel and earlier Homecoming environs: the 2003 concert that took place at T. D. Jakes's Potter's House megachurch in Dallas, Texas, that yielded the 2004 videos *We Will Stand* and *Build a Bridge*; and the 2005 concert in Jerusalem that yielded the videos *Israel Homecoming* and *Jerusalem Homecoming* (2005). These events are "outside" (and "inside") southern gospel and the Homecomings in different ways. The Potter's House videos are among the worst-selling in the Homecoming catalogue—especially in comparison to the other Homecoming products released around the same time. The Israel videos are among the Homecoming's later platinum sellers. Unlike Homecomings that take place in the friendly confines of Gaither Studios, or even in southern and midwestern sporting arenas, these Homecomings have vacated the old home places. To the extent that the old home places remain, the Gaithers must transplant them or reconstruct them.

To be sure, the Gaithers did not totally vacate the old home places in the twenty-first century. The weekend-long Gaither Family Fest that I attended in 2009 is the third event on which I will focus. Specifically, I will examine the array of women and femininities present onstage and in the audience during that Memorial Day weekend in Gatlinburg, Tennessee. Although the role of Homecoming men changes after the deaths of the "legends" celebrated in the first Homecomings, the problem of Homecoming "regeneration" is especially salient for Homecoming women after the likes of Vestal Goodman, Eva Mae Lefevre, and Faye and Mary Tom Speer leave the stage. As I will show in this and the final chapter, twenty-first-century Homecoming women (and "womanhoods") proceed in several directions—none of which recapitulate the southern gospel matriarchs of the 1990s.

FADING MARGINS

In a press release the week before the collaboration between "America's Best Preacher" and "The Gospel Songwriters of the Century," Bishop T. D. Jakes and Bill Gaither both expressed excitement over their upcoming event.[10] "I'm elated about the opportunity to commemorate the cultural and ethnic diversity of gospel music with a man who has contributed so much to the gospel community for so many years," said Jakes. "This event comes at an opportune time displaying unity while there is so much uncertainty and division in the world." Bill said, "For years it has been a dream of mine to create an experience where musicians from various ethnic backgrounds come together for an event like this. Now to see this dream is reality, particularly alongside someone like Bishop Jakes, is quite unbelievable."[11] This was to be full gospel, in concert.

Bill was not exaggerating about his dream. The *We Will Stand / Build a Bridge* event was the completion (or resumption) of a project Bill began in 1994. That year, given the outpouring of interest in his celebrations of *white* gospel music, Bill decided to orchestrate an African American version of the Homecoming programs. He hoped to showcase classic black gospel, to pay tribute to pioneering African American gospel musicians, and perhaps to approximate the returns of the early Homecomings. Proceeds from the video would be used to set up a trust fund for struggling and ailing black gospel musicians—akin to the Gospel Music Trust Fund, started in the early 1980s by Nashville talent agent Herman Harper to help gospel musicians in Nashville circles (the Gaithers were strong supporters).

In 1994, Bill assembled a large group of black gospel singers in his studio—among them such gospel "legends" as Albertina Walker, the Barrett Sisters, Ralph Goodpasteur, and the Mighty Clouds of Joy. As was the case with their Homecoming counterparts, the group sang for hours as the tape rolled (on this occasion for three separate six-hour sessions), the singers passing the solo microphone among themselves during the songs. Canonical black gospel songs such as "Take My Hand, Precious Lord" and "Great Day" comprised the setlists. The sessions were almost as loosely organized as the first *Homecoming* video; judging by the degree to which the choir seemed occasionally caught off guard by transitions in the music, the setlists were guidelines, not rules. As in the Homecomings, the musicians sometimes wept, embraced, laughed, and told stories in between songs, though this element of the program tended to be more formulaic than it was in the early Homecomings; many of the "testimonies" and autobiographical accounts took place outside of the sessions and were edited back in to the final programs. Still, the two resulting videos, *Through It All* and *On My Way to Heaven*, remained sparsely edited; at times, the video shows the one hundred-plus chorus (and accompanying instrumentalists, whose live playing prohibited significant editing) performing for twenty successive, unspliced minutes.[12] The Gaithers are absent from the studio footage, only materializing in introductory voiceovers and in periodic interviews with some of the musicians—interviews in which musicians narrate black gospel history and explain some of the genre's stylistic idiosyncrasies.

Star Song printed a few test copies of *Through It All* and *On My Way to Heaven*. Although the Gaithers organized, recorded, and produced the videos out of their own studio, they did not own the performance rights for most of the musicians in the sessions. Nearly all of these rights belonged to Savoy Records, whose proprietor did not release them, citing to Bill his failure to see the need for a charity for black gospel musicians, in the era of "Bill and Hillary" (Clinton).

This was a major setback, but the Gaithers did not wallow in their annoyance. While the Gaithers already were executing a slow integration of the Homecomings in 1994—manifest in Doris Akers and the Fairfield Four's performances and in the front-row presence of Lillie Knauls—their interracial project became more pronounced after the *Through It All* / *On My Way to Heaven* fiasco. Jessy Dixon, a performer and key historical resource in *Through It All* and *On My Way to Heaven*, made his Homecoming debut in the 1994 session that produced *Precious Memories* and *Landmark*. From then until the late aughts, he would be a regular Homecoming performer. Larnelle Harris, member of a lesser-known (among southern gospel fans) 1980s incarnation of the GVB, appeared in the same videos. Although he was more known for his grandiose duets with Sandi Patty than he was for performing traditional black gospel numbers, and although he never became the Homecoming mainstay that Dixon did, Harris's dexterous vocal modulations and insistence on groove (in his *Landmark* feature performance, he playfully teases the assembly when he encourages them to clap on the eighth notes: "Now I know this is not '1' and '3,' but you can do it!") signal the presence of an African American—or, at least a distinctly nonsouthern-gospel—form of music.

Until 2003, Homecoming integration meant adding black musicians to its normatively white performance space. When the Homecoming came to T. D. Jakes's Potter's House Church in Dallas, things changed. The resulting videos, released in 2004, are certainly not normatively white. When Jake Hess and Vestal Goodman assume the Potter's House stage, they are not assumed to be home. Performing for the most visibly diverse audience and among the most visibly diverse performers of any live Homecoming, the Homecoming regulars are well received, but suddenly more conspicuous.[13]

These 2004 videos communicate some of the things the Gaithers wanted to say in 1994. *We Will Stand* and *Build a Bridge* represent the Homecomings' most forthright complication of southern gospel's primacy in the broader American Christian landscape. The videos also manifest Gaither pedagogy at its most democratic. While it is important never to lose track of their control over their products' narratives, Bill and Gloria assume minor roles in these videos, preferring to step back and let other people tell other stories, just as they did in the unreleased 1994 programs. The Potter's House videos contain clips of several offstage interviews between Bill and the performers. The first of these on *We Will Stand* takes place between Bill, Delores Washington, and Albertina Walker. "We are sitting in the presence of history here," Bill says by way of introduction of Washington and Walker. The latter, he points out, is known as "the queen of gospel music and the originator of the famous

Caravan[s]." Bill's sparse comments in all of his interviews with black gospel musicians evince his familiarity with black gospel history (my 2006 spelunking in the cavernous, fireproof, temperature-controlled safe that contains Bill's LP collection revealed a substantial collection of black gospel records). But Washington and Walker take the lead. At Bill's prompting, Walker tells her story in gospel music by way of roll call, rattling off the names of people and churches with whom, for whom, and in which she sang:

> WALKER: West Point Baptist Church in Chicago, James Cleveland, Willie Webb, Robert Anderson—those singers, they sang with Roberta Martin—New Covenant, Reverend Thurston, All Nations Pentecostal Church, which was Elder Lucy Smith, used to be on Oakwood Boulevard, First Church of Deliverance, Reverend Clarence H. Cobb . . .
>
> GAITHER: . . . and Ralph Goodpasteur was the music director of that church for many years . . .
>
> WALKER: . . . oh yes. Inez Andrews, Bessie Griffin.[14]

Walker's glossary (and roadmap) of twentieth-century African American pastors and musicians (in her case, mostly Chicago figures) is a common genre in African American church culture, where landmark ministers rhetorically are wedded to their landmark institutions. In the context of a Gaither video, the roll calls viewers to acknowledge a big American story. Even limited to Chicago (admittedly a monumental gospel city), the story of black gospel and African American Christianity looms sufficiently large to render white gospel as but one component of American Christianity and its music. White Homecoming fans may not recognize any of Walker's places or names, but they have heard roll calls before. Walker calls to Homecoming viewers who have heard Bill Gaither regularly call a roll that includes Jake Hess, Denver Crumpler, Burl Strevel, J. Bazzel Mull, and Mull's gospel radio show.[15] Walker brings viewers' attention to a gospel legacy at least as hefty as southern gospel's. Walker's (and Bill's) invoking of the institutions and churches in black gospel complicates Bill's claim in the 1993 *Turn Your Radio On* video, that the transmission of black gospel heritage is mostly private. In any case, Bill has been waiting to give this history his public attention. He says in the interview that he has known Walker "for about ten years," which means they met around the time of the *Through It All / On My Way to Heaven* sessions.

While *We Will Stand* communicates a distinct black gospel history, it also communicates the traffic between white and black gospel. Although segregation was (and is) a gospel reality, black gospel was not and is not *wholly* other from southern gospel. The Gaithers tell of the traffic by historicizing canonical styles and songs. When Jake Hess takes the stage to sing Genser Smith's "Sweeter as the Days Go By"—a well-known song in white gospel circles—Bill prefaces the performance with a voiceover: "Jake Hess sang with the Statesmen Quartet back in the early 60s a song that came out of the black church."[16] *Build a Bridge* features a tribute to Dorothy Love Coates, writer of "Get Away, Jordan"—another song made popular in the mid-century white gospel world via an early Statesmen recording. A few years after *Build a Bridge*, "Get Away, Jordan" would roll back onto the Homecoming stage via vivacious, choreographed performances by Ernie Haase and Signature Sound.[17] The videos certainly leave the impression that white gospel owes much to black gospel. The most "distinctly white" music in the programs is of two sorts: centuries-old European music or contemporary, often Gaither-authored songs—though the latter bear the mark of stylistic cross-pollination. The all-white family trio, the Martins, bring the house down with a harmonically intricate, nearly flawless *a cappella* rendition of the 1561 hymn "All People That on Earth Do Dwell." While the Martins commonly perform *a cappella* songs on Homecoming stages, their selection and arrangement in *this* video seems to stand for the high-water mark of European Christian music. The Potter's House choir sings the Gaithers' "Let's Just Praise the Lord." Their version contains a number of black gospel music signatures: abrupt caesuras followed by fortissimo vocal explosions (*let's just* [rest, whomp of the kick drum] *PRAAAAISE THE LOOOORD*), tenor-soprano-alto harmony, and an instrumental mix that features the drumset far more than it is featured in most Gaither programs. The choir closes *We Will Stand* with a rousing version of the Gaither/Richard Smallwood piece, "Jesus, You're the Center of My Joy." As this song was a cross-genre, interracial collaboration from the outset, and as the video culminates in its performance, the song seems to represent the Gaithers' ideal synthesis of cross-cultural exchange. The song is the Gaithers' proof of their interracial purchase. It signals that they are more than tourists in black gospel worlds. Two years before the Potter's House event, Delores Carpenter's and Nolan Williams Jr.'s *African American Heritage Hymnal* included "Center of My Joy," along with five other Gaither songs.

Aspects of the Potter's House videos' gospel history remain whitewashed. The friendly, abbreviated stories of songs and adaptations across racial boundaries imply neighborly lending—love, not theft. The Gaithers' own 1994 difficulties surrounding copyrights prove that interracial exchange does not preclude profound racism. It would be easy for white viewers to transpose the videos' very pertinent lessons—that there always has been continuity between races in gospel music, and that black gospel has a rich history—into a major key: the races have always basically gotten along, separate but cordial. The question of how much it is reasonable to expect from a Homecoming event in the way of complicated history-telling is especially difficult to answer in the case of these videos. In this instance, the Gaithers intentionally abandon the white, southern gospel normativity of most of their videos. How much dissonance—or what balance between unity and dissonance—should these videos attempt to achieve? To return to the language of Anderson and Foley (see chapter 3), are these videos mythic or parabolic—the occasion for celebrating Christian unity across difference, as Jakes's comments in the press release suggest, or the occasion to bring attention to past and current divides? Is the very filming of an alternative mythic (beloved, unified, *interracial*) community a parabolic gesture, problematizing the Homecomings' old mythic (beloved, unified, normatively *white*) community? Or are the Gaithers simply augmenting mythic with mythic, playing around all of the unresolved chords?

Much depends on white fans' views—or, in this case, how one interprets fans *not* viewing. That the Gaithers had a difficult time selling *We Will Stand* and *Build a Bridge* suggests that the videos introduced *some* significant discontinuity and discordance into the Homecoming world (it is important to note, too, that the covers of these videos do not include the word "Homecoming," though they are identified as being in the "Gaither Gospel Series"). The Homecoming engine was in high gear when the Potter's House videos hit the shelves. During and shortly after that flush year of 2004, the Gaithers had few problems moving most products. The Potter's House videos may have remained on the shelves because they were parabolic interruptions of the mythic Homecoming catalogue. If black bodies themselves signified discord to white Homecoming fans, *We Will Stand* and *Build a Bridge* could remain on the shelves and still be parabolic; all it took were the visages of Jakes and Mom Winans on the DVD covers.[18] If fans viewed the programs and interpreted the prominence of nonwhite people, cultures, and histories as dissonant, the videos served a parabolic purpose.

However, in the videos, the Gaithers and Jakes proffer a vision of racial reconciliation that might sound familiar to Homecoming fans—perhaps to most conservative white evangelicals. During the longest narrative interlude of *We Will Stand*, Bill interviews Jakes about his ministry.

BILL: You don't promise easy solutions for difficult problems.
JAKES: You have hit the core of what my ministry is all about.
BILL: Sure.
JAKES: I walked up on the stage terrified that if I told the truth that they'd laugh me off the stage.
BILL: Sure.

JAKES: That if I talked openly about the pains people confront and the crises that they go through, it wasn't popular . . .

BILL: Sure.

JAKES: . . . and I was terrified. And it was amazing to me—instead of running from me, people started running to me, saying, "me too! I've been there, too. I feel you. I understand you." And it wasn't just black people. It was white people. It was brown people. And gradually we started translating the material to other languages.

But I tell people that pain is a common denominator. We all experience it. We all go through it. And when we can't relate to anything else about each other, we can relate to the struggles and the turmoil that we go through. You start talking to the Jew about the Holocaust, and you start talking to a black man about slavery, and you start talking to a poor man about a starving child that he lost, and you start talking to an Indian who's locked up in a cage, and it doesn't matter the details are different, because the pain is the same.

If you don't believe it, go into the nursing home and watch how the old people don't argue with each other—just elderly people in the same situation, perhaps becoming friends for the first time, sitting down eating with people that thirty years ago they'd have never ate with before. But crisis brings us together in a way that we would never come together before. Or look at the Vietnam veterans—guys in the foxhole together. What's great about what we're doing is, without some terrible situation occurring, we came together just because we wanted to. And there we were, up on the stage singing together. We're not in the foxhole, we're not in the nursing home, we're not in a crisis. We're just there because we want to be—black, white, young, old, lifting our hands singing our songs. And maybe we're starting to learn that we don't have to wait till we're at the funeral home or the nursing home before we join hands and start singing together. We can do it now.[19]

When Bill tells Jakes, "you do not promise easy solutions to difficult problems," Bill is articulating his own ministerial intent. If there is one thing I am sure about regarding the Gaithers' self-conscious intent, it is that they do not want to promulgate what they view as a dubious "prosperity gospel" or "faith-healing" message. In nearly every in-depth conversation I had with Bill or Gloria, they differentiated health-and-wealth ministries from their own. I regularly heard them make similar overtures on their live stages. They do not discount the possibility of Christians experiencing financial blessings or miraculous healings, but they do not intend to proclaim the end of Christianity as a this-worldly escape from hardship, or to encourage fans to believe that one can measure one's faith by one's health or wealth. Andraé Crouch's "Through It All" is a standard in Homecoming setlists—*through* it all, not *over* it all.

The Gaithers' anxiety about being likened to "health-and-wealth" ministers is understandable. Televised Homecomings often run adjacent to such ministers' broadcasts. Furthermore, the Homecomings run on the power of positive singing. While the very visible deaths and physical declines of Homecoming performers check any belief that optimistic faith necessarily yields temporal deliverance from pain, many of the tears that flow during the Homecoming are tears of once and future joy. Although the Gaithers are critical of southern gospel music's historic obsession with the heavenly rewards that await the saints, death gives way to victory—somehow, always—in the Homecomings. Skeptical toward prosperity gospels' meretricious meritocracies, yet willing to broadcast in the high resolution of heaven, the Gaithers feel the burden of delineation—a burden that is perhaps endemic to anti-prosperity gospel, heaven-believing evangelicals, and perhaps explains why such evangelicals are among the harshest critics of health-and-wealth evangelists. How, precisely, does proclaiming heaven's *ultimate*, happy resolution for the faithful differ from proclaiming *temporal* happy resolutions for the faithful? Do not both proclamations promise a final certitude, peace, help for pain? Evangelicals have theological answers to these questions—answers that vary in their consistency and depth.[20] But the theological answers must be loud and repetitious to circumvent practical family resemblances. The Gaithers work hard to clarify *their* version of gospel deliverance.[21]

It is not surprising that Bill's conversation with Jakes provides an occasion for clarification. Jakes likely feels Bill's burden of delineation. He airs his programs in the same milieu as do the Gaithers. His messages often thematize personal deliverance through the power of the Holy Spirit. His best-selling book *Woman, Thou Art Loosed!*, published the same year as the *We Will Stand / Build a Bridge* videos, became an annual conference and was adapted into a movie and stage play of the same name. Addressing himself to Christian women, Jakes recommends members of his audience regard themselves as fully liberated in Christ—free from substance addictions, from insecurity, from physical and psychological abuse. *Woman, Thou Art Loosed!* epitomizes Jakes's broader messages of personal empowerment and Christian freedom. Coupled with his enormous congregation and television ministry, these messages result in him being grouped with "prosperity gospel" ministers. The distinction between "the gospel of empowerment" and "the prosperity gospel" is hard to pinpoint. It often depends on the distinguisher's suspicions of the minister in question or unwillingness to engage the full content of the minister's message. It is not clear how Jakes is or is not a prosperity gospel minister. He wishes to clarify.[22]

Jakes's description of his ministry, peppered with Bill's affirmations, provides a glimpse into how the two Christian media giants understand their difference from health-and-wealth gospels. The primary difference: honest acknowledgment of the ubiquity of pain, even among the faithful. It is unclear what painful, pain-filled truth once "terrified" Jakes to speak; the general third person ("the pains people confront and the crises *they* go through") implies Jakes did not speak about his own struggles. But the empathetic responses he received suggest the pains sounded like firsthand experience. Multitudes responded; *all* have experienced pain and crises. Jakes's health-and-wealth peers cannot or will not acknowledge this truth.

As Jakes continues to speak, it becomes less clear how his ministerial lens corrects the health-and-wealth vision. Jakes translates the common fact of pain into the commonness of discrete painful experiences: "pain is a common denominator," *ergo*, "it doesn't matter the details are different, because the pain is the same." Jakes then offers a litany of examples of general pain cloaked in particularity: "the Jew"/Holocaust, "a black man"/slavery, and so on. Although American slavery and the Holocaust are particular historic atrocities, in Jakes's rendering they also stand in for present-day personal suffering. As rhetorical placeholders, they shunt attention away from present bodies undergoing present suffering—often due to present oppressors. True, some present-day black men or Jews might have direct or strong second-hand experience with slavery or the Holocaust, but more will have experience with other kinds of suffering. Talking with actual, present people would prove the details of suffering do matter—not simply because one must look in the eyes of discrete suffering persons, living in dynamic and discrete contexts, but because one would be forced to confront the reality of discrete oppressors with discrete motivations. Jakes names examples of human suffering that occur(red) at human hands, but he does not render salient human culpability. The erasure of the interpersonal nature of these conflicts effectively synonymizes them with, say, the pangs of aging or cancer. If "the pain is the same," losing a loved one to an Auschwitz gas chamber is the same as losing a loved one to a heart attack. It is a tragedy if one suffers a heart attack or genocide. But faith will allow us to endure through the pain, even unto death.

Surely, there are Homecoming viewers for whom Jakes's message is a challenge. Surely some people—all people, sometimes—are callous to the mere fact of others' pain and need provocation to countenance it. Moreover, if Jakes's (and perhaps Bill's) implication that their televised health-and-wealth peers are "pain-deniers" is correct, Jakes's solutions to life's difficult problems are indeed more honest, less easy. However, to countenance actual pain is to countenance actual, differentiated human beings. Jakes's denial of particularity or its import—evident in his nursing home analogy—suggests an unwillingness or inability to countenance human beings. During much of my research project, my spouse was a chaplain at an assisted living facility. I have heard the tales and talked to the citizens of that space (not just "watched" them). A minister would have to be under heavy sedation to walk through those halls and detect no signs of interpersonal conflict.

If the details do not matter, and if pain is an ineluctable fact of life, Jakes leaves himself few resources for addressing unjust suffering directly traceable to human oppressors. The year after the *We Will Stand / Build a Bridge* videos were released, T. D. Jakes joined Oprah Winfrey in the New Orleans Superdome, speaking over the public address system to console the thousands of people displaced during and after Hurricane Katrina. Jeff Stout reports that the community organizers present—most of whom were Christians—took issue with Jakes's attempts at consolation: as one organizer remembered it, his advice to the displaced to "just trust in God [...] . Everything is going to be fine." Some of the community organizers managed to gain access to the public address system, to challenge Jakes's theology, and to call local civic and church leaders to begin organizing meetings inside the Superdome. Several hundred came together to pray, to share stories about what had happened in their locales, and to explore concrete measures that local citizens could take to repair community breaches and prevent further damage. Likely, Jakes understood himself to be responding compassionately to victims of a natural disaster. The organizers understood themselves to be responding to and preparing for less natural disasters.[23]

If the theological anthropology of suffering that Jakes articulates in *We Will Stand* is an alternative to health-and-wealth gospels, it is not a significant departure from the theological anthropology of other Homecoming programs. The Gaither-Jakes treatment of pain depends upon and rearticulates Homecoming apoliticism as an eschewing of interpersonal conflict. As was the case with Gaithers' vision of community that I explored in chapter 3, this eschewal works against the apparent goals of the Potter's House concert and videos: racial reconciliation and harmony. The Gaithers have more than a passing interest in racial reconciliation and harmony. Harmony usually contains the promise of consonance and eventual resolutions, but it also requires multivocality. The best harmonizers in history have known how to use dissonance and suspension to new ends.

✳ ✳ ✳

On more than one occasion, Bill told me that "good theology is good psychology." His chief example: the past can and should be left behind. God's forgiveness and grace washes sinners white as snow. One need not live under the burden of the past. It is finished. The account is settled. Given that the Homecomings' currency *is* a southern gospel past, this seems contradictory; Bill cashes in on usable pasts and rejects others. However, when Bill is talking about the past in a psychological/theological context, he is not imagining people who have been oppressors or who have been the beneficiaries of oppression. He has another population in mind.

The evening session of Gloria's inaugural songwriting workshop had ended. It was July 2011, and given where Alexandria was located in the time zone, even nearing ten o'clock, even with some gathering clouds, there was some faint light in the sky. I exited Gaither Studios with Bill, Gloria, and a handful of workshop leaders. We nearly tripped over a woman sitting on the short step just outside the door. She was crying and clutching her right ankle. It was swelling quickly; it looked like a bad sprain. Despite the fact that the woman could not put weight on the ankle, she did not want an ambulance or hospital care. In a panic-stricken voice, she told us that she had recently lost one job, she was just starting another, and she did not know if her new insurance plan was in effect yet. She also was upset at the prospect of missing the rest of the workshop, because she had saved and saved to attend. Bill told her not to worry about the medical costs and had an assistant call an ambulance to take the woman to Anderson's hospital, about twenty-five minutes away. Because the woman needed to go home straight from the hospital—she lived about forty-five minutes away from Anderson (in the opposite direction of Alexandria) and commuted each morning to the workshop—someone would have to drive her car to the hospital. I volunteered, since I was one of the few people not needed for the workshop early the next morning. Bill came in his car, too (he did not have to get up early, either). He would drive me back to Alexandria.

After following a lead-footed Bill through Madison County backroads that he knew by heart, Bill and I sat together for over an hour or so in the hospital waiting room. "There's no way she is going to be able to drive home on that ankle," he said. Around midnight, the doctor let us in to the woman's room. It had taken some time because the woman was taking numerous prescription drugs, and the staff had to sort out which painkillers were safe to give her. The tearful woman was affable and grateful to Bill and me—even a little jokey about her clumsiness. But at one pause in the conversation, her countenance dropped. "Pastor Bill," she said, "can I share something with you?" She looked apologetically at me; I took the hint and went into the hall. About ten minutes passed before a visibly shaken Bill came out to get me. I reentered. The woman had been crying hard. "This young lady has really been through it," Bill said.

As Bill and the woman divulged portions of her story to me, I learned that she was in a relationship with an abusive man. Whatever the nature of the abuse was, it involved both her and her teenage daughter. The woman felt conflicted; she knew the man was harmful, but she had been with him for some time, and she felt like she was letting God down if she shirked her commitment. "Let me see your palms," Bill said to her. "Just what I thought. No nail scars." Bill proceeded to counsel her out of her sense of responsibility for this man and the guilt she felt when she considered leaving the relationship. She was not this man's Messiah. The woman calmed down.

As Bill had suspected, the doctors did not clear the woman to drive. With Bill following us, I drove the woman, in her car, the forty-five minutes to her home (due to a wrong turn, it became an hour-long voyage). As we drove, we chatted about our lives; she had worked as a flight attendant for a now-defunct airline and was in the middle of a tumultuous career change, living currently in a transitional apartment. We arrived at her apartment to the tune of thunderclaps; lightning blasted the sky. Bill and I helped her up the steps to her third-floor apartment. She only had a couple of water bottles to give us for our troubles, but we assured her that no payment was necessary. As we started across the parking lot, a particularly close bolt of lightning and loud clap of thunder sent us jogging back to Bill's car.

As he sped undeterred in and out of torrential rain, Bill let me in on a little more of the woman's story, though he also (rightly) guarded her privacy. This led us to talk about crises in American manhood, the defense budget, convention singing, good theology, and good psychology. Uneasy in such storms, I was ready to come through to Alexandria. Our progress was slowed, though, when a policeman pulled Bill over in the dark, broad Indiana countryside, a few miles from our destination. Bill handed the stoic officer his license and explained why we were on the road so late on such a night. As the unresponsive officer walked back to his squad car with Bill's license, Bill rolled up his window, grinned at me, and said, "well, I sure hope he likes gospel music."

Bill did not get a ticket. We returned to Alexandria around 3:00 a.m. Late the next morning, well after the workshop had begun, I ate my breakfast alone with Bill, ASCAP's Gospel Songwriter of the Century, in the vacated workshop dining area. Our minds not yet rested from travel, we laughed a little as we reminisced about our odyssey.

When the Gaithers proclaim release from the past, they imagine themselves proclaiming release to captive audience members such as this woman. Conscious carriers of the American Wesleyan-Holiness tradition, these Andersonians want to wake their neighbors to the possibility of liberation from their historical accusers and abusers—the possibility of receiving and

communicating the spontaneous love of God firsthand. This is the woman
whom they want to want to be well. This is one of the women for whom
Gloria clears the outer courts. This is the woman who needs to know it is not
too late to seek a newer world. This is the woman to whom the Gaither gospel
speaks when it says, *thou art loosed!*

But such women are not the only ones listening. Members of the Homecoming world are not only captives. Many have been, if not captors, the beneficiaries of others' captivity to religious, racial, and sexual persecution. An
aging Hovie Lister, bald and emaciated because he is undergoing cancer treatment, performs on the Homecoming stage in the final years of his life, the
turn of the century. Lister perhaps did more to revolutionize mid-century
white gospel stages than anyone else. He injected fanfare into these stages
and made some of the first moves to racially integrate them. I watch his final
Homecoming appearances; it is hard not to like him—at once bristly and affable, happy to be a part of the show for a little while longer. He is immensely
pitiable, because of his illness and because he represents a senior population
that is rendered irrelevant and invisible by a youth-oriented, death-denying
American popular culture. He represents a rural southern population that is
often the subject of unqualified ridicule in the same culture—a culture that
he helped to build. At the same time, Lister has been the beneficiary and per-
petuator of some of the worst racism in southern gospel.[24] He helped to build
a culture of racial abuse. The cancer-ridden Lister's final pains are very real,
but they are not the same as the pains he has inflicted and from which he
has benefited. It does not seem that Lister has been forced to reckon with his
abuse—certainly not in the Homecomings. Are the Homecomings the occasion for this reckoning?

The turn-of-the-century Homecomings function partly as (sometimes
preemptive) eulogies for a dying generation. Eulogies extend forgiveness
and absolution, implicitly or explicitly, often when neither are requested, or
even would be recognized by the dead as warranted. Eulogies are never true,
entirely. If we consider our own pending eulogies, we might not want them to
be. But eulogizing is not the only function of turn-of-the-century Homecomings. The Gaithers want harmony and reconciliation—racial and otherwise.
This cannot happen without a *full* reckoning of the past. And the literature
on abuse and reconciliation agrees: abusers and the beneficiaries of abuse do
not get to determine the occasion of this reckoning. They do not get to assess
the pain of the abused and tell the abused when or how to get over it.[25] If, as
Bill Gaither or T. D. Jakes suggest, various pains are basically the same, or the
past is truly passed, these conclusions only can be reached through substantive, often painfully honest contact across difference. What transpired on the

Potter's House stage in March 2003 is a welcome and in many ways successful attempt at such contact, unprecedented in the published Gaither video catalogue. But when Bill and Jakes synonymize all human pain, they provide an escape hatch for viewers who do not wish to countenance the concert's more difficult and promising implications. If no such countenancing occurs—if, in essence, Homecoming audiences look on as Lister and his generation pass away without them having to render an account—no reconciliation or harmony will happen. Without the reckoning, if history is any indication, the sins of the fathers will be visited upon the heads of the daughters.[26]

* * *

The Potter's House videos are not simply black and white. Consider Lily Isaacs, a stylish, short-haired woman who prefaces the performance of her family bluegrass band with this autobiographical sketch:

> I am born Jewish. My parents are both full-blooded Jews, and when World War II broke out, my parents were victims of the Holocaust, and they spent five years of their lives in the concentration camps: first in Poland, and then in Germany. They were liberated in nineteen and forty-five. Then I was born in 1947 and came to New York, and I grew up in New York City, in the Bronx and I lived there for over 20 years [applause]. And 31 years ago, a Jewish kid got acquainted with the real Messiah [applause].[27]

Standing by Lily, Bill then tells the story of Lily's mother appearing in the 2002 Homecoming concert at Carnegie Hall (she appeared onstage that night to say, in a heavy Polish accent, "I'm proud to be an American"). Bill proceeds to introduce the Isaacs—sisters Becky and Sonya, brother Ben, with their mother, Lily—as a bluegrass band, "but every now and then backstage I hear them doing this minor stuff [Becky jokes, halfway into the microphone, "Jewgrass," to much laughter]. It all goes together, and it's beautiful. And they were doing this, and I said, 'you've got to do this for the taping in Dallas.'" Lily introduces the song—based on Psalm 133:1—as one she learned growing up in New York, attending summer camp, learning about Israel and "just wanting to be there on a kibbutz all my life." She recites the verse in English ("Behold, how very good and pleasant it is for brethren to dwell together in unity," NKJV). The Isaacs then sing the psalm in Hebrew.

There is more to Lily's story. She was one-half of the short-lived women's folk duo Lily and Maria (Fiszman and Neumann, respectively), who played the Greenwich Village folk scene in the late 1960s. Their eponymous 1968 "acid folk" album is a cult classic among folkees—a highly experimental mix of jazz, folk, and rock infused with organ, jazz brushwork on the drumset, and lush vocal harmonies. The folk scene put her in contact with a number of southern bluegrass musicians—including Joe Isaacs of the Greenbrier Boys, son of a Pentecostal minister, whom she married. In 1971, at a memorial service for Joe's brother, who had died in a car accident, she converted to Christianity. The conversion resulted in a profound break with her parents. Lily later reconciled with them. Her father converted to Christianity. Lily remains public about her wish for her mother to do so as well; as evident in the fact that the Carnegie Hall concert was the first time Lily's mother had seen her grandchildren perform at a gospel concert, some tensions remained. Joe and Lily divorced in 1998 but remained on relatively good terms (Lily and "The Isaacs" continue to feature Joe's music on their website).

The Isaacs were among the most skilled musicians in the Homecoming world. Becky, Sonya, and Ben play guitar, mandolin, and upright bass, respectively. Their vocal blend was astounding. While they were the Homecoming musicians about whom my fan interviewees were most vocal in their distaste, they were also frequently singled out as favorites. *All* fans awed at their talent. On several fronts, the Isaacs were familiar outsiders. As bluegrass musicians from Tennessee, they were well within the southern sphere. Before her rise on the Homecoming stage, Sonya Isaacs had been a backup singer for country stars such as Vince Gill, Dolly Parton, and Reba McEntire. Involvement in other "southern" forms of music did not necessarily help them. Given the efforts Bill had made to connect southern gospel to country via the Ryman Auditorium, and given the 2003 release of the two-volume video *A Gospel Bluegrass Homecoming*, I was surprised how often those fans who told me they did not like the Isaacs couched their dislike in a general distaste for bluegrass music. However, any fan who mentioned Lily's autobiography and the Hebrew-language songs based on Greek Dorian or Phrygian modes (the "minor stuff") did so in praise.[28] The Jewish element of the story made the difference.

There is a strong supersessionist component to the Gaithers' deployment of Lily's Jewish heritage, but the Gaithers do not seem to believe that the only good Jew is a Jesus-worshipping Jew—or even a particularly religious Jew. In 2009, Gloria published in *Homecoming Magazine* her interview with author Mitch Albom—among his best-selling books, *Five People You Meet in Heaven*. Albom talks with Gloria about his 2009 book *Have a Little Faith*, in which Albom recounts the story of getting to know a rabbi from his home town and eventually delivering his eulogy. The book and the interview are about spirituality and a journey of faith, but not a journey that follows all of the old, familiar evangelical roads.[29] If her interview with Albom is any indication,

Gloria regards Judaism as an outside-but-kindred religion and Jews as fellow spiritual seekers who possess an intelligible and trustworthy approach to faith. Gloria is not alone among evangelicals in this attitude toward Jews, even those who pray for the conversion of Jews to Christianity.[30]

If nostalgia is the longing for a home that never existed or no longer exists, evangelicals' fascination with their "parent religion"—one which they code as ancient or passed away but still cherished—is a kind of nostalgia. Because Lily Isaacs actually grew up Jewish, and because her conversion to Christianity recapitulates many evangelicals' sense of the chronological and theologically normative march of religious history, she is the perfect avatar and spokesperson for evangelicals' nostalgia for a religious homeland—one that must be both present and passed over. That is, she is the perfect avatar this side of the homeland itself.

DISPATCHES FROM THE NEW JERUSALEM

Does the Jordan possess a discernible current? The water, green and glassy, hardly stirs as the camera pulls back, as Bill Gaither says in voiceover, "the Jordan has a sense of home about it. And still today, believers come to be baptized in these peaceful waters." When Bill stops speaking, a harmonica plays what sounds like "How Dry I Am"—an American folk tune standardized in Irving Berlin's 1919 song "The Near Future." Possibly originating as a work song or spiritual, "How Dry I Am" was a common chorus during Prohibition and shortly afterward, often used ironically as a drinking song. As the camera turns and expands, viewers finally see the music's source: Buddy Greene, multi-instrumentalist, harmonica virtuoso, singer-songwriter, and Homecoming regular. Like a middle-aged Huck Finn, Greene sits on a rock beside the river, his pant legs rolled up just below his knees. When the Georgia-born Greene concludes his playing, he speaks into the camera, with a distinct but qualified southern accent common in border states, especially common among Nashvilleans: Yankee with Dixie inflections or Dixie with Yankee inflections. Upon his rock, this revelation:

> How poignant the words of Psalm 137: "By the rivers of Babylon we sat and wept when we remembered Zion. There on the poplars we hung our harps, for our captors asked us for songs. Our tormentors demanded songs of joy. They said, 'sing us one of the songs of Zion.' How can we sing the song of Zion in a strange land?" But captivity can't steal identity. Abba Eban once wrote, "there were many Babylons in Jewish history, but Zion always beckoned through the

tears." And for all of us, the songs of home will never be sung as they were intended until we all get home.[31]

In *Israel Homecoming*, filmed and released in the winter of 2005, Bill sets up his Christian viewers to regard the Jordan River as a home site—not an arcane metaphor, given the common usage of the river to symbolize the passage into one's true home, either as site of baptism or site of crossing into some promised land. But Greene subtly complicates the picture. He may be beside the Jordan, but his recitation of Psalm 137 narratively locates he and his "we" beside Babylonian rivers—the rivers of exile. He is playing an American tune on the harmonica—that quintessentially American "harp." Greene also ceases his recitation before he reaches the psalm's most territorial, vindictive, and violent verses:

> If I forget you, Jerusalem, let my right hand wither! Let my tongue cling to the roof of my mouth, if I do not remember you, if I do not set Jerusalem above my highest joy. Remember, O Lord, against the Edomites, the day of Jerusalem's fall, how they said, "Tear it down! Tear it down! Down to its foundations!" O Daughter Babylon, you devastator! Happy shall they be who pay you back what you have done to us! Happy shall they be who take your little ones and dash them against the rock! (NRSV)

Greene does *not* speak these words on Jordan's bank, near the closing of the Second Intifada, in which approximately 3,000 Palestinians and 1,000 Israelis were killed. Where is Greene, exactly? Where is he hanging his harp? And whose song does he play on it?

The waters further stir. The camera leaves Greene and returns viewers to the main performance venue of the video: the base of the Tower of David, in Old City Jerusalem. The outdoor concert, which began in daylight and at this point has extended into the evening, now features Jeff and Sheri Easter, along with Charlotte Ritchie. Among early twenty-first-century Homecoming regulars, the Easters stylistically were the most akin to Nashville's contemporaneous country music exports. Jeff sings and speaks with a pronounced twang—one that gets augmented in his comedic exchanges with Bill, which in nonsouthern concerts often thematize the simple southern country boy's experience of urban, international, or otherwise "noncountry" spaces. The Isaacs are sometimes visible in the Easter shot, sitting on their own pedestal, slightly above and beyond the rest of the singers. Captivity can't steal identity.

In this performance, the Easters and Ritchie showcase their *a capella* dexterity in a one-minute version of James McNaughton's and Brent Dowe's 1969 song, "Rivers of Babylon"—a song that employs both Psalm 137 and Psalm 19:

> By the rivers of Babylon, where we went down
> And there we wept when we remembered Zion
> for the wicked carry us away in captivity
> require from us a song
> How can we sing King Alpha's song in a strange land?
> So let the words of our mouth
> And the meditations of our heart
> Be acceptable in thy sight Oh God.[32]

Few selections in the entire Homecoming corpus are as replete with interpretive possibility as this song, appearing at this point in the video. McNaughton and Dowe were founding members of the Jamaican rocksteady group the Melodians, and "Rivers of Babylon" has become a standard in Jamaican music. The Easters' version retains the Rastafari components of the song. They sing of "King Alpha"—the common Rasta moniker for Ethiopian Emperor Haile Selassie I, whom Rastas regard as divine. Although Homecoming viewers likely would assume this refers to Jesus, "the Alpha and the Omega" (cf. Revelation 1:8, 21:6), "King Alpha" is an obvious revision of the psalm that Greene just quoted.[33] The first four measures of "Rivers of Babylon" are almost identical musically to "How Dry I Am." The first four notes are the same as those of the chorus of the Gaithers' "Because He Lives." Whose song are the Easters singing? Whose song was Greene playing?

To recap: Buddy Greene, looking like Huckleberry Finn beside the Mississippi, plays what could pass as an American folk tune, on the folksiest of instruments, near the Jordan—in most evangelical Christian art and literature, the river of rebirth, return, homeland, resolution. His segment concludes with a psalm of exile, after which the Nashville-countrified Easters, appearing in Jerusalem, sing a song that recalls three songs: a "secular" tune that itself may have been inspired by a spiritual, a song from an Afro-Caribbean belief system rooted in Judaism and Christianity, and the Gaithers' best-known song. Inside the walls of the city of Zion—under the portion built and rebuilt by Jews, Christians, and Muslims throughout history—the Easters sing from the vantage of exile. After witnessing with Greene the supposed river of home, rendered as American pastoral, viewers lyrically experience with the Easters the supposed rivers of exile—through a Rastafari song in which captivity connotes the slavery and oppression of African and Afro-Caribbean peoples.

Their song contains the same passage quoted by Greene—the open question concerning homebound religious identity in exile. This is all transpiring as the Second Intifada comes to an end.

The water still stirs. After the Easters' performance, the camera leaves off the night and David's Citadel for a daytime shot of the Mount of Olives. Viewed from the Old City, it focuses first on Seven Arches (the Jordanian-owned hotel on top of the Mount in East Jerusalem) and the large ceme-tery that covers the western slope—part of which was bulldozed during the construction of Seven Arches. This is the cemetery that houses the Tomb of the Prophets. Filling up the measure, the view widens to encompass one end of the Temple Mount. Visible are the trees inside the Temple complex, the long body of Al-Aqsa mosque (not its dome), and for a second the entirety of the Western Wall, with people gathered at its base. During this shot, Gloria Gaither speaks: "How can I love this place so much and yet not worship the place? How can I love the Word that *he was* and not worship the words themselves that carried such eternal truths?"[34] With these shots, a viewer would need more than passing knowledge of Jerusalem to recognize, specifically, what they are seeing. But as Gloria's narration continues, things change. Facing the camera, apparently standing at the Old City overlook atop the Jewish cemetery, below Seven Arches, on the Mount of Olives, Gloria is shown speaking. Slightly decentered in the frame, she shares space with the (an)iconic gold Dome of the Rock resting on her right shoulder. She contin-ues her narrative:

> How can I, as he himself said, be in this world but not of it? No one reminded us more than Jesus that we are pilgrims, sojourners in search of a better land, even better than this he loved so much. Here a parade began of restless pil-grims, wandering from this place across times and places, looking for a place, the place, where their souls would finally be at rest. No matter how much we settle in, there is something deep in our spirits that makes us know we'll never really be at home until we're at home with him.[35]

Gloria's nodding toward the merit of different faiths while ultimately reaf-firming the superiority of Christianity potentially could resonate with a range of inclusivist and exclusivist Homecoming fans. As viewers look at the sacred sites of Jewish and Muslim Jerusalem, Gloria recalls Greene's nar-rative, suggesting that places do, in fact, have sacred worth. Gloria narrates Jesus himself as loving his home deeply, though it is unclear if Gloria's "this he loved so much" signals all of "the Holy Land" or the Jerusalem over which he lamented.[36]

The tendency for place-love to morph into place-idolatry is central to Gloria's message. She does not point rhetorical fingers at particular faith traditions, but the footage of Jewish and Muslim sacred sites leaves little doubt which religious peoples apparently tend toward such idolatry. Muslims receive the most obvious visual condemnation. While not particularly Muslim, Seven Arches' location in Arab East Jerusalem and its connections to Jordan invokes, at the very least, a non-Israeli population. Homecoming viewers might not know the history or import of Seven Arches, but the Dome of the Rock certainly registers as a Muslim site. The most recognized monument in the segment, the golden dome, remains in the frame longer than any other structure—counterpoised to a golden-haired, Western Christian woman who is preaching the delocalization of sacrality. Jewish populations come under indictment as well. Only Jews appear in person, albeit briefly and blurrily, in the ostensible act of place-worship: gathered at the base of the Western Wall. The only other Jewish bodies "present" in this footage are those lying in the cemetery on the slope of the Mount of Olives. With them, supposedly, lie those prophets whom Jesus claimed were killed by the Pharisees' ancestors.

Gloria does not exempt Christianity from judgment. However easy it is to miss as the sunlight dances off of the high places on the Mount of Olives, the second question Gloria poses in her narrative is monumental. If Gloria here extends and riffs on the psalmic mode to which Greene and the Easters just alluded—as I showed in chapter 4, Gloria is both willing and able to write so scripturally—the parallelism of the first and second questions suggests that *place* equals or is intensified by *word*.[37] The second question implies that Gloria's (and by extension evangelicals') temptation to place-worship takes the form of word-worship—which, since she is apparently discussing Jesus's biblical words, implies text-worship. Evangelical bibliolatry is no less idolatry than place-idolatry. Gloria's gestures toward a Truth/Christ/Word signaled by, but transcendent over, truths/texts/words are consistent with her Holiness experientialism. Transcendent Truth transcends text-and/as-propositional content. However, Gloria's critique of Christians is quick and contains a back-handed recommendation of Christianity. Christians have advanced past place-idolatry to the point that they can succumb to a higher transgression, a more sophisticated idolatry. Mistaking *the Word's words* for *the Word* seems an honest wrong turn for pilgrims on the right path. At least Christianity, as Gloria conceives it, is not hung up on sacred sites. And a religion that is not hung up on sacred sites presumably has little to do with religious conflicts over place. When the camera scrolls back to capture the Mount of Olives, it stops just as it reaches the Church of Mary Magdalene, situated near the Garden of Gethsemane on the slope of the Mount of Olives. One dome that is *not* prominent in *Israel Homecoming* is the dome of the Church of the Holy Sepulchre. Neither does the Homecoming camera venture inside this church, to capture the stone-kissing, wall-touching tactility of Holy Land Christianity. *Jerusalem Homecoming*—the second video from the concert—ends with Geron Davis's "Holy Ground."[38]

Just as Bill's wariness about the past runs against his Homecoming employment of it, Gloria's wariness about place runs against the Homecoming deployments of the Ryman Auditorium, the rural South, and even Jerusalem. But it is worth bearing in mind two aspects of Gloria's wariness. First, against the backdrop of other Homecoming programs, Jerusalem is a sanctuary in and from "the" American southern gospel. Jerusalem is a locus of relatively higher sacrality from which Gloria can lodge an authoritative critique at *southern gospel*'s regional and theological provincialisms. Gloria's words are warnings to Homecoming citizens to be cautious about *any* place-worship, Dixie-worship included. As a recognizably holy other place, Jerusalem positions Gloria as a cosmopolitan vis-à-vis southern gospel culture—one who has achieved a larger view, from the outside. As a *recognizably holy* other place, Jerusalem sufficiently circumscribes Gloria's cosmopolitanism within familiar, honored walls. She is not some casual world traveler, speaking meddlesome words from some unknown pagan region. Gloria is speaking Holiness from the Holy City. The efficacy of her geo-critique depends in some measure on the very notion of geosacrality she criticizes.

Gloria also offers a warning for evangelicals who would make something more of the Holy Land than the Gaithers feel they should. The Gaither demographic is filled with apocalyptic Christian Zionists—fans who read Hal Lindsey's *The Late Great Planet Earth*, who watch tele-prophet Jack Van Impe, who are watchful for any archaeological evidence that confirms the literality of some biblical past, for any news from Jerusalem's present that confirms the literality of some biblical future.[39] It was easy to miss apocalyptic Zionism in my concertgoing, and even in my one-on-one fan interviews. Conversation did not organically turn toward "the Holy Land" as the site of Armageddon.[40] When I spent sustained time among *groups* of fans—at Gloria's songwriting workshop, overhearing conversations at Family Fest—I observed how matter-of-factly many of them declared in polite company that we were living in the end of days, or that Israel was instrumental in the unfolding ending. In some quarters of the Homecoming world, apocalyptic Christian Zionism at least endured, and may have prevailed.

Not so with the Gaithers. In my experiences with them on and off stage, they were never high on reading the end into the times, or particular places; the future, they thought, was not theirs to hold. In *It's More Than the Music*,

Bill described the mood of excitement in evangelical circles after the Six-Day War in 1967:

> "Surely," many Christians declared, "it won't be long now before we see King Jesus face-to-face." Gloria and I believed in the second coming of Christ, but we tended to focus more on serving God in this life than on speculating about the future. Besides, we were parents of young children; we were singing on weekends, writing songs, and teaching school during the week; we were too busy keeping up with the hectic here and now to pay much attention to the sweet by and by![41]

The Gaithers intend gently to instruct their "place-worshipping" Christian Zionist fans through the erasure and deployment of several sacred sites in *Israel Homecoming*. The video contains no talk of Jerusalem or Israel as the site of Armageddon or of Jesus's return. When the narrative turns toward "authentic" sites—where the Jesus of the Gospels *really* walked—the Gaithers do little speculating. Only when they film on location in the Garden of Gethsemane and at the old steps leading to Herod's Temple do they claim to stand where the Gospels' Jesus stood; given the scholarly archaeological consensus, such claims are here plausible. Granted, viewers are set up to fill in the gaps; when Christ-posing Guy Penrod wails the final verse of "Because He Lives" in front of the more dubious Garden Tomb, surely Homecoming viewers' hearts will burn within them. But the Garden Tomb is only identified as such by a quick caption, no narrative. The Gaithers do not commit themselves explicitly to the correspondences between history and speculation. They neither confirm nor deny.

Neither confirming nor denying is the formula of the entire Israel project. The Gaithers do not recommend that their Christian viewers forget Jerusalem; the sheer fact of the concert insists on Jerusalem's memorialization. But neither are Christians to set Jerusalem above their highest joy. This attempt at neutrality helps to explain why the Holy Land of the Homecomings seems all past, no discernible current.[42] Certainly, *Israel Homecoming*'s erasure of present peoples in a video built on biblical themes implicitly primitivizes them. The Gaithers could have addressed this problem by telling stories of current Jewish, Arab Christian, and Muslim inhabitants that complicate any narratives of impending apocalypse. Indeed, the Israel videos may have been an occasion on which the Gaither penchant for showing and creating unity would have been helpful. However, this would have required more penetrating contact with the tangled roots and branches than Holy Land tourism typically allows.[43] The Gaithers opt for conspicuous silence, conspicuous absence, regarding present matters. The silence and absence are conspicuous because many of the ministers with whom the Gaithers shared airspace around the time of this video's release were especially dedicated to interpreting present-day Israel in apocalyptic terms. Texas minister John Hagee—whose apocalyptic Sunday sermons aired adjacent to Homecoming programs throughout the nation—opened his book *Countdown to Jerusalem: A Warning to the World* (published in January 2006), with these words: "The final battle for Jerusalem is about to begin. Every day in the media you are watching the gathering storm over the state of Israel. The winds of war are once again about to sweep through the sacred city of Jerusalem." Later the same year, Hagee would form Christians United For Israel (CUFI), an organization designed to "provide a national association through which every pro-Israel church, parachurch organization, ministry or individual in America can speak and act with one voice in support of Israel in matters related to Biblical issues." While Christian Zionists were setting their faces toward Jerusalem long before Ariel Sharon controversially went to the Temple Mount in 2000, the Second Intifada, coupled with general concerns over Islam in post-9/11 evangelical America, made these years especially germane for American evangelicalism's Zionist revelators.[44]

Conspicuous silence and conspicuous absence are important tools in the Gaithers' apolitical toolkit. They are and are not blunt. I first witnessed the tools in use in a discussion of homosexuality with Bill. He told me of an instance in which he was cornered by a Christian man who wanted to know if a particular gospel musician was gay. Bill told the man, "I don't think it's any of my business. And frankly, I don't think it's any of yours, either." My first reaction to Bill's "don't ask don't tell" policy—and his obvious pride in his stand—was to dismiss it as safe moralizing. Bill's silence was not nearly as courageous as Bill thought it was.[45] However, it was not just silence; it was a silence that called attention to itself and demanded reciprocal silence. The insistent silence undermined his inquisitor's assumptions, (1) that he and Bill agreed on the kinds of personal knowledge of others to which they were entitled, (2) that they would share such knowledge between them if they had it (presumably since they were both heterosexual male Christians), and (3) that this kind of personal knowledge was worth passing around. "Don't ask, don't tell" was by no means a radically liberating policy, but when it came from a man whose broadcasts appeared alongside the likes of John Hagee, it rerouted the prevailing discourse. It cleared some of the outer courts for further invitations.

Given some Homecoming fans' interpretive maneuvers that I have already examined, it would seem that conspicuous silence and absence would have to be extremely conspicuous to challenge discursive norms. Fans are good at reading things into, around, and on top of Homecoming scripts. The erasure of present-day Israel in *Israel Homecoming* may not have been conspicuous enough; by virtue of choosing to film a program in Jerusalem, and by virtue of broadcasting it (though not by Gaither choice) alongside John Hagee's programs, the Gaithers benefited from the evangelical Israel-worship they were subtly problematizing. Unlike in Bill's "don't ask" anecdote, the Gaithers do not appear on screen saying to viewers, "present-day Israel is none of our business; and frankly, we don't think it's any of yours, either." Still, the erasure made it more difficult for Christian Zionist viewers to read the goings-on in modern Israel into their private, imminent apocalypses. Primitivizing a modern people by biblicizing them may be dehumanizing, but so is handing over a present population to be pawns in someone else's *eschaton*.[46] If such viewers want to read personal Armageddons into the video, they will have to work harder than they do when they read *Countdown to Jerusalem*.

UNMONUMENTED

There are a number of roads Homecoming fans will take when they think of their country.

Lynn and I drove from New Jersey to Gatlinburg, Tennessee, for the 2009 Family Fest, which had been held on every Memorial Day weekend since 1990. We split the trip into two days, stopping just north of Harper's Ferry one night before making the final push down Virginia's spine. An atlas junkie who delights in measuring the import of old tracks, I remarked *ad nauseum* to Lynn how our journey almost exactly reversed our 2006 move from North Carolina to New Jersey. It was also a rough reversal of the Confederacy's northern advance, the elongated rewind of Pickett's Charge. Trading duties behind the wheel, we made good time from Harper's Ferry.

Gatlinburg is located at the concurrent strip of US Highways 321 and 441. It is geographically and culturally continuous with Dollywood, nestled in the bosom of the Great Smoky Mountains. Entering from TN-66 off exit 407 on Interstate 40, the two-becomes-one roadway cuts through a constant cluster of "country" restaurants, hotels, motels, go-cart tracks, mini-golf courses, dinner theaters, and gun shops. Our hotel, the Park Vista, jutted out of the slope of a hill, behind the downtown area, on the opposite slope of the ski lift that extended up behind the other side of downtown. "The Highest Point in Gatlinburg," the Park Vista was a tall, cylindrical concrete building—the high-water mark of unregulated build-up. Development aspired no higher.

Gatlinburg fanned out street level through the increasingly dense valley, in the thin shadow of the Smokies.

The 2009 Family Fest was especially important because it marked the official debut of the post–Guy Penrod/Marshall Hall GVB. It was an all-star quintet. Bill had rehired former GVB standouts: the exuberant Mark Lowry; the soulful, larger-than-life, ever-returning prodigal Michael English, and the operatic super-tenor David Phelps joined Bill and Wes Hampton. Family Fest was primarily musical, but it included a significant element of spoken procla-mation and instruction, on the main stage and in smaller workshop sessions. In addition to *The Shack* author William Paul Young, Reformed theologian Dr. Steve Brown and motivational speaker Zig Ziglar made appearances. On the main stage, Gloria read *Three Cups*, a self-published children's book by the CFO of an Indianapolis real estate firm, which taught children the impor-tance of money management (the "three cups" divided one's money—one cup for saving, one for spending, one for giving). The GVB still performed "Give It Away," and Bill still gave away money to random fans. However, the economic bubble during which "Give It Away" had flourished had burst less than a year prior to this weekend. The Gaithers thought some additional economic les-sons on thrift, expressed in the common-sense language of a children's book, seemed appropriate.[47]

Family Fest 2009 was my first contact with a single set of performers and fans that extended beyond one evening. Consequently, I felt freed to spend large amounts of time backstage, in the audience, and in the merchandise area without fretting as much as I usually did about missing something else-where. The weekend audience seemed even less generationally diverse than the audiences I had experienced at other concerts; with a few exceptions, the age range appeared to be late forties to mid-eighties. There was little racial diversity, as usual; senior and middle-aged black women comprised a tiny (but not absent) population, conspicuous due to their skin color, their color-ful dresses, and the florid hats they wore during Sunday morning's gather-ing. In fact, although Homecoming masculinities remained as prominent and complicated as ever, this weekend I found myself wondering at the varieties of *femininities* contained on and off the stage. Family Fest was the first event I had attended at which Gloria was present. It was also my introduction to some singing groups not featured in previous Homecoming videos, in which women were featured performers.

The greatest discernible point of diversity among women concerned dress and makeup. While performing and viewing women did not show-case the famous augmented features of Dollywood's proprietor, some vis-ages seemed rather plastic. In many cases, the hairspray and makeup were of

Parton proportions. Backstage, many female performers and male performers' spouses seemed dedicated to perpetual self-maintenance; I always could count on seeing some individual peering into a handheld mirror, adjusting foundation or touching up eyeliner. (While male musicians also evinced a good deal of cosmetic labor on their persons, the labor was confined to private dressing rooms. Men did not wield mirrors.) The backstage area was an occluded front of nebulous perfumes; it was not unusual to run into similarly pungent patches of air amid the fans in the arena and its lobby. Some women's hairdos defied the laws of gravity. Far below the median age, Lynn and I were "darlins" to a number of the friendly "southern hons" present. There were moments in Gatlinburg—indeed, at every Homecoming concert I attended—when I would not have been surprised to learn at least a few men in drag were in attendance, so hyperbolic seemed some of the getup. Some explicit and intentionally humorous gender-play occurred at Family Fest; one of the weekend's biggest hits was Logan Smith, a twelve-year-old boy who executed a spot-on vocal impersonation of Vestal Goodman.[48]

At the other end of the spectrum was a significant population of conspicuously austere women. Old-order Mennonite women comprised the most recognizable denominational group, with their distinctive translucent head coverings, stiff-backed bonnets, and long, monochromatic dresses. Judging by the many huge gray buns of apparently huge amounts of hair bobbing through the auditorium, variously Pentecostal women were also a strong contingent. Neutral-toned knee- or ankle-length skirts were prevalent. Judging by the white handkerchiefs laid over the tops of a smattering of heads, Gaither concerts were at least enough like church for many women present to follow the Pauline injunction in 1 Corinthians to cover their heads in worship assemblies. Onstage, Kim Collingsworth represented one version of this austere brand of feminine (non)adornment. The mother and pianist in the Collingsworth Family band (also comprised of her spouse, Phil, their three daughters, and their son), Kim Collingsworth wore a skirt extending nearly to her ankles with a matching, button-up jacket that appeared to be of thick, woolen fabric. Her hair was tied tightly back into a bun. If she wore makeup, it was only minimal stage makeup. I had little sense of her age; the guesses I made based on her clothing did not jive with the guesses I made based on her wrinkle-free, white skin. Cognizant of the wide range of generational possibilities in evangelical families, I could not guess her age judging by her seemingly older husband and preteen daughters (why was Kim's age so important to me, during Family Fest, anyway?).

Kim Collingsworth played and sang from behind the piano during the Collingsworth Family's set, situated just outside and just a few feet below the circular stage at the arena's center. But the spotlight swung to her when she performed a solo piano arrangement of the "Hallelujah" chorus of Handel's *Messiah*. Backed by a prerecorded orchestral track, Collingsworth began the song quietly, leaning slightly over the piano, eyes closed, apparently murmuring words. As the arrangement grew, her motions became more pronounced. She began to perform more ornate, dexterous rolls up and down the keyboard to fill the space between the melody lines, all the while her arms and head gesticulating more wildly. Her hands lept quickly and highly off the keys as if she were touching burning coals. Her soft glossolalia became more pronounced. Her jaws worked wider. About two hundred feet away, I had the impression I could hear her speak (I thought of notably oral jazz pianist Keith Jarrett). The video screens above the stage showed her every move, but even some two hundred feet away, flush with Collingsworth at floor level, I could see her torso dancing up and down the piano. I did not need screens. By the last verse, orchestra and piano had reached their full volume. The arena shook as Collingsworth, on occasion leaping from the piano bench, punched and rolled at the keys, now clearly mouthing the words as she played, her visage bending and crinkling with every stab of her hand and whip of her neck toward the sky. When the song ended, her face was beaded with sweat. To say she received a standing ovation at the conclusion of the piece is not exactly correct; everyone had been standing for about five minutes by that point (customary during the "Hallelujah" chorus), everyone craning and leaning into the nucleus from which this atomic energy proceeded, silent in expectancy. As if they were reaching for some divine garment, several hands extended up and in to this performing core on the edge of the circular stage. When the piece ended, the crowd—which, I then noticed, included several Homecoming singers who had emerged from the green room to watch this performance—blew up in applause, whistles, and "praise Jesuses" for what felt like minutes. Collingsworth, eyes on the ceiling, refracted the applause heavenward. Never, in any Homecoming concert, did I witness a live crowd respond like that. Neither did I ever experience a more expressive performance from a woman in a Homecoming concert.

The spring prior to this performance, the national media were all atwitter with the "discovery" and federal raid of a massive Fundamentalist Latter-Day Saints (FLDS) compound in the Texas hinterlands. Women and girls wearing long, uniform, pioneer-era-looking dresses and coifs looked fearful and suspicious to news outlets' cameras. Some of the women, barely visible, peered from behind windows and screens, presumably because they were under the spell of some vigilant patriarchal power who forbade them a life exterior to his watchful eye. News cameras were everywhere. The amount and tone of coverage bespoke an obsessive, near-pornographic interest. I was interested, too—returning a fearful, suspicious gaze for what I told myself were professional, scholarly reasons. While neither Collingsworth nor even the Mennonite and Pentecostal women at Family Fest were dressed precisely like the FLDS women, the Family Fest modes of modesty signaled to me a resembling variety of conservative, arcadian, ostensibly male-determined patriarchalism. I wondered if Kim Collingsworth's performance would have been so powerful to me, or to many others present, if I had not assumed that such a public flex of her personal power discorded with her wardrobe. One month before Collingsworth's performance, a similarly modestly dressed woman, less attractive than Collingsworth by most media standards, had emerged from the Scottish countryside and caused television viewers to coo condescendingly when she performed on the reality talent television program, *Britain's Got Talent*. Susan Boyle and her golden voice quickly caused a stir in American media. The aura around Boyle demonstrated the state of popular femininity, especially when it came to musical women: how could a woman who looked like Boyle so confidently make such beautiful music?

With so many divining forms of femininity at Family Fest, I wondered how the different women present thought about the panoply. What did the head-covering Pentecostal women think when the Pentecostal Lee University Singers took the stage Sunday morning? The choir's young women were covered to fit all forms: all skirts and blouses of requisite knee and elbow length, but all skin-tight; long hair tied up, but lots of makeup; hands lifted in praise, heels lifted in pumps. Were the Lee Singers acceptably splitting the difference between acceptably Christian femininities? Which women in the audience would feel represented on the Family Fest stage—the same stage that sponsored the author who had cast God the Father as an African American woman? What fashions of femininities were the Homecomings staging?

✳ ✳ ✳

A number of women played important roles in the Homecomings of the 1990s. Eva Mae Lefevre helped catalyze the first video's jam session. Vestal Goodman was arguably *the* face and voice of the Homecomings' first decade. Faye and Mary Tom Speer held a prominent seat in every Homecoming video filmed in Gaither Studios. These women were not only key Homecoming citizens; they were key as *senior* citizens, especially relative to the women occupying pop and contemporary Christian music stages during the same period. The early Homecomings were one of the few musical stages available to postmenopausal women—particularly to women whose bodies show the "unrepaired" marks of old age. Even as Lilith Fair expanded the rock-and-roll stage to include a wide variety of women in the late 1990s, its marquee acts typically were but slightly grungier versions of *Cosmopolitan* models (organizer Sarah McLachlan did not exactly upend popular conceptions of beauty). The 1990s covers of *CCM* magazine, then the major publication of the Christian music industry, tell a similar story. While the women of the 1990s Homecomings and CCM's female performers resembled each other in the opacity of their attire, CCM women possessed the skin, the hair, and the trim bodies of the secular pop diva. Aspiring to offer an alternative to secular pop, CCM promoters replicated those attractive characteristics of secular musicians that most evangelicals either affirmed as a positive value or did not countenance as a candidate for affirmation or censure. The slender, unblemished female form—age to age, still the same—tested well.[49]

The Gaithers' featuring of women marginalized in the music industry was not merely a side effect of the program's orientation to bygone days. First, by the end of the twentieth century, the Homecomings had become more than memorials of mid-century gospel. Fans were celebrating the elderly musicians, male and female, for their *recent* Homecoming performances as much as for their mid-century performances. Eva Mae still could play. Vestal remained a force onstage.[50] For several artists, the Homecomings were a second career zenith. Second, the Gaithers publicly had protested (and continue to protest) the music industry's sexisms for some time—by word and deed. In *It's More Than the Music*, Bill tells the story of the signing of a young, overweight Sandi Patty when another Christian music label passed on her; the label "could not sell [Patty's] image." Bill writes, "the Christian music industry was following the lead of country and pop music in its search for the next slim and sleek artist [...] . That attitude made me sad, and it still makes me sad now."[51] In 2007, I attended a Homecoming concert months after *Playboy* playmate Anna Nicole Smith had died of a drug overdose—not a loss I expected anyone on the stage to take time to lament. While acknowledging that he did not know the particular demons with which Anna Nicole Smith wrestled, Bill used the occasion of her death to speak for several minutes about the trauma and identity struggles that loomed for all women in a culture that reduced women's worth to their physical appearance. He enjoined those audience members who had young daughters or granddaughters to tell the girls regularly, "you are a beloved child of God," and that, despite what anyone says, their value had nothing to do with their hair, their skin, or their weight. When in 2008 I attended the main Sunday service at the Gaithers' home church in Indiana, nearly all of the liturgical duties (sermon included) were performed by women. Bill was delighted when I expressed pleasant surprise as we drove from the service. In reference to the pastoral interns who came to their home church from nearby colleges, Gloria closed her book *Something Beautiful* with encouraging words for the next generation of Christian communicators: "preach it, sister, preach it!"[52]

Older women were especially prominent the first decade of the Homecomings, but as the 1990s gave way to the "aughts," younger women began appearing in greater proportion and assuming greater programmatic centrality in the Homecomings. Candy Hemphill Christmas, daughter of gospel singer-songwriters Joel and LaBreeska Hemphill, began appearing in the mid-1990s and was a regular until around 2002. Christmas was the most demonstrative of regularly appearing women. She usually sat near the front of the Homecoming circle, and the camera frequently found her. Christmas was also physically attractive by CCM standards, though like most Homecoming women, her big hair and heavy makeup harked back to CCM trends a few years old. Coupled with the confidence with which she assumed the stage, Christmas's long skirts and pantsuits also gave her the air of a Pentecostal/charismatic evangelist—a singing cousin to Paula White, Joyce Meyer, and Juanita Bynum. A cadre of women slid first into the back rows, then into the spotlight of the Homecoming choir around the same time—Joyce Martin Sanders and Judy Martin Hess of the Martins, Sheri Easter, Sonya and Becky Isaacs, and others. Although the Homecoming cameras fell for increasingly lengthy amounts of time on this new generation, as long as Vestal, Eva Mae, and their generation were present, the younger generation never dominated the camera. In contrast with CCM, the Gaither Homecomings were extremely intergenerational enterprises well into the twenty-first century.

But the old guard did depart, and changes did occur. One of the unusual characteristics of the Homecomings' second decade was the grandmatriarchal gap, which became most visible around the time of Vestal's 2003 death. Those younger women who had been present in the 1990s Homecomings did not replace Vestal or Eva Mae. Those who had familial connections to the legendary gospel families (Tanya Goodman Sykes, Allison Durham Speer, Candy Hemphill Christmas) did not fill their mothers' and aunts' seats—unusual, given the strong Homecoming narrative of "passin' the faith along" to the next generation. Cynthia Clawson, who had been the most prominent middle-aged woman in the 1990s Homecomings, left and co-pastored a church in Texas with her spouse. Connie Hopper of the Hoppers was a constant well into the twenty-first century, but she was never an outspoken, front-row presence. Candy Hemphill Christmas moved to Nashville, also to become the co-pastor of a church with her spouse and to start a ministry to the city's homeless population. Joyce Martin (then) McCullough went through a difficult divorce, and the Martins stopped recording from 2003 to 2011. Given their long Homecoming tenure, Janet Paschal and Sheri Easter were reasonable candidates to fill the chairs, except that they were relatively young and their domestic arrangements did not fit the script. Paschal had made her way in gospel music as a single woman until 1999, when she married at the age of forty-three. She had no biological children. Easter was not finished being a *mother*, let alone ready to become a grandmother. She delivered her third child in 2005, twenty years after her wedding, eleven years after her previous child (a chronology about which the Easters regularly joked onstage). Moreover, Paschal and Easter entered later seasons of life during an epoch of "age-defying" cosmetics. It was hard to look at them, as the first decade of the new century closed, and believe they actually were approaching the age of some of the "grandmatriarchs" of the first Homecomings. Already possessing some significant connections in the music industry outside the Homecomings, the Isaacs set off on their own seemingly as quickly as they arrived. Although Lily Isaacs was in the right age demographic to fill the grandmatriarchs' seat, Lily's southern gospel narrative was not (could not be) like Vestal's. No biologically matrilineal descent, and little institutionally matrilineal descent, occurred. Even the most powerful woman in the Homecoming world was powerful as a slight outsider—both due to the Homecoming narrative of her and to her increasingly infrequent appearances. Gloria Gaither seemed not so much a singer in the world but the voice hovering over it.

The period during which I attended Homecoming concerts was the period during which women were least present on the Homecoming stage—certainly as regular acts.[53] The GVB increasingly dominated the concerts. Bill seemed to be passing the scepter with which he had been entrusted to Ernie Haase and Signature Sound, the all-male group led by Haase, ex-Cathedral tenor and son-in-law of George Younce. The young Haase's familial, institutional, and stylistic link to Younce, the Cathedrals, and southern gospel music generally made him a sensible heir apparent. Homecoming descent looked to be patrilineal if it was going to be anything. No one was going to pick up Vestal's hanky and sit in her big plush chair. That center was gone.

ROUND WITH MANY VOICES

In all his dealings with legends' passing, Bill knew better than to try to force replacements. As I discussed in chapter 1, Bill was good at intuiting when to stop trying to recreate something, even as he acknowledged he had to maintain some continuity with old projects. He told me in 2008, "It seems like it's a lover's quarrel in the southern gospel field. 'We want you to be exactly like this, and if you aren't, we're going to give you a lot of static.' And maybe that's a compliment, you know? It's more like a family kind of thing, you know? 'You're still part of the family; I want you to behave like you are a part of the family.'" Moreover, as much as Bill loves southern gospel quartet music, stylistically he cannot rest from travel. He claimed he never wanted merely to recreate tribute after tribute: "I think the community angle is another reason why I did [the videos]. You could do one or two just for the sake of nostalgia. You couldn't do one hundred and fifty. I mean, I'd be tired of it after a point— say, 'okay, we've remembered all of the Big Chief [Wetherington, of the States- men] and Jake [Hess] stories we can tell, now why else are we doing this?' So you've got to find other reasons to do what you're going to do." In these state- ments, Bill echoes Gloria's emphasis on the community aspect of the Home- comings. The same dilemma appears. If you are in a community, this means that other community members can and will develop expectations of you. Bill feels somewhat confined by the southern gospel world's expectations (and confined by the works of his own hands over the past few decades, which have helped to create the expectations). However, he appreciates the respect implic- itly granted him: only family could develop such strong expectations of one another, and such a sense that they are entitled to having such expectations met. In a related fashion, this southern gospel community is built on having a shared history; expectations develop because of precedent. Bill consciously has enjoyed, perpetuated, and benefited from telling Big Chief and Jake Hess stories. He has passed their music along, literally and by way of the new/old GVB, Ernie Haase, and others. However, if a community is to be dynamic, it must allow its members some agency. Bill seems to want some freedom to work at the margins. He wants to strive for better quality, to seek different musical forms, to find new talent, and never to yield too much to conventions. But these very conventions shaped him and his Homecomings.

During the second half of the final main concert at Gatlinburg, Bill "did a homecoming." All of the musicians who had sung during the weekend gath- ered in seats on the circular stage in the center of the arena. The semicircle of the early Homecomings—from the viewers' point of view, a concave arc— became inverted. It was now a convex gathering of performers; we the viewers did not complete the circle but bore witness to its completion onstage. The passing of the solo microphone, the verse-long mini-ensembles, the joking and talking between songs, and the sing-along atmosphere made this "home- coming" related to the old programs. But the characters in the circle were dif- ferent—for a time.

As the set grew to its climax, as the ensemble began singing the "Home-coming classics," the circle doubled. The video screens, arranged above the stage in a convex circle so that they projected out in every direction, brought the legends forth: Jake Hess, George Younce, Glen Payne—all suspended in the pixillated sky above Wes Hampton, Ernie Haase, and Kim Collingsworth. The footage of them singing came from old Homecoming videos. Suddenly, Hampton was harmonizing with Hess, Haase with his father-in-law Younce. When Vestal Goodman presided over the circle, a roar of applause went up from the audience and from the singers gathered underneath her, as if she could hear it. The final song sung on the main stage that weekend was "Because He Lives." Wes Hampton—the most versatile singer in all of the Homecomings, the only GVB member not named Bill Gaither who remained in the group after the 2009 shakeup—wailed the first verse. The "live" ensem-ble—audience, performers, living and dead—sang the chorus in unison.

Some version of this video resurrection happened in Gaither shows throughout the twenty-first century. Years after Natalie Cole's Grammy-win-ning performance of "Unforgettable" with her deceased father Nat King Cole, a few years before deceased hip-hop artist Tupac Shakur would appear "live" as a hologram at the Coachella Music Festival in California, Bill Gaither had widened the lens, erased time, and reinvigorated the tradition that had made the Homecomings the biggest phenomena in gospel music. Death gave way to victory in the Homecomings' technocracy of the dead. The blessings fell from the chromakey heaven, from those confederated dead, sought among the living, onto the next generation of Homecoming singers. The final chapter is about one of that next generation.

6
HOME BOARDERS
LYNDA RANDLE AND RACE

MODERN, INTEGRATED, INTERPRETIVE

"Hello, all you vanilla people."

I laughed out loud and looked around, half-convinced I had misheard. The applause from the Salisbury, Maryland, audience was tapering from the song that had just ended, but it still popcorned loudly enough throughout the arena to cloud some of the stage audio. I could have misheard.

Lynda Randle spoke again, punctuating hard consonants with staccato bursts of air and lingering on long vowels like they were draughts of expensive wine:

"Hellohh from a CHoColaTe Giiiirl from Deee-Ceee."

I was certain I had heard correctly this time. As the clapping subsided, I noticed the calm smiles on the visages of my immediate neighbors, all middle-aged and senior white men and women. I had become well acquainted with these easy, summer-picnic grins—too muted to signal ecstasy, but sufficiently recurrent to signify hearts soon made glad, hearts ready to believe that things can get no worse than pleasant enough. White dress hanging loosely from her shoulders and cascading to the middle of her shins, tightly curled noodles of jet-black hair blossoming in all directions from the center of her scalp, Randle slowly strolled across the front of the stage, waving and rendering smile for smile.

I did not expect all smiling to stop, exactly, when Lynda Randle, the African American woman who appeared most regularly on the Homecoming stages, broadcasted, in high definition, her racial contrast. Those with eyes to see—and perhaps those with ears to hear—knew that Randle represented racial difference on a Homecoming stage. Her broadcast merely named the obvious. However, excepting the Potter's House concert videos, forthright speech about onstage racial difference was a rarity in Homecoming programs, especially before 2004. When race was invoked, it was typically done in a narrative voiceover, as in Bill's discussion of black children learning to sing on their mothers' knee in *Turn Your Radio On*. Even the two South African Homecoming videos, released just a few months before this Maryland concert, communicated little directly about race, nationality, or ethnicity—European, African, white, or African American. The lack of conversation about race, despite the presence of some racial diversity, had for me substantiated one of the claims of sociologists Michael Emerson and Christian Smith: white evangelicals who moved in overwhelmingly white social circles regarded silence as the proper response to racial difference. White evangelicals preferred not to "make an issue" of race; in fact, they blamed those who "made race an issue" for fanning the cooling embers of American racism.[1] Randle's rhetorical revelation of racial difference did not necessarily jar her white audience out of their racial assumptions. Her words did not preface the sort of address on systemic racism that Emerson and Smith might have advocated. She spoke euphemistically; *chocolate* and *vanilla* were more pleasing to the palate than were *black* and *white*. Still, Randle made race surface in a new way for a community whose members were accustomed to holding race talk below the discursive waterline. I expected to see some smiles unsettled.

No one batted an eye.

During that and all concerts, my attempts to ride the trains of gazes and sounds that ran between Lynda Randle and her audiences often left me perplexed. A few years after the Maryland show, onstage in Alabama, Randle recounted a story (at Bill's prompting) about her touring RV being stopped by the police in the South. Lynda was riding in the passenger seat as her spouse, Mike, drove. They noticed several sirens in their rearview mirrors and pulled over. The next thing they knew, a sheriff's deputy had his pistol pointed directly at Mike through the left window of the glass. The terrified Randles breathed a slight sigh of relief when the deputy screamed, "it ain't him!" (Lynda put on a white Florida panhandle accent to deliver the line.) Apparently, a white man had absconded with singer Crystal Gayle's RV after a show in a nearby town and was driving through the night somewhere. Lynda laughed as she said, "for once, the police weren't on the lookout for a chocolate man." Randle, Bill, and we in the crowd laughed at the punchline. I am not sure that we all laughed for the same reasons. Revisiting Randle's story in 2015—during and shortly after the highly publicized police killings of black men in Ferguson, Missouri, Baltimore, Maryland, Staten Island, New York, and numerous other locations—I was less sure.

That Lynda Randle could talk so candidly onstage about race demonstrated how embedded she had become in the Homecoming world. In the life of the Homecomings, no African American performer—and, in the twenty-first century, few women—would be so familiar and intimate with Homecoming audiences. Her solo sets and spoken banter with audiences separated her from Lillie Knauls. Unlike Jessy Dixon, who already had made a name for himself before he entered the Homecoming sphere, Randle basically became a known entity through her relationship with the Gaithers.[2] After making her debut video appearance in 1996—on *When All God's Singers Get Home*, in a brief ad-lib performance of Rex Nelon's "We Shall Wear a Robe and Crown"—Randle soon joined the Homecoming tour as a regular. In 2007, with the release of *The Best of Lynda Randle*, she became one of two African Americans (with Jessy Dixon), one of two women outside a family band (with Janet Paschal), and one of a handful of performers under the age of fifty to have her own Homecoming compilation video.[3]

Randle began her Homecoming career during those transitional, turn-of-the-century years when the Gaithers were supplanting in-studio videos for live concert videos, when members of the old Homecoming generation were beginning to die in quick succession. She arrived just in time to make it into the studio sessions with the "legends"—sessions that would later themselves become the object of Homecoming nostalgia. She thus could reasonably claim to be one of the "classic" members of the Homecoming troupe. In the first decade of the twenty-first century, Homecoming audiences not only expected to see Randle; they expected to hear her perform the particular songs that had become, by her rendering, "Homecoming favorites." Through these years, she recorded at the Gaithers' Indiana studios. The Gaithers' music company has released all but the first two of her major studio albums.

As she narrated herself and was narrated to Homecoming audiences, Randle was not simply a friendly Christian neighbor, an ambassador from the supposedly distant realm of black gospel. She was not simply the latest black person in the Homecoming rotation. As I will show through my examination of her Homecoming biography and her music, Randle and the Gaithers posit Randle as a kind of southern gospel singer. Granted, her membership had specific conditions. Like Lily Isaacs, Gloria Gaither, and even, to some extent, Guy Penrod, Randle had an insider-outsider story. She belonged insofar as she did not seem to belong. But as an African American woman, Randle represented an old difference newly lodged in the old home place. The difference she represented always had been present in the southern gospel field, and in the Homecomings. But Randle was centrally cast. *Her* difference was alight in the spotlight, and the hearth was constrained to find ways to contain it.

POTOMAC RIVER, DOWNTOWN

Gloria Gaither is correct about walking stories. Be they little brown churches in the glen or storefront sanctuaries nestled in between the great steel fingers of the city, the old houses of American Christianity perpetually ring with storytelling. Stories of God animating specific believers' circumstances stoke the fires of evangelicalism. To be sure, personal stories do not wield unfettered power; accounts that tug too forcefully at the tentpoles of a faith community's grand narrative meet revision or censorship. However, the "little" stories that individual evangelicals tell to themselves and to others constantly constitute and reconstitute the communities' broader narrative, each injecting new blood into an old redemption story.

For artists in the Christian music industry—artists whose careers depend upon their projecting a personal faith fundamentally consonant with that of their fan base—biographies possess immeasurable significance. What Jay Howard and John Streck note in their study of CCM holds true for most Christian music: "For many [CCM fans], the single defining characteristic of contemporary Christian music is the faith of the artists who produce it ... the end result, then, is a genre defined not by the texts (songs and albums) that constitute it, but by the individuals responsible for producing those texts."[4] Howard and Streck rightly identify theological and moral beliefs and practices as key rubrics fans use in assessing a Christian musical act's merit. Christian music fans want to know that musicians believe the right things and, perhaps more importantly, live the right way.

However, Howard and Streck isolate moral-theological considerations from other assumptions regarding (among many possibilities) race, age, class, gender, and region. Explicit moral-theological priorities always develop against a backdrop of other cultural assumptions and expectations. Embodied musicians do not appear as disembodied doctrines or practices to disembodying fans. An audience's sexual ethics will fall differently upon the bodies of male and female artists. An aging female artist will face a different set of expectations from an audience than would a young female artist. An artist who grew up in a single-parent apartment in the Bronx must make a different set of choices in telling her story to a fan base that values the nuclear family and "southern country living" than would an artist who hails from a two-parent home in rural Georgia. Guy Penrod and Mark Lowry have to be narrated through and around different "facts" of their lives to garner fans' trust. "Correct" doctrine and behavior might earn Christian artists a favorable response, but so too must artists play to (and with) other listener sensibilities to gain full acceptance. In turn, the particularity of artists' stories—especially if they conform at auspicious points to audience expectations—can precipitate slow, often unconscious alterations in their audiences' standards. This interplay illustrates well Pierre Bourdieu's concept of the "intentionless invention of regulated improvisation." Musicians operate under discursive regulations that allow for some (controlled) ad-libbing, and this ad-libbing can produce, unbeknown to musician and audience alike, changes in the regulations themselves. The rules governing Christian music communities are constructed in part as an effect of the behaviors that the rules themselves are supposed to manage.[5]

In such a milieu, Lynda Randle works out her acceptability. The details of Lynda Randle's life make her at once a favorable and unfavorable candidate for acceptance into the Homecoming fold. Stated simply, Randle grew up in Washington, DC, in a heterosexual two-parent household, with eight siblings. Her father drove a taxi and worked as a part-time minister, and her mother stayed at home with the children. After attending public school through the eighth grade, her parents enrolled her in a Christian school in one of Washington's Maryland suburbs, where she was the only African American student. Randle began her solo singing career during high school, at the prompting of her choir instructor, who encouraged her to develop her solo skills. She later attended Jerry Falwell's Liberty University in Lynchburg, Virginia, again as a racial minority in a largely white, heavily Christian school. Immediately after graduating from Liberty in 1989, Randle married Mike. The pair relocated to Liberty, Missouri, a major Kansas City suburb, where they lived while Mike worked as a youth minister in the nearby city, his hometown. Lynda took her music on the road, performing primarily at churches, music festivals, and women's conferences. At one of her performances at a woman's conference in the early 1990s, Gloria Gaither was in attendance. Impressed with Lynda's abilities, Gloria reported her find to Bill, and the Gaithers invited Randle to record an album at their studio in the mid-1990s. Soon after, Randle performed on her first Homecoming video. She quickly became a Homecoming regular. For the first seven years of the twenty-first century, a large majority of her concert appearances occurred on Homecoming stages.[6]

One purpose of the always-important spoken-word narratives in Homecoming programs is to clarify the link between singers and their "staple" songs. Singers at live performances regularly preface songs with personal stories that illustrate the songs' significance in their lives. As Randle and Gloria present them in *The Best of Lynda Randle Homecoming*, Randle's biography and signature song are just so wedded. As with all of the *Best of . . .* Gaither videos, the Randle program divides the musical features with shots of the Randle home and excerpts of Randle's interview with Gloria. The exchanges between Randle and Gaither, filtered through the Gaither editing process and saturated with references to Randle's suburban schooling and urban upbringing, illustrate the dually exceptional and representative role Randle must play for her Homecoming audience.

"You look like a person who's never had a problem in the world," Gloria Gaither says to Randle early in the video. Randle laughs.

> RANDLE: I don't have any sob stories as far as being raised in the inner city of D.C. For a while I did . . .
> GAITHER: You *were* raised in the city?
> RANDLE: Right. In the city. For a while I wondered why of all the places to raise a kid, God allowed me to be born in Washington, D.C. But that was definitely something that strengthened me and brought me to this place.[7]

Randle first invokes urban life generally and dismissively. She positions her experience against the general experience of "being raised in the inner city" and all of its accompanying misery and tragedy. She did not have *that* kind of life. Her labeling of accounts of inner-city plight as "sob stories" suggests some general skepticism regarding either the reality or the degree of the plight (one does not call a *true* tragedy a "sob story"). Randle prefaces her comments about her urban existence by disentangling herself from the typical, apparently melodramatic and contrived, inner-city narrative, thus rendering her own testimony more authentic, more honest. Randle has no sob story to tell, just a real one.

Gloria's interruption ("you *were* raised in the city") of Randle alters the interview's orientation toward the urban. Gloria obviously does not reiterate the location of Randle's childhood for her own clarity; she already knows this detail. The clarification that Randle, indeed, was raised in the city, draws Randle back into a tough city narrative from which her earlier comments began to remove her. Randle's self-distancing from "inner city sob stories" may make her personal story more trustworthy, but if she departs too dramatically from the peril-laden urban narrative that Homecoming audiences expect to hear from an African American woman, she risks forfeiting her status as a representative of urban (and black) life. Gloria seems to sense this, and immediately reinforces Randle's origins. The fact that a video edit occurs to show Gloria make the interjection—that there is a jump cut from Randle to Gloria back to Randle to capture each woman speaking—highlights how important this point is in the Homecoming setting. Gloria reminds viewers that, notwithstanding the *uniqueness* of Randle's story, it is still authentically *representative* of city life.

Following Gloria's interjection, Randle's DC upbringing seems fraught with hardship. The city burdened Randle at least enough for her to question God's justice in her youth. While Randle admits to wondering why God put her in DC, she exempts her parents from liability. The absence of Randle's parents from the account precludes the conclusion that her family simply could have moved if conditions were so terrible. Randle does not leave an opportunity open for Homecoming audiences to cast her parents as mobile masters of their circumstances, thus producers of (and wallowers in) their family's tribulations. Such an account would run the risk of becoming a sob story to those Homecoming fans who lionize hard work and are suspicious of structural, deterministic explanations of hardship—specifically urban poverty.[8] As in other Homecoming cases, here there are no named human victimizers. Just as Randle exempts her parents from liability, her silence regarding the racial and structural dynamics of her plight keeps white, middle- and upper-class societies off the judgment seat. As Randle must preserve the virtue of her family inside and along with the racially inflected "hard work" narrative, God becomes the nonhuman victimizer most suitable to invoke.

Acknowledgment of the divine root of her circumstances affords Randle a reasonable explanation for her afflictions. Because a loving and all-powerful God would not insist that beloved creatures suffer senselessly, Randle's suffering in DC must have possessed a purpose. Like numberless Christians before her, Randle understands her past difficulties as a God-kindled fire through which she passed in order to become "stronger." This justification of suffering occurs in numerous black and white gospel songs, from Charles Tindley's "We'll Understand It Better By and By," to the Gaither's own "It Won't Rain Always." However, unlike the speakers in these songs, Randle pairs her strengthening with physical deliverance from the environs of her trials. In her statement, "that was definitely something that strengthened me," the first "that" invites listeners to join place with experience, as "that" seems to refer to both the city and Randle's tumultuous life in the city. Washington itself *was* the trial; there is no question of seeking welfare in it, or seeking its welfare. If God designs only temporary trials—hurdles over which believers must jump to achieve a condition that is possible only on the other side of the trial— the city itself becomes purely instrumental, a proving ground that Randle had to endure for a time but ultimately one from which she achieved liberty. Not only did Washington strengthen her; it also "brought" her somewhere other than Washington—to an ambiguous "this place." Certainly, "this place" suggests arrival at a new spiritual plane. But as Randle speaks these lines— reclining in a plush easy chair, arms draped over the marshmallow cushions, addressing one of the wealthiest women in the music industry—the struggles of Washington seem a distant memory. The city was not a dwelling place by Randle's reckoning. It was a stop on the way to greener pastures.

In this portion of her interview with Gloria—which occurs immediately after the opening song on the video—Randle explicitly disavows "sob sto- ries," but she suggests that some degree of general difficulty accompanied her inner-city life. The biography on her website, around the same time, made the latter point more forcefully: "Growing up a part of the D.C. inner-city culture, Lynda experienced a pain and anguish that can rarely be imagined by the majority of Christian America. Since giving her life to the Lord Jesus Christ, He has used the scars of her youth to bring a distinct depth and richness to her ministry."[9] The inner-city wounds cut deeper and wider in this statement than they do in her interview with Gloria. The city left scars usable to God. Moreover, the "pain and anguish" of the inner city suddenly and unabashedly enter into a binary relationship with the apparently nonurban "majority of Christian America."

In both the interview and the website biography, it is understandable if Randle offers few specific details regarding her inner-city anguish. Limited space on the video and webpage, not to mention personal reluctance to expose private and perhaps painful memories, might restrict Randle from speaking in detail about her early life.[10] However, the details that Randle does volunteer complicate her account of her absorption and misfortune in the city. Immediately after Randle's statements regarding Washington, she leaps to a discussion of her adult life and the tragedies that provided the context of her "call" to sing her signature song—"God on the Mountain," a performance of which follows this interview clip. The abrupt leap leaves the adulthood trag- edies connected narratively to her inner-city youth. Randle explains that the song "came" to her at a time she had lost several family members. Her father died of cancer in old age (shortly after diagnosis), one of her brothers died of a brain aneurysm at fifty-four, one of her sisters died at thirty-seven for a rea- son Randle does not disclose, and a close friend "passed in her sleep" at thirty- eight—all in the span of a few months. While it makes sense that Randle would jump to a discussion of the overwhelming loss she experienced during the time she discovered "God on the Mountain" (this portion of the interview, after all, prefaces the song), the quick transition steers listeners away from the details of Randle's Washington existence, leaving them free to construct the city hardships themselves, using whatever preconceptions of urban space they have at their disposal. At the same time, Randle's adult losses, though they pertain to specific people in Randle's life, are universal in kind, and open empathetic territory between Randle and the aging Gaither audience, many of whom have experienced similar losses.[11] Randle's nod toward her urban upbringing reminds Homecoming viewers of the singularity of her witness; her city-born anguish is, indeed, such that audiences cannot imagine—even though the absence of particular details in Randle's account invites audiences to imagine. The allusion to specific deceased friends and relatives, conversely, highlights the commonness of Randle's pain. Both maneuvers establish Randle as authentically fit to perform Tracy Dartt's gospel hit:

> The God of the mountain is still God of the valley
> When things go wrong, He'll make them right
> And the God of the good times, is still God of the bad times
> The God of the daylight, is still God in the night.[12]

Randle's unique inner-city blues grant her a special dominion over the song; Randle *like no one else* understands the valley, the bad times. At the same time, Randle's familiar familial losses afford her representative status; she sings out of and on behalf of the suffering of the Homecoming audiences.[13]

The most peculiar variable in Randle's inner-city story is the large degree of contact she had at a young age with white suburbia. Starting in the ninth grade, Randle attended a private, Christian, and by her account all-white high school in Maryland. In the sixty-five-minute video, Randle mentions the school in three separate interview segments, each of which reveals her ambivalence regarding her location in the school. In the first of these segments, Randle begins to say that she went to a Christian school in Washington, then quickly corrects herself: "I went to a Christian school in Washington, D.C., you know, actually in the Maryland area, and I was kind of thrust into an all-white choir. And I was like the only chocolate kid in this choir. And they were singing these spirituals and songs, and one thing led to another and they asked me to sing."[14] Demarcating Washington from "the Maryland area" highlights the compartmental nature of Randle's youth, though in both cases Randle renders herself as an object to forces outside of her control. She lived in DC because God ordained it. An unidentified force "thrust" Randle into the all-white student choir. As the only African American in the choir, she apparently became the "authentic" renderer of the spirituals in the choir's repertoire. Randle passes over the process of her selection ("one thing led to another"). The general and putatively white "they" acted on the spirituals and on Randle. Randle renders herself object in other segments of the interview as well, claiming, "I was put in this Christian school." In contrast with her inner-city account, Randle's school narrative introduces her parents as determining agents in her education. God did not decide—directly—to enroll Randle in the suburban Christian school. Her parents acted. In none of her accounts of her school experiences does Randle cast herself in an active role.

More ambivalence is evident in Randle's discussion of the religious aspects of her youth. As Gloria probes the religious dimensions of Randle's background, Randle immediately transports viewers to her home in Washington: "Every single night around our kitchen table, there in the inner city of Washington, we would have family devotions and read the Psalms and the Proverbs."[15] These were *family* devotions—led by her father, as Randle later notes. But this Rockwellian scene, so celebrated in southern gospel culture, occurred "there in the inner city." Emphasizing that urban context, Randle seems to think this will provoke quiet exasperation in an audience who equates "inner city" with moral or religious emptiness. If audience preconceptions of an essentially irreligious urban landscape hold, Randle's family comes off as possessing miraculously exceptional piety. There in the decadent American Nineveh, a father spends quality time with his family, providing regular religious instruction. But if the religious dedication of the Randle family functions representationally vis-à-vis the inner city, audiences cannot maintain perceptions of the city as unequivocally profane. A part-time taxi cab driver, part-time preacher leads his family in nightly Bible reading. In many ways, that *is* Christian America, as Homecoming audiences likely understand it. If that is true, the god of those country mountains of Gatlinburg is also the god of the metropolis.

These two possible understandings of Randle's family devotion story can and probably do coexist in some proportion among fans. But given Randle's heretofore equation of the inner city with depravity and misery, Randle family exceptionalism in the face of inner-city degeneracy seems the interpretation likely to prevail. Randle's perpetual tracing of religious boundaries along municipal (and concurrently racial) borders further promotes such a reading of Randle and the city:

As much as I tease about it, it was a predominantly white Christian school, and you coming straight out of the inner city and to a school with predominantly white kids, it was kind of weird at first. And my parents, though, taught us to love people. They made no issues of color of skin or anything like that, so it wasn't really that hard to adjust. But being in that school and having Bible [instruction] and those kinds of things all day, um, has a way of working deeper into your personal life.[16]

Randle's narrative vacillates between two poles: easy assimilation and apprehensive adaptation. In this passage, the "weirdness" Randle initially feels derives from racial and regional difference. The inner city opposes the white school, and matriculation in the latter marks more than a mere change in location. But Randle immediately places the racial aspects of her transition under erasure, noting that her parents did not "make an issue" of race in their tutelage of their children.[17] Retracting her invocation of race requires Randle to minimize the "weirdness" she experiences. Due to her parents' "color-blind" moral training, the adjustment proved smooth and fleeting.

However, Randle does not let go of the difference she experiences in the school. Instead, she transmutes her feelings of difference to a discussion of religious training. By the end of her account, Randle identifies the ubiquity of the Bible as the Christian school's most striking departure from the inner city. Randle does not express the difference as a function of private versus public education. She positions the "inner city" in general, not the public education system, against her private Christian school and its uninterrupted religious instruction ("Christian" is the one adjective that prefaces "school" every time Randle mentions the Maryland school). A mere minute after she fondly and proudly recalls her family's inner-city Bible time, Randle nullifies the inner city as a viable site of religious devotion by opposing it to the pious private school. Coming out of the city to a white school was strange at first, but Randle easily adjusted because she had learned from her parents to "make no issue" of race. Coming out of the city to a place where people regularly read the Bible necessitated a more prolonged and profound adjustment, even though Randle had learned from her parents the value and practice of regular Bible reading. Randle minimizes the racial difference between Washington and her private suburban school—a difference that, by Randle's own admission, is a stark reality but apparently has no bearing on her story. She enlarges the religious difference between Washington and the school—a difference that Randle's devout urban-dwelling family undermines but a difference that is nonetheless central to Randle's story. All racial considerations supposedly set aside, the conclusion seems clear: the god of the suburbs is not the god of the metropolis.

What is Lynda Randle's *true* domain? Is Randle "of the city" or "of the suburbs?" Is Randle "in but not of" one or both of these worlds? Randle's biography contains, and must contain, multitudes. So too her music.

ANOTHER GOSPEL, ANOTHER COUNTRY

"God on the Mountain" begins in the tonal valley. The first line of the song, "Life is easy when you're up on the mountain," requires the vocalist to hit the song's lowest note twice in her first breath. The opening words gradually ascend from a low F—not an impossibly low note for an alto, but very deep nonetheless—to an A, pauses, then lands back on the F: "Life (F) is (G) ea (A)—sy (F)." The singer starts by ascending the musical scale—scaling the mountain—but immediately falls back onto the note—into the valley—whence she came.

That "God on the Mountain" would become Randle's signature Homecoming song makes stylistic as well as thematic sense. Randle is not a "mountaintop" vocalist. In comparison with contemporaneous leading female vocalists in black gospel music, she possesses a limited and low vocal range.[18] She cannot improvise rapidly up and down musical scales—a highly valued if not essential characteristic for late twentieth- and early twenty-first-century female black gospel performers. However, Randle has a nearly flawless sense of pitch (an attribute that helped her earn the only perfect score ever given to a singer at the Christian Artist Music Seminar Talent Contest, a major Christian music industry event). She also sings with a cavernous, wide-mouthed intonation that fills concert halls despite her low register. Randle performances do not peak on explosive high notes or a string of high-velocity vocal improvisations. Rather, they slowly swell and shrink like a river at the bottom of a gorge—within very closed parameters, with no aspirations to the whirl of the mountaintop that so often distinguishes black gospel performances.

But is "mountaintop black gospel" the only type of black gospel? What determines the "blackness" (or "whiteness") of gospel music? Intricacy, frequency, and scalar quality of vocal modulation? Instrumentation? Tempo? Song repertoire? Racial makeup of the audience? The musician's self-identification with a genre? Who sets the terms of one's belonging in a genre? The question of genre is not foreign to musical circles. But addressing the question of *gospel* music's parameters requires the recognition of the interplay between style, race, and religion in the construction and preservation of what would seem, at first glance, a primarily musical descriptor. Stylistic choices are racialized choices. In varying degrees and with varying consequences, one could say the same of rap, country, and a number of other musical genres. But with gospel, the confluence of the underground cultural rivers that feed this body of music occurs very close to the surface of performers' and listeners' awareness, often breaching that surface. Race consciously *and* unconsciously matters in gospel music communities. Randle's music—and her reflection on her music—demonstrate the crosscurrents that pull Randle as she stands in the middle of converging racial and stylistic streams.

A Way Through, Randle's first album under Gaither sponsorship, released in 1995, bears few stylistic similarities to later Randle recordings. Unlike those later recordings, *A Way Through* includes several Randle-penned songs.

Heavily syncopated percussion programming and layer upon layer of synthesizer parts—reminiscent both of the early 1990s *nouveau* R & B of Bobby Brown and the "adult" R & B of Peabo Bryson—drive the quick cadence of several tracks. Occasional nods to older gospel styles—most prominent on the Hammond organ-driven title track—occur on *A Way Through*, but arrangements of the 1990s R & B variety remain the norm throughout the album. Despite the thickness of the instrumental production, however, Randle's vocals receive little studio tweaking—no effects, few of the stacked harmonies that typically add body to vocals otherwise swallowed by such multitiered instrumentation. Randle's solitary and undistilled voice jarringly juts from songs that are otherwise the audio progeny of digital effects processors and loop machines. On the album cover, Randle, dressed in what appears to be a pantsuit, her hair tightly braided, croons into an old-fashioned RCA microphone against a backdrop of another, more obscured figure (perhaps also Randle) standing arms outstretched in front of a large red door. The image captures well the anomalous meeting of tradition and modernity on the album.

Whether or not *A Way Through* felt like an awkward fit to Randle, it certainly proved a tough sell for Randle and the Gaithers' Spring House Music Company. The album saw limited production and distribution from the outset. As of 2008 it was commercially available only through Randle's personal website and at her concerts (as of 2016, it is extremely hard to find). Randle's 2000 release, *Soul Shower*, evidences several changes. More polished studio production and greater coherence between vocal and instrumental tracks set the album apart from its predecessor. Like *A Way Through*, *Soul Shower* conforms to some of the pop music *du jour*—acoustic pianos, drums, and guitars creep back onto the sonic landscape, joining more subdued incarnations of the previous two decades' electronic instrumentation. *Soul Shower*'s discreet grooves and phlegmatic, quasi-acoustic voicings proved a good fit for Randle, and they worked well in an era that hoisted into the limelight irenic pop female vocalists such as Natalie Imbruglia and Leigh Nash, lead singer of the Christian music crossover group Sixpence None the Richer.[19]

Soul Shower's success, however, would pale in comparison with the popularity of her two-volume follow-up release in 2002 and 2001, *Timeless* and *Timeless II*.[20] Although Randle had been touring regularly with the Gaithers for about four years, no prior solo Randle recording captured her renditions of the songs that had endeared her to Homecoming audiences. The two *Timeless* albums feature the Randle of the Homecoming videos and stages. Several tracks on the first volume are actually remixed versions of live Homecoming performances, complete with smatterings of audible spoken affirmations from the aging choir of "Homecoming legends." Such vocal affirmations—popular in white and black gospel music gatherings alike—accentuate Randle's broader acceptance into the southern gospel fold. Randle seems at home in Homecomings.

In a number of ways, the *Timeless* albums mark Randle as a southern gospel musician. The arrangements lean heavily on the front portions of the four-count rhythm sequences. Bass drum and bass guitar square with each other prominently and exactly on the first and third beats; neither ever venture syncopated improvisations. The snare drum, which occurs on the third beat, all but disappears in the mix. The handclapping that occasionally emerges from the choir and/or audience aligns with the bass instruments on the first and third beats.[21] Piano dominates the recordings, serving as both the rhythmic and harmonic locus of the accompaniment. Guitar and harmonica solos occasionally fill the transitional space between verses and choruses. Unlike African American choral arrangements, which often have only soprano, alto, and tenor parts, a fourth, bass part is prominent in most of the *Timeless* choral arrangements, as is the case with nearly all southern gospel hymn singing. The song selections also mark the *Timeless* albums as southern gospel. The overwhelming majority of the twenty-six songs on the two albums derive from known southern gospel songwriters—writers such as Dottie Rambo, Ronnie Hinson, Squire Parsons, and Tracy Dartt, all of whom made livings as performers of southern gospel. Four African American-penned songs appear on the two albums; Andraé Crouch and Charles Tindley get one credit apiece on each record. Bill and Gloria Gaither wrote or cowrote three *Timeless* selections.

The prevalence of southern gospel hallmarks on the *Timeless* albums makes sense given the Gaithers' hand in the releases during the Homecoming heyday. While the Gaithers exercised administrative control over Randle's previous projects, the first volume of the *Timeless* collection belongs to the Gaither Gospel Series, a subgroup of Gaither-managed products that contains many of the Homecoming albums and videos, most of the post-1991 GVB albums, and several remastered compilations of mid-twentieth-century southern gospel quartets and family bands. Artists whose products bear the Gaither Gospel Series logo reside in the green room of the Homecoming world. Randle's association in this select series, with such canonized acts as the Statesmen and the Speer Family, positions her as a vital member of the Homecoming version of the southern gospel community. It is among this community that Randle sells most of her wares.

Considered together, style, musical catalogue, marketing, and audience provide strong cause to label Randle a southern gospel musician. However, none of these criteria themselves are stable, and none unequivocally solve the question of Randle's genre. Even with all of the stylistic "southern gospelness" of Randle's music, Randle's execution does not resemble that of most female southern gospel vocalists. Her combination of forceful attack, nearly imperceptible roll-ups to initial pitches, confident casualness in interpreting rhythmic patterns, and placement of dramatic pauses and crescendos within phrases, are not signature southern gospel technique. They have many parallels in black gospel. White songwriters prevail on Randle recordings, but black and white gospel musicians have transported songs across racial borders throughout the twentieth century. Some of the white-authored pieces on the *Timeless* recordings such as "Down at the Cross" and "If the Lord Wasn't Walking by My Side" issue from black churches and black gospel stages as frequently as they do from white venues. The Gaithers market Randle inside the Homecoming southern gospel, but already I have noted how the Gaithers try to push, however gently, at the edges of the genre's boundaries—how Gloria, in fact, resists thinking of Homecoming music as essentially southern gospel. It is tough to tell where Gaither expansion of the genre ends and their departure from the genre begins. Randle indubitably appears in front of mostly white, and mostly Homecoming, audiences. However, the same is true of Jessy Dixon. For extended periods in their careers, Mahalia Jackson and Ethel Waters performed for mostly white audiences as well. This does not necessarily make them performers of a "white" genre of music.[22]

Granted, Randle's relationship to her white audiences differs from the relationship between these latter performers and their white audiences. White patrons of Jackson and Waters *expected* them to perform "black" music, according to "black" conventions. Conversely, the *similarity* of Randle's music to "white" southern gospel music, not its exotic departure from "white" musical forms, accounts for much of Randle's appeal. Yet Randle is not the gospel version of Charley Pride, the popular African American country musician of the 1960s and 1970s. Pride's twangy-voiced, heavily orchestrated recordings shimmer with the rhinestone gloss of white Nashville; his albums no more bear the sonic imprint of African American influence than do contemporaneous recordings of Dolly Parton or Kenny Rogers. Pride's success in country music required a supposedly complete purging of racial identity, and he knew it: "I don't have no skin hang-ups. I'm no color. I'm just Charley Pride, the man." [23] Randle's parents may have raised her to make "no issue" of color, but she does not claim to be colorless. Randle needs southern gospel audiences to code her as black. And Randle's success depends upon her ability to supply just the right kind of blackness in just the right, tastiest dosage. Like her reflections on her upbringing, her music demonstrates a cautious and intentional broadcasting of a particular blackness—"chocolate," as Randle dishes it.

The tenuous relationship Randle possesses with white (and black) gospel forms and communities starkly manifests itself when music and autobiography come together—when Randle speaks about her music. The first question Gloria Gaither smilingly poses to Randle in the interview on the *Best of Lynda Randle* video invites Randle to synthesize race and music genre: "So, Lynda, what is a black girl doing singing southern gospel country music?" Gaither likely intends her diminutive reference to the middle-aged Randle as a "black girl" to signal the pair's familiarity with each other, to indicate that race is an available and germane topic for discussion.[24] With respect to Randle's inclusion in the southern gospel fold—a fold Gaither further blanches by connecting it to overwhelmingly white "country" music—Randle humorously avoids committing herself in reply: "You know, Gloria, it's going to be kind of hard to answer that question. It's just [pauses] it's a God thing. It's something that I never dreamed of for myself. You couldn't have paid me any amount of money to believe that this would happen one day. But I'm just [pauses] I'm just here." Hesitations in the otherwise fast-talking Randle's speech are significant markers of self-editing. Randle begins to answer, stops to scan the cards in her rhetorical hand, then plays the wild card of evangelical personal testimony: "it's a God thing." The phrase both vocalizes Randle's faith and relieves her of responsibility for her career trajectory. She then braids the clichés of humble and grateful celebrity self-awe ("I could never have dreamed I would be *here*," "I could not have imagined *this* would have ever happened to *me*") with strands of cynicism and regret ("I would not have written my story *this* way," "you could not pay me enough money to do *this*"), to manufacture a suspiciously appreciative response. Perhaps feeling herself sinking deeper into the bog of ambivalence, Randle cuts herself off and ends by reasserting the premise of the question: "I'm just here." Question averted.

After briefly nodding toward her experience in the Maryland school, its choir, and her tenure in Liberty University (about which Randle gives no details), Randle names the Gaithers as her southern gospel godparents:

RANDLE: After my college days at Liberty University, I kind of hooked up with you guys, the Lord put us together, and I guess when you hang out with the Gaither folks, Bill, he can get you to do anything. [laughs].

GAITHER: [laughs] Things you would never imagine.

RANDLE: I would have never dreamed. [pauses] As a matter of fact, I still don't consider myself southern gospel per se. But it's fun. Y'all are [pauses, looks to the side, smiles] different kind of folks. And it's nice.[25]

Although the "kind of" softens the intentionality of Randle's initial contact with the Gaithers, Randle casts herself as a willing if not active agent in the "hooking up." Immediately, however, Randle withdraws her agency. *God* was responsible for "putting her together" with the Gaithers. By the time she concludes, Bill Gaither assumes the providential role: "he can get you to do anything." Be it God or Bill Gaither, someone besides Randle launched Randle's southern gospel career. When Randle resumes speaking of herself in the active voice, it is to claim distance from southern gospel. Even the proceeding qualification that she has fun in her southern gospel environs comes with mischievous glances and transparent attempts to protect an unspoken opinion. Randle's playful and amicable demeanor invites Gaither audiences close even as the content of her communication pushes them away.

But if Randle insists upon her friendly, wayfaring stranger status vis-à-vis southern gospel music, she does not consequently claim black gospel music as her homeland: "I call myself a chocolate rocker, 'cause, you know, black folks are typically stereotyped as black gospel music, you know. You have to do black gospel music. [Laughs] I almost killed myself trying to sing like CeCe [Winans] ... and Whitney [Houston], all these people. That was not the call I had."[26] Equating black gospel with vocally dexterous sopranos prohibits Randle from seeing herself as a black gospel artist, however much she desired at some point in her life to be one. Her resignation to sing according to her "call" reflects her acknowledged inability to reproduce the vocal stylings of CeCe Winans. Furthermore, Randle never calls *herself* a black person in this segment; "*black folks* are typically stereotyped ...," "*you* have to do black gospel," but "*I* call myself [...] chocolate." However, Randle's surrender of black gospel aspirations is not a forfeiture of *racial* identity. Understanding that black gospel represents the most authentically African American musical genre to many black and white audiences, Randle understands that it becomes more incumbent upon her to assert forthrightly her "blackish" identity for audiences to read her as an "authentic" black artist. Randle does not succeed as racial representative in the Homecoming world if she divorces herself too completely from African American culture as her audience understands it. She needs to connect herself to a black musical lineage—one that her audience will recognize as distinctly black. Randle's "rock" must be palatably, euphemistically black—"chocolate."

It is. Randle's claiming of a "call" separate from black gospel music occurs in the context of a discussion of Mahalia Jackson. Gloria Gaither asks Randle to name her heroes. After naming her parents (a nearly automatic response in the "family-centered" Homecoming material), Randle names Jackson, praising the gospel star for the racially integrated concerts she gave in a society still largely segregated. Randle's praise of Jackson immediately precedes Randle's "chocolate rocker" comments, and Randle returns to a discussion of Jackson immediately after her invocation of Winans and Houston:

> . . . that was not the call I had. I mean, I can do a couple little rolls here and there, but I'm kind of a [pauses] Mahalia, she was a *modern day rocker*. I mean she just [pauses] it's not like major rolls, you know, where people can do these tricks and things with their voices, but she was a good screamer.[27]

Randle refers to the vocal "rolls" present in black gospel of the Winans/Houston variety in increasingly dismissive terms, eventually reducing them to ostentatious vocal stunts. By noting that Jackson did not do "major rolls" like this, Randle weakens the chain that links Jackson with Winans and Houston—Jackson's supposedly direct gospel descendants. At the same time, Randle fortifies her own connection to the legendary gospel singer. Jackson and Randle seem very similar by Randle's reckoning. Randle is a chocolate rocker. Jackson was a modern-day rocker. Randle can do only a "couple little rolls." Jackson doesn't do "major rolls." Randle performs for mostly white audiences. Jackson performed for integrated audiences. By the end of Randle's commentary, it is Randle, not Winans or Houston, who appears as the heiress of the most iconic black gospel singer in history. Randle's interruption of her own sentence unintentionally articulates the gist of her claim: "I'm kind of a . . . Mahalia." If Randle's musical jury required further evidence of her lineage, they could consult her Dove Award–winning *Tribute to Mahalia Jackson* album, released in 2004 through the Gaithers' Spring House label.[28]

From a musical standpoint, Randle is "kind of" a lot of things. Her partial musical likeness parallels her never-complete sense of belonging to black and white musical traditions and the cultures of which they are functions. In one sense, Randle faces no new dilemma in her search for a musical or cultural "home." No musical style or culture possesses static and impermeable boundaries, so all social actors' sense of belonging will be ever in flux. Randle's case is peculiar, however, in the centrality of flux to her success. Randle denies being "southern gospel per se" from a forum made available to her because she is at least *southern gospel enough*. Were Randle not so apparently southern gospel, or did she not so evidently transgress certain racial and stylistic parameters surrounding southern gospel, neither the question of her "southern gospelness" nor her denial would be necessary. Ultimately, it is this denial that gives her an identity in the southern gospel community. Her role in the Homecomings is to trouble her own belonging in the Homecomings, at the same time troubling the borders of the Homecomings themselves—the culture they represent and to which they have been targeted. Randle is the supreme example of the Gaithers' centralization of erstwhile margins, their re-formation of southern gospel.

RUNNING ON BORDERLANDS

I made my first trip to a Homecoming performance in 2006—a concert in eastern Pennsylvania, a location many mid-Atlantic residents refer to as the "Deep North." Before the show began, I noticed that the four video screens— perched from the stage light scaffolding, facing outward in all directions away from the circular, centered stage—displayed a series of quotations in quick succession. As ticketholders settled into their seats, their gazes defaulted toward the screens at the center of the Homecoming panopticon; the screens were the only moving images in the stage area. Most of the quotations came from evangelicals of note—Billy Graham, Chuck Swindoll, and Dwight Moody, to name a few. Others the Gaithers seemed to have culled from some reservoir of American aphorisms—words from Ralph Waldo Emerson, Martin Luther King Jr., and Benjamin Franklin. I was surprised by none of these. However, some did surprise me. There was Gandhi. Most shocking to me, there was Betty Shabazz. I looked around at my fellow concertgoers. No surprises. Most attendees were sixty years of age or over, by my reckoning. A small but significant minority of women wore head coverings and opaque, ankle-length dresses. Virtually everyone was white. I watched the video screens run completely through the repeating litany of quotes three times in order to confirm I actually had seen the name of Malcolm X's widow. Every time her name appeared, I dropped my head to scan the crowd. Several people scanned the screens. No one batted an eye.

At a later concert—at which ran the same preshow word reel—I asked Bill Gaither about the quotes—the Shabazz quote specifically. Bill smiled his big, bleached, toothy smile, satisfied at my taking notice. He said that he only had a given audience's attention for a few hours on a single night; every moment of that time mattered. If the concert could expand that audience's horizons just a little bit in that time, the concerts did their job. Bill and Gloria Gaither, the former high school English teachers, ever remained educators.

From the outset, the Homecoming enterprise has been instructive—downright intraevangelistic. The first Homecomings sought to bring old musicians to new audiences. Every Homecoming video contains narrative interludes that tell the history of songs, musical groups, and significant moments of musical and religious revival. Some of these history lessons escort viewers all the way back to the eighteenth century.[29] Notwithstanding the heaping help-ings of nostalgia embedded in these episodes, the attention to history stands out in an evangelical milieu that so often leapfrogs every item of Christian history between the apostle Paul and the present.

Without explaining all African Americans present in the Homecom-ings as separate cogs in a single heuristic wheel—a reduction that too easily casts the Gaithers as undisputed arbiters of the Homecoming space and that fails to account for the difference between black Homecoming regulars—it is nonetheless important to attend to the pedagogical elements of African American presence in the Homecomings. Just as the Gaithers intended for the Shabazz quote to widen their audience's horizons, the Gaithers expected Randle's presence to instruct and to illuminate. However, precisely what Afri-can Americans broadly, and Randle specifically, illuminated was not easy to discern. As with Albertina Walker's "roll call" in the *We Will Stand* video, concertgoers probably did not recognize Betty Shabazz, but they probably could have guessed that the Shabazz quote came from outside the bounds of their immediate culture; no one with a name like "Shabazz" ever sang with people named Denver Crumpler or Eva Mae Lefevre. But did a presumption of cultural difference matter, especially when no one seemed to notice? Did "intraevangelism" require acknowledgment on the part of the evangelized that something—something slightly *other*—was being preached? To what extent could a cultural outsider, rendered in pixillated doses of easy-to-accept truisms, broaden a community's horizons or substantially alter a commu-nity's self-understanding? And how broad were the Gaithers willing to go? What did it matter that Shabazz—or Martin Luther King Jr., for that matter—were present in the Homecoming space if their presence was solely aphoris-tic, and if only that portion of their public speech which most conformed to audience conventions appeared? How was Randle's presence like Shabazz's presence? Was she a walking aphorism? No one batted an eye when Randle appears onstage—not even when she spooned out racially flavored phrases like "vanilla people" and "chocolate girl." So where, if anywhere, were Randle and the Gaithers taking the Homecoming audiences?

In one sense, nowhere. Marla Frederick's concern regarding the racially diverse megachurches of American suburbia and television applies to the Homecomings. In language similar to Michael Emerson's and Christian Smith's, Frederick frets over the potentially deleterious effects of multicultur-alism if it occurs without a discussion of the structural aspects of racism:

> To say that pastors . . . who have historically encouraged multiculturalism without a serious critique of racism have been most popular among television

audiences is not an overstatement. The theology of this type of simple multicul-
turalism pervades much of what is presented on television, even when churches
themselves may be more heavily involved in combating racism. Such silenc-
ing (color-blind/race-neutral discourses) can have the effect of reproducing the
racism if the structural dynamics of racism are not addressed.[30]

If a dominant group controls the terms of diversification when members of
nondominant groups enter the former's social space, the change that takes
place in that space is at least incidental and at worst a fortification of the
dominant group's dominant narrative—a narrative that has its being *qua*
dominant vis-à-vis the nondominance of others. Masquerading as mutual
cultural exchange and enfranchisement, the dominant group's adoption and
absorption of members of nondominant groups allows a dominant group to
cast itself as diverse, integrated, and democratic. The dominant group thus
constructs for itself a rejoinder to the accusation that it contributes to and
depends upon the inequality of nondominant groups. How could the Homecomings be racist? One of the Gaithers' most popular performers was an African American woman—not just any African American woman, but a *really*
African American woman, one who grew up in the inner city and who traces
her musical lineage through Mahalia Jackson. As I have shown, numerous,
often pernicious assumptions regarding an essential African American experience remain intact and become fortified in this narrative. That Randle herself sustains and relies upon many of these assumptions does not mean that
they are less toxic.

In another sense, though, Randle and the Gaithers were taking the Homecoming audiences—and southern gospel—somewhere. The Gaithers' engagement with African Americans and traditionally African American musical
forms was more than a simple parading of black bodies across a stage. The
Gaithers' commitment to history-telling led them to render a "new past"
salient to their audience. If such stories sometimes projected (sometimes tacitly) too much friendly reciprocity in cross-racial exchanges, the stories nonetheless drew attention to the historic traffic between black and white gospel.
They also demonstrate the Gaithers' commitment to giving credit where
credit was due for specific items in the southern gospel canon.

While Randle indubitably functioned as one of the Gaithers' early twenty-
first century avatars, it would be hasty to dismiss her as a mere pawn in the
game. If Randle understood black gospel as predominantly a domain of pitch-
shifting sopranos, if Randle believed she could not sing in such a fashion, and
if Randle could thrive in the Homecoming world without sacrificing what she
understood as essential components of her identity (perhaps even thriving

because of those components), the Homecomings no doubt struck her as an auspicious fit. It is also important to understand Randle's secondary and university education as providing spaces in which she developed the tools necessary to thrive as a minority presence in a white evangelical world. To dismiss Randle as being simply duped into adopting a white evangelical ideology, first by her Maryland schoolteachers, then by Jerry Falwell and company at Liberty, then by the Gaithers, is to embark upon a mythic quest through time in search of Randle's unadulterated agency as an African American woman—a fool's errand that requires an impracticable parsing of Randle's life and that eventually reduces an investigator to essentialist assertions of race identity. To be sure, Randle's passive-voice rendering of her schooling and her relationship with the Gaithers suggests that she has been the clay in the hands of several white potters. But that which made Randle ripe for Gaither fashioning also equipped Randle to fashion the Gaither stages. Randle knew white evangelicals—those people she called "vanilla," a term which playfully, simultaneously casts them as racially distinct, tasty, and/or humdrum. If Randle sought community with other African Americans who worked under similar racial circumstances, she need have looked no further than her immediate family. Randle's brother Michael Tait was the sole African American member of dcTalk, one of the most successful recording groups in CCM history. As of this writing, he is the front man for another popular, mostly white Christian rock band, the Newsboys.

Given the strict segregation that has kept the inner sanctum of southern gospel music lily white for decades, the centrality of Randle in the Homecomings—perhaps *especially* because no one batted an eye at it—suggests a significant shift took place in southern gospel audience expectations. In the twenty-first century, Randle's occupation of center stage came to be taken for granted. It would not have been taken for granted in the first Homecoming videos. The fans I interviewed had a wide range of opinions on Lynda Randle specifically and race in the Homecomings generally. Indeed, it often seemed that individual fans harbored a range of difficult-to-parse opinions. Early in my fieldwork, I realized that, outside the world of East coast academe, I had to abandon my own prejudices and presumed associations between specific word choices and progressive or retrograde racial attitudes. Sitting in his cowboy church, Roy initially shocked me by using the term "colored people." His bewildering alternations between "colored people" and "people of color" left me wondering whether Roy had learned his race-talk from George Wallace or Alice Walker. Although he used a jarring, nonacademic, and (to my ears) outdated lexicon, Roy was among the most vocal of fans I interviewed in his insistence on intentionally closing the racial divide that had plagued southern gospel music. He believed the Gaithers were deliberately trying to close that divide, and he was happy about it. Roy also was one of the few people whom I did not need to prompt to talk about race; he wanted to talk about it. By contrast, Nick was an older man with a mellifluous, "nonaccented" radio voice (in contrast to Roy's southern drawl). Ours was a fruitful conversation; Nick possessed an encyclopedic knowledge of the Homecomings and an amazing memory of the concerts he had attended, even the people he had met at different venues. He was willing and able to talk about Lily Isaacs's Jewish identity in a sophisticated fashion. Near the end of our conversation, I turned the subject to demographics—age, denomination, and finally race. He said, "stuff like that [race] only comes out to me when somebody does something . . . stupid . . . and I say, 'yeah, it figures.' But normal, day-to-day stuff, I don't think of . . . I don't even think of Lynda Randle as being black." This interview was on my mind when Randle told the story of being pulled over in the South; would *Nick* have been laughing, and if so, why? Nick did not live far from Ferguson, Missouri. Occasionally, I got a humorous glimpse of the nervousness that fans experienced when Randle came up, and with her, race. I interviewed Dan and his spouse, Hannah, in their living room. Dan had just finished saying that Randle was one of his favorite Homecoming singers when he had to receive a phone call in the other room. Hannah took that time to say that she did not care for Randle. She craned her head to search the hallway Dan had just entered, then leaned toward me. As if to dodge Dan, the tape recorder, or perhaps Randle herself, she whispered an addendum: "*and it's not because she's black.*"

If comments posted on YouTube video clips of Randle performances are any indication—comments that allude approvingly to Randle's "reserved" and "respectful" renditions of gospel songs—Homecoming viewers neither desired nor expected Randle's performances to possess the Pentecostal fervor of, say, Jessy Dixon's performances.[31] Not simply as an African American, but as an African American *woman*, Randle performed under an especially watchful eye. However, the watchfulness did not reduce simply to racism and misogyny. As Bill suggested with reference to southern gospel fans' stylistic expectations, one knows one belongs to a family when one is held accountable to familial expectations. The expectations facing Randle may have been unfair (would Mark Lowry have been praised for being "reserved" or "respectful?") and unilinear (did Randle feel free to harbor and express *her* expectations of her audience?). The fact that the expectations were often implicit might have made them more difficult to navigate, even though Randle had been navigating implicit white expectations nearly all of her life. But in any case, these expectations were not there for Doris Akers or the Fairfield Four in the early videos. Randle was no guest artist. She was undeniably a member of the central cast. On *We Will Stand*, Randle sings "His Eye Is on the Sparrow" with black gospel matriarch Mom Winans and Vestal Goodman. The photo on the DVD cover that captures this performance places Vestal in the center of the triad—Winans on the left, Randle on the right—suggesting that white gospel has a privileged position in the Gaither Gospel Series. However, read dialectically from left to right, Randle is the synthesis of the two older women. Vestal was not, and could not be, replaced. After Vestal's death, Randle became the face of the Homecoming feminine. Fans could protest a black woman's centrality in the Homecoming version of southern gospel if they wished, but the burden of proof had shifted. They now had to issue their protest like Hannah did—in whispers in the margins, out of time with the beat of the present: *it's not because she's black.*

Homecoming audience members feel solidarity with the performers based on a common inclusion in "the human" narrative—a narrative whose normativity is both assumed and constructed in the Homecomings themselves. Paradoxically, universality requires particularity. An account of a common human experience becomes most plausible when a discernible, recurring thread runs through many stories that otherwise bear no likeness to one another. Dissimilar storytellers spinning similar stories help affirm a universal narrative. Enter the strangely familiar Lynda Randle—attached to the exotic inner city and white evangelical suburbia alike, channeling and tracing black and southern gospel, self-consciously chocolate in a vanilla world.

EPILOGUE

LET US NOW PRAISE . . .

I walk over more aphorisms—James Baldwin, Ralph Waldo Emerson, William Hazlitt, and others. The words of these figures are etched, in fine masonry, into the sidewalk of downtown Greenville, South Carolina—my hometown after I left New Jersey. Of the twenty-seven quotations in Main Street's sidewalk, two are identified as coming from women.

The details vary from account to account, but generally most residents of the Upstate's celebrated emerald city will tell you a story of well-laid plans and hard-won yet steady progress. Most stories begin with Max Heller (1919–2011)—an Austrian Jew who came to South Carolina shortly after the Nazi takeover. With the help of a well-heeled Greenville woman, Heller escaped Vienna (the Moses comparisons are not lost on many Greenvillians), came to Greenville, rose through the ranks of a local clothier, and eventually started his own business. Heller's winning personality and hard work endeared him to many locals. Heller wanted to be well, and he wanted his city to be well. He was the city's mayor through the 1970s, and he helped lead the city through what was by some accounts and comparisons a smooth (if belated) process of desegregation. In this, he apparently allied with some powerful local white businessmen—who, some stories have it, let the more bellicose white populations know that Upstate integration would be orderly, without incident. Greenville, South Carolina, would not be Greensboro, North Carolina. In 1979, Heller ran for Congress as a Democrat against Republican Carroll Campbell Jr. Campbell's campaign regularly asked voters if they would rather have a native South Carolinian or a Jewish immigrant representing them.[1] Voters responded by electing Carroll, who later became the state's governor. Heller became the chairman of the South Carolina State Development Board.

The decline of the textile industry decimated many Upstate towns. Not Greenville. So the story goes, due to the efforts of a handful of men, starting

with Heller, Greenville embarked on a decades-spanning strategic revitaliza-
tion project to beautify the city and to attract a more cosmopolitan business
community to the region (the causal relationship between these two aims
varied from account to account). A Michelin plant came to Greenville in the
1970s, and its North American headquarters followed in the late 1980s. BMW
set up a major facility between Greenville and Spartanburg in the 1990s.
Major hotels and banks set up shop in Greenville's downtown. A seventeen-
mile paved bike trail, the Swamp Rabbit Trail, was completed in 2010. It runs
through the heart of the downtown—notably, through the downtown's lovely
Falls Park, where visitors and residents walk and bike year-round along the
Reedy River as it cascades from the base of Appalachia. The road that used to
hide the falls has given way to the stunning Liberty Bridge. The curved pedes-
trian suspension bridge, completed in 2004, has become Greenville's symbol.

I lived for two years near the southern terminus of the Swamp Rabbit
Trail, about a five-minute walk to Nicholtown, a historic African American
neighborhood on the other side of the Reedy. Nicholtown was connected to
the main trail by a series of spurs in 2011. On two different instances within
my first year in Greenville, I woke up to find graffiti on the main trail near
Nicholtown—swastikas, the number 777 (key in white supremacist numerol-
ogy), and arrows pointing up the Nicholtown spurs with "GHETTO" written
under them. Within months of my moving to Greenville, Jacqueline Woodson
won the National Book Award for her young adult novel *Brown Girl Dream-
ing*—based partly on Woodson's experiences splitting her childhood between
Brooklyn and Nicholtown. Woodson became a known entity in the national
media after the National Book Award Ceremony in late 2014. In his introduction of his friend Woodson, presenter and author Daniel Handler said,
"Jackie's allergic to watermelon. Just let that sink into your mind." No one
who read Greenville's local news in 2014 would have known this—or known
that Woodson, an African American gay woman who won the National Book
Award and used to live in the Upstate, existed.[2]

On occasion, Lynn and I used to ride our bikes all the way to the northern terminus of the Swamp Rabbit Trail: Travelers Rest (TR), a bucolic little
town north of Greenville, closer to Appalachia, that has experienced its own,
trail-related economic boom. Cyclist George Hincapie, Greenville resident
and Lance Armstrong's former teammate, runs a high-end hotel that mainly
caters to cyclists who come to the area. If one travels just north of TR, one will
see the Dixie Republic—self-described as "The South's Largest Confederate
Store"—where one can buy things like Confederate flag bumper stickers that
say "We Fought the First War Against Terrorism," and "Lee Surrendered . . .
We Didn't." To reach the Dixie Republic, one must navigate the crossroads;

Highway 25, the 25 Business Loop, and Highway 276 meet and separate in Travelers Rest. Part of the junction is named after one of the county's famous native sons: Hovie Lister Interchange.

More typically, I biked the three miles on the Swamp Rabbit from my home to the Greenville downtown to work in a coffee shop. I sat alongside bowtied, seersuckered men who liltingly theorized about the SEC football season, men in Italian shoes who in muted German and French speculated about final quarters, college-aged women in pairs who discussed the book of Ephesians, weekenders from surrounding counties who came in huffing and sweaty after walking or running in Falls Park. A vibrant slam poetry collective—comprised largely but not entirely of young African Americans—regularly hosted readings at this coffee shop.

A year after I moved to South Carolina, a twenty-one-year-old white man named Dylann Roof walked into Emanuel AME Church in Charleston, sat for about an hour during a Wednesday night Bible study, pulled a gun, and murdered nine of the congregants—among them Clementa Pinckney, a state senator and Emanuel's pastor. It did not take long to discover that Roof's shooting spree was racially motivated. He apparently told his victims, "you rape our women and you're taking over our country and you have to go." He admitted that he wanted to start a race war. Pictures surfaced of Roof waving a gun and Confederate flag, wearing a jacket that bore the flags of Rhodesia and apartheid-era South Africa.

Among state and national citizenry, the Charleston murders sparked the same back-and-forth concerning gun control, the same incredulity, the same heartfelt and impotent expressions of regret that happened in the United States every year or so, or whenever another white American male decided to go on a shooting spree. But this was different. By the time of the Charleston killings, the entire nation had been forced to reckon with racism for three years, as we considered clashes between public and private security forces and black citizens in Florida, Ohio, New York, Missouri, Maryland, and, just two months before Roof's attack, in North Charleston, South Carolina. Every incident involved a black man killed by security forces. Every incident involved one part of the citizenry insisting that these events were undeniably about race, and another part insisting they were undeniably about something else. The Charleston mass murder was different. Despite the herculean efforts of some 2016 presidential hopefuls and media pundits to erase or minimize the fact, the Charleston murders could not be "unraced" sanely. The 2015 events at Emanuel AME, Charleston smacked too much of the 1963 events at Sixteenth Street Baptist, Birmingham.

In the South—and, to some extent, around the nation—Roof's act reignited a rather unexpected debate concerning the Confederate flag, which flew on public and private grounds all over the South (and elsewhere), including the South Carolina State House grounds in Columbia. Where, if anywhere, was the flag appropriate? Whom did the flag represent? What was the flag's meaning? Who decided the flag's meaning, and for whom did they decide it? Of course, the flag was but a crystallizing symbol; replace "flag" with "South" and you approach the marrow of the debate. I followed the public and private conversations in the South. I heard southern nativity defined and deployed all kinds of ways. I witnessed the same Upstate populations who cheered as their low taxes attracted international businesses now complain about outside agitators. I looked on as 10 state representatives—5 from the Upstate—vote against even having a conversation in the legislature about removing the flag from the State House grounds. They were defeated by 103 other representatives. I watched an African American woman named Bree Newsome shimmy up the flag pole in Columbia and remove the flag herself. I watched her get arrested. I watched two state employees—both African American men— run the flag back up the pole. As of this writing, the flag has come down in Columbia. Just before I left Greenville, in 2016, I had begun seeing more cars in the parking lot of the Dixie Republic. I also had begun seeing a greater proportion of Confederate flags adorning cars in the New South's emerald city than I ever had in rural Laurens County, where I worked, just to the south of Greenville. As of this writing, the southern representatives continue to debate.

* * *

The Gaither Vocal Band rolled into Greenville in May 2015, a month before the Charleston murders. I had not been to a GVB concert since the fall of 2013, when the group consisted of Bill, Michael English, Wes Hampton, Mark Lowry, and David Phelps. English and Lowry had left. Bill added Adam Crabb, a member of the famous gospel-singing Crabb family. He also added baritone Todd Suttles, a former fitness director at Vanderbilt University. Just north of five feet tall and built like a tank, Suttles contrasted with the tall, slender Crabb. Possessing a wide range for a baritone and a confident yet unassuming tone, Suttles harmonized well with the entire group. Suttles was an African American with deep skin tones; he contrasted with the assembly.

The names on the sides of church vans in the parking lot, and the general carriage and dress of the people in attendance, made me suspect this was not an audience of Greenville's citizens. It was certainly not an audience that would appear on the websites of the city's visitor center or chamber of commerce. I was back among oxygen tanks, wheelchairs, opaque and muted dress, and unorthodox orthodoxies of hair. The two upper-middle-aged women who sat in front of Lynn and me at the concert spent the duration crying, lifting their hands, singing, and very frequently popping some assortment of pills whose effects I could not discern. Before the show, Bill, Lynn, and I talked in a tiny, austere backstage room, when Deana, Bill's longtime stage manager, pulled Bill into the hall to meet an old couple. The man was in a wheelchair and could hardly speak. The woman spoke for him when words were necessary. They informed Bill that they had been married for sixty-seven years, and both had been music ministers at a little church in rural South Carolina for four decades. Bill leaned in to listen to them, graciously received their compliments, posed for a photo, said his farewell, grabbed his handheld microphone, and walked with Lynn and me down the corridor to the arena. We emerged at floor level, watching longtime Gaither stage captain Kevin Williams prep the crowd. A couple of people seated near the mouth of the corridor saw Bill. They pointed, smiled, and pulled their neighbors' shirt sleeves. Bill had escorted us to the very edge of his spotlight; I had never been this close. He turned to me and joked, "wanna come onstage?" I laughed and said no. For what must have been the hundred thousandth time, Bill flipped his microphone on and started into his banter with Williams as he crossed over, into the crowd's full field of vision. Lynn and I waited for Bill to clear the area before we moved to our assigned seats.

As had become our routine, Lynn and I went backstage again after the show. It was always astounding to me how much energy Bill had after his lengthy concerts. I know firsthand that one often exits a spotlight with a visage shining in afterglow, but I am not a nearly eighty-year-old man who has been performing for nearly sixty years. Bill was especially excited to introduce me to Suttles. As ticketholders exited and the tear-down crew entered, as the stage came down around us and our backstage became once again continuous with the arena proper, I talked with Bill and Suttles for about an hour, about everything from competitive weightlifting (Suttles and I shared this interest) to different genres of gospel music. Bill got pulled into some side conversations, and I asked Suttles about what challenges he had experienced since joining the GVB. He said the toughest thing was learning not only all of the songs, but in some cases, more than one part to the songs. While there were some anchoring numbers in every show—songs he could be fairly certain would be on any setlist—Bill always operated like a skilled quarterback: calling audibles. "He's not reading what's going on out there," Suttles said, indicating where the audience had been. "He's reading what's happening onstage." Bill trusted that whatever magic was happening onstage would translate to the audience. The entire ensemble had to be ready for Bill to call any tune in the catalogue based on his assessment of the space. Indeed, the Greenville show included a humorous, very public example of one such moment: when David Phelps arrived late for the second set, caught in a photo-op with fans, Bill asked, in front of the entire crowd, bassist Gene McDonald to sing Jerry Reed's (famously, Johnny Cash's) "A Thing Called Love" while we waited for Phelps. McDonald did. While we were speaking after the show, Wes Hampton, who was nursing allergies, talked with Bill about trading harmony parts with Crabb on a particularly challenging song for the next night's concert. Whatever works.

At this point in his career, Bill's understanding of "whatever works" is second nature. I partially agree with Suttles's observation. Since gospel shows run on the interaction between audience and performers, it seems to me that Bill makes a least a sidelong interpretation of his audiences, even as he focuses on his stage. Still, it did seem that Bill had honed a kind of trickle-out approach to his concerts: get everything right onstage—the music, the energy, and even the love—and the audience will respond accordingly. The last time the GVB had a regular African American member was 1987—years before the first Homecoming, even more years before Greenville's conservative Christian Bob Jones University officially lifted its ban on mixed-race student dating. Suttles's first solo that night—a low, low bass line in the high-energy "Love Is Like a River"—received thunderous applause. Only Bill's joke about the new GVB looking like a gospel "Rat Pack" called attention to Suttles's racial difference (after a deliberate, laughter-filled pause, during which all musicians' eyes turned toward Suttles, the latter said, "well, I guess that makes me Sammy Davis"). The audience seemed right with him all night.

We talked a long time after the show. It was approaching midnight, and the tour bus had to load up and head to the next night's venue: Roanoke, Virginia. Bill, Suttles, Lynn, and I wished one another well. Lynn and I walked out of the Bon Secours Wellness Arena, the partial illumination of Greenville's booming little downtown sparring against the heavy southern darkness. We had work to do the next day. Somewhere under the same sky, Dylann Roof was making plans.

THAT IS THE TUNE BUT THERE ARE NO WORDS . . .

In 2013, the Gaithers invited Lynn and me to Alexandria. I had sent Bill and Gloria an early copy of this book months before, and one purpose of the trip was to get their feedback. Another purpose was to attend Anderson University's performance of the 1973 Gaither cantata, *Alleluia! A Praise Gathering for Believers*. I use the word "cantata," though it is difficult to pinpoint the genre.

Alleluia! first appeared during the Gaithers' most fecund period of songwriting. Some of the "big" Gaither songs of the 1970s, such as "Because He Lives" and "Let's Just Praise the Lord," comprise the musical score. The arrangements vary in scope; *Alleluia!* requires a full orchestra and choirs, but scaled-down solos also occur. *Alleluia!* also is more than the music. Solo, spoken-word segments occur between the songs. Some are Gloria's scripted glosses on Bible stories (e.g., the "woman at the well" narrative from the Gospel of John). However, the Gaithers also script the unscripted in this work. They intentionally leave narrative spaces open, to be filled by the personal narratives culled from the particular population putting on the show. *Alleluia!* would never be the same show twice, exactly.

The Anderson University version of *Alleluia!*—which had not been performed in its entirety for many years—gave me a glimpse into the complicated world of American Holiness Christianity. An Anderson drama teacher composed and delivered a stirring oratory concerning the experience of a present-absent God. An old woman who had been one of Anderson's first African American graduates stepped out of the choir to tell her story—one that did not cast Anderson's racial history in unequivocally negative or positive light.[3] One middle-aged white woman gave an emotional account of her struggles with substance abuse—an account that led me to believe the woman felt she was winning but had not won.

I left *Alleluia!* convinced, more than ever, that one had to reach far back into Gaither history to understand how and why the Homecomings were so successful. More than that, though, Anderson's *Alleluia!* performance reminded me how much of the Gaither history was not a southern gospel history—not theologically, not culturally, not stylistically. The morning after the program, right before the Gaithers and I would sit down for a five-hour discussion about this book, I ran into the Gaithers' daughter Amy in Gloria's coffee shop. Amy had been in attendance the previous night; as both a Gaither and a professor of communications and theater at Depauw University, she had a good eye for detail. As we chatted about the show, Amy told me she felt that *Alleluia!*, and the era from which it came, was the quintessence of her parents' career. Conceding the significance of the Homecomings, she worried that the Homecomings' success tended to overshadow much of this earlier period.

Bearing in mind that Amy spent some of her formative years during this period, and that this might account for her strong feelings about it, I believe she is right. However, one would be hard-pressed to find studies on twentieth-century Christian music, or twentieth-century American evangelicalism generally, that pay much attention to the Gaithers of the 1960s and 1970s. This is not because such studies do not exist. In addition to the significant works on

American Christian music I already have discussed (see the Introduction), several scholars have produced much-needed work on "pre-Moral Majority" American evangelicalism in the 1960s and 1970s. Many were published between this book's inception and completion. Focusing on moderate and progressive (and often nonsouthern) evangelicalism, these scholars trouble what now seem like intuitive affinities between conversionistic, bibliocentric forms of Christianity, and thoroughly or simplistically conservative politics. This work is important in part because these affinities once again seem questionable with respect to early twenty-first-century American evangelicalism. While I believe the quantity and the timing of these studies could lead one to overestimate the varieties of 1960s and 1970s evangelicalism, they provide a helpful corrective to the accepted associations between red state America and "red-letter Christianity."[4]

None of this literature discusses the Gaithers with any sustained seriousness. Neither does the literature on conservative evangelicalism of the same time period. One reason, I believe, is that the Gaithers do not fit easily within even the rightly complicated historical narratives. The Gaither Trio did not protest the Vietnam War with evangelical progressive Jim Wallis and his post-Americans. However, as Bill informed me, Greenville's own Bob Jones University discouraged its students from attending this same Trio's concerts in the 1970s (too "Pentecostal," whatever that may have meant). I admit some personal bias as I note the Gaither omission; when I find the Gaither name missing from the index of nearly every potentially relevant monograph, I experience that same mixture of relief and frustration that all scholars feel when they find no one has paid much attention to their subjects. Still, I hold that the Gaithers' *entire* career deserves more attention than it has garnered— precisely because they represent and speak to a vast, messy middle in modern American evangelicalism. I hope that recent scholarship (mine as well as the aforementioned) has cleared the courts for more work on such populations.

Another reason I believe the Gaithers have received scant attention in this literature is that scholars still struggle with how to discuss music as a constituting and constituted element of American evangelicalism. There are many excellent studies of evangelical music. There are many excellent studies of evangelical social engagement and politics. But we have work to do to synthesize the conversations. The Gaithers' pre-Homecoming endeavors may or may not warrant book-length treatment, but I hope my book offers one model for how one might examine musical and extra-musical elements of American evangelical culture in a way that illumines the entire landscape.

America. Gospel. South. Evangelical. These are and always have been shifting landscapes. Even within the Homecoming world, everyone was—and is—a citizen of worlds that move and slip under foot. Music. More than the music. South. More than the South. Some are better adjusted to the motions than others. Even the tightest cords of American evangelicalism do not keep the ground from shifting; knowing who holds the future does not mean the course is definitively charted. Even the simplest, seemingly sturdiest land-scapes contain earthflows that their creators set in syrupy motion, that they direct only to a big, vague something that is partially hidden to them, not quite understandable—something deceptively small and proximate, that they see only as in a convex glass.

NOTES

INTRODUCTION

1. Gloria won only one pre-Homecoming Gospel Songwriter of the Year Award.

2. Qtd. in Ken Abraham, "A Most Unlikely Mogul," *Saturday Evening Post*, September/October 2003, 58. The ASCAP award was given based on the frequency with which the organization granted licenses for the performance of Gaither songs.

3. These are the figures as of 2012. Not included are awards Bill has won for albums he has produced. The Gaithers release corresponding videos and music albums; the videos typically outsell the albums.

4. Statistics originally published in Pollstar, reported in "Gaither's Homecoming Celebrates 10 Years," *Christian Examiner*, last modified August 20, 2005, accessed February 10, 2013, http://www.christianexaminer.com/Articles/Articles%20Aug05/Art_Aug05_07.html.

5. For my fuller definition of southern gospel music, see Ryan Harper, "Music: White Gospel," in *Encyclopedia of Religion in America, Vol. 3*, ed. Charles Lippy and Peter Williams (Washington, DC: CQ Press, 2010), 1491–96.

6. CCM and Christian rock studies: Andrew Beaujon, *Body Piercing Saved My Life: Inside the Phenomenon of Christian Rock* (Cambridge, MA: Da Capo, 2006); Jay Howard and John Streck, *Apostles of Rock: The Splintered World of Contemporary Christian Music* (Lexington: University Press of Kentucky, 1999); David Stowe, *No Sympathy for the Devil: Christian Pop Music and the Transformation of American Evangelicalism* (Chapel Hill: University of North Carolina Press, 2011). African American gospel studies: Jerma Jackson, *Singing in My Soul: Black Gospel Music in a Secular Age* (Chapel Hill: University of North Carolina Press, 2004); Anthony Heilbut, *The Fan Who Knew Too Much: Aretha Franklin, the Rise of the Soap Opera, Children of the Gospel Church, and Other Meditations* (New York: Knopf, 2012); Alan Young, *Woke Me Up This Morning: Black Gospel Singers and the Gospel Life* (Jackson: University Press of Mississippi, 1997). Country music studies: Jeffrey J. Lange, *Smile When You Call Me a Hillbilly: Country Music's Struggle for Respectability, 1939–1954* (Athens: University of Georgia Press, 2004); Kristine McKusker and Diane Pecknold, eds., *A Boy Named Sue: Gender and Country Music* (Jackson: University Press of Mississippi, 2004); and Richard A. Peterson, *Creating Country Music: Fabricating Authenticity* (Chicago: University of Chicago Press, 1997).

7. James Goff Jr., *Close Harmony: A History of Southern Gospel* (Chapel Hill: University of North Carolina Press, 2002); Michael Graves and David Fillingim, eds., *More Than "Precious Memories": The Rhetoric of Southern Gospel Music* (Macon, GA: Mercer University Press, 2004); and Douglas Harrison, *Then Sings My Soul: The Culture of Southern Gospel Music* (Champagne-Urbana: University of Illinois Press, 2012). Another book of note is David Bruce

Murray's self-published *Murray's Encyclopedia of Southern Gospel Music* (Musicscribe, 2005). Like many of the southern gospel fans I have encountered in my research, Murray has a broad knowledge of the personnel history of the major southern gospel singing groups of the past fifty years. Although his book is not an authoritative, comprehensive source of information on the genre (his information on the Gaither Vocal Band is scattered), it provided a helpful starting point in many of my inquiries.

8. There is no single record of Bill Gaither's conceiving of the Dove Awards. However, multiple industry insiders attest to the fact that, in a 1968 GMA board meeting, Bill proposed the idea for an awards ceremony for gospel artists.

9. I will refer to the "Homecoming world" throughout the book. I use the term like sociologist Howard Becker uses the term *art world*: to signal all of the people whose activities are necessary to the production and sustenance of the franchise. This will include primarily the Gaithers (as writers, producers, performers), musicians, songwriters, staff, and fans. As Becker points out, membership in art worlds is not stable; people can make decisions that exclude themselves or others from the space. This is true of the Homecomings as well. But to conceive of the Homecoming as such an art world is to call attention to a cooperative network of meaning-making that includes but does not reduce to the Gaither Music Company. See Howard Becker, *Art Worlds* (Berkeley: University of California Press, 1982), 34–39.

10. On church homecomings, see Gwen Kennedy Neville, *Kinship and Pilgrimage: Rituals of Reunion in American Protestant Culture* (New York: Oxford University Press, 1987). Although Neville argues that the roots of homecomings extend into the late eighteenth and early nineteenth century (especially in the cemetery associations that flourished in the late nineteenth century), she notes that the name "homecoming," as well as a number of contemporary homecoming rituals, began to appear only in the middle of the twentieth century.

11. Burpo and Vincent, *Heaven Is for Real: A Little Boy's Astounding Story of His Trip to Heaven and Back* (Nashville, TN: Thomas Nelson, 2010). The book chronicles Sonja and Todd Burpo's son Colton's near-death experience—his voyage to heaven during a difficult medical procedure. Key to the verification of Colton's story is his reporting of family members' presence in heaven—family members he had not met (a miscarried sister, and great-grandfather about whose salvation the family had been anxious).

12. Cleanth Brooks, "The Heresy of Paraphrase," in *The Well-Wrought Urn: Studies in the Structure of Poetry* (New York: Mariner, 1956).

13. For a study that takes seriously evangelical propositionality—and evangelical propositions about propositionality—see Molly Worthen, *Apostles of Reason: The Crisis of Authority in American Evangelicalism* (New York: Oxford University Press, 2013). It is worth noting one of the first points on which Gloria disagreed with me when she read an early draft of this book. Gloria believed *evangelical* properly should refer to a Reformed, usually Calvinistic strand of Christians, and she was worried about my using the term also to describe a range of other Christians (especially people from her own Wesleyan-Holiness tradition). In her opinion, either *evangelical* means something as specific as her definition, or it is really too broad to be meaningful. Gloria's definition certainly has some merit; ironically, many Wesleyan scholars for some time have contended that this Reform-centered definition of evangelical has prevailed *unjustly* in the historiography. See Donald Dayton, *Discovering an Evangelical Heritage* (Ada, MI: Baker Academic, 1988). I hold that *evangelical* signals a conversionistic and bibliocentric version of Christianity that is sufficiently broad to include, say, most Wesleyans, yet narrow enough to exclude a number of liberal Protestant, Catholic, and Orthodox Christians. Given that Gloria also identifies herself in her first Homecoming appearance as coming from a "northern evangelical background" (see chapter 1), I feel justified using the term. However, my

definition is admittedly not absolute. In fact, as I will show in chapter 4, Gloria herself might be the best example of how much could fit under the umbrella *evangelical*—and how little, perhaps, the term then might signify.

14. Stanley Cavell, *The Senses of Walden* (Chicago: University of Chicago Press, 1972), *In Quest of the Ordinary: Lines of Skepticism and Romanticism* (Chicago: University of Chicago Press, 1994); James Boon, *Verging on Extra-Vagance: Anthropology, History, Religion, Literature, Arts . . . Showbiz* (Princeton, NJ: Princeton University Press, 1999); Helen Vindler, *Invisible Listeners: Lyrical Intimacy in Herbert, Whitman, and Ashbery* (Princeton, NJ: Princeton University Press, 2007); Jeffrey Stout, "The Transformation of Genius into Practical Power: A Reading of Emerson's 'Experience,'" *American Journal of Theology and Philosophy* 35, no. 1 (January 2014): 3–24, *Blessed Are the Organized: Grassroots Democracy in America* (Princeton, NJ: Princeton University Press, 2012); Amy Hungerford, *Postmodern Belief: American Literature and Religion Since 1960* (Princeton, NJ: Princeton University Press, 2010); John Lardas Modern, *Secularism in Antebellum America* (Chicago: University of Chicago Press, 2011).

CHAPTER ONE

1. "He Touched Me" was the title track of Presley's 1972 now-platinum gospel album under RCA. The album earned Presley the second of his three Grammy Awards and featured the southern gospel singing group the Imperials on background vocals. Cash recorded "He Touched Me" for his 1979 collection *A Believer Sings the Truth* (Cachet/Columbia). Although the song did not make the final cut for the two-disc album, it appeared on the 1984 extended-session reissue, *I Believe* (Columbia). Columbia did not convert either of these records to compact disc format, but the posthumous 2012 release, *Bootlegs, Vol. IV: The Soul of Truth* (Columbia), contains all of the tracks from both releases.

2. Gaither-penned or Gaither co-penned songs are most likely to appear (and most likely to appear in greatest number) in one of three types of hymnal: trans-denominational hymnals popular among evangelicals—such as Word Music's best-selling *Celebration Hymnal* (Nashville, TN: Word, 1997), which contains four Gaither songs; hymnals published in and used by heavily evangelical denominations—such as the Southern Baptist Convention's *Baptist Hymnal* (Nashville, TN: Lifeway, 2008), which contains ten Gaither songs; and hymnals used in denominations in the Wesleyan trajectory of Christianity—such as *The United Methodist Hymnal* (Nashville, TN: Abingdon Press, 1989), which contains four Gaither songs. Gaither songs also appear in a variety of other hymnals. Of particular note are the Disciples of Christ's *Chalice Hymnal*, ed. Daniel B. Merrick (Atlanta, GA: Chalice Press, 1995), which contains three Gaither songs, and *The African American Heritage Hymnal*, ed. Delores Carpenter and Nolan E. Williams Jr. (Chicago: GIA Publications, 2001), which contains six Gaither songs.

3. Generally, the phrase "close harmony" describes a musical arrangement in which the notes in a chord are near to one another in pitch—rarely more than an octave apart. The "closest" harmonies are those in which the notes in a chord are the nearest possible consonant notes in a given scale. Sophisticated close harmony vocal arrangements often employ odd close intervals—such as stacking firsts and seconds, or fifths and sixths—before resolving into more assonant triads. To the extent that southern gospel musicians sometimes do this, the genre is akin to barbershop quartet music. Bill Gaither is aware and proud of this connection. He told me in 2010 that, among the many honors he has received, few mean as much to him as his honorary membership in the Barbershop Harmony Society (awarded in 2006), because, according to him, barbershop quartet culture places a premium on vocal precision and careful ensemble blending.

4. Bill Gaither, with Ken Abraham, *It's More Than the Music: Life Lesson on Friends, Faith, and What Matters Most* (Nashville, TN: Warner Faith, 2003), 2.

5. Nitty Gritty Dirt Band, *Will the Circle Be Unbroken* (New York: EMI, 1972). The Dirt Band's title track itself recalls a long gospel story. The 1972 version of "Will the Circle Be Unbroken" (or, "Can the Circle Be Unbroken?"), well known in country circles, is actually A. P. Carter's 1935 rewrite of a 1907 hymn with the same title, by Ada Habershon and Charles Gabriel. The song was first made popular by Charles Alexander, who sang it as he toured with popular evangelists Reuben Torrey and John Wilbur Chapman. Alexander published the song in *Alexander's Gospel Songs* (Philadelphia, PA: Westminster Press, 1908).

6. *The Gaither Vocal Band Homecoming Video Album* (Nashville, TN: Star Song, 1991).

7. Doug Harrison notes that *Homecoming* was filmed less than a year after Bill had organized a tribute and concert for Rusty Goodman, of the gospel singing group the Happy Goodmans. The 1990 concert was also a benefit for Rusty, who was dying of cancer but who had very little money for palliative care. For this event, Gaither assembled CCM, country, and southern gospel musicians—among them Amy Grant, Ricky Skaggs, and BeBe and CeCe Winans. Complete with a reading from Gloria and a video montage of past Goodman performances, the concert was a sort of proto-Homecoming. See Harrison, *Then Sings My Soul*, 126–28.

Harrison reads the story of the Goodman concert as one of the "less well-known" histories of the Homecomings. The Goodman tribute certainly proves that Bill knew something about whom to assemble in 1991, and what might be the emotional effect of the assembly. Harrison is correct about it being "less well-known" in the sense that Bill's *organization* of the concert is somewhat downplayed in the famous Homecoming nativity story. Still, Bill does not hide the fact of the Goodman concert. He discusses it in *It's More Than the Music*, 238–39. He shows clips from this concert in the first Homecoming compilation video, *Special Homecoming Moments* (Alexandria, IN: Spring House, 1997). The concert fits into the Homecoming saga as a prequel—a sign of what kind of gathering and what kind of emotion would happen, even as one of the events that sparked Bill's interest in doing the Homecoming video.

One must go farther back in Gaither history to understand Bill's ability to assemble and orchestrate musical-revival events. Aside from his early experience as a church music director, and as an organizer of the Bill Gaither Trio concerts (events that often involved many more than three musicians or one act), the Gaithers' 1973 musical showcase, *Alleluia! A Praise Gathering for Believers* is an important Homecoming predecessor. I will discuss *Alleluia!* in some detail later, but suffice it to say here that the showcase is partly scripted and partly contingent on the particular community putting on the show. The Gaither-written musical numbers are the tentpoles of *Alleluia!*, as are some narrative scripts. However, explicitly written into the event are spaces in which "local" individuals give their testimony or recite some spoken word piece of their own design. The synthesis of structure and improvisation in *Alleluia!* is a key forerunner of the Homecomings.

8. The only fan I interviewed who followed the GVB in the 1980s was a self-described fan of contemporary Christian music, which suggests something of the GVB's style before *Homecoming*. In 2009, Bill Gaither released the two-volume album and video, *Gaither Vocal Band: Reunion* (Spring House) a program that reunited every former member of the GVB in Gaither studios to perform and reminiscence. Two years later, Bill released the twenty-disc limited edition box set, *Gaither Vocal Band: The Ultimate Collection* (Spring House). The massive anthology only included those albums recorded under the Gaithers' record label, thus all of the albums of the 1980s—and even the first few albums of the Homecoming era—were absent. The *GVB Reunion* products recall a pre-Homecoming GVB; some fans told me they watched

the video and were surprised to see that African American singer and sometime-Homecoming performer Larnelle Harris had been a member of the group.

9. For a fuller discussion of *Field of Dreams* in the context of late 1980s politics, see Alan Nadel, *Flatlining on the Field of Dreams: Cultural Narratives in the Films of President Reagan's America* (New Brunswick, NJ: Rutgers University Press, 1997), 48–85. Nadel interprets the final "stream of headlights to the enchanted field" scene as signifying the triumph of consumer nostalgia over American agriculture—"the private sector's willingness at twenty dollars a head to subsidize ghosts more than farms" (52).

10. Cohen, *A Consumer's Republic: The Politics of Mass Consumption in Postwar America* (New York: Knopf, 2003). For a discussion of 1980s music's refusal to "buy in," see Bradford Martin's *The Other Eighties: A Secret History of America in the Age of Reagan* (New York: Farrar, Strauss, and Giroux, 2011), particularly Martin's fifth chapter on 1980s post-punk music. While Martin concedes that post-punk had a materialistic, market-driven component, he nonetheless argues for an essential "authenticity" in post-punk, arguing that the music "wrought a greater concern with the authenticity of musical expression and diversified approaches to songwriting and has emerged as a culturally venerated music that is fundamentally about something" (95).

Debates rage regarding the nature of 1980s pop appropriations of 1950s America—the central issue being whether the appropriations support or subvert Reagan-era conservatives' idealization of the Eisenhower years. For an example of how this debate plays out in reference to *Back to the Future,* see Michael Dwyer, "'Fixing' the Fifties: Alex P. Keaton and Marty McFly," in *The 1980s: A Critical and Transitional Decade,* ed. Kimberly Moffitt and Duncan Campbell (Lanham, MD: Lexington, Books, 2011), 201–23; Elizabeth McCarthy, "Back to the Fifties! Fixing the Future," in *The Worlds of Back to the Future: Critical Essays on the Films,* ed. Sorcha Ní Fhlainn (Jefferson, NC: McFarland, 2010), 133–57; Nadel, *Flatlining on the Field of Dreams,* 76–77; Graham Thompson, *American Culture in the 1980s* (Edinburgh: Edinburgh University Press, 2007), 104–5. For a look at how one company adapted its marketing along the lines of newness, nostalgia, and authenticity from the 1980s on, see Constance Hays, *The Real Thing: Truth and Power at the Coca-Cola Company* (New York: Random House, 2004).

11. For examples of rejections and reappropriations of the "neon dreams" to ends other than Reagan's, see Bradford, *The Other Eighties,* esp. 67–94. Philip Glahn, "Counterpublic Art and Social Practice," in *The 1980s: A Critical and Transitional Decade,* 251–70.

12. The longing for authenticity in an age of presumed artifice—expressed often by the artificers, via the artifice—is not new, certainly not in American history. European Americans imagine themselves occupants of an unspoiled garden. Americans build machines. The machines mean progress (less labor, increase in leisure), but they also threaten to spoil the garden. Some keepers of the garden call for the machines' removal—amplifying and broadcasting their calls as far as the machines permit. Americans ride their industrial, technological creations over the horizon, into the next millennium—so automatically that some Americans wonder if it is humankind that is being ridden out over a cliff. Many scholars have explored this narrative as it has occurred in American history. See Leo Marx, *The Machine in the Garden: Technology and the Pastoral Ideal* (New York: Oxford University Press, 1964). The Progressive Era is a favorite epoch for scholars of material culture who explore artifice and authenticity. Miles Orvell argues that during this period, American culture shifted from valorizing imitation, even illusion, in art works and techniques, to valuing the supposedly "original" authentic works and techniques. See *Real Things: Imitation and Authenticity in American Culture, 1880–1940* (Chapel Hill: University of North Carolina Press, 1989). In his introduction, Orvell makes a telling claim about the "synthetic" culture in which he himself writes: "during

the last twenty-five years Americans have not merely tolerated the facsimile representation with grudging humor. They have loved it. One has to remind oneself of this fact or one will utterly fail to understand something as innocent as the recent report in a news magazine that the most fashionable designers are making polyester clothes for the richest people in America. As one designer in this mode put it, 'I love it when they don't try to look real'" (xxiii).

Some scholars have added their own plaintive protests to the narrative of machination. See, for example, the 1983 preface and concluding pages of T. J. Jackson Lears's *No Place of Grace: Antimodernism and the Transformation of American Culture, 1880–1920* (1981, repr., Chicago: University of Chicago Press, 1983), xi–xiv, 309–12. Lears's monumental text is itself important as an artifact of cultural history, published as it was at the onset of Reagan's presidency. The same year of *No Place*'s first reprint, George Lucas would conclude his lucrative *Star Wars* trilogy with *The Return of the Jedi*. Set in the past ("a long time ago, in a galaxy far, far, away"), Lucas nonetheless filled his world with unfathomable special effects and high-tech machinery. The final conflict in the film was resolved largely through the uprising of forest-dwelling "primitives" who used their wooden weapons to defeat a laser-wielding, steel-clad empire. By the end of the battle, some of the primitives literally occupied the empire's vehicles of death. The garden was in the machine.

Although he does not make explicit connections to post-Reagan freemarket concerns, Doug Harrison's examination of Bill Gaither's publicly narrated anxiety strongly suggests that such concerns haunted Bill as he built the Homecoming franchise. As Harrison notes, Bill's 1992 memoir, *I Almost Missed the Sunset: My Perspectives on Life and Music* (Nashville, TN: Thomas Nelson), is replete with stories of the psychic turbulence Bill experienced in the sixties—episodes that Bill explains as being a result of personal-professional insults, worldwide communism, the assassination of Kennedy and Martin Luther King Jr., and general cultural unrest. Harrison reads Bill's anxiety as partially "symptomatic of a cold war predisposition to worry over invisible enemies and hidden forces waiting in the shadows to destroy faithful Christians in moments of vulnerability" (121). Explicitly following Lears, Harrison notes that Bill's calls in this memoir for a return to a former, godly manhood both expresses and constitutes resistance to the perceived weightlessness of modern life: a modern/antimodern protest against the modern. That Bill feels the need to rehearse earlier anxieties publicly in 1992—in the twelfth and final year of a Republican White House, during a significant recession, and at the end of a pyrhhic US military victory in Iraq—suggests that the old anxieties and old longings have been renewed when the Homecomings begin.

13. On the market and Protestant theology, see Colin Campbell, *The Romantic Ethic and the Spirit of Modern Consumerism* (New York: Oxford University Press, 1987), 71–77; R. Laurence Moore, *Selling God: American Religion in the Marketplace of Culture* (New York: Oxford University Press, 1994), 35–39, 49–60, 220–37; James Hudnut-Beumler, *In Pursuit of the Almighty's Dollar: A History of Money and American Protestantism* (Chapel Hill: University of North Carolina Press, 2007), 220–25; Anne Borden, "Making Money, Saving Souls: Christian Bookstores and the Commodification of Christianity," in *Religion, Media, and the Marketplace*, ed. Lynn Schofield Clark (New Brunswick, NJ: Rutgers University Press, 2007), 67–89.

14. Evangelical critiques of megachurches and consumerist Christianity often get combined with critiques of putatively "soft," relativistic theology of the emergent church movement. See, for example, David F. Wells, *The Courage to Be Protestant: Truth-Lovers, Marketers, and Emergents in the Postmodern World* (Grand Rapids, MI: Eerdmans, 2008). Ironically, some of the Christians in this same "emergent" orbit have equally strong criticisms of megachurches and consumerist Christianity. See, for example, Tony Jones, *The New Christians: Dispatches from the Emergent Frontier* (San Francisco, CA: Jossey-Bass, 2008), 72–76. For a criticism from a more

ambiguous, mainline Protestantism, see historian Robert S. McElvaine's *Grand Theft Jesus: The Hijacking of Religion in America* (New York: Crown, 2008).

15. Smith argues that American evangelicals proliferate largely because of their sense that their faith is under siege and perhaps on the decline. Communal urgency creates solidarity. See *American Evangelicalism: Embattled and Thriving* (Chicago: University of Chicago Press, 1998), chapters 4 and 5. On Bill Gaither's productive anxiety, see Harrison, *Then Sings My Soul*, 122.

16. My interviews with fans left me with the suspicion that the Homecomings have made it easier for many elderly members of "contemporary-leaning" churches to stomach their congregations' musical changes. Most fans presumed CCM was the genre that attracted young people and young families—a desired demographic. Those who preferred to stand by the old ways had Homecoming videos, and often-daily Homecoming television programs, as consolation prizes. Judging by early twenty-first-century conversations within evangelical communities, the effects of this compartmentalization of generations were (and are) by no means viewed as positive by all evangelicals. See, for example, Thomas Bergler, *The Juvenilization of American Christianity* (Grand Rapids, MI: Eerdmans, 2012). For a nonevangelical academic study of youth (and suburban, and white) culture in American Christianity, see Eileen Luhr, *Witnessing Suburbia: Conservatives and Christian Youth Culture* (Berkeley: University of California Press, 2009).

17. The concept of "authenticity" has been the subject of much scholarly discussion—in media studies (e.g., Orvell, *Real Things*), studies of popular music (e.g., Richard Peterson, *Creating Country Music*), in literary studies (e.g., Lionel Trilling, *Sincerity and Authenticity* [Cambridge, MA: Harvard University Press, 1971]), and in ethics (e.g., Charles Taylor, *The Ethics of Authenticity* [Cambridge, MA: Harvard University Press, 1991]). The moment and content of Taylor's text make it most germane for my purposes.

Published the same year as the first Homecoming, Taylor's book expresses and addresses the anxieties over the neoliberal free market that underwrite the first Homecoming and its narration. Taylor builds off of Trilling's work, taking for granted a simple starting definition of authenticity: to be authentic is to be "true to oneself"—self-determining, self-realizing. Taylor primarily aims to disjoin self-realization and self-determination from narcissism—a conjunction that undergirds antiliberal critics' argument that neoliberal individualism necessarily produces social atomization. Taylor therefore spends most of *The Ethics of Authenticity* examining how individuals might be true to themselves *within a community*. Although his project is not to identify the criteria by which one person may reasonably judge another person's authenticity, on two points he provides a vocabulary that helps to clarify, if not to resolve, how Homecoming viewers code the Gaithers and the Homecomings as "authentic"—or, to use the more common word I heard from fans that I took to be a synonym for "authentic," "real."

First, Taylor builds off of the rather mundane observation that individuals' "authentic" identities are forged in social contexts. Individual identities require recognition. He argues that individuals who live in a culture of relative social mobility, and one that places a premium on individuals' "inwardly derived, personal, original" identities, have to "win" their recognition through exchange with others—and these exchanges as such entail the possibility of loss (48). Unlike in previous ages, when more rigorously circumscribed social classes made the question of identity and recognition moot, in the modern neoliberal world, identity and recognition are (mutually) contingent. Taylor separates the recognition-exchanges into two categories: the "intimate" and the "social," and he claims that the need for and achievement of recognition is most evident in the former case: "On the intimate level, we can see how much an original identity needs and is vulnerable to the recognition given or withheld by significant others" (49).

Second, Taylor distinguishes between the *manner* and *matter* of discovering and articulating one's authentic self. Taylor takes for granted that, in the modern age, authenticity is self-referential; the manner in which I become authentic is to become true to myself. However, my "true self" might be committed to any number of ends outside of or beyond myself. The matter—the content—of my authenticity need not be self-referential, inwardly focused, simply because my achievement of my authenticity is self-referential. I could be "true to myself" by executing my devotion to a political cause, to a particular community need, or to God (81–82).

When he speaks of "significant others," Taylor seems to mean "love relationships" (50)—something akin to spousal partnerships. But the euphemism suggests a broader possibility, and it begs a question that Taylor does not address: how do some of one's "others" come to be "significant," to the extent that they become one's signifiers? Even conceding that I cannot choose all of my "significant" constituents, I can choose some of them, and to some extent I can regulate the terms and pitch of the intimacy with those whom I choose. This is important if one admits (as I think Taylor would admit) that "significant others" are not only parents, guardians, siblings, or other people with whom one's relationship was or is, to some extent, compulsory. In noncompulsory relationships, significance and the right to signify do not precede the exchanges of identity recognition; it is not exactly true that, because of their significance to me, my significant others help constitute my original identity through recognition or the withholding of recognition. It is true that a personal history with these others makes possible and meaningful the exchanges I have with them, but the personal history itself is a series of these sorts of exchanges. Others become, remain, or cease to be significant to me—and I to them—through such exchanges.

Under what conditions are such exchanges likely to take place, and to continue to take place, between significant others who are in a relatively voluntary relationship? What binds them such that the exchanges are not simply mirroring affirmations and such that the discord in any one exchange does not necessarily cut off subsequent exchanges? Perhaps one condition is the matching of the "matter" of the parties' respective individual identities—if, say, both "true selves" profess an allegiance to the Christian God. This common object orients all recognition and withholding. If one party interprets the other party's withholding of recognition as the formers' abdication of the common object, the relationship is in danger of ending. But if the parties never disagree about the object, it may seem to them, and it will certainly seem to others, as if the relationship is merely personality mirroring—not a relationship of true selves, distinct significant others.

This is the situation in which the Gaithers, and to some extent all Homecoming artists, find themselves vis-à-vis their fans, those "significant others" whom the Homecomings are designed to make feel intimate—"at home" in the Homecomings. If one pronounces one's "true" self" to be committed to an object shared by loosely organized others—others who not only assume the manner of individual self-discovery but who also recommend the manner as the normative manner through which all people realize commitment to the matter—the social dimensions of authenticity get complicated. The celebrity evangelical Christian who would be "authentic" lives a constant paradox. If he is to be recognized as an authentic celebrity evangelical *Christian*, his manifest Christianity must accord with the ideas of Christianity that his "significant others" take to be their shared object—a difficult task, since there are a lot of others, they sometimes change, and their expectations are not always explicit or internally consonant. If he is to be recognized as an authentic celebrity *evangelical* Christian, his faith must be *demonstrably his own*. He has a *personal* relationship with Jesus. If his faith seems too formulaic, too coldly cognate with even "correct" versions of Christianity, he forfeits authenticity. If his self-disclosure seems either mendacious or incomplete, he forfeits authenticity. If he is to be an authentic *celebrity* evangelical Christian, not only must he follow the light of faith that is his own—against all social scripts, especially the temptations of the market—he also must exhibit to society (to the market) the faith that the significant others recognize as true Christianity. Manner and matter overlap.

18. Richard Peterson notes this dilemma with respect to the country music industry's attempts to (re)produce "authentic" artists and products based on older tropes: "there is an accent on being 'real,' and yet in the mechanical system each copy is a paler replica of the authentic original" (*Creating Country Music*, 229).

19. Bill writes extensively about the ease with which skepticism regarding his motivations affects him in *It's More Than the Music*, 138–44.

20. According to Gloria, even in this second video, Bill (still a novice in video production) was resistant to too much orchestration. He chafed at the production team's attempts to smooth the edges of the program and sacrifice the raw edge that the first video contained.

21. *Reunion: A Gospel Homecoming Celebration* (Nashville, TN: Star Song, 1992).

22. Both of the hymnals used in this session are later editions of Stamps-Baxter shape-note hymnals: *Heavenly Highway Hymns* (Nashville, TN: Brentwood-Benson, 1989), originally published in 1956, and *Great Gospel Songs and Hymns* (Grand Rapids, MI: Zondervan, 1992), originally published in 1976. The former was compiled in part by Ben Speer, the youngest son in The Speer Family gospel singing group, who would be the longest regular in the Homecoming franchise.

23. *Reunion: A Gospel Homecoming Celebration*.

24. The Ryman's online interactive timeline suggests what the displays in the building itself make clear: this building was built for American evangelicalism. The second item on the interactive timeline, after "Thomas Green Ryman is born," is "Thomas Ryman hears the Rev. Samuel P. Jones" speak. See "History," Ryman Auditorium, accessed November 21, 2012, http://www.ryman.com/history/. However, the major scholarly histories of country music tend to pick up the story of the Ryman in 1941, when the Grand Ole Opry program—and with it, country music—became a resident in the building. As Bill Malone notes, the capacious balcony area of the building, which now houses exhibits of costumes and instruments from early country performances, was once a Confederate memorial. See Malone, *Country Music, U.S.A.*, 2nd rev. ed. (Austin: University of Texas Press, 1985), 75. For the "country era" Ryman, see also Lange, *Smile When You Call Me a Hillbilly*, 41–43.

25. For a full discussion of these tropes in country music—and some of the tensions that result as country becomes "mass market," see Cecelia Tichi, *High Lonesome: The American Culture of Country Music* (Chapel Hill: University of North Carolina Press, 1994), esp. 135.

26. On authenticity and Garth Brooks's short-lived "Chris Gaines" alter ego, see Chuck Klosterman, "The Passion of the Garth," in *Eating the Dinosaur* (New York: Scribner, 2009), 103–16. One source of pointed backlash against Brooks was his 1992 single, "We Shall Be Free." Sonically and thematically, the song borrowed heavily from African American gospel. Brooks cowrote the song with Stephanie Davis on the heels of the post–Rodney King verdict and Los Angeles riots of 1992. Its lyrics expressed subtle support for gay rights and more explicit advocacy for environmental justice. See John Leland, "Garth Takes a Brave Stand," *Newsweek*, October 12, 1992, available on EBSCOHOST.

27. It is also worth noting that the videos often mark pending earthly departures. The final song of *Turn Your Radio On* is Cynthia Clawson's version of Albert Brumley's "If We Never Meet Again"—a country waltz that speaks of an eventual reunion in heaven between two intimates (Brumley also wrote "Turn Your Radio On"). Clawson sings over a photo montage. The last three photos, in order, are the joined hands of Lillie Knauls and Gloria Gaither (interracial

solidarity), Jake Hess embracing Vestal Goodman (two likely candidates to be soon "departed," especially given Hess's poor health at the time), and Howard Goodman's tear-soaked profile. Gloria closes the program with a reading of Rudyard Kipling's 1896 poem "L'Envoi," a meditation on life in heaven. She reads over a still shot of an old, cathedral-style wooden radio resting on a table.

28. *Reunion: A Gospel Homecoming Celebration.*

29. Ibid. Gloria's essay is prefaced with Bill's singing "Tho' Autumn's Coming On"—a Stuart Hamblen song that I heard Bill sing in several live shows when Gloria was present. It is sung from the point of view of a spouse to his partner as they both enter old age.

30. The recitation is included in its entirety on *Special Homecoming Moments* (1997). Bill's preface of the reading on this compilation emphasizes Gloria's outside stance vis-à-vis southern gospel—particularly stressing her education. Bill notes half-jocularly that, if she had not met him, she probably would have earned her doctorate and be "teaching English at Harvard or Yale or something."

31. Michael Graves, "The Gaither Homecoming Videos and the Ceremonial Reinstatement of Southern Gospel Music Performers," in *More Than "Precious Memories": The Rhetoric of Southern Gospel Music*, ed. Michael Graves and David Fillingim (Macon, GA: Mercer University Press, 2004), 163. Neither Graves nor I want to suggest that Lefevre's story gets resolved *only* at the end of the first series of videos. Certainly, each video contains partial returns—as Lefevre's emotional performance of "Without Him" on *Reunion* indicates. Lefevre's very presence is a sort of homecoming. However, Lefevre's transformation over the course of the videos is important—especially with regard to the four videos from *Turn Your Radio On* to *Landmark*, which Bill films during two different sessions but releases and internally orders in such a way as to accentuate Lefevre's "landmark" return in "Great Is Thy Faithfulness," which I will discuss shortly.

It is worth noting that most of the Homecoming studio sessions of the nineties—and some of the live concerts—yield two videos (as indicated by the personnel and wardrobe continuity). Thus *Turn Your Radio On* and *Old Friends* derive from the same session, as do *Precious Memories* and *Landmark*, and so forth. This "two-in-one" methodology will remain through the twenty-first-century live concerts (see, for example, *Live from Toronto* and *Canadian Homecoming* [Alexandria, IN: Spring House, 2006]). It calls attention to the Gaithers' editorial choices. Songs from the session are chosen and matched to appear on particular videos, in a particular order, to convey a product-specific narrative.

32. Graves, "The Gaither Homecoming Videos," 162.

33. American art is replete with ambivalent racial exchanges—exchanges that simultaneously undermine and fortify race as a meaningful category by which society is organized. In her work on Mark Twain, Shelley Fisher Fishkin argues that Huckleberry Finn's imitating a kind "blackness"—an imitation that is improvised, somewhat spontaneous—undermines the racial hierarchies that supposedly structure society. Tracy Fessenden offers a helpful corrective to Fishkin, noting that, while some undermining can happen, it is also possible that "dominant power is mobilized in gestures of empathy, improvisation, and imitation." This is an important possibility to remember with respect to the Fairfield Four's performance. The call-and-response, hand-clapping Homecoming chorus "puts on" the gestures of black church spaces (although such displays are not limited or endemic to black churches, something clearly changes when the Four take center circle; the chorus is suddenly clapping on the backbeats, Cynthia Clawson's shoulders are ducking and dodging in a new way). This imitative gesture closes the gap between the black performers and white audience; there is empathy and improvisation. However, it is an irruption into the typical order of things, and *as an irruption*

it calls attention to the order of things. See Fishkin, *Was Huck Black? Mark Twain and African American Voices* (New York: Oxford University Press, 2003), 95; Fessenden, *Culture and Redemption: Religion, the Secular, and American Literature* (Princeton, NJ: Princeton University Press, 2007), 112–13. Fessenden builds intentionally on Eric Lott's work on blackface minstrelsy in the nineteenth century and the ambivalence of imitative, "staged" blackness. See Lott, *Love and Theft: Blackface Minstrelsy and the American Working Class* (New York: Oxford University Press, 1995).

34. James Goff notes that "stage-sharing" among black and white gospel groups was relatively common, even in the South, before 1954. However, he argues that *Brown v Board of Education* hardened white southern attitudes toward integration, and groups such as the all-white Statesmen and the all-black Golden Gate Quartet had to limit their joint appearances. See Goff, *Close Harmony*, 210–12. Bill includes the Four's performance of "Dig a Little Deeper" on *Special Homecoming Moments*. Prefacing the song on that video, Bill calls attention to George Younce's ecstatic response. Indeed, Younce's position in the chorus means he and all of his actions are visible in most of the shots of the Four. Bill's preface also has the effect of licensing the African American singers via southern gospel royalty. Younce, the celebrated Cathedrals' bassist, is beside himself with joy; southern gospel viewers have permission to respond accordingly.

35. Discussing this moment in 2013, Bill told me that he actually wanted the Four to stay, but the group's manager insisted that their feature songs fulfilled their contract; the conditions of contact between white and black gospel musicians are difficult to discern on both sides of the veil.

36. *Turn Your Radio On* (Alexandria, IN: Gaither Music Company, 1993).

37. On the "essential" emotional-musical religiosity of African Americans, see Curtis Evans, *The Burden of Black Religion* (New York: Oxford University Press, 2008).

38. See, for example, the comments on "Doris Akers—He Touched Me," YouTube, last modified March 18, 2009, accessed January 22, 2013, http://www.youtube.com/watch?v =spzvrMyWSg. At the height of the civil rights movement, Akers collaborated with the Statesmen on the album *Sing for You* (New York: RCA Victor, 1964). Akers would be one of the first gospel singers to record an album entirely of Gaither songs, with *All God's Children: Doris Akers Sings the Best of Bill and Gloria Gaither* (Vancouver, BC: Heart Warming Records, 1974).

39. While "racial others" demonstrate most starkly the simultaneous undermining and affirming of the boundaries of southern gospel, all "others" of the third category have this double effect. African American singer Larnelle Harris and CCM star Ray Boltz appear in the following videos, *Precious Memories* and *Landmark*. Each performs a single solo during the session. As with the Fairfield Four, Boltz and Harris each receive enthusiastic support. They occupy the center of the circle when they perform their one or two feature songs, and they drift to the back rows and margins of the semicircle for the rest of the session, only visible when the camera sweeps by. Like the Fairfield Four, they do not appear in the next video— though Harris's professional relationship with Gaither extends before the Homecomings and after *Landmark*.

40. For some time, J. D. Sumner held the world's record for the lowest vocal note ever recorded. Currently, the record belongs to Roger Menees, a semiprofessional southern gospel bass singer from southern Illinois. See Tom Barker, "Anna Man Sets World Record for Lowest Note," *Southern Illinoisan*, June 17, 2010, accessed November 10, 2012, http://thesouthern.com/news/local/anna-man-sets-world-record-for-lowest-note/article _20cdc8c0–79c9–11df-9c74–001cc4c002e0.html.

41. The National Quartet Convention was started by J. D. Sumner in 1957. It is the major annual gathering of southern gospel musicians and industry insiders—a week-long showcase

of old and new talent. Although it began in Memphis and was held in Birmingham, Nashville, and Atlanta in its first few decades, the NQC has been held in Louisville, Kentucky, since 1993. In 2013, it left Louisville for Pigeon Forge and Gatlinburg, Tennessee, near the Southern Gospel Music Hall of Fame and Museum in Dollywood.

42. Singing conventions date to the middle nineteenth century. Prevalent in the rural South, singers in a region would gather once or twice a year for several days to perform with (and for) one another, practice, and try new material. It was with this phenomenon in mind that songwriters and music publishers eventually began to write "convention songs"—pieces that employed three- or four-part harmony and typically several counterpoint lyrical lines to test and titillate conventions. See Goff, *Close Harmony*, 38–39.

43. For a discussion of barrelhouse piano playing in history, see Peter J. Silvester, *The Story of Boogie-Woogie: A Left Hand Like God* (Blue Ridge Summit, PA: Scarecrow Press, 2009), and Stuart Isacoff, *The Natural History of the Piano: The Instrument, the Music, the Musicians—from Mozart to Modern Jazz and Everything in Between* (New York: Knopf, 2011), 162–85.

44. One notable hymnal appearance of "Looking for a City" is Brentwood-Benson's *Great Gospel Songs and Hymns*, used in the *Reunion* video.

45. One YouTube version of this "battle" between Goodman and Cook had 514,000 views as of this writing, after five years of being posted. See "'Looking for a City' by Vestal Goodman and Johnny Cook (1974)," YouTube, last modified August 19, 2007, accessed February 1, 2013, http://www.youtube.com/watch?v=rf8f32cDAXA. The comments section was host to a debate between those who thought this video had nothing to do with religion, but with good vocals, and those who thought the "gospel" message essential.

46. The song takes its title from a passage in the New Testament book of Hebrews that likens Abraham's pilgrimage to the spiritual journey of the early Christ-followers: "By faith [Abraham] sojourned in the land of promise, as in a strange country, dwelling in tabernacles with Isaac and Jacob, the heirs with him of the same promise: For he looked for a city which hath foundations, whose builder and maker is God" (Hebrews 11:9–10, KJV). According to the previous verse, Abraham did not know where he was going, but he proceeded on faith.

A few scholars have noted that "Looking for a City" is a favorite song in drag culture (Vestal and her vestments are not unusual in drag culture). For homosexual men and transgendered citizens, the song can express (and create, in collective singing) the dream of an (urban) home, free of struggle and persecution. See Edward Gray, "Looking for a City: The Ritual and Politics of Ethnography," in *Out in the South*, ed. Carlos Dews and Carolyn Leste Law (Philadelphia, PA: Temple University Press, 2001), 173–84; Jeffrey Bennett and Isaac West, "'United We Stand, Divided We Fall': AIDS, Armorettes, and the Tactical Repertoire of Drag," *Southern Communication Journal* 74, no. 3 (2009): 307.

I was sitting in a lawn chair on the edge of Bill's home pool, as he waded casually in the shallow end, when I first told Bill that I noticed a substantial number of gay men in Homecoming audiences. Naïvely worried that my observation would be a bombshell to him, I spoke when his back was turned so I would not have to see his reaction. "Oh, sure," he said, not breaking a stride, raising a casual hand. "They have always been around." He then stopped, turned around, and grinned wide before adding, "and they were *really* around when Vestal was alive." On Vestal's flamboyant stage show, see Harrison, *Then Sings My Soul*, 141–42.

47. "Looking for a City," Cooper/Hartford Music Company, 1949.

48. The Cathedrals and the Statesmen both recorded "This Old House" in the early sixties. See the Statesmen with Hovie Lister, *Stop, Look & Listen for the Lord* (Camden, NJ: RCA Camden, 1962), and Cathedral Quartet, *Cathedral Quartet with Strings* (Vancouver, BC: Heart Warming Records, 1965). As on their album version, the Statesmen typically combined the song with "When the Saints Go Marching In."

49. For Hauerwas's position, see his sequel to his more famous *Resident Aliens*, published the same year as the first Homecoming: *After Christendom: How the Church Is to Behave if Freedom, Justice, and a Christian Nation Are Bad Ideas* (Nashville, TN: Abingdon Press, 1991). Critics of Hauerwas often accuse him of licensing (explicitly or implicitly) a version of escapism that does not depart from fundamentalist versions. For a consideration of Hauerwas, the Duke professor, in his southern context, see Robert P. Jones and Melissa C. Stewart, "The Unintended Consequences of Dixieland Postliberalism," *Crosscurrents* 55, no. 4 (2006): 506–21.

50. See, for example, Earl Scruggs's 1975 recording on *The Earl Scruggs Revue, Anniversary Special, Volume One* (New York: Columbia, 1975). Joan Baez opens the song, singing the chorus. Johnny Cash sings the first verse.

51. *Kennedy Center Homecoming* (Alexandria, IN: Spring House, 1999). For an example of Gordon Mote's version, see *Give It Away* (Alexandria, IN: Spring House, 2006), DVD. The song appears on the 1991 GVB album *Homecoming*.

52. Although this verse evokes a circumscribed, familiar gathering to which the "ship" is headed, another notable "optional" verse sometimes added to the song—for example, in the 1975 Scruggs version—plays up the joyful lawlessness of the ship: "The ship will make no stops / and on board there will be no cops / we are going far beyond the sky / hey we all jump up and down / and dance to that happy sound / let's bid this world goodbye."

53. Like authenticity (n. 14), the concept of sentimentality has been the subject of much scholarly discussion. Following merely the decades-spanning conversation surrounding American women's literary history, the studies are still numerous. See, for example, Ann Douglas, *The Feminization of American Culture* (New York: Knopf, 1977); Jane Tompkins, *Sensational Designs: The Cultural Work of American Fiction* (New York: Oxford, University Press, 1985); Lauren Berlant, *The Female Complaint: The Unfinished Business of Sentimentality in American Culture* (Durham, NC: Duke University Press, 2008). Of the many works that explore sentimentality, Michael Tanner's 1976 essay "Sentimentality" best helps explain why I feel cautiously confident in calling "Old Friends" sentimental but I typically will refrain from using the word in reference to Homecoming material. I refer to Tanner's essay as it appears in *Art and Morality*, ed. José Luis Bermúdez and Sebastian Gardner (New York: Routledge, 2003), 95–110.

Tanner gives qualified endorsement to Oscar Wilde's suggestion that an emotion is sentimental when one hasn't "paid for it"—when one can simply step into and out of feelings without any regard for the actual, material circumstances that should elicit, prevent, or delimit the feelings. The "payment" can go two ways. First, an emotion has been paid for if there is a story behind it—usually a story of struggle. If poor parents have labored to save for their daughter's college education and cry with happiness at their daughter's commencement, one reasonably might say they earned their emotion. The second way is forward-looking. Those works of art that call one to action—in other words, that require one eventually to "make the payment"—are resistant to sentimentality. Tanner claims that the worst music "urges an illusion of order, or offers the exciting and appalling temptations of disorder" (109). In other words, bad music incentivizes inner and outer passivity; the world is either already ordered or need not or cannot become so (on evangelical painting and sentimental order, see Paul Maltby's *Christian Fundamentalism and the Culture of Disenchantment* [Charlottesville: University of Virginia Press, 2013], esp. 130–71). Tanner does not claim that sentimentality always can or should be avoided; at the close of his essay, he judges the emotional deadness Eliot describes in *The Wasteland* as far worse than sentimentality's excessive emotion. Still, Tanner recommends avoiding art that causes or results from these two "failures of payment."

"Old Friends" requires no payment for its filial sentiment. While it names the hardships that friends help one another to endure, it gives little indication that the friendships *themselves* are dearly bought. There is a passive, retrospective resolution to the song. The friend was sent by

God (the hard labor of friendship is erased). It narrates backward from some supposedly stable position. Although there was a time of instability, the friendship—the object of sentimentalization—is not challenged. Nor did it have to be, because the time of instability, like the time of "tears," is over. There is a vast illusion of final order.

I feel *cautiously* confident in calling "Old Friends" sentimental because the song contains a number of interpretive possibilities. If the Gaithers are the speakers in the song—this seems plausible, given that they are the song's cowriters, and given that being once relatively poor and now "big winners" describes their gospel career—the song takes on a particularity that minimizes the sentimentality. Presumably, there are people sitting in the Homecoming studio who *were* these very friends to Bill and Gloria—who stuck by them in good times and bad times. The Gaithers paid for the emotion. Moreover, the other singers, and the viewers at home, might sympathize with the Gaithers' feelings, having had (earned) experiences of friendships like the one in the song. These other singers and viewers did not pay for the emotion they are experiencing, in the sense of having been players in the particular friendships that inform and are expressed in the song, but it seems callous to claim they are consequently merely taking their emotions "on the cheap." The choices are not only between payment and no payment. In this case, it might be more appropriate to say that viewers are renting to own.

It is this nebulous lease on lives in the Homecomings that presents difficulties. It is the problem of high-resolution evangelicalism. Nearly everything in the Gaither catalogue presumes triumph. The Gaithers are singing about their old friends who stuck by them through thick and thin while they sit in a room thick with friends, on top of the gospel world. The triumph may be an accurate description of their lives, but it is not necessarily an accurate description of their viewers' lives. What do the resolved chords of the Homecomings communicate to people who constantly make the same payments as the Gaithers but do not get the promised product? (for an exploration of unresolved-thus-untold stories on Gaither stages, see Lynn Casteel Harper, "Family Fest," *CALYX: A Journal of Art and Literature by Women* [Summer 2012]: 47–52). Stories are never told on the decline, because there is no *ultimate* decline. To be clear, Bill and Gloria strive to demonstrate in their programs that Christians are not promised a life free of hardships; as I will discuss in later chapters, there is plenty of death, illness, and setback manifest on their stages. But there can be nothing but triumph, in the end. The Gaithers, and *all* evangelicals who insist that all will be made well—at least for Christians, maybe for everyone—always will be open to the charge of sentimentality from those who define the term according to emotional "payment." There will always be perceived excess in some direction; either evangelicals can never pay enough for eternal resolution, or they are not really paying anything, since the end product has already been forwarded to them, and its worth infinitely exceeds the price exacted for it. With sentimentality so conceived, one could label all people who "hope for things unseen" as hopelessly sentimental.

At the risk of being sentimental, I want to hang onto a distinction between, say, Martin Luther King Jr. and Thomas Kinkade. Conceptualizing sentimentality as lack of payment for emotion helpfully calls attention to the potential dangers that arise when emotions are divorced from concrete, differentiated experiences. However, one should not draw the line too definitively when one considers the range of emotions possible and manifest in so complex an enterprise as the Homecomings. In the case of the Homecomings, I find sentimentality hardly a clarifying term. I will use it hardly in this book.

54. The Speer Family was the second of several mid-century gospel groups to which the Gaithers would devote a documentary video, in their Hall of Honor series (the first being the Goodman family). See *Bill and Gloria Gaither Present the Speer Family: A Love Story*, directed by Bill Gaither and Donald Boggs (Alexandria, IN: Spring House, 1994).

55. *Landmark* (Alexandria, IN: Spring House, 1994).

56. William and Gloria Gaither, "The Family of God," Gaither Music Company, 1970.

57. Charles Johnson is well credentialed in black and white gospel music circles. Early in his career, he sang with the legendary black gospel group the Nightingales. The Revivers were one of the few groups who deliberately borrowed from white quartet music and who shared stages regularly with them throughout the 1980s and 1990s. James Goff recounts visiting with Johnson at his home in Durham, North Carolina. Johnson gives Goff a mini-sermon on the color-blind quality of gospel music—a colorblindness based on the universal "gospel" it proclaims. See Goff, *Close Harmony*, 199–200.

58. See Jim Bessman, "Gaither Sees Bigger Home for Gospel," *Billboard*, May 3, 1997, 29. In 1997 and 1998 some of the first videos were certified by the Recording Industry Association of America (RIAA) as platinum sellers.

59. The two exceptions to the southern/midwestern rule during the nineties are *Kennedy Center Homecoming* (1999) and *Hawaiian Homecoming* (Alexandria, IN: Spring House, 1998). As I will discuss in chapter 5, the former program is a celebration of gospel music as an "American institution." The latter is not one of the popular videos, but its transplanting of the Homecoming chorus to a popular vacation destination anticipates the Homecoming cruises of the Bahamas and Alaska that the Gaithers will organize in the twenty-first century.

60. Boym, *The Future of Nostalgia* (New York: Basic, 2001), xiii–xiv.

61. Although there are limits to the amount of time that can transpire between nostalgic moments and their objects (e.g., it is difficult for me to be nostalgic about the Byzantine Empire), the fact that the Homecomings on either end of the 1990s possess the same core cast means that there is still discernible continuity across time. The early programs are retreating further into history, but the living relics of those programs are not yet dead. In this case, nostalgia increases as urgency increases; the Homecomings rage against the dying of their original lights.

62. Boym, *The Future of Nostalgia*, 49.

63. Ibid.

64. *All Day Singin'* (Alexandria, IN: Spring House, 1995).

65. For one evangelical's take on the American evangelical fascination with the Amish—particularly in romance novels—see Eric Miller, "Why We Love Amish Romances," *Christianity Today*, last modified April 25, 2011, accessed February 1, 2013, http://www.christianitytoday.com/ct/2011/april/loveamishromances.html. Although Miller says little about evangelical exoticizing of Amish culture, he recognizes that the strict, closed societies of Lancaster County represent simultaneously an attractive and potentially dangerous counterpoint to permissive, "anarchic" American culture. Amish fiction—which often casts a young Amish person struggling between fully accepting the strictures of her religious community and casting off into the "freedom" of broader culture—dramatizes the question of freedom and law with which evangelicals perpetually wrestle. Miller fails to wrestle with the question of the Amish's draw among white evangelicals who idealize (white) rurality as a "pure" way of life, connected to a past that can and should be rendered present. Playing with the term "Old Order Amish," the subtitle to Miller's article points to this idealization: "In our brave, liberated new world, more American evangelical readers are seeking freedom in the Old Order."

66. A single sepia-toned photo of an "old-timey" black family occurs in *Precious Memories*.

67. Faulkner, "A Rose for Emily," section V.

68. The terms "diegetic" and "extradiegetic" are commonly used in film studies. "Diegetic" music occurs within the world of the characters; it is music that both they and the film audience hear (e.g., a character enters a bar and a pianist is playing there). "Extradiegetic" music

does not occur within the characters' world; only the audience can hear it (e.g., an orchestra plays a lush piece over a love scene). Claudia Gorbman coined the term "metadiegetic" music to describe a soundtrack heard by the film audience but one that seems to be heard by a character in a film, even though the music may not be playing in the literal setting. For example, if every time a man is depicted as thinking of his lover, the audience hears the same orchestral score, they might reasonably understand the man to be hearing the music in his head. Although it is difficult to discern precisely if a character is internally hearing a song, Gorbman's term provides a way to describe the ways soundtracks blur the spaces between the audiences (and their inferences) and those of the characters. See Gorbman, *Unheard Melodies: Narrative Film Music* (Bloomington: Indiana University Press, 1987). The Homecomings are replete with such musicial moments.

69. Although it was not as publicized as the Swaggart or Bakker controversies, Oral Roberts's 1987 call for supporters to donate to his ministry or he would die ("the Lord would call me home") caused a brief media stir. See Richard Ostling, Barbara Dolan, and Michael Harris, "Raising Eyebrows and the Dead: Oral Robert Stirs Controversy with a Remarkable Claim," *Time*, July 18, 1987, available at EBSCOHOST. On Bakker, Roberts, and Swaggart, see Steven P. Miller, *The Age of Evangelicalism: America's Born-Again Years* (New York: Oxford University Press, 2014), 81–83.

70. The fallout over the Swaggart saga as it is narrated in the pages of *Christianity Today* reveals the range and fluctuation of responses inside evangelical culture regarding not only Swaggart but televangelism in general. In June 1988, Rodney Clapp took Swaggart to task for refusing his Assembly of God denomination's proposal for discipline, imposing instead his own ninety-day exile from his church. "Swaggart's flouting of the denomination's discipline is symptomatic of a misguided individualism that infects the entire American church." In March 1989, after musicians such as Ozzy Osbourne and Little Feat lampooned Swaggart and the Bakkers in lyrics and stage shows, Peter Crescenti took a decidedly more defensive tone regarding the "disgraced" ministers. He ended his article with a question: "anyone for a boycott of the record industry?" See Rodney Clapp, "Swaggart's Own Worst Enemy," *Christianity Today*, June 17, 1989, 17; Peter Crescenti, "Pop Stars Blast Evangelists," *Christianity Today*, March 3, 1989, 63.

71. For "Dr. Pathos's" original appearance, see John Bowman and Buddy Sheffield, "Hour of Power: Tag Team Evangelists," *In Living Color*, season 2, episode 19, directed by Paul Miller, aired March 17, 1991 (Los Angeles, CA: 20th Century Fox Television, 1991). The same year, progressive rock band Genesis released their album *We Can't Dance* (London: Virgin). It included the song "Jesus He Knows Me," which satirizes a sexually miscreant, money-grubbing televangelist. In the music video, which aired in 1992, Phil Collins plays the televangelist, adorned in an orange leisure suit. Also in 1992, Steve Martin starred as a huckster minister in *Leap of Faith*, directed by Richard Pearce (Hollywood, CA: Paramount, 1992).

CHAPTER TWO

1. Two years after *Homecoming*, the GVB released *Southern Classics* (Nashville, TN: Benson, 1993).

2. Many fans to whom I spoke claimed that there was an "energy" at the live shows that they missed in the videos, though because of sound quality (and control), not as many unequivocally preferred the live concerts to the televised and videotaped events. A number of fans above the age of seventy noted their preference for the spirit of the live concerts, but they remarked on the difficulty of traveling to and from the shows with great frequency. Many belonged to

churches that purchased blocks of tickets when the Homecomings visited a nearby city (parking lots at Homecoming concerts always contain plenty of church buses).

3. English's history was indeed replete with southern gospel. Before joining the GVB, he had already earned a name for himself performing with several southern gospel groups—most notably the Goodman Family and the Singing Americans.

4. See "Adultery Muzzles Careers of Singers," *Christianity Today*, June 20, 1994, 64. English's fall from grace not only generated discussion about his career; it also produced widespread conversation in Christian entertainment regarding the nature of popular Christian music and the importance of entertainers' images. President of the Star Song label Darrell Harris—who was instrumental in the recording and release of the first Homecoming videos—published a piece in the July 1994 issue of *Christianity Today* titled "The Burden of Celebrity." Written explicitly on the heels of the English-Jordan controversy, the essay is part apology for CCM's executives' right and duty to "discipline" wayward performers, part call for CCM labels to provide counsel and accountability for their contracted musicians (in *Christianity Today*, July 18, 1994, 19).

5. In an interview in December 1994, English stated that Bill Gaither "advised me to handle this situation privately" ("English Launches Second Career," *Christianity Today*, December 12, 1994, 56). But no Christian media outlets attached Gaither to English's "sin." Gaither invited English to a Homecoming taping in 1999. A "ceremonial reinstatement" of English ensued, and is captured on *Good News* (Alexandria, IN: Spring House, 2000), and discussed in Graves, "The Gaither Homecoming Videos," 153–81.

6. Penrod did not immediately follow English. In 1994, Buddy Mullins joined the GVB. Mullins replaced English on the GVB's *Testify* (Nashville, TN: Chapel, 1994), an album English had planned to record with the quartet. But Mullins only joined the GVB on the condition that he could continue singing with his family's band; his GVB membership did not feel permanent to anyone. The lead singer spot remained in relative flux.

7. Joel and LaBreeska Hemphill, Trumpet Call Music, 1995, *Ryman Gospel Reunion* (Alexandria, IN: Spring House, 1995). This live video is not to be confused with the 1992 *Reunion* video, whose setting is split between Gaither Studios and the Ryman. The song's first audio release occurred on the album *Southern Classics, Volume 2* (Nashville, TN: Chapel, 1995). It was the GVB's first Penrod-era studio album. The first volume of *Southern Classics* (Nashville, TN: Benson, 1993) was Michael English's last GVB project during his first GVB tenure.

8. As of this writing, Mark Lowry and David Phelps have logged more nonconsecutive years than Penrod in the GVB—Lowry singing from 1988 to 2001, then rejoining the group from 2009 to 2013, Phelps singing from 1997 to 2005, then again from 2009 to the present. In 2008, Bill Gaither informed me that Penrod had been unable for a few years to go out and stand by the merchandise tables to talk to fans during intermissions and times he wasn't needed onstage—as was done by nearly every Homecoming artist—because "he would never be able to get away."

9. In his 1969 essay "What Is an Author?" Michel Foucault argues that the author provides a unifying center, a critical terminus at which all apparent contradictions in a series of texts can be explained or resolved "by the principles of evolution, maturation, or influence." Although Foucault focuses on producers of texts, his theory is applicable to artists. It is the living, "growing" creator of art who gives perhaps disparate creations apparent cohesiveness. The "unified" corpus, in turn, at least in part enforces the notion of the artist as a stable site of production. See *The Foucault Reader*, trans. in 1979 by Josué V. Harari, ed. Paul Rabinow (New York: Penguin, 1984), 111.

10. Although they focus on CCM, Jay Howard's and John Streck's analysis of the demands on Christian musicians to be "holy personalities" is relevant to Homecoming artists and fans. See Howard and Streck, *Apostles of Rock*, 9.

11. *The Best of Guy Penrod* (Alexandria, IN: Spring House, 2005).

12. Gloria later indicated to me that she and Bill also had on their minds the circuit rider of American Wesleyan history—another solitary, rugged, but in this case (like Penrod) explicitly Christian, frontier figure.

13. John Darin Rowsey, John Starnes, and Daryl Williams, "Singing with the Saints," Centergy Music, Centergetic Music, 1997.

14. "On the Authority," Suzanne Jennings, William Gaither, Woody Wright, Townsend and Warbucks Music, Gaither Music, Would He Write Songs, 2000.

15. For a discussion of rurality in the American imagination, see Marx, *Machine in the Garden*, especially chapters 1 and 3. For a British perspective, that focuses more pointedly on the city/country, order/disorder dichotomy, see Raymond Williams, *The Country and the City* (New York: Oxford University Press, 1973), especially chapters 1, 7, and 25. Rebecca Kneale Gould's attention to the array of practices among modern homesteaders in New England highlights the debates about what constitutes "order/disorder" and "nature/artifice." See *At Home in Nature: Modern Homesteading and Spiritual Practice in America* (Berkeley: University of California Press, 2005), 42–53.

16. The first line in Penrod's biography on his webpage spelled out what type of man Penrod's fans were supposed to see in him: "Guy Penrod is in every sense of the word a man cut from the cloth of rugged individualism." "About," guypenrod.com, accessed August 12, 2010, http://guypenrod.com/index.htm?id=17927.

17. For an extended study of Sallman, see David Morgan, *Icons of American Protestantism: The Art of Warner Sallman* (New Haven, CT: Yale University Press, 1996).

18. See Kathryn Joyce, *Quiverfull: Inside the Christian Patriarchy Movement* (Boston, MA: Beacon Press, 2009). For a provocative insider's take on the complicated world of American conservative "homesteading" and homeschooling, see Rod Dreher, *Crunchy Cons* (New York: Crown Forum, 2006).

19. Christian theologians have been wrestling with the tension between metaphorical, literal, and ideal speech at least since Aquinas. The late twentieth-century philosophical/linguistic turn to regard language as constructive of thought and reality has recast metaphor as a cause and root, not an offshoot, of conceptualization and experience of the objective world. In short, we experience and conceptualize the world *through* metaphors, rather than developing metaphors after experience and conceptualization. See George Lakoff and Mark Johnson, *Metaphors We Live By* (Chicago: University of Chicago Press, 1980). Janet Martin Soskice's examination of religious language, specifically, borrows from Lakoff and Johnson. See Soskice, *Metaphor and Religious Language* (Oxford: Clarendon, 1985).

20. On Penrod's website, he further suggests that he does not regard his particular familial arrangement as normative: "I don't presume that everyone lives the same lifestyle. I have my wife, Angie, who's been the love of my life for twenty-five years, and we have eight wonderful kids, seven boys and one girl ages eighteen down to four that we homeschool. I live in the country on a farm in a log house and drive a tractor and a Ford F-350. As a family we've tried to put God at the center of our lives and we've found peace even in the middle of life's storms. Those listening to the new music may live in Manhattan in a high rise and go to work in a limo, but at the end of the day—'life is life' and we all have joys and heartaches as well as similar basic needs and desires." Penrod quoted in "About," guypenrod.com, accessed August 12, 2010, http://guypenrod.com/index.htm?id=17927.

21. Although he does not investigate religious language, Sean Zwagerman's study of women's humor highlights the transgressive, power-laden potential of jabs such as Jen's. See *Wit's End:*

Women's Humor as Rhetorical and Performative Strategy (Pittsburgh: University of Pittsburgh Press, 2010), esp. chapters 1 and 4.

22. Many scholars of American religion have worked on gendered renderings of Jesus. See Colleen McDannell, *Material Christianity: Religion and Popular Culture in America* (New Haven, CT: Yale University Press, 1995), 180–82, David Morgan, *Icons of American Protestantism*, 163–64. However, many of the scholarly discussions of Jesus as sexual object come from historians of Medieval Renaissance art and iconography. See Leo Steinberg, *The Sexuality of Christ in Renaissance Art and in Modern Oblivion* (Chicago: University of Chicago Press, 1983), and Caroline Walker Bynum, *Holy Feast and Holy Fast: The Religious Significance of Food to Medieval Women* (Berkeley: University of California Press, 1987), 246–59.

23. On evangelicals' sensitivity to demographics, and their willingness to adjust liturgical practice to fit demographic desires, see James K. Wellman Jr., *Evangelical vs. Liberal: The Clash of Christian Cultures in the Pacific Northwest* (New York: Oxford University Press, 2008), 80–82, 133–36; Shayne Lee and Phillip Luke Sinitiere, *Holy Mavericks: Evangelical Innovators and the Spiritual Marketplace* (New York: New York University Press, 2009), especially chapters 2 and 6. Little yet has been written on "cowboy-themed" churches, though they are numerous in middle America.

24. The (western) cowboy has not always been a staple character in country music—especially that strand of country that traces itself to and through the Ozark and Appalachian region. See Jeffrey J. Lange, *Smile When You Call Me a Hillbilly*, part 1; Peterson, *Creating Country Music*, chapters 5–6; Bill C. Malone, *Country Music, U.S.A.*, chapter 5.

25. Penrod did not grow out his hair until he left Liberty University—a school that, until 2015, still required that men's hair "shall be cut in such a way that it will not come past the middle of the ears, or over the collar or eyebrows at any time. Ponytails for men are unacceptable." See "Dress Code for Men," Liberty University, accessed September 18, 2014, http://www .liberty.edu/studentaffairs/deanofmen/index.cfm?PID=2925. It is a relatively recent development among many conservative evangelicals that I Corinthians 11:16 ("But if anyone should be contentious—we have no such custom, nor do the churches of God," NRSV) has come into play in discussions of the "hirsute" verse in Corinthians. Only after the 1970s, when there was a good deal of "contention" about long hair, and when Christian rock established itself as a viable Christian medium, did the matter begin to get dropped (and it never dropped in some circles, as the example of Liberty suggests). Roy wrestles with this issue, in part, because he straddles these epochs.

In a reflection that parallels the Gaithers' reactions at Penrod's audition, Billy Graham notes that he objected to his son Franklin's long hair when the latter was a teenager. Again, a woman intervened. It was Graham's wife, Ruth, who reminded him "it wasn't a moral issue." See Graham, "A Father's Heart," BGEA, accessed June 16, 2010, http://www.billygraham.org/articlepage .asp?articleid=1552.

26. The covers of *Singing News* over the years tell the story of their conservative preference in clothing. The most telling piece of evidence is the relative infrequency of the relatively boundary-pushing GVB's appearance on the cover. When the group does appear, all members wear coordinated suits and ties—not their typical performance attire (see the October 2009 cover of the magazine). The National Quartet Convention's rules can best be summarized by looking at an exchange between Clarke Beasley of the NQC and southern gospel blogger and industry insider Daniel Mount. Wanting clarification on the NQC's dress code, Mount asked, "is there any requirement that men be dressed in suits and ties or be clean shaven?" Beasley replied, "Thank you for your e-mail. Contrary to popular myth, there is no contractual

requirement regarding dress that we place on our artists. We depend on our artists to make wise decisions about dress and song selection based on where they are and who they are singing to. Unfortunately, we are sometimes disappointed." Beasley added, in another reply to Mount, "the same applies for hairstyles." The moralistic yet noncommittal tone of Beasley's response bespeaks the unwritten rules governing appearance in the southern gospel world, and the malleable space that concert promoters carve for themselves should they need to "exercise discipline" regarding some artists' choices. The GVB did not appear at the NQC from 2004 to 2007. See Mount, "NQC: No Dress Code," southerngospelblog.com, October 9, 2006, accessed November 20, 2010, http://www.southerngospelblog.com/archives/70.

27. See Beth Myers, "NOW Promises 'No Surrender' to Right Wing Promise Keepers," *NOW*, October 1997, accessed August 1, 2010, http://www.now.org/nnt/10–97/pk.html. The NOW anti-Promise Keeper campaign—called the Promise Keeper Mobilization Project—No Surrender Campaign—remained up and running as of August 2010. The latest PK-related article on the NOW website at this time, which was written in 2004, basically repeated the organization's 1990s anti-PK arguments. This demonstrates that NOW still regarded the PKs as a serious threat in the 2000s, and that the organization had little awareness of (or concern for) the changing face of evangelical masculinity after the 1990s. "Promise Keeper Mobilization Project," National Organization for Women, accessed August 12, 2010, http://www.now.org/issues /right/promise/project.html. Studies that saw PKs as uniformly and unequivocally patriarchal typically were published closer to the time of the PK's greatest popularity. See Jean V. Hardisty, *Mobilizing Resentment: Conservative Resurgence from the John Birch Society to the Promise Keepers* (Boston: Beacon Press, 1999), and Michael A. Messner, *The Politics of Masculinities: Men in Movements* (Thousand Oaks, CA: Sage Press, 1997). Later scholars and journalists chiseled away at the monolith. See John P. Bartkowski, *The Promise Keepers: Servants, Soldiers, and Godly Men* (New Brunswick, NJ: Rutgers University Press, 2004). Rosin, "Promise Weepers," *New Republic*, October 17, 1997, available at EBSCOHOST; Susan Faludi, *Stiffed: The Betrayal of the American Man* (New York: William Morrow and Company, 1999), 260; W. Bradford Wilcox, *Soft Patriarchs, New Men: How Christianity Shapes Husbands and Fathers* (Chicago: University of Chicago Press, 2004).

28. See Clifford Putney, *Muscular Christianity: Manhood and Sports in Protestant America, 1880–1920* (Cambridge, MA: Harvard University Press, 2003), and Stephen Prothero, *American Jesus: How the Son of God Became a National Icon* (New York: Farrar, Strauss, and Giroux, 2004), 87–122.

29. It could be debated how antiracist the PKs were, in effect; NOW took this issue on (see "Myths and Facts about the Promise Keepers," *NOW*, accessed August 12, 2010, http://www .now.org/issues/right/promise/mythfact.html#racism). But racial reconciliation was certainly a strong part of the group's official message. Number six on the "Seven Promises of a Promise Keeper" list was "a Promise Keeper is committed to reaching beyond any racial and denominational barriers to demonstrate the power of biblical unity." ("Seven Promises," *Promise Keepers*, accessed August 12, 2010, http://www.promisekeepers.org/about/7promises). On race in the PK movement, see Miller, *The Age of Evangelicalism*, 111–13.

30. Barry and Suzanne Jennings, "A Few Good Men," Townsend and Warbucks Music, 1990. First recorded on the Gaither Vocal Band, *A Few Good Men* (Nashville, TN: Star Song, 1990). The song also appeared on the Promise Keeper compilation, *A Life That Shows* (Nashville, TN: Sparrow, 1994). Playwright/screenwriter Aaron Sorkin also would use "a few good men" as the title of his award-winning 1992 movie starring Tom Cruise and Jack Nicholson.

31. *Wild at Heart: Discovering the Secret of a Man's Soul* (Nashville, TN: Thomas Nelson, 2001), 7. For a look at readers' responses to Eldredge's book, see Sally K. Gallagher and Sabrina

L. Wood, "Manhood Going Wild? Transformations in Conservative Protestant Christianity," *Sociology of Religion* 66 (Summer 2005): 135–59. I discuss Eldredge and his epoch more fully in Harper, "New Frontiers: *Wild at Heart* and Post-Promise Keeper Evangelical Manhood," *Journal of Religion and Popular Culture* 24, no. 1 (Spring 2012): 97–112.

32. Eldredge, *Wild at Heart*, 22.

33. John Eldredge, *The Way of the Wild Heart: A Map for the Masculine Journey* (Nashville, TN: Thomas Nelson, 2006). Wild at Heart *Field Manual: A Personal Guide to Discover the Secret of Your Masculine Soul* (Nashville, TN: Thomas Nelson, 2002). John and Stasi Eldredge, *Captivating: Unveiling the Mystery of a Woman's Soul* (Nashville, TN: Thomas Nelson, 2007).

34. James Dobson, *Bringing Up Boys: Practical Advice and Encouragement for Those Shaping the Next Generation of Men* (Wheaton, IL: Tyndale, 2001). Eric Ludy, *God's Gift to Women: Discovering the Lost Greatness of Masculinity* (Sisters, OR: Multnomah Publishers, 2003); Eric Ludy, *The Bravehearted Gospel: The Truth Is Worth Fighting For* (Eugene, OR: Harvest House, 2008). Erwin McManus, *The Barbarian Way: Unleash the Untamed Faith Within* (Nashville, TN: Thomas Nelson, 2005).

35. See Christina Hoff Sommers, *The War against Boys: How Misguided Feminism Is Harming Our Young Men* (New York: Simon and Schuster, 2000), and Lionel Tiger, *The Decline of Males: The First Look at an Unexpected New World for Men and Women* (New York: St. Martin's, 2000).

36. Dobson's behaviorism is on fullest display in *The New Dare to Discipline* (Wheaton, IL: Tyndale, 1992), 79–80. Although Dobson claims to "resoundingly reject" behaviorism of B. F. Skinner's variety, he endorses the "reinforcement theory" of Skinner's predecessor in educational psychology, E. L. Thorndike. In Dobson's application of the principle, it is hard to tell precisely how Dobson departs from behaviorism except in principle. To see how this plays out in Dobson's treatment of boys specifically, see *Bringing Up Boys*, 15–16. See also Joseph and Linda Ames Nicolosi, *A Parent's Guide to Preventing Homosexuality* (Downers Grove, IL: InterVarsity Press, 2002). The first chapter of the Nicolosi's book is titled "Masculinity Is an Achievement." See also Tanya Erzen, *Straight to Jesus: Sexual and Christian Conversions in the Ex-Gay Movement* (Berkeley: University of California Press, 2006), 134–48.

37. The Carnegie Hall version of "A Few Good Men" features a number of New York City firemen and policemen walking onstage during the coda. *Let Freedom Ring* (Alexandria, IN: Spring House, 2002).

38. Quotations from Penrod come from *The Best of Guy Penrod*. Quotations from Eldredge come from *Wild at Heart*—pages 12 and 20, respectively. In *The Way of the Wild Heart*, he identifies the "cowboy stage" as one stage in males' development (he devotes two chapters to this stage).

39. For a discussion of southern masculinity and Christianity, see Ted Ownby, *Subduing Satan: Religion, Recreation, and Manhood in the Rural South, 1880–1920* (Chapel Hill: University of North Carolina Press, 1990). Susan Friend Harding's work on Jerry Falwell also highlights the minister's play with "manly" symbols, language, and acts. See *The Book of Jerry Falwell: Fundamentalist Language and Politics* (Princeton, NJ: Princeton University Press, 2000), 176–81.

40. For an excellent collection of essays on the history of masculinity in the postbellum South, see *Southern Masculinity: Perspectives on Manhood in the South since Reconstruction*, ed. Craig Thompson Friend (Athens: University of Georgia Press, 2009).

41. As a rule, these gestures are available to, and perhaps required of, males alone. Male singers are far more kinetic and effusive than their female counterparts—who more frequently (though not exclusively) appear as solo acts, whose gospel mettle seems to depend upon their

decorous physical isolation from other acts. The family-band-saturated world of southern gospel means that a significant proportion of women who appear are mothers (and many in the southern gospel demographic are postmenopausal). Women are not entirely disallowed tactility—tactility with relatives, primarily, as putatively sexless older women. But women onstage are notably more reserved.

Reporting on mid-century female country stars Charline Arthur and Kitty Wells, Emily C. Neely suggests that the domesticated, unaffected propriety of female honky-tonk performers was largely a 1950s phenomenon—that women were more vivacious performers before the post-WWII nationalization of the music. See Neely, "Charline Arthur: The (Un)Making of a Honky-Tonk Star," in *A Boy Named Sue*, 44–58.

Doug Harrison is at his strongest when he writes about the gender-bending theatricality of southern gospel music. Although I believe he overestimates the number of performative identities available to *women* on Homecoming stages (119), he rightly notes the "queerness" of southern gospel as it is manifest in male performances. As Anthony Heilbut does in his study of homosexuality in black gospel (*The Fan Who Knew Too Much*), Harrison notes the "open secrecy" of homosexuality in southern gospel music industry—the fact that gay men abound in an insistently heteronormative world. See Harrison, *Then Sings My Soul*, 137–61.

42. *Singin' with the Saints* (Alexandria, IN: Spring House, 1998). Other notable Penrod performances of "It Is Finished" occur on *Red Rocks Homecoming* (Alexandria, IN: Spring House, 2003), and *Australian Homecoming* (Alexandria, IN: Spring House, 2003). Because the *Singin'* version I discuss here features Penrod with the Bill Gaither Trio, it is worth looking at Michael English's equally passionate but less strident performance on the Gaithers' pre-Homecoming video, Bill Gaither Trio/Gaither Vocal Band, *Live in Concert* (Alexandria, IN: Spring Hill, 1991).

43. William and Gloria Gaither, "It Is Finished," Gaither Music Company, 1976.

44. Penrod's song selection is not the only sign that the Homecomings were leaning more deliberately toward country in the late 1990s and first years of the twenty-first century. The twangy Easter Family and the family bluegrass band the Isaacs became more regular Homecoming presences starting around 2000. In 2008, the Gaithers released the two-volume *Country Bluegrass Homecoming* (Alexandria, IN: Spring House, 2008), which featured country and bluegrass artists such as Marty Stuart and Ricky Skaggs. Perhaps the most monumental gesture the Gaithers made toward country music was their celebration of the Oak Ridge Boys, captured primarily on *The Oak Ridge Boys: A Gospel Journey* (Alexandria, IN: Spring House, 2009), CD and DVD. The move brought the Oaks back more definitively into the southern gospel community in which they began their careers—a community that had held them at arm's length for decades.

45. Numerous country and gospel singers recorded "Jesse Taylor" before the GVB's rendition on their 1999 album *God Is Good* (Alexandria, IN: Spring House, 1999), the 1998 Homecoming video *Down by the Tabernacle*, filmed at a rustic Wesleyan camp meeting site in rural Indiana (Alexandria, IN: Spring House, 1998), and, in an unusual turn, the post-Penrod GVB album *New Edition* (Alexandria, IN: Spring House, 2014), on which African American bass singer Todd Suttles sings lead. The best-known pre-GVB version appeared on the Oak Ridge Boys' eponymous 1974 album.

46. Dallas Frazier and Sanger D. Shafer, "The Baptism of Jesse Taylor," Sony/ATV Acuff-Rose Music, Inc., 1972. Frazier experienced a kind of "baptism" himself. He retired from songwriting in the late 1980s, and he became the pastor of a nondenominational church in Tennessee.

47. The titillating narration of sin in personal testimony has long been a subject of evangelical discussion as well as an issue among ethnographers of evangelicals. See Susan Friend Harding's treatment of Jerry Falwell and his own rendering of his "wild youth," 88–100.

48. Benjamin Gaither, Gloria Gaither, William Gaither, Doug Johnson, and Kim Williams, "Jesus and John Wayne," Mountain Manna, Sony/ATV Timber, 2007. The song appears on *Country Bluegrass Homecoming Volume 2* (Alexandria, IN: Spring House, 2008), the GVB album *Lovin' Life* (Alexandria, IN: Spring House, 2008)., and the post-Penrod GVB album and video, *Happy Rhythm* (Alexandria, IN: Spring House, 2015), with Adam Crabb singing lead.

In 1999, independent country/folk artist Pat Green released a song titled "John Wayne and Jesus" on his album *Here We Go*. Unlike the Gaithers' song, Green *compares* Jesus to John Wayne—in a rather tongue-in-cheek fashion: "I met John Wayne and Jesus when I was just a kid, / they both had on their cowboy hats just like I pictured them, / I stood up at the front of the class waving my American flag, / saying the pledge sang amber waves of grain." I have not found any evidence that the Gaithers, Kim Williams, or Doug Johnson were aware of the song.

49. Ed and Patsy Bruce wrote "Mammas . . ." in 1975, the same year Ed Bruce first recorded it on *Ed Bruce* (Los Angeles, CA: United Artists, 1975). The famous, number-one Jennings/Nelson recording appeared in 1978 on *Waylon and Willie* (New York: RCA Victor, 1978).

50. Even more striking about Dugan's clip is that it opens with a clip from a John Wayne film, in which Wayne is pontificating about taking a stand for what is right, in a universe where there is clearly a "right" and "wrong." In this case, John Wayne seems to be on Jesus's side, as Dugan would have it. "Jesus and John Wayne mp.4," YouTube, April 20, 2010, accessed December 8, 2010, http://www.youtube.com/watch?v=FtZBqtj_2JQ.

51. First criticism, User: xovampireprincessxo, August 2009, comment on "'Jesus and John Wayne' By The Gaither Vocal Band (2008)," YouTube, October 29, 2008, accessed December 8, 2010, http://www.youtube.com/watch?v=izneCqdrJHw. The Ethiopian viewer, user: 3ir7uclye, October 2009, comment on ibid. Another viewer asks a similar question in Portuguese.

As Paul Gutjahr notes in his study of Amazon.com reviews of the *Left Behind* series, several caveats are important to make regarding online commenting on media artifacts: the self-selectivity of a computer-literate clientele, the self-selectivity of people who possess, and want to share, strong opinions on the artifact, and the inability for scholars to assess commenters' true identities. Gutjahr sent follow-up surveys to Amazon.com respondents to attempt to close the gap between him and the anonymous reviewers, though he acknowledged even that exercise was fraught with self-selectivity. See Gutjahr, "No Longer Left Behind: Amazon.com, Reader-Response, and the Changing Fortunes of the Christian Novel in America," *Book History* 5 (2002): 209–36.

These caveats will be important to keep in mind throughout, as I will revisit blog comments and YouTube clips in later chapters. In the case of the "Ethiopian," the commenter may be lying about his/her country of origin. Even if this is the case, though, the fact that the commenter thinks to situate him/herself outside the culture that created "Jesus and John Wayne" illustrates some awareness that the song will not resonate outside of a specific American subculture. The "Ethiopian" identity draws out that subculture's insiders to justify publicly the song on more cosmopolitan (but still Christian) grounds without feeling like the call for justification is a challenge. If the "Ethiopian" were in fact, say, a white male Baptist preacher from Texas, the point still holds that there is a debate to be had surrounding the song; it just refashions the debate into a friendlier, cross-cultural dialogue.

52. User: oldguycode, October 2009, comment on ibid.

53. "Lucifer" comment by User: bubbaj232, August 2009, comment on ibid. "Both Jesus and John Wayne" comment by User: shefrog42, October 2009, comment on ibid.

54. Britt quotation from e-mail message to the author, August 21, 2010. See Britt's online defense at "Jesus and John Wayne," Musicscribe, March 10, 2009, accessed December 2 2010, http://www.musicscribe.com/blog/wordpress/?p=1394. Britt: "Why do some think the song is comparing Jesus to John Wayne (it's not) or giving a brief for sin (it's not doing that either)?"

55. Penrod's solo album, *Breathe Deep*, was released soon after Penrod's GVB departure—in February 2010, on the Gaithers' Spring House label.

CHAPTER THREE

1. "Mark," in response to Daniel Mount, "Sarah Palin to Appear at NQC," southerngospelblog.com, April 5, 2010, accessed September 8, 2011, http://www .southerngospelblog.com/archives/4692.

2. Sue Smith, "Thursday's Blog on Friday," *writeaboutjesus.com*, September 17, 2010, http://www.writeaboutjesus.com/Sues_Blog/Blog/Entries/2010/9/17_Thursday's_blog_on _Friday.html. Smith quickly removed her post after Doug Harrison reposted her comments on his website. She was concerned, apparently, that she was being quoted out of context. Harrison—who had provided both a block quote and a link to Smith's blog—noted her concern in an updated post and relinked her site. In the updated version of her original post, Smith acknowledged that Palin obviously did not know southern gospel music but insisted that this was "no big deal." Doug Harrison, "NQC 10: Sideshow Sarah Palin Post-Mortem," Averyfineline: Criticism and Commentary on Southern Gospel Music, September 17, 2010, accessed September 8, 2011, http://averyfineline.com/2010/09/17/nqc-10-sideshow-sarah-palin-post-mortem/. Sue Smith, "Homesick," *writeaboutjesus.com*, September 18, 2010, http://www.writeaboutjesus .com/Sues_Blog/Blog/Entries/2010/9/18_home_sick.html.

3. "DixieDawg," in response to Doug Harrison, "NQC 10: Sideshow Sarah Palin."

4. The most extensive study of the American "apolitical" impulse is Nina Eliasoph's *Avoiding Politics: How Americans Produce Apathy in Everyday Life* (New York: Cambridge University Press, 1998). Examining a rather wide, eclectic assortment of social, recreational, and activist groups, Eliasoph finds that nearly all parties use "politics" to refer to that arena which opposes or lies beyond those concerns and activities on which they place great value. In her examination of church congregations that are wrestling with the issue of homosexuality, Dawne Moon demonstrates that Eliasoph's conclusions apply to American Christian groups. Moon notes that church attendees across the "conservative-liberal" spectrum share a suspicion toward "politics" in the church; they differ, though, in their understanding of what constitutes "politics." *God, Sex, and Politics: Homosexuality and Everyday Theologies* (Chicago: University of Chicago Press, 2004), especially chapters 4–5.

5. In *It's More Than the Music*, Bill recalls the ambivalent reception his Trio received in the 1970s. While people were mostly cordial in face-to-face encounters, most of the crowd left during the Trio's performance (Bill: "I have never seen the backs of so many heads in my life!"). After this episode, reports Bill, "almost by accident we took our music in a different direction [. . .] . Over the next twenty years, we developed our own audience, one accustomed to our soft and easy approach to the music" (135–37).

6. In his book-length treatment of American antigovernmentalism, Garry Wills notes this tendency to regard professional politics as no arena for honest people. Tracing one cause of the mistrust to an interpretation of the Constitution and its authors—one that emphasizes their cynicism toward governance—Wills notes the tendency for antigovernmentalists to "assert[s] that the founders had such a low opinion of politics that no honest man could make it his profession." Wills seeks to debunk and complicate this view. At the same time, he acknowledges that the logic that undergirds this version of apoliticism has a tight (perhaps self-fulfilling) circularity to it that is difficult to answer with historical argument: professional politics is essentially a dishonest game, so it attracts only dishonest people; because it attracts dishonest

people, it is essentially a dishonest game. See Wills, *A Necessary Evil: A History of American Distrust of Government* (New York: Simon and Schuster, 1999), 22.

7. The joke dots the internet. The *National Review*'s Byron York reported that Tony Perkins, head of the Family Research Council, used a version of the same joke at the 2007 Values Voters Summit in Washington, DC. See York, "Values Voters Humor," *National Review Online*, October 17, 2007, http://www.nationalreview.com/corner/150679/values-voters-humor/byron-york.

8. For an account of Graham's involvement with Nixon, see William C. Martin, *With God on Our Side: The Rise of the Religious Right in America* (New York: Broadway, 2005), 146–47; Grant Wacker, *America's Pastor: Billy Graham and the Shaping of a Nation* (Cambridge, MA: Harvard Belknap, 2014), 212–14.

9. That the Gaithers feel compelled to answer to the fiercest heteronormative Christians in their audience was evident to me early. When I first met the Gaithers, Bill was just extinguishing the last embers of a controversy involving he and a fellow Christian songwriter, Marsha Stevens. In 1979, Stevens, the person behind several popular Christian songs of the 1970s, publicly affirmed her homosexual orientation and divorced her husband. Consequently, Christian labels refused to record her songs, Christian radio refused to play them, and most Christian musicians shunned her. The Gaithers continued to perform her song "For Those Tears I Died" at Homecoming events. After Bill learned that Stevens was in attendance at a 2002 Homecoming concert in Phoenix, he invited her backstage and posed with her for a picture. Stevens posted the picture on her website, along with a message that suggested that Bill Gaither still "fully" endorsed her. According to Bill, "some fundamentalist website" reprinted a copy of the picture, alongside an article that identified Gaither as a liberal, homosexual sympathizer. Word spread. Bill convinced Stevens to take the posted picture down and grudgingly released a statement to the press explaining his (not-too-vehement) stand against homosexuality. See "Bill Gaither Issues Statement Regarding Misrepresentation," *Singing News*, last modified May 4, 2006, accessed August 10, 2006, http://www.singingnews.com/news/sg_wire/story_detail .lasso?id=35494. Although Bill's public statement expressed frustration that Stevens exploited the photo on her site, much of the frustration he expressed to me was that this had become an issue at all; Bill's tone did not suggest to me that Bill meant "some fundamentalist website" as a compliment. Still, that "fundamentalist website" dictated the terms of Bill's public statement.

10. Stated simply, the Campolos were famously split on the issue of homosexuality—Tony believing homosexuality to be a sin "in practice," Peggy believing monogamous marriages were acceptable venues for same-sex practices. In the first decade of the twenty-first century, the pair regularly engaged in public debates on the legal and religious upshots of their convictions. For a recording of one of their discussions, see "Building Bridges on Homosexuality: Tony and Peggy Campolo on Homosexuality," The Gay Christian Network, 2010, accessed October 20, 2011, gaychristian.net/campolos.php. In 2015, Tony Campolo announced his full support of gay marriage. See "Tony Campolo: For the Record," tonycampolo.org, last modified June 8, 2015, accessed June 20, 2015, http://tonycampolo.org/for-the-record-tony-campolo-releases-a-new -statement/#.VXXFXM9Viko.

11. Gloria Gaither, *Something Beautiful: The Stories behind a Half-Century of the Songs of Bill and Gloria Gaither* (New York: FaithWords, 2007), 5–6. Gloria's sympathy with progressive causes certainly would not have been unprecedented among evangelicals in the early 1970s, as recent scholarship on the evangelical moderates and progressives demonstrates. See Miller, *The Age of Evangelicalism*, chapters 1 and 2; David R. Swartz, *Moral Minority: The Evangelical Left in an Age of Conservatism* (Philadelphia: University of Pennsylvania Press, 2012).

12. Baldwin, *No Name in the Street*, 1972, rpt. in *Collected Essays* (New York; Modern Library Association, 1998), 467–70.

13. Gaither, *Something Beautiful*, 6.

14. Two of Guthrie's verses do not appear in the Homecoming version: (1) "Was a high wall there that tried to stop me / A sign was painted said: Private Property, / But on the back side it didn't say nothing / This land was made for you and me." (2) "One bright sunny morning in the shadow of the steeple / By the Relief Office I saw my people — / As they stood hungry, I stood there wondering if / This land was made for you and me." Given the published 1944 version of the song, the Homecoming omissions are not unusual. There is an irony in the Guthrie song's appearance: Guthrie wrote the song as a critical response to "God Bless America"—the title track of the Carnegie Hall Homecoming video on which "This Land" does not appear. See Sheryl Kaskowitz, *God Bless America: The Surprising History of an Iconic Song* (New York: Oxford University Press, 2013).

15. *God Bless America* (Alexandria, IN: Spring House, 2002); *Let Freedom Ring* (2002).

16. Benjamin and Gloria Gaither, "Give It Away," Gaither Music Company, Hook, Line and Music Publishing, 2006.

17. Although this championing of charity occurs throughout Christian history, Anders Nygren's *Eros and Agape* is one of the most important articulations of the belief that Christian love is essentially charity. The Swedish Lutheran theologian's definition of *agape* as gratuitous benevolence leads him to reject justice as a motivation for true Christian love—which should be an *agape* love of the sort God gives to undeserving humans. For a Christian analysis and critique of Nygren, see Nicholas Wolterstorff, *Justice: Rights and Wrongs* (Princeton, NJ: Princeton University Press, 2008), 98–110.

18. Thoreau, "Economy," *Walden*, 1854, rpt. in *Walden and Other Writings* (New York: Barnes and Noble, 1995), 62–63.

19. Weber, *The Protestant Ethic and the Spirit of Capitalism* (1904–1905; repr., Mineola, NY: Dover, 2003), 175–76. Italics in Weber's original.

20. Williams, *The Country and the City*, 32–33.

21. Jeffrey Stout catalogues the systematic assault on middle-class, usually African American, New Orleans neighborhoods. Stout points out that a number of outside developers and legislators used the evacuation of the city during and after Katrina as an opportunity to hasten their plans to redistrict, rezone, and clean out the Gentilly and Lower Ninth Ward sections of the city for their own benefits. It took (and continues to take) local populations organizing, educating, and advocating for themselves in court, council meetings, and other public spaces to counter their immensely wealthy, well-organized opponents. See Stout, *Blessed Are the Organized*, chapter 2.

22. Benjamin and Gloria Gaither, "Give It Away," 2006.

23. Population statistics come from the US Census Bureau, http://factfinder.census.gov /servlet/ACSSAFFFacts?_event=Search&geo_id=&_geoContext=&_street=&_county =anderson&_cityTown=anderson&_state=04000US18&_zip=&_lang=en&_sse =on&pctxt=fph&pgsl=010.

24. Jeremy W. Peters and Micheline Maynard, "A Town in Danger of Dying Out as GM Falters," *New York Times*, February 20, 2006, http://www.nytimes.com/2006/02/20/business /worldbusiness/20iht-gm.html. It is important to note some characteristics of Anderson that distinguish it from Flint, Michigan. While Anderson wagered and lost a great deal on success of the domestic automobile industry, the city had some side bets on the table. In 1905—long before GM drove into town—Anderson became the headquarters of a Wesleyan/Holiness denomination that eventually called itself the "Church of God, Anderson, Indiana" (to distinguish itself from the many other "Church of God" institutions—specifically the Pentecostal Churches of God headquartered in Cleveland, Tennessee). Anderson Bible School—the

denomination's flagship education institution—was founded in 1917. The school is now Anderson University—an institution with two thousand undergraduates and another five hundred graduate and professional students.

Anderson also benefits from its agricultural surroundings. As in many midwestern locales, farmland is losing out to suburban sprawl in this region. But farming remains a major enterprise in the area—which means, among other things, that there is a significant population dispersed over a wide geographic region for whom the services of a small city remain important. Along with nearby Muncie, Anderson provides many of the amenities endemic to a sizable town while remaining more accessible (by mileage and by temperament) to the rural populations than is Indianapolis. Anderson's hospital, St. John's Medical Center, is the largest employer in Madison County.

As of this writing, the city has begun to court industry back to town with some success, advertising its wealth of available factory spaces. That the city's website proclaims in a large font that Anderson is one of the top-100 small American cities for business—and that the website is available in English, German, Chinese, and Korean—demonstrates city officials' designs (see cityofanderson.com). In 2009, Nestlé opened a massive factory and beverage distribution center in Anderson.

25. Bill discusses the temptation of moving to Nashville in *It's More Than the Music*. According to him, he and Gloria decided (and continue to decide) to remain in Alexandria largely because it allows them "to separate our 'real lives' from our 'stage lives'" (131). Of course, this is complicated, given they live about a mile from the studio in which the early Homecomings were recorded. Bill also talks about his desire to care for a particular plot of land over time (90–91).

26. Franzen, "The Joy Breaks Through," in *The Discomfort Zone: A Personal History* (New York: Picador, 2006), 62.

27. I was inconsistent in this strategy. For example, I was bolder about injecting race—another taboo topic—into the space. But unlike race—which I could bring up more easily by invoking conspicuous "racial others" like Lynda Randle or by asking about the stylistic characteristics of black and white gospel music—*politics* possessed no Homecoming avatar.

28. Frederick, *Between Sundays: Black Women and Everyday Struggles of Faith* (Berkeley: University of California Press, 2003), 133.

29. Ibid., 142–59.

30. The Homecomings differ from the televised ministries Frederick examines in two important ways. First, they are a more holistic enterprise, in that several types of communication occur in them. Second, most Homecoming viewers (and performers) are white evangelicals. Certainly, the programs are in the white evangelical tradition. White evangelical churches certainly are not historically bereft of social engagement, but rarely do they self-consciously possess a (factual or fictitious) narrative of sustained, explicit social engagement as do black churches. Unlike black television ministers—who easily can be read as departing from "the legacy of Martin Luther King Jr." when they eschew social engagement—the Gaithers are not as likely to be read as departing radically from such a legacy.

31. Frederick is aware of and concerned about the effects of televangelism on local churches, but it is not her primary focus. She tends to think more broadly than will I in this section when she posits "social engagement" against televangelistic individualism. First and foremost, Frederick worries that this individualism weakens individuals' ability or willingness to tackle complicated and divisive issues like structural racism and classism. I share this worry, but here I explore how the Homecomings may weaken individuals' ability to participate, even mundanely, in a relatively homogeneous local community of faith. Frederick wonders if so-individualized

Christians will care about societal injustice; I wonder if so-individualized Christians will be equipped even to debate the color of the sanctuary carpet with one another.

32. In evangelical circles, personal "testimony" usually signals two, sometimes-overlapping autobiographical narratives. Most narrowly, such a testimony is one's profession of faith; it recounts the moment that one came to accept Jesus as one's personal savior, and perhaps what transpired immediately afterward. However, the personal testimony also can be a broad, spiritual autobiography—one that highlights setbacks, sins, redemption, and transformation (thus the "saved" can deliver testimonies without needing to narrate a second born-again experience). Testimonies of the kind I will examine in this chapter assume a Christian audience, though testimonies may be designed as evangelistic tools. In all cases, testimonies tend to be delivered from the point of some moment of significant resolution; obviously, the "unsaved" would not deliver a testimony in an evangelical assembly, and testifiers must be sufficiently free of taint (i.e., not mired in the wrong kind of sin) that their self-knowledge—their authority—is trustworthy. Relevant to my discussion, Tanya Erzen argues that the Christian Right's "testimonial politics" deploys the personal testimony to show the superfluity of government welfare programs and to shunt attention from structural injustice. Change happens as individuals fall under "conviction" and repent. The triumphalistic arc of personal testimonies suggests that change (always) happens only when individuals as such fall under "conviction," repent, and are transformed. See Erzen, "Testimonial Politics: The Christian Right's Faith-Based Approach to Marriage and Imprisonment," *American Quarterly* 59, no. 3 (September 2007): 991–1015.

33. *Homecoming Kitchen Cookbook* (Brentwood, TN: Salem Publishing, 2008), 16.

34. In chapter 5, I will discuss an example of a fan who feels precisely this relationship with the man she calls "Pastor Bill." For another example of how individuals came to feel "pastored" by a public evangelical, see Grant Wacker's discussion of letters to Billy Graham, in *America's Pastor*, 266–82.

35. Herbert Anderson and Edward Foley, *Mighty Stories, Dangerous Rituals: Weaving Together the Human and the Divine* (San Fransisco, CA: Jossey-Bass, 1997), 31–32.

36. Gloria and William Gaither, "Let's Just Praise the Lord," Gaither Music Company, 1972. The song contains a provocative shift in point of view. In the first verse, the singer(s) are a "we" and they speak to a "you"—presumably, the audience. Often using the song to close programs, the Gaithers sum up in the verse what has transpired—ostensibly during the previous concert. At the end of the verse and into the chorus, the first-person plural seems to open up and include the audience, so that all of "us" are "just praising the Lord." The song thus lyrically executes the unification of performer and audience that happens so often in the Homecomings.

37. When Gloria and I discussed the Homecomings and community in 2008, she mentioned two motifs she and Bill notice in fan mail. First, people told the Gaithers that their local churches began to put on their "Gaither Homecomings," essentially replacing the "Homecoming Friends" with members of the congregation and formatting a Sunday evening according to the videos. The degree to which the Gaither Homecomings were utterly supplanted varied; some churches ran the videos on a screen as the congregation sang along, and others simply borrowed the videos' format. All cases involved actual local groups sitting together with one another and singing. A couple of fans told me that their churches conducted similar "*sans*-Gaither Gaither Homecomings." These sorts of moments seem rich with mythic possibility. It alleviated my concern that Homecomings tend to be vicariously communal experiences.

The second motif did less to ease my concerns. Gloria noted that she and Bill regularly receive letters from parents and grandparents of young and adult children with Down

Syndrome. These children adore the Homecomings; they know all of the singers' names, each singer's signature song, which songs appear on which video. Again, this matched with some of my experiences in the field. At two different live concerts, I watched Jessy Dixon leap from the stage and dance with a person with Down Syndrome (by my guess, both ages eighteen to twenty-five). After they stopped dancing, these individuals ran up and down the aisle, laughing and clapping. Their elation was contagious. Few Homecoming moments filled me with more joy. What this says about community, however, is unclear. Gloria believed it demonstrated that the Homecomings could be a kind of community for these women and men, who may not have had much community in the rest of their lives. I would not downplay or begrudge the intimacy that these individuals feel toward the Homecomings, but it does not suggest the sort of sustained reciprocal intimacy that I believe is necessary to have a community. Rather, it might suggest the failure of local Christian bodies to involve congregants with cognitive disability in the full life of the body.

38. Doug Harrison discusses the precarious issue of privacy and intimacy in the southern gospel community in his post, "Riding the Southern Gospel Tiger," Averyfineline, March 30, 2011, accessed May 11, 2012, http://averyfineline.com/2011/03/30/riding-the-southern-gospel -tiger/. See also Goff, *Close Harmony*, 254–55.

39. Putnam, *Bowling Alone: The Collapse and Revival of American Community* (New York: Simon and Schuster, 2000), 411. Italics in original.

40. Benedict Richard O'Gorman Anderson, *Imagined Communities: Reflections on the Origin and Spread of Nationalism* (New York: Verso, 1983), 31–32. Anderson's second point continues as follows: "The most messianic nationalists do not dream of a day when all the members of the human race will join their nation in the way that it was possible, in certain epochs, for, say, Christians to dream of a wholly Christian planet." I drop this sentence so as to avoid confusion about the particular messianism of the Homecoming audience, and of modern evangelicals in general. While a number of members of the latter group certainly like the idea of a "Christian planet," when all boundaries disappear, I do not sense that a large number view this as an imminent or achievable reality inside of history. I follow Charles Taylor in assuming that in this secular age—this "certain epoch"—such a dream is not prevalent. See Taylor, *A Secular Age* (Cambridge, MA: Harvard Belknap, 2007), 2.

41. Although he himself was a member of a Protestant denomination, David Hume voiced concern about Protestantism's tendency toward violent atomization due to antinomian "enthusiasm." See "Of Superstition and Enthusiasm," rpt. in *Collected Essays*, ed. Stephen Copley and Andrew Edgar (New York: Oxford University Press, 2008), 38–42. This is a recurring synopsis of Protestantism in general, especially among its Roman Catholic critics. See George Weigel, *The Truth of Catholicism: Inside the Essential Teachings and Controversies of the Church Today* (New York: Harper Perennial, 2001), 35–52.

42. Danielle Allen, *Talking to Strangers: Anxieties of Citizenship since* Brown v. Board of Education (Chicago: University of Chicago Press, 2004), 12–13. In his book *A Theology of Public Life* (New York: Cambridge University Press, 2007), Charles Mathewes makes some points similar to Allen's, though the Augustinian Mathewes speaks self-consciously to Christians. He encourages Christians to cultivate a sense of restlessness in the world that does not seek escape from conflict but enters into it, as a sort of liturgical practice. Both Allen and Mathewes are wary of "consensus models" of public engagement, though Allen is more specific with her alternative proposals.

43. Ibid., 54.

44. Ibid., 63.

45. Ibid., 17. Allen borrows deliberately from Benedict Anderson in this passage. Like any guiding metaphor, wholeness helps citizens explain their role in a democratic community that

is hard to actually see; it requires "expending a significant amount of conceptual and *imaginative* labor to *make* themselves part of an invisible whole" (italics mine). Allen suggests here that imagination of community *creates* citizenship.

46. Ibid., 91.

47. See Rorty, *Contingency, Irony, and Solidarity* (New York: Cambridge University Press, 1989), part 1.

48. William J. and Gloria Gaither, "He Touched Me," William J. Gaither, 1964. Gloria Gaither, "I Then Shall Live," Gaither Music Company, 1981.

CHAPTER FOUR

1. For an excellent anthology of mid-century writing on Freud and art, from Freud himself to the critics and theorists, see William Phillips, ed., *Art and Psychoanalysis* (New York: Criterion, 1957). The most important immediate predecessor to Trilling's essay—one to which he is certainly responding—is Edmund Wilson's "Philoctetes: The Wound and the Bow," the final essay of Wilson's collection, *The Wound and the Bow: Seven Studies in Literature* (New York: Oxford University Press, 1941). Trilling's concern over the conjunction of art and madness reappears in the final pages of *Sincerity and Authenticity* (written after Trilling has likely encountered Foucault's work on the social history of madness). Later, a number of artists and critics would testify to and expand upon Trilling's decoupling of art from mental illness—notably Trilling's ambivalent admirer Susan Sontag in *Illness as Metaphor* (New York: Farrar, Strauss, and Giroux, 1978), and William Styron in *Darkness Visible: A Memoir of Madness* (New York: Random House, 1990).

2. I quote from the most widely read version of Trilling's essay, as it appears, slightly revised from 1945, in *The Liberal Imagination* (New York: New York Review Books Classics, 1950), 164.

3. Trilling most explicitly lays out his theory of culture in "Reality in America": "A culture is not a flow, nor even a confluence; the form of its existence is struggle, or at least debate—it is nothing if not a dialectic" (ibid., 9).

4. See Amy Hungerford, *Postmodern Belief*, especially the introduction and chapter 5; Susan Friend Harding, *The Book of Jerry Falwell*, esp. chapter 1; and Tanya Luhrmann, *When God Talks Back: Understanding the American Evangelical Relationship with God* (New York: Knopf, 2012), esp. chapter 10.

It is worth bearing in mind the ways Søren Kierkegaard's "knight of faith" resembles and diverges from the myth of the sick artist. The isolated, unintelligible sojourner, Kierkegaard's knight of faith "knows it is terrible to be born in solitude outside the universal, to walk without meeting a single traveler. He knows very well where he is, and how he is related to men. Humanly speaking he is insane and cannot make himself understood to anyone." See *Fear and Trembling*, trans. Alastair Hannay (1843; repr., New York: Penguin, 1985), 103. The knight of faith is conscious of his distance from society yet cannot close the distance through intelligible disclosure. For this reason he appears out of his mind. Kierkegaard—the "sensitive person" who claims neither to understand the knight nor to possess his faith—is drawn to the knight despite the latter's inability to disclose (63). Possibly unlike the sick artist—and certainly unlike Kierkegaard's tragic hero—Kierkegaard's knight of faith does not purport to "express the universal"—to assess and then to articulate a vision of how things are or should be, from the vantage of his isolation. His goal is not to express, but to be.

5. Harding claims that it is "Bible-based language"—language that both uses Bible stories and takes the Bible as its object—that "persuades and produces effects" (xii). Believers' practices

(e.g., speech surrounding the text) generate shared meaning. The Bible creates solidarity only insofar as its "believing" readership has cultivated common habits of reading it and speaking about it. Hungerford makes a similar point in her discussion of a debate between two characters in Marilynne Robinson's novel *Gilead*: "the scene presents theological questions and theological discourse as something to produce thinking, not conclusion, but also, perhaps more importantly, as something that can become a productively shared discourse only between, as Ames says, 'people who have . . . sympathy for it'" (118). Even if full-bodied faith requires assent to propositional content, some sort of pre-assenting faith—some experience of sympathy or will-to-sympathy for the religious believer and her testimony—must unlock the door. One must be a kind of "sensitive person" to engage seriously in theological discourse.

6. Evangelical struggles over reason vs. nonrational or supra-rational experience have something to do with the multifarious deployment of the term "belief" in evangelical discourse. Often, the term means belief in the propositional content of a statement—as in "I believe Jesus Christ died on the cross and was resurrected from the dead." To believe in this sense does not necessarily entail scientific-empirical rationality (one can believe something that goes against the available "objective" evidence), but it implies an agent who willfully can limit some forms of reasoning and selectively can employ them to enhance the comprehensibility of nonrational or supra-rational claims. The ability to comprehend propositional content remains central. For example, many evangelicals posit an "age of accountability"—a point in life at which children possess the capacity to understand the gospel message, thus rendering their subsequent professions of faith legitimate and their rejections of it damning.

Also circulating in the discourse, though, is a Kierkegaardian sense of belief—one that posits belief as operating outside of, if not in opposition to, belief-as-comprehension. See part 2, chapter 2, "Appendix to A," in Kierkegaard's *The Sickness unto Death*, trans. and ed. Howard and Edna Hong (Princeton, NJ: Princeton University Press, 1980), 87–104. To believe in this way is to abandon the quest for comprehension and to give oneself over to the absence of completely satisfying evidence. Referring to Wilfred Cantwell Smith's exegesis of the 1611 King James Bible, Tanya Luhrmann notes that "belief" has for some time in Christian history carried the connotation of adoration and trust. Although late nineteenth-century developments in conservative evangelical Christian circles prioritized belief in doctrinal statements over belief in people ("I believe *that* X" over "I believe *him*"), Luhrmann argues that belief-as-trust has made a comeback in late twentieth-century- and early twenty-first-century evangelicalism. To contemporary evangelicals, God "is so real, so accessible, and so present, and so seamlessly blends the supernatural with the everyday, that the paradox places the need for the suspension of disbelief at the center of the Christian experience. The supernatural is presented as the natural, and yet the believer knows that it is not" (320).

7. Young and book retailers categorize *The Shack* as fiction, but critics understandably treat the text as a theological treatise. For a book-length example of evangelical criticism of prosperity gospel ministries, see David Jones and Russell Woodbridge, *Health, Wealth, and Happiness: Has the Prosperity Gospel Overshadowed the Gospel of Christ?* (Grand Rapids, MI: Kregel, 2011).

8. A text that manifests and responds to evangelical adoption of secular music is Steve Stockman's *The Rock Cries Out: Discovering Eternal Truth in Unlikely Places*—published in 2004 by the book division of Relevant Media, an evangelical media group that, as its name suggests, seeks to cultivate conversation with secular culture. Stockman—also the author of a 2001 book on the spirituality of U2—devotes each chapter of *The Rock Cries Out* to a different secular musician and the redemptive possibility in his/her music. Among the artists he discusses are Kurt Cobain, Radiohead, Joni Mitchell, Bruce Springsteen, and Tom Waits.

9. Qtd. in Gloria Gaither, *Something Beautiful*, xiii.

10. The Association of Theological Schools (ATS) found that, in 2011, the number of male instructors at ATS-accredited institutions was 2,706, while the number of women was 849. Men outnumbered women at the level of full professor 1,298 to 296. See "2011–2012 Annual Data Tables," The Association of Theological Schools, accessed January 10, 2013, http://www .ats.edu/Resources/PublicationsPresentations/Documents/AnnualDataTables/2011 –12AnnualDataTables.pdf. These findings did not specify subfields (e.g., systematic theology, New Testament studies), nor did it include theological schools not accredited by the ATS. If the publications in biblical and theological studies by academic presses carried by evangelical-leaning booksellers are any indication, men would outnumber women in even greater proportion in these fields. Clicking on christianbook.com's link to "academic" titles, I had to scroll through 67 publications before I came to a woman author (and she was a coauthor). See "Category: Academic," Christianbook.com, accessed February 10, 2013, http://www.christianbook .com/Christian/Books/easy_find?event=HPT&category=Academic&N=1107463&Ne =1000000&Nso=1&Nu=product.endeca_rollup&Ns=product.number_sold&view =default&Nao=50.

11. For a discussion of the appeal of "strong" heroines in evangelical romance fiction, see Lynn Neal, *Romancing God: Evangelical Women and Inspirational Fiction* (Chapel Hill: University of North Carolina Press, 2006), ch. 5.

12. A few Gaither songs contain spoken-word sections—interludes recited over music, usually to say something lengthier about the song's theme (e.g., "There's Just Something about That Name" and "The Church Triumphant"). Gloria employs the device mostly in the songs she wrote during the 1970s—a time when a number of country and gospel musicians were using spoken word to revivify the ballad genre. These interludes allow Gloria to pack a more pointed theological lesson into a small time frame.

13. Over the twenty-first century, Gloria's appearances on the live stages grew increasingly limited—partially due to health issues, partially due to other speaking engagements. She is often present in concerts that become videos.

14. During much of the time I attended Homecoming concerts, Gloria was literally the wounded artist. She had suffered severe knee pain for several years. She underwent double knee replacement surgery in 2011.

15. Starting around 2007, Gloria gradually began to pass scriptwriting duties to Emily Sutherland—a gregarious young woman whom the Gaithers first hired as an executive assistant and then as a content manager for their website, gaither.com. Judging by my encounters with Sutherland and the Gaithers at Gloria's 2011 songwriting workshop, Gloria places an immense trust in Sutherland's vision and writing abilities.

16. By their own public count, Bill and Gloria have written or cowritten around seven hundred songs (as of 2012). "Gloria Gaither," gaither.com, accessed January 10, 2013, http://gaither .com/artists/gloria-gaither. The numbers pale in comparison to Fanny Crosby's legendary eight thousand hymn lyrics. However, when one figures in those Crosby and Gaither songs that fizzled in obscurity, and the number of Gaither songs anthologized in hymn collections and recorded by contemporary artists, the comparison is apt.

17. A reverse reading is also possible: fans committed to women's visible spiritual leadership could be frustrated at Gloria's excessive self-effacing. But I have yet to meet someone who interprets Gloria this way. Even a self-effacing Gloria is a highly visible Gloria. For a sustained discussion of the potential power of "submission" rhetoric among evangelical women, see R. Marie Griffith, *God's Daughters: Evangelical Women and the Power of Submission* (Berkeley: University of California Press, 1997).

18. I do not mean to suggest that Gloria's life story and songwriting will not figure in to this chapter. I have already shown how evangelical culture requires its celebrities to integrate all of

their public and private endeavors to establish their trustworthiness. However, rather than rendering *primarily* a biography or song catalogue/analysis, I will attend to the details of Gloria's life and songwriting insofar as they inform (1) the Gloria Gaither who is constructed in and for the Homecomings, (2) the Gloria who constructs the Homecomings, and (3) the Homecoming matter that Gloria constructs.

19. Bill and Gloria both possess this risk-taking impulse to some degree, but Gloria tends to realize the impulse more forthrightly. Bill has admitted to me that Gloria is the bigger risk-taker of the two. His narrative of the division of disposition and labor—the practical, penny-pinching businessman, the risk-taking, idealistic, imaginative woman—conforms to a dubious gender dichotomy (even though Bill admits he is glad that Gloria counterbalances his more miserly tendencies). Based on my observations of how they work, though, the narrative matches the reality (recall the story of Guy Penrod's hiring). Bill was skeptical about Gloria's songwriting workshop venture; Gloria dared to try it because she thought it needed to be done. If it were up to Bill, Gaither Family Resources probably would not carry copies of the Qur'an, Steinbeck novels, and an assortment of Penguin Classics; Gloria thinks the store's visitors at least need to see these items in the space, even if they do not purchase them.

20. The notion that "conversion" pertains to a person's becoming particularly, especially devoted in belief and practice inside a large body (say, "Christians") rather than pertaining to a person *joining* such a body (e.g., "I became a Christian") antedates evangelical language—and, to some extent, modern definitions of "religion." For an example of converts inside Christianity in the Middle Ages, see John Van Engen, *Sisters and Brothers of the Common Life: The* Devotio Moderna *and the World of the Later Middle Ages* (Philadelphia: University of Pennsylvania Press, 2008), 14–19. While a simple, unilinear connection has been complicated, older scholarship on the pre-Luther pietists connects them to later Protestant Piety movements. See Anne Hudson, *The Premature Reformation: Wycliffite Texts and Lollard History* (New York: Oxford University Press, 1988).

21. I have not been able to detect a consistent difference between the "universal" and the "absolute" in Gloria's writing and speech, and I will follow her and use the words interchangeably. Following C. S. Lewis's version of natural law reasoning (as is the case with many evangelicals, Lewis is a go-to apologist for Gloria), she uses both terms to characterize (a) material conditions that have always been the case ("all humans die" is a universal or absolute truth), (b) states of mind or consciousness that either some humans in all societies or every human in some societies have experienced (Gloria seems to regard "existential doubt" as universal or absolute; in Christian circles, the form of this doubt, which she suggests all Christians experience, entails doubts about God's nature and/or existence), and (c) principles that should govern morality and ethics, in all cases (it is absolutely and universally true that arbitrary killing of others is wrong). Conflating descriptions and prescriptions allows some Christians to cast the particularities of their moral codes as both universal and universal*izing*. So the argument goes, if Christianity's diagnosis of the human condition is correct, its prognoses and prescriptions for all humans are probably correct, too. This conflation is what Gloria worries about when she speaks of the "personal stamp," yet it is a difficult conflation to escape for a people who believe they can and must proclaim the one true gospel.

22. The paradox is akin to one examined by political philosopher Seyla Benhabib in the 2004 Tanner Lectures at the University of California-Berkeley: the paradox of democratic state sovereignty in an age of proliferating cosmopolitan norms. If every human being has rights that no discrete states can or should deny, but discrete states presumably are (and should be) in charge of legally establishing and protecting those rights, whence does the authority of the states and the norms originate? Whose legitimacy is founded on whose? If a state derives its legitimacy from its conformity to some set of universal rights, the state loses its particularity

and some of its self-determining power—a contradiction, as self-determination of local populations is an implicit and explicit value in most statements of universal rights. If the universal
rights derive their legitimacy from the support of discrete states, any tangible execution and
enforcement of the rights would be subject to the governing powers in those states. The norms'
"universality" would seem quite locally contingent, not universal.

The situation is further complicated by rapid, expansive global migration. Any given
democracy might have citizens, refugees, and documented and undocumented workers living
in its jurisdiction. If these possess a set of rights that are "universal," presumably the state is
obliged to honor those rights. But some of these populations possess little or no decision-
making power within the state framework (some cannot vote, some cannot be prominent in
the public discourse because their residence is "illegal"). There are limited to no means within
the official power structure by which members of these groups can hold the state accountable
for its rights violations. If the state has the unique power to confer or deny "universal legislation," and such populations cannot effectively assert their basic human rights within the state
framework, do these populations truly have "universal" rights?

Benhabib notes that this is an unresolvable paradox. Her hope is that the widely accepted
discourse of cosmopolitan norms will provide a way for marginal groups to exert power in
those localities where power is officially denied them. Appeals to the translocal can cause a
local, power-holding citizenry to reexamine and revise its "legal" treatment of marginal citizens
and noncitizens, and perhaps improve its very concept of citizenship. It is not just a matter of
clearing the outer courts; it is a matter of moving the walls and empowering new populations
to move them further. Concerned with the relationship of insiders and outsiders, Benhabib
discusses Kant's notion of hospitality at length in her first lecture.

To return to Gloria Gaither's hospitality: By Gloria's reckoning, every human being has an
invitation (a right) to "come to God's temple" if they will. However, there are people in the temple who want to limit the invitations—who place undue conditions on membership. Perhaps
Gloria or some other persons or group already inside the temple comes along and clears the
temple—establishes and protects the universal invitation. Well and good. However, the people
invited into the outer courts did not have an official say in their inclusion. It required someone
already inside, who possessed ears to hear the appeals from beyond the discrete entity—a kind
of insider/outsider, a local cosmopolitan—to extend and sustain the invitation (Christianity
traffics heavily in such insider/outsiders: a Galilean Jew, a Roman citizen/Jewish convert to the
Jesus religion, a Michigan-born evangelical who married a southern gospel fanatic).

If Gloria extends the invitation while she herself stands in the outer court, she is at least
extending an invitation into a process to which she is subordinate. If "whosoever will come"
accepts the invitation, they arrive no longer as subordinates but as fellow citizens ("not
disciples but friends"). They will have a future say in the height and thickness of the outer
walls. However, if Gloria is extending the invitation from the inner court, she is extending to
outsiders an invitation into a kind of second-class citizenship; members of the outer court
have rights and powers, but not the same rights as Gloria or whoever stands in (and polices)
the recognized inner court of evangelical life. In the former case, Gloria's self-subordination to
the contingency of the universal invitation means possibly relinquishing her particular, local
control; she (and the constituency she represents) will no longer be the sovereign (or the only
sovereign) who determines the character of the temple—which may look very different after
the invitees begin exercising their new power. In the latter case, Gloria (and the constituency
she represents) retains a more exclusive power. Her local authority is intact, but the "universal"
invitation seems little more than an exercise of her particular, local power. The universal is
subordinate to her; it will always be the case because the invited outsiders are not invited into
the seat of power.

Benhabib's Tanner Lectures are published, complete with responses from Jeremy Waldron, Bonnie Hong, and Will Kymlicka, as *Another Cosmopolitanism*, ed. Robert Post (New York: Oxford University Press, 2006).

23. Gloria faces the same dilemma of catholicity and parochialism that faces other evangelicals with universal (if not universalistic) leanings. One's particular commission requires one to proclaim the particular Jesus who is the (only) way, truth, and life, through whom (and only through whom) all humans may come to the Father. One's finitude—the fact that one sees through the glass dimly—requires one to qualify one's knowledge of this Jesus, the nature and character of his leading, and the Father to whom he leads. This is a simultaneously known and unknown God.

Diana Eck touches on this dilemma in her discussion of religious "inclusivists"—who, unlike exclusivists, believe God is "listening" to people of all faiths, but who, unlike pluralists, still believe it is "God-as-conceived-*by-us*" who is doing the listening. Eck lays out the dilemma well, but she assumes a too-stark divide between inclusivism and pluralism. See Eck, *Encountering God: A Spiritual Journey from Bozeman to Banaras* (Boston, MA: Beacon, 1993), 167–99.

24. Gloria Gaither, "John Steinbeck: From the Tidal Pool to the Stars: Connectedness, Is-Thinking, and Breaking Through—A Reconsideration," *Steinbeck Quarterly* 25 (Winter/Spring 1992): 45–46. I add the italics to *what is* for syntactical clarification. Gloria read this essay at an international conference on Steinbeck in France in 2006; it reappears (in English) in the proceedings of the conference. See Claude le Fustec, ed., *Lectures de Steinbeck: les raisins de la colère* (Rennes: Presses Universitaires de Rennes, 2007), 115–24. The cover art of this publication: Antoine Jean-Baptiste Thomas's 1822 painting, *Le Christ chassant Les marchands du Temple*—"Christ chasing the merchants from the Temple."

The presumption that evangelicalism is a deductive theological system appears time and again throughout American evangelical history. See George Marsden's discussion of "the Baconian Ideal" that funded early fundamentalist exegesis, in *Fundamentalism and American Culture: The Shaping of Twentieth-Century Evangelicalism, 1870–1925* (New York: Oxford University Press, 1980), 55–62.

25. John Steinbeck and Edward Ricketts, *The Log from the Sea of Cortez* (New York: Viking, 1951), 257.

26. Emerson, "The Poet," 450. Citation from the Library of America edition of Emerson's *Essays and Lectures* (New York: Penguin, 1983).

27. Lest Gloria's presupposing of overarching principles that unify disparate realities seem a necessity of Homecoming scriptwriting, not necessarily a part of her general writing process, consider her description of songwriting in the introduction of *Something Beautiful*: "At first, even before we were married, I began 'fixing' the lyrics to Bill's songs, giving him a line here, a phrase there, an ending or an opener. But gradually we began to develop a system that almost always involved us both searching for the right way to express—Bill in music, I in words—a great idea that would not be silenced. It was the idea that drove us both—always the idea" (xxi–xxii) (in our interview, Gloria outlined a similar method). Granted, "idea" does not necessarily mean "universal truth" or "overarching, unifying principle." When Gloria expressed her "idea-driven" process to me, she illustrated her point by talking about the inception of "Peace Be Still," a song she wrote after a visit to the Sea of Galilee. She and Bill decided there had not been many good songs written about that particular place or about the gospel story of Jesus quieting a storm on the sea. But just as importantly, they did not feel that a good song had been written about the *feeling* that the Sea of Galilee symbolized for or created in people who took the gospel story to heart. The lyrics to "Peace Be Still" do not catalogue the features of the Sea of Galilee; they describe the feeling of standing before a storm (physical and psycho-spiritual), of wondering if one's redeemer lives, and of experiencing eventual reassurance through that redeemer's

calming, commanding presence. The "idea" of the song, in this case, derives from a particular experience of a particular material place, but it clearly uses the particularity as a means to express a broader truth—less Galilee-specific—about tribulation, doubt, and deliverance.

28. Rothko and Adolph Gottlieb, reprinted in Rothko, *Writings on Art*, ed. Miguel López-Remiro (New Haven, CT: Yale University Press, 2006), 36.

29. Madeleine L'Engle, *Walking on Water: Reflections on Faith and Art* (New York: North Point Press, 1980), 28.

30. A few pages after this passage, L'Engle acknowledges that she begins with particular Christian presuppositions when she encounters and interprets other texts: "Of course, because I'm a struggling Christian, it's inevitable that I superimpose my awareness of all that happened in the life of Jesus upon what I'm reading, upon Buber, upon Plato, upon the Book of Daniel. But I'm not sure that's a bad thing. To be truly Christian means to see Christ everywhere, to know him as all in all." She does not entertain the possibility that she is superimposing something on her particular Christianity; although she hedges with the term "*struggling* Christian," she assumes her particular vision of Christ is the particular vision of Christianity. However, she uses even this narrowly Christocentric broadening gesture to call into question pernicious types of Christian parochialism as the passage continues: "I don't mean to water down my Christianity into a vague kind of universalism, with Buddha and Mohammed all being more or less equal to Jesus—not at all! But neither do I want to tell God (or my friends) where he can and cannot be seen! We humans far often tend to codify God, to feel that we know where he is and where he is not, and this arrogance leads to such things as the Spanish Inquisition, the Salem witch burnings, and has the result of further fragmenting an already broken Christendom" (32). This sounds remarkably like Gloria's worries over "personal stamps."

31. "Probable Impossibles" is the name of the fifth chapter in L'Engle's *Walking on Water*. She borrows her terms explicitly from Aristotle, who writes in chapter 25 of *Poetics*, "with respect to the requirement of art, the probable impossible is always preferable to the improbable possible." Aristotle is writing specifically of art (L'Engle cuts off the prefatory, qualifying clause when she quotes Aristotle). He even seems wary of attempts to render the impossible in art. However, for L'Engle, neither the artist in her fictions nor the Christian in her convictions are contained by impossibility. Describing the virgin birth and incarnation in the same chapter, L'Engle writes, "the whole story of Jesus is confounding to the literal-minded. It might be a good idea if, like the White Queen [in Lewis Carroll's *Through the Looking Glass*], we practiced believing six impossible things every morning before breakfast, for we are called on to believe what to many people is impossible. Instead of rejoicing in this glorious 'impossible' which gives meaning and dignity to our lives, we try to domesticate God, to make his mighty actions comprehensible to our minds" (82). Turned one way, L'Engle's words are judgments against dogmatic naturalism or miracle-barren Christianity: following Kierkegaard, belief entails the rationally incomprehensible. Turned another, way—the way I believe Gloria turns it—L'Engle's "glorious impossible" is a condemnation of fundamentalists who try to codify and systematize faith. Belief is not about comprehension of a text.

L'Engle's appropriation of Aristotle has a powerful influence on the Gaithers. The sixth song on the GVB's album *Give It Away* is titled "Glorious Impossible." The phrase first appears in *Walking on Water*, but L'Engle used it as the title and motif of her children's book about Jesus's birth (New York: Simon and Schuster, 1990). Although the Gaithers did not write the song, they are immensely proud of having "discovered" the piece (it was written by Joe Beck, Carl Cartree, and Wendy Wills; the latter is the lyricist). The song is about the incarnation and Jesus's birth—two "glorious impossibles" whose unorthodox, unexpected nature is accentuated through the song's 3-to-4 beat hemiola.

32. In *Walking on Water*, L'Engle recounts a time early in her life when she handed in a story to her writing teacher. He returned it and told her, "it's well written, Madeleine, but I don't believe it." She continues the story: "'But it's true,' I defended hotly. 'I wrote it exactly the way it happened. It's true.' Calmly he replied, 'If I don't believe it, it isn't true'" (147). Gloria quoted L'Engle, calling her by name, in my 2008 interview with her: "Fact is what happened once. Story is what always happens."

33. For an excellent study of Paul's hermeneutic *from* a Wesleyan, see Richard Hays, *The Conversion of the Imagination: Paul as Interpreter of Israel's Scripture* (Grand Rapids, MI: Eerdmans, 2005). Some debate surrounds the relationship of the four points on Wesley's "quadrilateral." Historian Albert Outler has expressed regret for introducing the phrase "Wesleyan Quadrilateral" in the 1960s, because it suggests that Wesley regarded scripture, tradition, reason, and experience as coequal, when Wesley actually believed scripture was the "first authority." See Outler, "The Wesleyan Quadrilateral in Wesley," *Wesleyan Theological Journal* 20, no. 1 (Spring 1985): 16. Many contemporary Wesleyan theologians have revisited the quadrilateral, insisting that Wesley prioritized the rule of scripture while retaining the other three "rules" as subordinate but essential elements of theological discernment. See, for example, Randy Maddox, *Responsible Grace: John Wesley's Practical Theology* (Nashville, TN: Kingswood Books, 1994). However, either through applications of Wesley's actual theological methods (which, Outler acknowledges, display a sophisticated interrelating of the four items) or through deployments of Outler's concept, the notion that reason, experience, and tradition positively affect scripture reading has informed modern Wesleyan teaching and practice. For example, the Gaithers' own evangelical Church of God–Anderson, Indiana, says very little about biblical authority in its public statement of beliefs. Their closest approximation to a statement on scriptural authority is vague by evangelical standards—more descriptive than prescriptive: "One of our early church songs says: 'The Bible is our rule of faith and Christ alone is Lord.' That still summarizes the core belief of most Church of God people." See "Our Beliefs," Church of God of North America, accessed February 1, 2013, http://www.chog.org/node/6. In an essay published in an "antifundamentalist" Wesleyan theological anthology, Fuller Theological Seminary professor Joel Green argues that Wesleyan hermeneutics are especially resistant to fundamentalism. See Green, "A Wesleyan Understanding of Biblical Authority: The Formation of Holy Lives," in *Square Peg: Why Wesleyans Aren't Fundamentalists* (Kansas City, MO: Beacon Hill, 2012), 127–37. For an excellent collection that demonstrates the variety of hermeneutics alive in evangelical circles, see *Evangelicals and Scripture: Tradition, Authority, and Hermeneutics*, ed. Vincent Bacote et al. (Downers Grove, IL: InterVarsity Press Academic, 2004).

34. Gloria's connection to Emerson is more than incidental. In her 1992 essay in the *Steinbeck Quarterly*, not only does she note Steinbeck's attraction to Emerson's concept of the "Oversoul"; she also makes specific reference to the passage in Emerson's Harvard Divinity Address in which he admonishes his listeners to go beyond imitation (even imitation of the "good models") and to claim their true identity as "new-born bards of the Holy Ghost." Gloria says, "Emerson, too, insisted that there was a much bigger picture and in his speech to the Harvard Divinity School condemned the cataloguers of religion, and there is evidence that it was the writings of Emerson and Thoreau that had the most early influence on Steinbeck's theory of 'breaking through' and *is* thinking" (122–23).

Another concrete connection between Gloria and Romanticism runs through England—from L'Engle back to Samuel Taylor Coleridge. In *Walking on Water*, L'Engle claims that Aristotle's "probable impossibles" are "all tied in with Coleridge's 'willing suspension of disbelief.'" L'Engle believes that a good artist can make whatever "impossibles" appear in her art seem probable (79). The artist realizes a world that does not accord with statistical or even material probability. As in the case with Aristotle, L'Engle uses a concept culled from Coleridge's writing on art to express something about her Christian religion.

35. Emerson, "The Poet," 454. As in Trilling's case, it is hard to imagine Emerson, even at his most democratic, having in mind something like an evangelical gospel songwriter when he describes his "Poet." In Emerson's case, there are specific reasons it should be hard to imagine. In "The Poet," Emerson delineates between the poet and the mystic—at the same time expressing his preference for the first: "[the mystic] nails a symbol to one sense, which was a true sense for a moment, but soon becomes old and false. For all symbols are fluxional; all language is vehicular and transitive, and is good, as ferries and horses are, for conveyance, not as farms and houses are, for homestead. Mysticism consists in the mistake of an accidental and individual symbol for an universal one" (463–64). The poet's and mystic's imaginations are both tuned to the discovery and articulation of the unified whole permeating the particular facts and symbols they observe. However, recognizing the flux of her imagination, and the vast fluidity and volatility of nature, the poet, unlike the mystic, resists universalizing any one symbol, one fact.

Although he never gives specific advice as to how to identify "homesteads," and although in other passages Emerson exalts humans' (universal) sense that "a thread runs through all things," he would likely wince at Gloria's devotion to an evangelical Jesus. There is not enough flux in her universals; she settles all things too quickly. Indeed, Emerson later expresses precisely this frustration at his "representative" mystic, Immanuel Swedenborg (cf. *Representative Men*, 683). However, the very protest Emerson levels against mysticism sounds like Gloria's concern over "personal stamps." Gloria's concern over dogmatists and their theological attachments is also a protest against presumptuously universalizing the particular/incidental matters of the faith.

Gloria's "particular-universal" tension might be rooted in American aesthetics as much as it is in evangelicalism narrowly defined. One can detect the tension between particularity and universality, and unity and diversity, in a number of post-Emerson poets' work—especially A. R. Ammons. Ammons explicitly talks about this tension in a 1973 interview with Mike Erwin and Jed Rasula (published first in a special "Ammons" issue of the *Chicago Review* 57, no. 1/2 [Summer/Autumn 2012]: 142–53). Questions of the relationship between universality and particularity fuels a number of his poems of the 1960s and 1970s (see, for example "One:Many" and "Corsons Inlet").

36. When I use "literalist" here, I primarily refer to those Christians who, starting in the nineteenth century, understood "literal" biblical meaning to pertain to correspondence between word and object, and who imagined a "literal reading" being one that attended only to the strict grammatical construction of the words. These are not the only ways Christians have used the term. Ian Christopher Levy discusses a prominent late-medieval assumption that *literal* meaning was equal to the author's intent—thus scripture, presumably authored by God, could potentially have many literal senses that may or may not be connected obviously to word-object correspondence or grammatical construction. Writing about the period just before Levy's, Alex Novikoff notes that Christians often accused Jews of being too literal in their reading of prophecy—in these cases, "literal" meaning something like overattending to strict word-object correspondence and strict grammatical construction. Thus there may be kinds of literalism in Christianity that match Gloria's hermeneutic, but they are not the "literalism" of most contemporary evangelicalism. See Levy, *Holy Scripture and the Quest for Authority at the End of the Middle Ages* (Notre Dame, IN: University of Notre Dame Press, 2012), 11–23, 209–17; Novikoff, *The Medieval Culture of Disputation: Pedagogy, Practice, and Performance* (Philadelphia: University of Pennsylvania Press, 2013), 187–90.

37. Having described the fiasco that was the Bill Gaither Trio's first NQC performance (which "devastated" Gloria), Bill writes in *It's More Than the Music*: "It was the continuation

of a complicated relationship between Gloria and southern gospel music. The gospel singers respected Gloria for her success as a songwriter (although many of them secretly thought that I was the real lyricist, and I was merely placating my wife by putting her name on the songs), but for many years they regarded Gloria as that 'smart Yankee woman,' and she regarded them as rude, insolent, arrogant, and ignorant" (137). Even if the Gloria–southern gospel relationship changed over time (presumably it did), if Bill is telling the truth on this point, a profound chasm separated Gloria from her spouse's first musical love.

38. There actually may be better historical reasons to separate country and western than there are to separate country from southern gospel. On the animosity between western "cowboy" music and southern "hillbilly" music, see Peterson, *Creating Country Music*, 83–94. It is also worth noting that Broadway singer Larry Wayne Morbitt is an Oral Roberts University graduate who worked for over a decade in church ministry before he came to *Phantom of the Opera* on Broadway in the late 1990s. See "Introduction," Larry Wayne Morbitt," accessed January 31, 2013, http://www.larrywayne.com/ccm_intro.asp.

39. Harrison, *Then Sings My Soul*, 144–48.

40. This "real America" southern rurality is not new. Gloria is speaking against the backdrop of early-to-middle twentieth-century southern writers who promoted their particular region (or, particular aspects of their particular region) as embodying national if not universal values. The promotion was complicated, because they sometimes connected it to a defense of the idea of localism: the South was their particular locale, but it was universally true that particular locales trumped universal abstractions—for artists and for all. In 1962, upon being given an award by the Georgia Writers' Association, Flannery O'Connor said, "I believe that for purely human reasons, and for some important literary ones, too, awards are valuable in direct ratio to how near they come from home." She went on to argue against what she viewed as the romantic "myth of the lonely writer" (who, judging by her description, is related to Trilling's "sick artist"): fiction writers, she said, aimed at communication, and communication always meant talking inside a particular community. While she conceded that attention to local particularity was not exclusively southern ("The best American fiction has always been regional"), she implies that there is some particular quality of southernness—of the South and its writers— that binds each to the other: southern writers "are not alienated, they are not lonely suffering artists gasping for purer air. The Southern writer apparently feels the need of expatriation less than other writers in this country." O'Connor's "Southern writers" do not seem to include writers who watched their relatives get lynched. See "The Regional Writer," in the Library of America collection, *Collected Works* (New York: Penguin, 1988), 843–52.

Before O'Connor, the Nashville Agrarians lodged a critique of modern industrial capitalism that depended on a conception of the North (and the encroaching "New South") as a nonplace; the progressivism, modern humanism, and addiction to profit that prevailed outside old Dixie did not allow for particularity but delighted in leveling and departicularizing labor forces and consumer markets. Like O'Connor, the Agrarians purported to be recommending a system that transgressed southern borders. In the introduction to the Agrarian manifesto, *I'll Take My Stand: The South and the Agrarian Tradition* (1930; repr., Baton Rouge: Louisiana State University Press, 1977), John Crowe Ransom wrote, "The members of the present group would be happy to be counted as members of a national movement" (xxxix). However, a few paragraphs before this sentence, Ransom describes the situation as a conflict between "a Southern way of life against what may be called the American or prevailing way" (xxxvii). The idealized Old South was not "real America" on the ground, but it ought to have been.

Wendell Berry, the Agrarians' most prolific and capable heir, softens Agrarian racism and is much less wistful about the Old South. Unlike most of the Nashville Agrarians, Berry is actually a farmer—working a very particular tract of land—and for that reason is more cautious about recommending his particular way of addressing his particular contingencies to people in other localities. He is more pronounced in his criticism of modern industrial capitalism's erasure of *all* locales' uniqueness; myths about a monolithic South were dangerous dis-placing devices, too. See "A Regional Motive," in *A Continuous Harmony: Essays Cultural and Agricultural* (Berkeley, CA: Counterpoint, 1970), 61–67. But even Berry wars with antiurbanity. In his 2003 essay "Two Minds," he speaks fondly about his former home in the Lower West Side of Manhattan as once a thriving community, but regrets that the World Trade Center complex "utterly dis-placed" the place. While Berry's critique of globalized corporate capitalism is trenchant, he constantly teeters on nostalgia for the old urban home place. He does not acknowledge the possibility and reality of community in the Lower West Side, even in the shadows and ruins of global capitalism. See "Two Minds," in *Citizenship Papers* (Washington, DC: Shoemaker and Hoard, 2003), 85–105. Both Gloria and her daughter Amy have expressed to me their love of Berry's poetry. As of this writing, Gloria is still hoping to interview Berry for a feature in *Homecoming Magazine*.

41. A number of scholars have explored North/South literal and cultural migrations from the early twentieth century to the civil rights movement. Most recently, see Wallace Best, *Passionately Human, No Less Divine: Religion and Culture in Black Chicago, 1915–1952* (Princeton, NJ: Princeton University Press, 2007); Chad Berry, *Southern Migrants, Northern Exiles* (Champagne-Urbana: University of Illinois Press, 2000); and James Gregory, *The Southern Diaspora: How the Great Migrations of Black and White Southerners Transformed America* (Chapel Hill: University of North Carolina Press, 2007).

42. John Egerton, *The Americanization of Dixie: The Southernization of America* (New York: Harper's Magazine Press, 1974). For studies of this cross-pollination as it occurs in specific venues, see Joshua Newman and Michael Giardina, "NASCAR and the 'Southernization' of America: Spectatorship, Subjectivity, and the Confederation of Identity," *Cultural Studies ⬄ Critical Methodologies* 8 (November 2008): 479–506; Mark Shibley, "Southernization of American Religion: Testing a Hypothesis," *Sociological Analysis* 52, no. 2 (1991): 159–74.

43. Lyle Lovett, Willis Alan Ramsey, and Alison Rogers, "That's Right (You're Not from Texas)," Polygram/Lylesongs Publishing, Wishbone Music, Red Baton Music, 1996.

44. One of the best proofs for the widespread, if not universal, quality of Gloria's southern-rural equation is the frequent combination of antisouthern with antirural rhetoric. Southerners get generalized as small-town, country people. Southernness and rurality together signify a foolish antimodernity, a failure to adopt and adapt to changing times. Rural southern people (in this construct, one is necessarily both at once) are irredeemably close-minded, thus potentially dangerous to the forward march of civilization. Fortunately, they are doomed to be trampled by the march or utterly reconstructed under it. This South appears in radical caricature in twenty-first-century reality television shows. Even so charitable and hopeful an essay as George Packer's 2013 retrospective on the South and the 2012 presidential election has a condescendingly didactic tone. Isolation from the "modern" nation was the region's problem: "Every demographic and political trend that helped to reelect Barack Obama runs counter to the region's self-definition: the emergence of a younger, more diverse, more secular electorate, with a libertarian bias on social issues and immigration; the decline of the exurban life style, following the housing bust; the class politics, anathema to pro-business Southerners, that rose with the recession; the end of America's protracted wars, with cuts in military spending bound to come. The Solid South speaks less and less for America and more and more for itself alone." Normative worries over this (real or imagined) South's proclivities aside, Packer leaves unidentified that "who" whom he thinks can (and should?) speak for America. See Packer, "Southern Discomfort," January 21, 2013, accessed February 10, 2013, http://www.newyorker.com/talk /comment/2013/01/21/130121taco_talk_packer#ixzz2KE8akIhG. Again, Wendell Berry writes on this issue. See "The Prejudice against Country People," in *Citizenship Papers*, 107–12.

45. As of December 6, 2009, *The Shack* held the number-three spot on the *New York Times* list of best-selling Paperback Trade Fiction. A June 24, 2008, *New York Times* article reported that the book had sold 350,000 copies according to Nielsen Bookscan—which typically accounts for about 70 percent of a book's actual sales. The highest reports of 2009 indicated about 10 million copies sold (Nielsen does not account for sales at retailers such as Walmart or sales from private websites). The last point is important to remember, as Young sold (and continues to sell) the book through his own website—http://www.theshackbook.com. The article also includes a picture of Young about to take the microphone at a small gathering. Although the caption includes few details ("William Paul Young, author of 'The Shack,' being introduced to an audience in suburban Indianapolis on Saturday"), Homecoming fans would recognize his venue and introducer: Gloria Gaither, at Gaither Studios. Motoko Rich, "Christian Novel 'The Shack' Is Surprise Best-Seller," *New York Times*, June 24, 2008, accessed December 1, 2008, http://www.nytimes.com/2008/06/24/books/24shack.html.

46. Papa's quote—*The Shack*, 120. On patripassionism—ibid., 164. Jesus's quote—ibid., 182. Mohler's criticism of *The Shack* is contained mostly in a radio program he aired on April 11, 2008 ("A Look at 'The Shack,'" http://www.albertmohler.com, last modified April 11, 2008, accessed October 8, 2009, http://www.albertmohler.com/?cat=Radio&cdate=2008-4-11.) Evangelical apologist Norman Geisler provides on his website the most exhaustive theological panning of the book. See Geisler, "Stay Out of 'The Shack,'" http://www.normangeisler.net, accessed October 8, 2009, http://www.normangeisler.net/theshack.html. While it is difficult to tell how far the criticisms extend, they did result in Windblown Media offering a point-by-point defense of *The Shack* against charges of heresy. See Wayne Jacobsen, "Is *The Shack* Heresy?" Windblown Media, accessed December 1, 2009, http://www.windblownmedia.com/about-wbm/is-the-shack-heresy.html.

47. Harrison rightly notes "non-believers'" participation in and enjoyment of religious music, from sacred harp singing to its southern gospel offspring (*Then Sings My Soul*, 154–58). The "choir" to whom I say the Gaithers are preaching contains such people. But even fans who do not share the evangelical faith of the majority in the Homecoming world have been initiated into the discourse. In this sense, I can say with confidence that very few Homecoming fans would find an evangelical soteriology, expressed through an altar call, unintelligible. For a discussion of the tension between singers' personal (dis)belief and the content of the "traditional" southern Christian music they sing, see Kiri Miller, *Traveling Home: Sacred Harp Singing and American Pluralism* (Champaign: University of Illinois Press, 2010), 188–200.

48. This joke appears in several videos. See, for example, *Australian Homecoming* (Alexandria, IN: Spring House, 2008).

49. Young claims that God "travel[s] all roads to find" an individual (Young, 182). Young hangs on to the agency of the individual in the experience (Young's "Papa": "reconciliation is a two-way street, and I have done my part" (192)). Young would not call this soteriology universalistic (Young: "most roads don't lead anywhere").

50. *A Billy Graham Music Homecoming, Vol. 2* (Alexandria, IN: Spring House, 2001).

51. Gloria 3:16 bears some similarities to John 3:16 as it appears in Eugene Peterson's paraphrased edition of the Bible, *The Message*: "This is how much God loved the world: He gave his Son, his one and only Son. And this is why: so that no one need be destroyed; by believing in him, anyone can have a whole and lasting life."

52. Earlier in the video, Bill and Graham's longtime songster George Beverly Shea converse about their common Wesleyan roots. There are numerous instances in the Homecoming catalogue in which the Gaithers deliberately call attention to their Wesleyan background. Gloria has communicated to me that she believes Wesleyans' emphasis on experience situates them especially well to respond to the needs of post-Enlightenment, postmodern citizens.

53. In the "Our Beliefs" section of their website, the Church of God–Anderson, Indiana's qualitatively and quantitatively places far more emphasis on sanctification than on biblicism. See "The Spirit-Filled Life" section of "Our Beliefs," www.chog.org.

54. *A Billy Graham Music Homecoming, Vol. 2.*

55. On Graham's style of "conversion," see Wacker, *America's Pastor*, 255–66.

56. I do not want to suggest that John, or elderly people generally, do not have the capacity to distinguish between cognate phenomena. Rather, I am claiming that some distinctions do not matter in retrospect—especially if other continuities override them. John does not have the same interest in isolating the Homecomings as I do.

57. Ruben Studdard, *I Need an Angel* (New York: J Records, 2004). The Gaithers discontinued the Praise Gatherings around 2005. Harrison notes that these events, like the Goodman tribute concert, demonstrate that Bill had cultivated and exercised his impresario skills well before the Homecomings began (*Then Sings My Soul*, 117).

58. In 2015, I expressed to Bill my surprise that the northern Homecoming audiences I had experienced seemed much more effusive than their southern counterparts. Bill agreed with my theory that this had something to do with the fact that southerners were awash in evangelical culture in a way that northerners were not (the Homecomings were not utterly novel in Greenville, South Carolina, where we had this conversation). The residue of southern propriety combined with old intraevangelical rifts also may have been an explanation; Bill noted to me how, years before the Homecomings, members of Greenville's Bob Jones University community had been discouraged from attending Gaither shows, due to their dubious Holiness enthusiasm. Bill added, though, that he experienced some of the greatest Homecoming audience exuberance in concerts in the greater Boston region—in his opinion, due to the strong charismatic Catholic population there.

59. Rebecca's hesitations, self-interruptions, and frequent "you knows" contrasted with the presentation on psalm-singing I had just heard her deliver—*sans* notes, never stumbling over a word. Difference of venue accounted partially for the change: talking about a subject she knew well versus fielding questions from an ethnographer.

Nevertheless, Rebecca's halted speech seemed to arise from her search for appropriate words—particularly when she attempted to articulate her problems with the Homecomings. By the time I talked to Rebecca, I had grown accustomed to the laborious work of extracting criticisms from interviewees. They were *fans*, after all. Coupled with a deeply embedded "if you can't say anything nice . . ." ethic and with the suspicion that their interviewer must be a Homecoming devotee since he was bothering to write about the Gaithers, collecting criticism could be like pulling teeth.

60. I borrow the term "narrative gaps" from Stanley Fish. See *Is There a Text in This Class? The Authority of Interpretive Communities* (Cambridge, MA: Harvard University Press, 1980), esp. 268–92.

61. The Gaithers have told me stories of receiving fan mail from people who fit each of these descriptions.

CHAPTER FIVE

1. The Kennedy Center website explains its Honors Series: "Since its inception in 1978, the Kennedy Center Honors has redefined America's perception of its artistic legacy and reinvented the way this nation rewards its artists. The Honors have been compared to a knighthood in Britain, or the French Legion of Honor—the quintessential reward for a lifetime's endeavor." See "About the Honors," Kennedy Center for the Performing Arts, accessed February

22, 2013, http://www.kennedy-center.org/programs/specialevents/honors/about.cfm. While the Honors' recipients are an even more select group than the performers in the center's concert hall, the hall is typically reserved for performers whose impact and respect approaches Honors-level.

2. *Kennedy Center Homecoming*.

3. Ibid.

4. Where the NIV uses "goodness," the NRSV uses "generosity." The former translation is more popular among most evangelicals.

5. The *Kennedy Center Homecoming* version of "Old Friends" amends one line: "I'm a rich millionaire in old friends" becomes "we are all millionaires in old friends."

6. Although Patty appears sparsely in the Homecomings (she typically is brought in for major venues like the Kennedy Center and Carnegie Hall), the Gaithers released *The Best of Sandi Patty* video in 2011—a compilation that includes not only many of her Homecoming performances but also many of her performances on the Gaither stages during the 1980s.

7. On Crouch's significance in black and white Christian music, see Stowe, *No Sympathy for the Devil*, 87–97.

8. In 2010, the Alaskan cruise became a Hawaiian cruise, though the cruise returned to Alaska in 2011. *Alaskan Homecoming: Live from the Gaither Alaskan Cruise* (Alexandria, IN: Spring House, 2011) was the first video filmed on a Homecoming cruise.

9. See Benjy Gaither, *The Great Divide* (Alexandria, IN: Spring House, 2001), and *The Legend at Gaither's Pond* (Alexandria, IN: Spring House, 2003). The central conflict in both videos is the failure of the animals to rise above petty differences to defeat their "landed" foes (a gang of beavers). The beavers want to stop up motion (literally and figuratively) and to rule the pond by fear; it is an indictment of intra-Christian disputes, theological and musical dogmatism.

10. The September 17, 2001, issue of *Time* magazine featured Jakes on the cover. Superimposed over the picture was the question, "Is this man the next Billy Graham?" The feature article named Jakes "America's Best Preacher," which caused much discussion in evangelical Christian media.

11. "Bishop T. D. Jakes and Bill and Gloria Gaither Unite in Concert," PR Newswire, last modified March 6, 2003, accessed August 21, 2012, http://www.prnewswire.com/news-releases/bishop-td-jakes-and-bill—gloria-gaither-unite-in-concert-74591452.html. The concert took place on March 12, 2003.

12. It should be noted, in this case and in the case of the "white" Homecomings, that editing and shot selection did occur. Of particular note is the fact that the videos were not filmed single-shot. Cameras move around and capture individual faces, sometimes weeping, sometimes laughing. But the basic song order is preserved—a fact necessitated by the instrumentalists' presence in the room and the songs' bleeding into one another.

13. While the most prominent examples of interracial, intercultural encounters in the Potter's House videos are between black and white Christians, the concert seeks to build bridges between other demographics. The Samoan Katinas are back for this concert. Their performance appears on *Build a Bridge*, as does the fiery, Spanish-language performance of the Latino El Trio del Hoy (which features a playful invitation to Bill and Jakes to dance to the music, to which they respond briefly and positively). The bringing together of the young women of gospel group Mary Mary, the middle-aged Blind Boys of Alabama, and the older Barrett Sisters also suggests the intergendered, intergenerational aim of the bridge-building *within* black gospel.

14. *We Will Stand* (Alexandria, IN: Spring House, 2004). For discussions of Martin, Smith, Walker, Goodpasteur, and Cobb, see Best, *Passionately Divine, No Less Human*; Horace Clarence Boyer, *How Sweet the Sound: The Golden Age of Gospel* (Washington, DC:

Elliott and Clark, 1995); Robert Darden, *People Get Ready! A New History of Gospel Music* (New York: Bloomsbury Academic, 2005); Michael W. Harris, *The Rise of the Gospel Blues: The Music of Thomas Andrew Dorsey in the Urban Church* (New York: Oxford University Press, 1992); Anthony Heilbut, *The Gospel Sound: Good News and Bad Times*, 25th Anniversary ed. (New York: Hal Leonard/Limelight, 1997).

15. It is worth noting Bill's "roll calls" as they occur in live concerts. At every concert I attended, from Pennsylvania to Alabama, Bill always took several moments to call attention to the musicians, promoters, radio stations, and sometimes ministers in the particular region who contributed to southern gospel history.

16. *We Will Stand*. Bill is partially correct on "Sweeter's" origins. Smith's version of the song did, indeed, come out of the black church. However, the song is a reworked version of white hymnist James Rowe's 1914 song of the same name.

17. For these groups' first recordings of the Coates song, see the Statesmen Quartet, *Get Away, Jordan* (Memphis, TN: Skylite Records, 1959); Ernie Haase and Signature Sound, *Get Away, Jordan* (Alexandria, IN: Spring House, 2007).

18. The cover of *We Will Stand* features separate photos of Bill and Jakes (at the top), Russ Taff and Jessy Dixon singing with hands raised and joined (in the middle), and Vestal Goodman with Lynda Randle and Mom Winans on either side of her (at the bottom). The *Build a Bridge* cover features larger photos of Bill and Jakes, the Mighty Clouds of Joy in the background between them, and the GVB with Lillie Knauls and Gloria on either side of them at the bottom.

19. *We Will Stand*.

20. For an overview of evangelical conceptions of heaven written by a Classical Arminian theologian, see Roger Olson, *The Westminster Handbook to Evangelical Theology* (Louisville, KY: Westminster John Knox, 2004), 195–99.

21. The Gaithers released two "heaven-themed" videos in the twenty-first century: *Heaven* and *Going Home* (Alexandria, IN: Spring House, 2003), recorded during the same session. That *Going Home* is among the platinum-selling videos suggests the otherworldly bent of the Homecoming audience. However, it is important to note that the videos offer a variety of speculations about the afterlife—some of them on-screen musings by toddlers, some quotations from famous Christian writers past and present. Although they are circumscribed (forthright universalists need not apply—but neither need people who want to talk about hell), the array of attitudes regarding the afterlife that the videos broadcast qualifies the sweep of any specific heavenly gazes—the very gazes that might be attracted to heaven-themed videos. As I will show with the Homecomings filmed in Jerusalem, the Gaithers know how to use what they know to be attractive phenomena to subtly undermine the attraction of the phenomena.

22. I am not prepared to make a normative claim about what constitutes "the prosperity gospel ministry," nor will I argue here for or against the Gaithers' or Jakes's inclusion in such a group. Shayne Lee takes it for granted that Jakes belongs in such a group, citing Jakes's pride in his personal wealth and several of the fundraising letters that Jakes disseminates to his supporters. I find these items important but insufficient evidence in proving that Jakes regularly centralizes the financial returns of faith to the extent that, for example, Creflo Dollar and Fred Price do. A proudly wealthy minister may be problematic, but if "the prosperity gospel" means anything specific, more information about Jakes's messages is required before I would label such a minister a "prosperity gospel" pastor. If the verbiage in fundraising letters were the sole criterion, I suspect that many, many evangelical churches in America would be "prosperity gospel" churches. See Lee, *T. D. Jakes: America's New Preacher* (New York: New York University Press, 2005), 99–113.

Rather than labeling the Gaithers or Jakes "prosperity" ministers, I'm interested in how these figures differentiate their enterprises from some of the ministries that surround them. It is clear that neither Jakes nor Gaither *wants* to be seen as an "easy-answer" ministry, and this segment illustrates what sorts of values and practices they believe would exonerate them from such a charge.

23. Qtd. in Stout, *Blessed Are the Organized*, 71–72. Although Stout assumes rather than investigates his informant's close association of Jakes with health-and-wealth gospels, the challenges Stout makes to Jakes's "apolitical" theology later in his book, concerning human agency and community conflict (cf. 198–200), could be made of health-and-wealth gospels as well. If Jakes is sincere in his concern for others' pain—and if he does not pose "easy answers,"—it is possible that he is better equipped to hear and respond to challenges such as Stout's than are some of his prosperity-preaching peers.

24. Harrison chronicles a number of public instances of Lister's racism (see *Then Sings My Soul*, 100–101). As Harrison notes in a footnote, though, Lister's racism has some of the same complicating features of that of many Jim Crow–era southern white men. Lister toured with African American groups; Bill told me that Lister once stormed out of a southern Illinois diner in the 1950s when the manager refused service to the all-black Golden Gate Quartet with whom he was touring. However, two members of the younger generation of Homecoming musicians told me of their horror upon hearing Lister go on "nigger"-laced tirades—one in an Atlanta mall around the time of the Georgia Dome recordings. As Harrison points out, Lister likely saw no contradiction between his efforts at staged integration and his prejudices. Lister seemed to like his version of integration.

25. On victim-initiated, "restorative justice" approaches to domestic violence, see Marie Fortune, "Forgiveness: The Last Step," in *Violence against Women and Children: A Christian Theological Sourcebook*, ed. Carol Adams (New York; Continuum, 1995), 201–6. On memory and justice in racial reconciliation, see Ronald Walters, *The Price of Racial Reconciliation* (Ann Arbor: University of Michigan Press, 2008), 5–7, 40–55, 155–61. For a self-consciously Christian approach to reconciliation, see John Berkman's "Being Reconciled: Penitence, Punishment and Worship," and Emmanual Katongole's "Greeting: Beyond Racial Reconciliation," both published in *The Blackwell Companion to Christian Ethics*, ed. Stanley Hauerwas and Samuel Wells (Hoboken, NJ: Wiley-Blackwell, 2006). Telling a long history of Christian approaches to sin and crime, Berkman argues for a revamped model of retributive justice that has reconciliation as its end. Although the title of Katongole's essay suggests that he eschews racial reconciliation (or at least regards it as an incomplete process), Katongole critiques a particular, generalizing view of racial reconciliation—one that denies or ignores the particular histories of particular racial prejudices and seeks to reduce all sorts of difference and prejudice to the same type. The "same kind of different as me" approach that Katongole criticizes is akin to what I find troublesome about Jakes's collapsing of all sorts of pain.

26. *Rocky Mountain Homecoming* is one of the first videos released after Lister's death. As is customary when such deaths happen, the video includes a tribute to Lister—several clips from his early and later career, a few interview clips. The final song he sings in the tribute montage is the Gaithers' 1969 "Thanks to Calvary (I Don't Live Here Anymore)." The song recounts how a once-abusive man underwent a conversion and ceased his abusive ways. In the second verse, the man's son sees his father coming in the room and hides. His father tells him he no longer has to fear; thanks to the conversion, "we don't live here anymore." Like "The Baptism of Jesse Taylor," the song focuses on the change wrought in the converted man's life and downplays the lingering effects of the man's "preconversion" self on the abused. Given his

known twenty-first-century racism, it is not self-evident that Lister even reached the point of recognizing a need to convert his behavior or thoughts.

27. *We Will Stand.*

28. This "Jewish-sounding" minor—which can be produced on a keyboard by starting on the "E" and playing all of the "white key" notes to the next-highest "E"—is prevalent in evangelical music based on Old Testament scripture. See Craig Terndrup's "Blow the Trumpet," which serves as the theme song for *Israel Homecoming.*

29. Gloria Gaither, "With a Little Faith: Mitch Albom," *Homecoming Magazine*, November/ December 2009, 36–40.

30. See Yaakov Ariel, "'It's All in the Bible': Evangelical Christians, Biblical Literalism and Philosemitism in Our Times," in *Philosemitism in History*, ed. Jonathan Karp and Adam Sutcliffe (New York: Cambridge University Press, 2011).

31. *Israel Homecoming* (Alexandria, IN: Spring House, 2005). Greene quotes Abba Eban, prolific Zionist author, dignitary, and Israel's foreign minister during the Six-Day War. Although Eban wrote numerous popular books, published by major commercial presses, on the subject of Zion and the Jewish people, this particular quotation comes from a relatively obscure essay: "Israel: Portrait of a Society," which appeared in 1981 in *Optima* magazine, a publication funded by the multinational mining corporation, Anglo-American, plc. (the corporation is a major shareholder in the De Beers diamond company). The line that Greene quotes also appears in Eban's essay after Psalm 137 is invoked. Eban uses the passage to explain all Jews' (even non-Israeli Jews') profound connection to and solidarity with the land now known as the nation of Israel. After citing the "if I forget thee, Jerusalem" portion of the Psalm, along with some other "return to Zion" scripture passages, Eban argues that the effects of the repetition of such scriptures "day by day over the centuries was to infuse Jewish life with a peculiar nostalgia, strong enough to prevent any sense of finality or permanence in any other land. 'By the waters of Babylon we sat and wept when we remembered Zion.' There were many Babylons in Jewish history, but Zion always beckoned through the tears. To add to the memories, there was an unbroken physical link; small Jewish communities clung to Jerusalem, Safed, and Hebron. Most invaders thought them too insignificant to be interfered with, and only the crusaders challenged their foothold with any measure of determination. But the Jews alone, few and poor as they were, had an indigenous sense of attachment. Their conquerors always had a home somewhere else; for them, Judea was merely a province, while for Jews it had a central, metropolitan connotation. The result was that the association of this people with their original land endured long after they had left their sovereignty behind." Eban, "Israel: Portrait of a Society," *Optima*, September 30, 1981, 128–29.

32. "Rivers of Babylon," Brent Dowe, Frank Farian, James McNaughton, George Reyam, Gallico Music, Universal Polygram, 1969.

33. One of the GVB's staple songs was Robbie Trice's 1974 "Alpha and Omega."

34. *Israel Homecoming.*

35. Ibid.

36. It is important to consider the kind of love that Jesus expressed for Jerusalem and his home region. As Simone Weil notes, "there is not the least indication that Christ experienced anything resembling love for Jerusalem or Judaea, save only the love which goes wrapped in compassion." See *The Need for Roots*, trans. Arthur Wills (1949; repr., New York: Routledge, 2006), 168. If Gloria has in mind the same kind of lamenting love to which Weil points, Jesus is not simply the person who renders physical homeland as a secondary concern for his followers; he himself models appropriate nonattachment.

37. For an analysis both of the types of parallelism in Hebrew biblical poetry and of the history of the study of such parallelism, see James Kugel, *The Idea of Biblical Poetry: Parallelism and Its History* (New Haven, CT: Yale University Press, 1981).

38. It is an open question whether or not the varieties of Eastern Orthodox Christianity represented by these structures would count as *Christian* to the Homecomings' evangelical audience—or if the audience even would be aware of Orthodox practices. However, Gloria possesses at least one connection to Eastern Orthodoxy: Madeleine L'Engle's discussion on iconography, which I discussed in the previous chapter. Situated as the Israel concert is between the (Arab) Christian and Armenian quarters of the Old City, it seems likely that the Gaithers were in close contact with some kinds of Orthodox Christianities when they organized and performed the concert.

39. On evangelicals' reading current affairs in Israel and Palestine through the lens of end-times prophecies, see Paul Boyer, *When Time Shall Be No More: Prophecy Belief in Modern American Culture* (Cambridge, MA: Harvard Belknap, 1992), 187–224; Victoria Clark, *Allies for Armageddon: The Rise of Christian Zionism* (New Haven, CT: Yale University Press, 2007), esp. part 2; and Mark Amstutz, *Evangelicals and American Foreign Policy* (New York: Oxford University Press, 2014), esp. 134–37.

40. The great majority of fans I interviewed listed the Homecomings from Israel among their favorite videos—a fact that may have been due to their conspicuousness (it is easier to differentiate between *Israel Homecoming* and the 1990s Homecomings than it is to differentiate between, say, *Landmark* and *Old Friends*). With little variation, the reasons they gave were of a Christocentric Travel Channel variety: it was neat to see where Jesus had lived and preached. This was the extent of speculation about biblical history. As I will explain, while the Gaithers are not above playing on the myths and legends of Jerusalem, they keep their *narratives* of the places rooted closely to scholarly consensus and reasonable archaeological probability.

41. Gaither, *It's More Than the Music*, 108–9.

42. Numerous scholars have pointed out how Western tourists to Middle Eastern "sacred" lands have for centuries viewed those lands as exclusively historic; even the present populations of those lands are relics. Most of this literature is built upon post-Veblen studies of leisure, specifically as it borrows from and responds to Dean MacCannell's *The Tourist: A New Theory of the Leisure Class* (New York: Schocken, 1976). See John Davis, *The Landscape of Belief: Encountering the Holy Land in Nineteenth-Century American Art and Culture* (Princeton, NJ: Princeton University Press, 1996), 32–52. Anne McClintock, *Imperial Leather: Race, Gender, and Sexuality in the Colonial Contest* (New York: Routledge, 1995), 21–74. Lester Vogel, *To See a Holy Land: Americans and the Holy Land in the Nineteenth Century* (University Park: Pennsylvania State University Press, 1993). Melani McAlister and W. J. T Mitchell both articulate American evangelicals' simultaneous backward- and forward-looking appropriations of Holy Land residents. See McAlister, *Epic Encounters: Culture, Media, and U.S. Interests in the Middle East Since 1945* (Berkeley: University of California Press, 2001), 13–15; Mitchell, "Holy Landscape: Israel, Palestine, and the American Wilderness," *Critical Inquiry* 26 (Winter 2000): 197. For a quantitative study of Christian tourism to Israel in the twenty-first century, see Noga Collins-Kreiner et al., *Christian Tourism to the Holy Land: Pilgrimage during Security Crisis* (Burlington, VT: Ashgate, 2006). The issue of tourism and religious (mis)appropriations is not limited to Western-Middle Eastern relations. See Myra Shackley, "Managing the Cultural Impact of Religious Tourism in the Himalayas, Tibet, and Nepal," in *Tourism and Cultural Conflicts*, ed. Mike Robinson and Priscilla Boniface (New York: CABI, 1999), 95–111. "Primitive" people within US borders also are often the subject of (and complicit in) their own brand of

this historical-cultural entrapment. See Aaron Ketchell's *Holy Hills of the Ozarks: Religion and Tourism in Branson, Missouri* (Baltimore, MD: Johns Hopkins University Press, 2007), ch. 6.

43. The Gaithers do have one significant connection in Israel, and they pay an on-camera visit to her home on the Sea of Galilee: Polly Grimes. Grimes was inducted into the Southern Gospel Music Association's Hall of Fame in 2008. Widely regarded as the promoter responsible for introducing some of the foundational southern gospel groups to West Coast markets, Grimes is the chairperson of "Tours Through the Book"—a group that organizes and leads Christians in tours of the Holy Land (see http://toursthruthebook.org/). She also helps to run Exodus, Ltd., "a non-profit organization of Christians from various denominations working together for the cause of Zion." See "About," Exodus, Ltd., accessed February 21, 2013, http://www.exodusltd.org/index.html. The latter organization is unequivocally pro-Israel. In 2004, Grimes herself reports providing services through Exodus to the Israeli soldiers fighting in the Second Intifada.

The Gaithers only name Grimes as a "friend," and they know her through her work in southern gospel concert promotion. They make no mention or endorsement of her causes and organizations in the videos. Grimes would not be the person to facilitate understanding across the various populations in Israel and Palestine. For an evangelical organization with more sustained, non-tourist interests in the region, see "Evangelicals for Middle East Understanding," accessed February 21, 2013, http://www.emeu.net/index.html.

It is also worth noting that Bill makes one vague allusion in *Israel Homecoming* to the state of affairs in modern Israel-Palestine. When he sings the first verse of "Because He Lives," he pauses after speaking of the newborn child facing "uncertain days," and says, "I don't care what the headlines on CNN say tomorrow." After a smattering of applause, he repeats the verse's last line, and the song continues. Although everyone in the space likely reads this as a reference to the tumult in Israel, this interruption and repetition of the verse is common in twenty-first-century Homecoming renderings of the Gaithers' most famous song—as are vague references to an unsettled world. Indeed, when Bill tells and retells the story of the song, he often calls attention to the fact that the world has *always* been an unsettled and unsettling place. See Gloria's description of "Because He Lives" in *Something Beautiful*, 4–6.

44. Hagee, *Countdown to Jerusalem: A Warning for the World* (Mary Lake, FL: Frontline, 2006), 3. "About Christians United for Israel," cufi.org, accessed February 26, 2013, http://www.cufi.org/site/PageServer?pagename=about_AboutCUFI. The degree to which evangelicals were involved in US policy during the Second Intifada is difficult to determine. Writing near the end of the conflict, Robert Smith claimed that American evangelicals' erstwhile near-unanimous support for Israel was already waning when the conflict began, and that Israeli prime minister Ariel Sharon's level of aggression toward Palestinians further soured many. See Smith, "Between Restoration and Liberation: Theopolitical Contributions and Responses to U.S. Foreign Policy in Israel/Palestine," *Journal of Church and State* 46, no. 4 (Autumn 2004): 833–60. In 2009, Stephen Spector devoted a full chapter of his book on evangelical Zionism to the conflict. Spector argued that it was a cadre of evangelicals—then-Kansas senator Sam Brownback and John Hagee among them—who pressured George W. Bush to commit more unequivocal support to Sharon. See Spector, *Evangelicals and Israel: The Story of American Christian Zionism* (New York: Oxford University Press, 2009), 212–33. Collins-Kreiner et al. report a substantial drop in North American tourists to Israel from 2000 to 2003 (32–37).

45. On the problems with the "open secrecy" of homosexuality in southern gospel spaces, see Harrison, *Then Sings My Soul*, 137–61.

46. Not all evangelical "end of days" scenarios end with evangelicals on one side, Jews on the other. Many "end-times" preachers—most notably John Hagee—believe that God's convenant

with the Jewish people still holds. While Hagee believes that the Second Coming will reveal to Jews the error of their rejection of Jesus as the Messiah, he believes they will be brought (back) into the fold. Hagee does not believe in proselytizing Jews. For more on the complex web of evangelical attitudes toward Jews, see Yaakov Ariel, *Evangelizing the Chosen People: Missions to the Jews in America, 1880–2000* (Chapel Hill: University of North Carolina Press, 2000).

In 2009, I was present at a Gaither Christmas concert that included country music singer-songwriter Larry Gatlin. Gatlin performed a song he had written a few years prior, titled "No Stars Tonight in Bethlehem." Although it called attention to contemporary Israel more than did the Homecomings filmed in Israel, the song was a nonpartisan lament over the bloodshed and violence in the region. Gatlin—the occasional conservative television pundit—conspicuously steered away from assigning blame. Given Gatlin's penchant for simplistic, patriotic grandstanding (see the Gatlin Brothers' 2011 song, "Americans, That's Who!"), the performance suggests a shift in what can and cannot be assumed about Israel on an American evangelical stage.

47. Hokanson Companies CFO Tony Townsley came up with the story of *Three Cups*. Mark St. Germain wrote the version that appeared in the book. It was illustrated by April Willy. *Three Cups* had a publishing story similar to that of *The Shack*: originally it was self-published and sold in the Indianapolis region, but word spread, and eventually Townsley started a website to sell the book. Unlike *The Shack*, *Three Cups* got picked up by a commercial press. Tommy Nelson, a division of Thomas Nelson, republished the book in 2011.

48. For one of Logan Smith's impersonations of Vestal Goodman, see "What a Lovely Name," YouTube, last modified December 8, 2009, accessed March 1, 2013, http://www.youtube.com/watch?v=liUWyOSngIQ. For a discussion of the creation and marketing of the "southern hon," see Mary Rizzo, "The Café Hon: Working-Class White Femininity and Commodified Nostalgia in Postindustrial Baltimore," in *Dixie Emporium: Tourism, Foodways, and Consumer Culture in the American South*, ed. Anthony Stanonis (Athens: University of Georgia Press, 2008), 264–85. See also Gray, "Looking for a City."

49. The sacralizing of such a trim female image occurs in Christian circles that purport to be profoundly removed from mainstream culture. At the time of the Homecomings, Pat Robertson's *700 Club* included segments devoted exclusively to weight loss and age-defying nutritional tips. Gwen Shamblin's popular Weigh-Down Workshops are the latest in what Marie Griffith identifies as a long line of weight programs marketed toward conservative Christians. See R. Marie Griffith, *Born Again Bodies: Flesh and Spirit in American Christianity* (Berkeley: University of California Press, 2004).

50. Although "The Happy Goodmans" had recorded nothing more than a 1990 tribute to Rusty Goodman since 1983, the Homecomings led Howard and Vestal to reunite with gospel singer/pianist Johnny Minick (with whom they had worked in the 1970s) to record five albums during the Homecoming era—four of which were released on the Gaithers' label.

51. Gaither, *It's More Than the Music*, 185.

52. Gaither, *Something Beautiful*, 306. Gloria guards the gender of her hypothetical interns until the final lines of the chapter; the late point of attack augments the lines' punch.

I do not want to suggest that the 1990s Homecomings and the Gaithers do not objectify the featured women. The programs often exalt female cast members according to narrowly circumscribed domestic roles. They are good wives, mothers, and grandmothers. When Suzy Hamblen speaks in *Landmark*, she appears as the avatar of her deceased spouse, gospel songwriter Stuart Hamblen—though she exhibits great skill in elucidating her spouse's struggles and musical aims. Eva Mae Lefevre is the longsuffering mother of a prodigal returned. Vestal Goodman is that high-haired "southern hon'" who calls everyone "darlin'" and whose chocolate cake recipe gets discussed reverently on the Homecoming stage as if it were a buttery Eucharistic host. That Faye and Mary Tom Speer leave the Homecomings shortly after Brock Speer's death suggests that they are defined by their relationship to a man. However, while these women were present, they were present *as musicians*; Mary Tom took the piano several times in the early videos. Doris Akers owned the space—at one point, literally shoving Bill off the piano bench (to much laughter) because she was dissatisfied with how he was playing one of her songs. Vestal Goodman may have suggested the eternally smiling Christian grandmatriarch, but her command of the microphone was just as suggestive of the revivalist preacher.

53. This changed somewhat in the years to follow. In 2013, the Gaithers released a two-volume feature of the women in the Homecomings. While obviously a number of the old guard were deceased, the two videos highlighted the stylistic, racial, and to some extent intraevangelical diversity of the past decades' gatherings. See *Women of Homecoming, Vols. 1 and 2* (Alexandria, IN: Gaither Music Group, 2013).

CHAPTER SIX

1. See Emerson and Smith, *Divided by Faith: Evangelical Religion and the Problem of Race in America* (New York: Oxford University Press, 2000), 80–83; Patricia J. Williams, *Seeing a Color-Blind Future: The Paradox of Race* (New York: Farrar, Strauss, and Giroux, 1997). For an ethnographic extension of Emerson's and Smith's work that factors in the effect of *Divided by Faith* on evangelical communities themselves, see Nancy Wadsworth, *Ambivalent Miracles: Evangelicals and the Politics of Racial Healing* (Charlottesville: University of Virginia Press, 2014).

2. Dixon recorded several albums under the Gaither label. However, it was not Dixon's Gaither-sponsored records that earned him fame, or even earned him a spot on the Gaither stage. Most of Dixon's Spring House recordings occurred late in his career, not during the middle of his rise.

3. *The Best of Lynda Randle* came out in June 2007—two weeks after the Gaithers released *The Best of Janet Paschal* CD and DVD. *The Best of Jessy Dixon* was released the year prior. In 2010, the Gaithers released *The Best of Sue Dodge*.

4. Howard and Streck, *Apostles of Rock*, 9.

5. Bourdieu, *Outline of a Theory of Practice* (New York: Cambridge University Press, 1977), 79.

6. Randle's website lists thirty-three appearances on her 2008 concert itinerary (the year after *The Best of Lynda Randle* DVD was released). I exclude from this number the week-long Gaither Alaska cruise, appearances on NBA All-Star Weekend, National Day of Prayer in Washington, and two conferences, one of which is Randle's own women's conference. Of the thirty-three shows, twenty-three are Homecoming shows. Of the remaining shows, five occur in Canadian churches (four of which are predominantly white). Other shows occur in larger festival/arena settings. See "Tour," Lynda Randle Ministries, February 5, 2008, http://www .lyndarandle.com/tour/index.php. Randle rolled back all of her concert appearances around 2010. A sign of her acceptance in the more general southern gospel world was her 2012 debut at the National Quartet Convention.

7. Bill Gaither, *The Best of Lynda Randle: Favorites from the Homecomings Series* (Alexandria, IN: Spring House, 2007). I add italics to indicate stress in speakers' voices.

8. The task of exempting poor urban African Americans—or any poor people—from responsibility for their own plight is crucial, because, if Emerson and Smith are correct, the belief that everyone controls their own destiny is built into the "cultural tool kit" of white

evangelical America. See *Divided by Faith*, 98–106. I have already shown this philosophy operant in the Homecomings in my discussion of the "takers and givers" in "Give It Away." Another
relevant phenomenon within the Homecomings is the presence and narrative of people with
physical disabilities. David Ring and Joni Eareckson Tada appear in early videos. Ring has
cerebral palsy and is a popular traveling preacher/singer; Eareckson Tada became paralyzed
from the neck down after a swimming accident during her teenage years, and she currently
runs an evangelical ministry specifically for the disabled. Later, blind piano virtuoso Gordon
Mote becomes a regular on Homecoming stages. The narrative is similar from case to case:
each person experienced obstacles out of his/her control that would have made it easy for him
or her to wallow in self-pity and to quit on life; none of these figures did so.

9. "About," Lynda Randle Ministries, accessed January 23, 2008, http://www.lyndarandle
.com/about/index.html.

10. As Randle mentions on the *Best Of* video, one of her brothers is in prison and at least
two of her sisters battled drug addiction at some point in their lives. Randle does not offer
many details in either case—she mentions both matters in passing, talking about her mother's
strength. At a show I attended in Pennsylvania, Randle mentioned her imprisoned brother to
the crowd as a prayer request (and expressed her reluctance to name him and his situation at
all).

11. The Gaithers are quite aware of how the deaths of Homecoming performers connect
them to aging members of their audience. See Bill Gaither, *It's More Than the Music*, 273–77,
and Gloria Gaither, *Something Beautiful*, 224–27.

12. Tracy Dartt, "God on the Mountain," Benson, 1975.

13. Comments on YouTube postings of Randle's "God on the Mountain" performances
demonstrate two trends. When people discuss Randle's performance particularly, people often
cite Randle as the "ideal" singer for the song. And quite often, people use the "comments" section to explain how the song relates to their lives—how it helped them through hardship. See
"Gaithers 'God on the mountain' with Lynda Randle live," YouTube, last modified February 16,
2007, accessed January 23, 2008, http://www.youtube.com/watch?v=Xipq208iNHg.

14. *The Best of Lynda Randle*.

15. Ibid.

16. Ibid.

17. I do not invoke Derrida's concept of putting terms "under erasure" (*sous rature*) to make
a complicated metaphysical claim. Rather, I find Derrida's graphic representation of erasure to
be an apt description of what Randle must do when she invokes and removes race. The term is
deleted, but remains visible (along with, perhaps due to, its deletion) and thus remains partially
in the discourse.

18. There are certainly popular low-voiced female singers in black gospel music, or singers who have roots in black gospel. Folk singer Odetta possessed a low voice. Ysaye Barnwell
of the singing group Sweet Honey in the Rock possesses a near-bass range. But it is rare for
women in the twenty-first century to have a solo gospel career as a deep alto or baritone. More
importantly, as will become evident later in the chapter, Randle believes that there are certain
expectations of female African American vocalists that prohibit singers with her particular
skills and range from pursuing certain gospel music avenues.

19. While the musicians I name here are white, several African American women emerged
near the end of the twentieth century who manifested a similarly scaled-down, acoustic driven
soul in their recordings, among them India Arie, Erykah Badu, and (as a soloist) Angie Stone.

20. Each *Timeless* album was recorded at Gaither Studios, and each was produced by Bill
Gaither. However, only the "first" volume was released through Spring House and distributed
through Chordant. The "second" volume, filled with songs from the same session, was actually

available a short time before the first volume through Lynda Randle Ministries. However, live Homecoming performances prove the best venue for sales of both albums, and both sell relatively well.

21. The emphasis on the downbeat (1 and 3) in southern gospel contrasts sharply with the emphasis on the backbeat (2 and 4) so prevalent in black gospel music. The former emphasis tends to hold the progression of the music back, giving it a good deal of verticality, while the latter pushes it forward, making the music feel faster. One need only compare any of the many Homecoming versions of "Leaning on the Everlasting Arms" with, for example, the African American choral version of Urban Nation to hear the difference. The emphasis on the first and third beat—an emphasis that southern gospel fans tend to accentuate by clapping on these beats—makes a song seem slower and less syncopated than the song rendered at the same tempo but with the emphasis (and hand claps) on the second and fourth beats. See Gaither, *Bill Gaither's Best of Homecoming 2001* (Alexandria, IN: Spring House, 2001), Urban Nation, *Church It Up: 30 Church Choir Classics* (Nolensville, TN: Madacy Christian, 2005).

22. Certainly the cases of Dixon, Waters, Robeson, and Jackson are different, both from one another and from Randle's. Although Randle's early recordings reveal that she had some knowledge of black gospel, it is not evident that she was immersed in black church music or jazz like Dixon, Jackson, or Waters. It is also not the case with Randle, as it is with the others, that notoriety came first in and through black gospel communities. Randle's popularity took off when she entered the Gaither world; she impressed the Gaithers because of her early music, but she did not have a large audience at the time.

23. Charley Pride quoted in Alanna Nash, *Behind Closed Doors* (New York: Alfred A. Knopf, 1988), 427. Pride is not popular because he brings "blackness" to country. This is not to say that there is no African American influence in country music, nor is it to suggest that Charley Pride's race is invisible in the country music world, or that his racial identity does not do particular things that help or hinder his career. But unlike Randle, Pride completely eschews race as a topic of conversation.

24. The "girl" comment is troubling but understandable given the demographic of the Homecomings. At the time of this video, Gloria is in her sixties. Given the age spectrum of the Homecoming performers, and given the high valuation on old performers, it is likely that such language is rooted in age rather than race (Bill called Lynn and me "kids" all of the time, though we were in our thirties during most of my fieldwork). The comment also has gender overtones as well. It is not uncommon to hear women of all ages be referred to or to refer to themselves as "girls" on the Homecoming stage. The diminutive term is operating primarily in a culture heavily inflected with patriarchal bias. Be that as it may, terms such as "girls" have a particularly pernicious history when applied to black females by white females (another function of this particular patriarchal context). It is also important to note that Gloria can and does use the term "black," whereas Randle uses the "chocolate" euphemism, suggesting that Gloria has more freedom to "make an explicit issue" of Randle's race than does Randle.

25. Gaither, *Best of Lynda Randle*.

26. Ibid.

27. Ibid.

28. Randle's *Tribute to Mahalia Jackson* won the 2005 Dove Award for Traditional Gospel Album of the Year—an award that used to be called Traditional Black Gospel Album of the Year. As of this writing, the award always has gone to an album by an African American singer or group. The one possible exception is Mike Farris's 2010 Award-winning *Shout! Live*. Even in this case, the white Farris, erstwhile lead singer of the rock group the Screamin' Cheetah Wheelies, borrows intentionally and heavily from traditional blues and black gospel (the

African American trio the McCrary Sisters, daughters of the Fairfield Four's Sam McCrary, are featured heavily on the album).

29. The 1997 video *Down by the Tabernacle*, set in a Wesleyan camp meeting location, contains an extensive narrative interlude that recounts the story of the Wesley brothers' ministry. Twenty-first-century Homecoming concerts almost invariably contain a segment during which Bill places an old-time RCA microphone in the center of the stage, explains how former singing quartets artfully maneuvered themselves around such a solitary microphone in the studio and onstage, and leads the GVB in an old-time "convention song."

30. Frederick, *Between Sundays*, 157.

31. See "'Eye Is On The . . .' By Lynda Randle/Alicia Williamson/Etc," YouTube, last modified February 19, 2007, accessed January 23, 2008, http://www.youtube.com/watch?v =XL2OlYhoWLs.

EPILOGUE

1. Campbell's tactics against Heller may have cost him a 1996 spot as a running mate for Republican presidential candidate Bob Dole. See Matthew Dorf, "Possible Dole Running Mate Could Send Jews Running," *Jewish Weekly*, last modified August 9, 1996, accessed June 1, 2015, http://www.jweekly.com/article/full/3801/possible-dole-running-mate-could-send-jews-running/.

2. As of June 2015, Woodson does not even appear on the Greenville's Wikipedia entry under "notable people"—a list that includes some of Greenville's one-term mayors. In April 2016, I worked with Presbyterian College and First Baptist Church Greenville to bring Woodson to do a reading at the church. Approximately 500-600 people attended.

3. David Swartz notes that several Anderson University (then College) students participated in the Selma March in 1965. See *Moral Minority*, 27.

4. See Larry Eskridge, *God's Forever Family: The Jesus People Movement in America* (New York: Oxford University Press, 2013) Brantley Gasaway, *Progressive Evangelicals and the Pursuit of Social Justice* (Chapel Hill: University of North Carolina Press, 2014); Miller, *The Age of Evangelicalism*; and Swartz, *Moral Minority*. For a collection that extends the discussion into the present, see Brian Steensland and Philip Goff, eds., *The New Evangelical Social Engagement* (New York: Oxford University Press, 2013).

CREDITS

The Baptism of Jesse Taylor
Words and Music by Dallas Frazier and Sanger D. Shafer
Copyright © 1972 Sony/ATV Music Publishing LLC
Copyright Renewed
All Rights Administered by Sony
/ATV Music Publishing LLC,
424 Church Street, Suite 1200, Nashville, TN 37219
International Copyright Secured. All Rights Reserved.
Reprinted by Permission of Hal Leonard Corporation.

God on the Mountain
Writer: Tracy Dartt
Copyright © 1988. Gaviota Music, Inc.
/BMI (admin. by ClearBox Rights).
All Rights Reserved. Used by Permission.

Give It Away
Writers: Benjamin Gaither, Gloria Gaither
Copyright © 2005 Hanna Street Music (BMI)
Hook Line and Music Publishing (ASCAP)
(adm. at CapitolCMGPublishing.com)
International Copyright Secured.
All Rights Reserved. Used by Permission.

It Is Finished
Writers: Gloria Gaither, William J. Gaither
Copyright © 1976 Hanna Street Music (BMI)
(adm. at CapitolCMGPublishing.com)
International Copyright Secured.
All Rights Reserved. Used by Permission.

A Few Good Men

Writers: Barry Jennings, Suzanne Jennings
Copyright © 1990 Townsend and Warbucks Music (ASCAP)
(adm. at CapitolCMGPublishing.com)
International Copyright Secured.
All Rights Reserved. Used by Permission.

Jesus and John Wayne

Writers: Benjamin Gaither, Doug Johnson,
Gloria Gaither, Kim Williams, William J. Gaither
Copyright © 2008 Hanna Street Music (BMI)
Hook Line and Music Publishing (ASCAP)
(adm. at CapitolCMGPublishing.com) / Sweet Radical Music ()
/ Sony Atv Cross Keys Pub (ASCAP).
International Copyright Secured.
All Rights Reserved. Used by Permission.

Jesus and John Wayne

Words and Music by Kim Williams, Gloria Gaither,
William J. Gaither, Benjamin Gaither and Doug Johnson
Copyright © 2008 Sony/ATV Music Publishing LLC,
Mountain Mamma Music and Publisher Unknown
All Rights on behalf of Sony/ATV Music Publishing LLC
and Mountain Mamma Music Administered by Sony/ATV Music
Publishing LLC, 424 Church Street, Suite 1200, Nashville, TN 37219
International Copyright Secured. All Rights Reserved.
Reprinted by Permission of Hal Leonard Corporation.

I Then Shall Live

Writers: Gloria Gaither, Jean Sibelius
Copyright © 1981 Hanna Street Music (BMI)
(adm. at CapitolCMGPublishing.com) / Harry Fox
International Copyright Secured.
All Rights Reserved. Used by Permission.

INDEX